AT THE CROSSROADS

MIDDLE AMERICA AND THE BATTLE TO SAVE THE CAR INDUSTRY

ABE AAMIDOR & TED EVANOFF

ECW Press

Published by ECW Press, 2120 Queen Street East, Suite 200,
Toronto, Ontario, Canada M4E 1E2
416.694.3348 / info@ecwpress.com

LIBRARY AND ARCHIVES CANADA CATALOGUING IN PUBLICATION

Aamidor, Abraham
At the Crossroads : middle America's battle to save the car industry /
Abe Aamidor, Ted Evanoff.

ISBN 978-1-55022-904-2

1. Automobile industry and trade—Social aspects—United States.
2. Automobile industry and trade—Indiana—Kokomo. 3. Kokomo (Ind.)—Economic
conditions. 4. Deindustrialization—Social aspects—United States. 5. Middle class—
United States. 6. Automobile industry and trade—United States. I. Evanoff, Ted II. Title.

HD9710.U52A35 2010   338.4'76292220973   C2009-905929-0

Cover and text design: Tania Craan
Cover image: © Abe Aamidor
Author photos: Ted Evanoff © Alan Petersime/*Indianapolis Star*;
Abe Aamidor © Frank Espich
Typesetting: Mary Bowness
Printing: Transcontinental   1   2   3   4   5

PRINTED AND BOUND IN CANADA

ECW PRESS
ecwpress.com

To Joe Aamidor, who had the idea for this book
— Abe Aamidor

For Abbay, Neely, and Mary
— Ted Evanoff

CONTENTS

INTRODUCTION

THREE HUNDRED AND FIFTY MILES southwest of Detroit, the roads run straight to the horizon in between tall cornfields and past gothic farmhouses, but also through small towns with traditional courthouse squares, brick-walled factory buildings, and now-cold smokestacks that tell of a faded industrial splendor. This is the heartland, the center of the center, the middle of the industrial Middle West. Once the vibrant core of America, it is becoming the New Appalachia. President Barack Obama's administration has shored up Chrysler Corporation and General Motors Corporation with $77 billion worth of federal loans, at least for the time being. But the 2009 bailout of Detroit failed to halt the "Rust Belt" deterioration afflicting Middle America.

Obama had the opportunity to harness GM and Chrysler to the greater task of not only reenergizing the American economy, but in leading the charge to a greener future less dependent on imported oil. It could have been an enterprise of massive scale, not unlike the Manhattan Project that produced the atom bomb during the administration of Franklin Delano Roosevelt, or perhaps the lunar landing first envisioned by John F. Kennedy. Instead the opportunity was largely squandered. *At the Crossroads* tells how that happened.

The book follows two parallel tracks. One story recounts the taxpayer bailout of General Motors and Chrysler and reveals in a coherent narrative the backstory of how these two industrial icons, as well as much of the nation's manufacturing industry, have been poorly served by Wall Street and Washington for at least the past generation. In the other track we see the consequences in the heartland. Hundreds of towns distant from Detroit are in themselves manufacturing satellites in the orbit of the big automakers. *At the Crossroads* tells the story of the auto industry crisis from the point of view of the people who live and work in such towns as they confronted their year of decision in 2009.

We meet small-town mayors who are the first line of defense against economic decline and the loss of community, but who often are the weakest players in a game where the rules are made elsewhere. We meet elected union leaders, dissidents and ordinary rank and file, but not through rose-colored glasses. The unions do not deserve all the blame for the auto industry morass, but they are not blameless either. We see small business owners and local activists who are trying to keep their communities intact in the face of what has been an economic tsunami.

We concentrate on Indiana because it has the largest proportion of manufacturing jobs of any state in the country, and is second only to Michigan in terms of automotive industry–related jobs. Indiana is a complex state demographically and socio-economically, but its automotive towns are smaller than Michigan's so the social and economic trends are more readily discernible. The state has three major research institutions in Indiana University, Purdue University, and the University of Notre Dame, as well pharmaceutical giant Eli Lilly and Company based in Indianapolis. But the state also includes large numbers of people who'd rather hunt and fish than taste wine and cheese, who'd rather vacation in Pigeon Forge, Tennessee, than Paris, France, and who drive Chevrolets because — yes — it's a union brand. This is not necessarily the stereotype of Washington, D.C., or Wall Street, where the fate of these workers was being decided.

In December 2008 talk of bankruptcy for either GM or

Chrysler was dismissed as misguided at best, heresy at worst, yet by the following summer both companies had emerged from remarkably quick, albeit carefully orchestrated, bankruptcies. Will they just die a slower, more humane death in the future, though? President Obama himself followed two tracks with the auto bailout — one was to at least save the domestic auto industry, no matter how downsized, as well as save the United Auto Workers. No reference to a GM or Chrysler bailout should ever be made without acknowledging that this was a UAW bailout by the Democratic president as well.

The other track was to pave the way for a partial or all-electric passenger car future in America. This was seen in the astounding increase in the Corporate Average Fuel Economy (CAFE) requirement set for 2015, as well as the distribution of big federal grants and loans for green and electric-powered vehicles the government began making in 2009. But by largely cutting GM and Chrysler out of that green future, at least temporarily, and by giving money to some foreign-owned companies such as Nissan instead, the Obama administration may have sealed the fate not only of these two still-important manufacturers, but of the industrial Midwest and important swaths in Canada and Mexico, too.

As this book will show, the entire region, what we call Middle America, has been scorched by the vicissitudes of a political and financial establishment in Washington and New York unattached to a manufacturing base that is essential to the national security and the overall economic prosperity of America. Since 2000, 5 million manufacturing jobs have vanished in America, eliminating more than $200 billion in annual payroll.[1] More than 23,000 factories have closed.[2] Some officers at the National Defense University, an arm of the Pentagon, fear America no longer has the industrial capacity to sustain the armed forces in a prolonged major war.[3] Meanwhile, the trade deficit has soared as the nation's appetite for imported oil and consumer goods far outstrips the exports that pay for all those imports. Now we borrow money to maintain our buying habits. China and Japan together hold more than $1 trillion worth of United States debt.[4]

At the Crossroads begins on November 19, 2008. Senior executives of Chrysler and General Motors were turned away by the Senate Committee on Banking after requesting $25 billion in aid. The senators, who just six weeks earlier had appropriated $700 billion for the troubled financial houses of Wall Street, refused any help for Detroit. Instead, they told the executives to return in December and show plans on how they would use any money to revive their companies. Some senators excoriated the executives for traveling to Washington, D.C., aboard their corporations' expensive jet aircraft, which was seen as proof that they were out of touch with the sentiment on Main Street. It all made superb political theater.

But for local leaders like Kokomo, Indiana, mayor Greg Goodnight (a former steelworker and truck driver), or Marion, Indiana, mayor Wayne Seybold (who grew up in a trailer park and later competed in the 1988 Calgary Winter Olympics with his sister Kim in the pairs figure skating category), or Jeff Shrock (a former Major League baseball prospect who injured his arm and later became an elected official of United Auto Workers Local 685), the snub pounded home a cruel reality: America was turning a cold shoulder not only toward arrogant, even imperious corporate executives, but to its true native sons as well.

"Doesn't anyone realize what is at stake?" said Mayor Seybold who had struggled with the loss of a major television tube manufacturer in 2004 and in 2009 was scrambling to help save a massive metal stamping factory in town owned by GM.

Yes, two giant auto companies were ultimately saved. (Ford was never in the same desperate shape financially as GM and Chrysler were, though its sales had plummeted almost as much during the crisis.) Yes, tens of thousands of jobs were saved. But the future was not assured. In a time when many believe the United States can maintain its economic might and standard of living on ingenuity and high technology alone, or by sending all young people to college instead of recognizing that many want to work with their hands, the industrial center has been reduced to an afterthought, even a cliché. Yet this industrial heartland also is home to most of America's engineers, manufacturing plant managers, and many skilled tradespeople. If the domestic auto industry is not reenergized, not only will communities fail, not only will talented, skilled people have to scatter with the wind, but we may lose our best chance to engineer an electric car or other alternative energy car that keeps the engineering brain-power in America (as opposed to an increasing reliance on foreign engineers and patents) and reduces our terrible reliance on imported oil, a reliance that has uncomfortably tied America to Middle Eastern wars and unstable societies in the Persian Gulf and South America.

This populist narrative ultimately is an exhortation: the auto industry can be recast larger than it has been left by this bailout. It is our opinion that Washington not only has failed to demonstrate a Manhattan Project–style commitment either to energy independence or to a role for American manufacturers in a green future, but it has also been unable to harness the country's sagging industrial base to a pro-jobs agenda able to repower the economy. Middle America will pay the price first, but in time all of America will come to understand the price of failure.

---

1. Alliance for American Manufacturing, Washington, D.C., http://www.americanmanufacturing.org/issues/economic/.
2. Employment in Manufacturing NAICS 31–33, U.S. Census Bureau, http://censtats.census.gov/usa/usa.shtml.
3. Ted Evanoff, "A Losing Battle: Our Industrial Base," *Indianapolis Star*, October 9, 2006: C01.
4. William Bonner, Addison Wiggin, *Empire of Debt: The Rise of an Epic Financial Crisis* (Hoboken, NJ: John Wiley & Sons, 2006) 37.

CHAPTER 1

The Perfect Storm

GREG GOODNIGHT WONDERED WHAT he had got himself into. The forty-four-year-old native Hoosier was in the first year of his first term as mayor of Kokomo, Indiana — a manufacturing hub with 46,000 citizens about an hour's drive directly north of Indianapolis. In his first State of the City address, delivered on an icy evening in February 2008 inside City Council chambers, Goodnight had warned local burghers, a couple of newspaper reporters, and a smattering of ordinary citizens — mostly older, the kind of people who always show up for these things — that the challenges facing the town were greater than ever and the plan of action more daring than anything people had seen before. Early in 2007, DaimlerChrysler, the major employer in Kokomo, had sold controlling interest in all its North American facilities, including its Kokomo auto and truck transmission plants, at a fire sale price to a private equity firm with no experience running a car company. The local economy had been reeling since October 2005 when Delphi, the other large auto industry employer in town and once a $29 billion corporate giant, filed for bankruptcy. The housing market had started to tank locally, too, well ahead of the subprime mortgage crisis that would strike the rest of the country by 2008. Rapidly rising gasoline prices had eaten into disposable income and eroded retail sales on the once-vibrant courthouse square and the city's two large shopping malls out by Highway 31, the major "four-lane" through Kokomo. Unlike the sanguine speeches presidents always make in their annual State of the Union addresses, Goodnight was here to deliver only bad news — Kokomo was in a deep recession.

"Our city's General Fund — our main operating account — will require us to take out almost $400,000 out of our already low cash reserves," he announced. "After this happens those cash reserves will have just $460,000 remaining," or less than 1.2 percent of projected annual revenue. The rules of good governance dictated that a healthy city have 5 to 15 percent on reserve, he told his audience. To balance the budget Goodnight would have to consider layoffs, including in the usually sacrosanct public safety sector. After all, payroll accounted for three-quarters of the city's annual budget.

The mayor said something else that was a surprising thing to hear from an elected official anywhere in Middle America today. "My labor union philosophy taught me to make decisions based not on what is best for the individual, but on what is the best for the group as a whole," he said, sounding like an amalgam of John F. Kennedy, who told citizens to "ask not what your country can do for you, ask what you can do for your country," and Karl Marx, who preached "from each according to his ability, to each according to his need." For, unlike most Indiana mayors, who often were licensed attorneys or successful businessmen, Goodnight was a mere high-school graduate, a long-time steelworker and factory hand who had nevertheless worked his way up the union ladder and local government to be elected mayor of his hometown in November 2007. He had been sworn in on January 1, 2008, just weeks before his State of the City address.

Goodnight — a Matt Lauer look-alike with an easy manner and a baritone voice, just a bit twangy from growing up locally — got his first good job out of high school in construction driving heavy equipment and tri-axle rigs between small Indiana towns. His father, Jimmy, a Teamsters Union official, got him the job. Later, he worked for Kokomo-based Haynes International, a manufacturer of high-tech nickel and cobalt-alloy metals. Goodnight wasn't active in the unions at first, but after one layoff he landed another factory job at a non-union shop where he worked twelve-hour shifts with no lunch and two twenty-minute toilet breaks. When he was called back to Haynes he decided his dad and all the guys he had grown up with were right — unions did matter. He was elected president of the United Steelworkers of America Local 2958, which represented twelve area factories in and around Kokomo, and was elected twice to the Kokomo City Council, winning the most votes of any council member in the 2003 election.

"I'm somewhat of the poster child for Kokomo, for the average person," Goodnight said. "I have a high school diploma, a limited amount of college, just a few classes. I've worked in the factories. If someone had trouble understanding the contract, or the attendance policies, I would help them. I've been laid off a couple of times as an adult. I'm very familiar with the average person."

Several months after that State of the City address Goodnight had begun making the tough decisions, trimming the city budget by six percent through involuntary layoffs and demoting two salaried administrators to hourly rate status, plus locking horns with the city's 121 firefighters over a proposed pay freeze. Then there was the annexation fight with two unincorporated areas on the edges of town — you receive city services, you have to pay city taxes, he told the resentful citizens to their faces, many of whom promised to punish him at the ballot box if and when they got to vote in municipal elections.

Then there was Goodnight's family life — just trying to maintain a semblance of normalcy in his family life was complicated by his wife Kelli's continuing battle with Huntington's, a degenerative brain disease. A second marriage for each, the Goodnights have four children — making theirs a blended family, yet another ongoing challenge. Several years ago on an early dinner date with Kelli and another couple at a family restaurant Greg pulled out discount coupons from his wallet and passed them around. "I figured she better know what I'm about before we went too far," he said.

The Goodnights live in what was Kelli's home before they were married, a wood-frame Colonial in what is called the Old

Silk Stocking neighborhood, but it's not as fancy as the name might suggest. Greg drives a 1997 Jeep Wrangler that he bought new and he earns $79,000 per year as mayor, but that's about the same as he made as a steelworkers' union president in the 1990s and less than what some skilled trades in the auto plants still make.

Kelli, from tiny Walton, Indiana, graduated from Indiana University Law School in 1996, after studying journalism as an undergraduate. She worked for years as a full-time UAW lawyer ironically specializing in bankruptcy matters for rank-and-file members. She says most autoworkers stayed out of financial trouble, but she also saw those who lived beyond their means, often with a track record of declaring bankruptcy every seven years like clockwork after spending their money on big boats, Harley-Davidson motorcycles, and more.

Indiana has disparate geography: broad flatlands and farm fields dominate just north of US 40, the old National Road that cuts through the state from east to west. Sandy beaches and Lake Michigan are at the far northern edge of the state, while deep woods dominate in southern Indiana. The Goodnights often take day trips and Greg likes to stop in to the many small manufacturing towns that dot the state. In part it's to remind himself that he doesn't want his city to end up like some others, he admits. Yet, sometimes, he sees something working right and he'll call and investigate how this or that city is managing. But he and Kelli also want to make sure their children study for the arts and other professions. Their youngest child has just started to learn the piano and their oldest son, Brody, was scheduled to enter Ball State University in the fall of 2009, intent on studying telecommunications. He wants to make documentary films one day, kind of like a young Michael Moore.

Only in December 2008, near the end of his first year in office, did Greg Goodnight have a chance for a friendly night out on the town. It was the annual United Auto Workers retiree Christmas party in the Howard County Civic Center. About 5,000 retired UAW workers still lived in and around Kokomo and their Christmas party was one of the big events on the community calendar each year, complete with a catered chicken dinner, prizes (floral arrangements this year), and rousing speeches by local union leaders and Democratic Party officials. It was a chance for Goodnight to set aside the constant budget battles and even forget an April 2008 *New York Times* spread on the city that he believes portrayed Kokomo as a town full of good old boys who sat in lawn chairs in the back of their pickup trucks and drank beer all day, a sad backwater not worth saving[1] and Goodnight liked to keep the clipping at hand as motivation — he would save his city just to prove the authors wrong.

Five hundred people showed up for the 2008 Christmas party, yet on the same evening, about 600 miles to the east, the United States Senate was meeting to vote on a proposed $14 billion aid package for two of the Detroit Three domestic auto manufacturers. Goodnight had been prescient in his State of the City address as an actual bankruptcy at any of the Detroit automakers, but especially Chrysler, would not only cost current employees their jobs, but would put in jeopardy the prosperity of all the retired UAW workers in the area, as well. Everybody at the chicken dinner knew about the Senate hearings; that's all they really wanted to talk about that evening. It was a Thursday, about thirty-one degrees Fahrenheit outside, with sleet and freezing rain falling as it often does early in the winter in north-central Indiana. Goodnight left the Christmas party about 9 p.m. and returned to his office in city hall to watch the vote on TV. The deliberations were broadcast live on cable news stations. The auto industry crisis had become the talk of the nation, second only in public interest to the subprime mortgage crisis and credit crunch of 2008.

"Everybody had been following the debate," Goodnight said. "I thought it was getting very partisan. I felt there was very little scrutiny given to the Wall Street package and very little discretion on how they were going to spend the money given to them, therefore I thought there was an overreaction to how they were going to give money to the auto industry. And there was a lot of animosity to the UAW. I saw that."

The bailout package never came to a vote that evening. Senate Democrats failed by a vote of 52–35 to "end debate" on the matter, so the bill authorizing the $14 billion aid package simply died. "We have worked and worked and we can spend all night tonight, tomorrow, Saturday, and Sunday, and we're not going to get to the finish line," Senate Majority Leader Harry Reid said at the time. "That's just the way it is."[2]

Jeff Shrock, a third generation autoworker and an officer of UAW Local 685, which represents Chrysler hourly employees in Kokomo, was also at the retiree party that night with his wife, Tina, and two children, Samantha and Cory. Shrock, forty, is a former Major League baseball prospect who injured his throwing arm while on scholarship at Western Kentucky University in Bowling Green, a town that's also home to Chevrolet Corvette production. When the "Tommy John" surgery (so named for a Major League pitcher who had his throwing arm successfully rebuilt after an injury) failed to save Shrock's career, he dropped out of college and returned to Kokomo where he waited for an opening at Chrysler, then jumped in. Shrock, too, was following the proceedings live on TV with a group of friends from the auto plants.

"Jaws dropped. They were worried," said Shrock, about six-foot-two and still fit, but with his thick, straight hair almost completely gray now. "They figured bankruptcy was inevitable. It was kind of a quiet time because everyone was speechless, not knowing what direction the company was going to take."

Shrock missed the final vote on "ending debate" in the Senate, but received a call at home later that evening from the office of Indiana Congressman Joe Donnelly (Democrat, second district). Donnelly represents part of Kokomo and Howard County and had worked closely with UAW representatives to support the aid package in Congress. "That's how I found out. It was like a death in the family," Shrock said.

As an elected Local leader, Shrock no longer works in the factories, though he visits them almost daily to deal with employee grievances, work rules, and the like. His offices are in a plain, single-story union hall south of downtown, which was built in stages beginning in the 1960s. The simple brick building is located in one of the city's family-style neighborhoods where many of the autoworkers have lived for decades. Large signs by each entrance to the parking lot declare that all "non-union" cars will be towed at the owner's expense.

Shrock is unapologetic about union activism in America. A relatively gentle, even laconic speaker, he has a soft accent that is not a drawl nor is it Southern. It's a voice that could very well be like that of pioneers in Indiana in the beginning of the nineteenth century. Just think of Gary Cooper in *Friendly Persuasion*, the movie about a pacifist Quaker family in Indiana during the frontier days. "As we followed the debate we knew the bailout was in trouble," Shrock said. "That was the word in the plants. Once the people heard [Tennessee Republican Senator Bob] Corker there was a lot of anger in their eyes."

Corker, who demanded UAW concessions as a condition for a bailout loan, had raised hackles in Kokomo when he stared down Robert Nardelli, the Chrysler chairman, during earlier congressional hearings. "Chrysler doesn't really want to be a standalone business," Corker told him, cameras rolling. "That's well-documented. Your plan is to hang around so you can date someone and hopefully get married soon before you run out of money."

But the people in Kokomo wanted Chrysler to survive, and they believed that Nardelli did, too. Some workers wrote Corker or called his office to protest his remarks. One fellow wrote to say he was canceling his annual fishing vacation to Tennessee.

Corker was an equal opportunity offender — he chastised both the failures and insularity of the Detroit Three management, but also what he perceived as greediness and poor shop-floor habits of the autoworkers. To people like Corker the unions were part of the problem, not the solution. But Shrock didn't see it that way at all. As a child he virtually grew up in this union hall — a hall with a full gym in back with basketball hoops, free weights, and more, plus a large banquet room for mass meetings on contract talks and weddings alike. Shrock says that as a child he'd come visit his dad, who also was a union officer here, and that retirees who now volunteer to run the place and clean up after people remember him as a boy. Today, they'll walk right into his corner office, too, and tell him what they think about things. The retirees are even teaching his boy, Cory, to shoot pool. They're like extended family, Shrock says.

Shrock was immediately bombarded by national media with requests for interviews after the Senate debacle. One reporter wanted to know which bars the autoworkers frequent so he could interview them there, while a cable news network correspondent did a live remote in front of the old Haynes-Apperson and Haynes Automobile Company plant on Home Avenue, an archaic factory that was closed in 1925, but which later was bought and operated by Chrysler well into the 1950s. The segment pictured what is now a used auto parts warehouse; it looks a lot like a decaying, Victorian-era factory, just a plain Jane rectangular brick cube several stories high with big steel casement windows and lots of broken glass panes. A large, teapot-dome water tower stands silent guard nearby. Shrock was furious at the reporter's choice of location: that's not a Chrysler plant anymore, he railed. Deep down, though, he knew that the old Home Avenue plant might be a vision of Kokomo's future, just like in a Charles Dickens tale.

The seat of Howard County in north-central Indiana, the city of Kokomo is a true microcosm of America. The cornerstone of the local economy has long been those well-paying auto-related factory jobs, though there were many second-tier parts suppliers in town, plus myriad corn, soybean, and dairy farmers in surrounding communities, as well as plentiful public service jobs in government and schools. Still, the car industry drove the local economy. In this city of over 46,000 people, most neighborhoods feature modest frame houses, often as not one-story homes over deep basements below and walk-in attics on top with small front yards that run right up to the city sidewalks. The courthouse square itself is moderately interesting, with disparate architecture including Teutonic and Italianate influences, plus a rectangular courthouse with lots of heavy metal trim in the windows, two large, vaguely Grecian-style urns in front and Art Deco bas-relief in the stonework.. It's not the kind of place *Architectural Digest* comes to looking for photo spreads, but Kokomo's homes have always been affordable and kids can still ride their bikes safely most anywhere in town. Oddly, there is no heroic statue or carefully preserved cannon on the courthouse square, which is quite atypical for jingoistic Indiana. The state sent 221,000 volunteers to the Union Army in the Civil War, for example, the third highest number of any state in the North, and the highest by proportion of its citizens.

Kokomo also sports a regional campus of Indiana University (IU). It's no bigger than some high schools, but is easily accessible inside the city limits, and there's a local branch of the state-run Ivy Tech Community College system. Many college-bound youth take their first two years of classes at either institution before going to the main campus of IU in Bloomington or Purdue University in West Lafayette. Even so, Howard County residents are much less likely to have finished college, though more likely to have completed high school, when compared to either state or national averages.[3] Most people will say it's because of the well-paying auto industry jobs — there just never was a need to go to college to earn a good living.

The city itself dates to 1841, when a local Miami Indian chief sold several acres of tribal land along Wildcat Creek for use as a trading post. An itinerant merchant, David Foster, named this plot of land Kokomo, after the Indian chief Ma-Ko-Ko-Mo.

Kokomo remained little more than a tiny hamlet until 1886, when a huge natural gas field was discovered underground. This led to several factories and especially glassblowing businesses in the area, as well as the Haynes-Apperson and Haynes Automobile companies, named for Elwood Haynes, an engineer who invented stainless steel, supposedly as a gift to his wife so her flatware wouldn't tarnish or rust. According to some sources, the first working prototype car made in America was a Haynes, built in 1893. Early samples of the single-cylinder model had a top speed of only seven or eight miles per hour. The company and its successor occupied the Home Avenue plant until a 1925 bankruptcy. Haynes International, the specialty steel company where Greg Goodnight worked for many years, is a direct descendent of that company. Over the years other companies established auto parts factories and even final assembly plants in the area. Besides owning the Home Avenue plant for years, Chrysler built its first automobile transmission plants in Kokomo in 1956, and now has three in the city. General Motors' prominence in the city dates at least to 1936, when its Delco Remy division developed the first push-button car radio.

More ignoble moments in Kokomo history include the state's largest Ku Klux Klan rally in a city park in 1923, and the expulsion of early HIV/AIDS victim Ryan White from a suburban Russiaville public school in 1985. Indiana in general has a mixed record on civil rights. Abraham Lincoln spent his formative years between the ages of seven and twenty-one living with his parents in southern Indiana, but a black man was very publicly lynched from a tree on the courthouse square in nearby Marion, another auto industry bastion in the state, in 1931. Texas-born and Oklahoma-reared D. C. Stephenson was long the leader of the Indiana Ku Klux Klan, which by some estimates attracted one-third of all white males in the state as members in the 1920s. In 1925 Stephenson was convicted of murder after poisoning and raping a young Indiana woman.

Chrysler, the biggest employer in Kokomo in 2008 with 5,300 workers, had set off the minivan craze in the 1980s, as well as the SUV craze shortly thereafter. The adventurous Jeep Cherokee and later the more upscale Grand Cherokee nurtured the baby boomer's sense of rugged independence. And Chrysler engineers hit another home run in 1994 with the muscular-looking, take-no-prisoners Dodge Ram full-size pickup, making it a serious contender for the first time ever against traditional best sellers from Ford and GM. Pickups were America's most popular vehicles for decades, outselling midsize sedans such as the Ford

Taurus, Toyota Camry, and Honda Accord two to one. Chrysler was selling 400,000 Rams a year by 1996, double the volume of 1993. The dependence on high-profit, gas-guzzling trucks, minivans, and SUVS was to haunt Chrysler and the other domestic manufacturers in time, of course.

The Midwest long has been the industrial heartland of the country, a heritage that traces to nineteenth-century machine shops, many run by skilled German immigrants. As the American interior filled with people, demand for manufactured goods grew. Thriving machine shops swelled into factories and gave way to the industrialization that supported cities like Kokomo for decades. And Kokomo's experience wasn't solitary. Indiana remains the number two auto-related manufacturing state in the country, and has been so for decades. Anderson, about forty miles northeast of Indianapolis, had in particular benefited from General Motors beginning early in the twentieth century. At one time Anderson was the largest GM parts manufacturing town in America outside of Flint, Michigan. In the 1920s GM added United Motors and Delco to Remy. Remy made electrical parts; it was founded in Anderson. GM soon moved Delco to town from Dayton, Ohio, where it previously had been based. In the same decade GM also purchased the Guide Motor Lamp Co. and moved its operations from Cleveland to Anderson. In the 1970s the number of people who worked in GM-owned plants in Anderson or surrounding Madison County, or in independent shops that supplied GM, was about 30,000 — a staggering sum that was equal to more than one-third of the city's total population. In the 1990s, however, GM spun off all its parts suppliers, including Delco Remy and Guide. The goal was twofold: make the parts suppliers more competitive in the marketplace while allowing GM to buy parts from other suppliers. The plan did not quite work as envisioned. The very last major auto industry employer, then known as Guide Corporation (it made taillight and headlight assemblies at the time), closed its doors in Anderson in January 2007, leaving 1,325 men and women without jobs. What Kokomo was facing, Anderson had already gone through.

"We are the first ones in modern history to recognize that General Motors is not part of Anderson's future," former Anderson mayor Kevin Smith said at the time of the Guide closing. "Truly, this has been an ongoing process since the 1970s. I look at this as the final closure. We don't like to see jobs lost, but business changes. A healthy, successful community changes with time."[4]

In 2008 Anderson elected a new mayor, former police detective Kris Ockomon who was working hard to diversify the local economy, building on recent successes in bringing a large food processing plant to town as well as a new casino. It remained an open question whether the city could ever compensate for those thousands of auto-industry jobs, however.

Other Indiana towns had been intimately tied to the auto industry over the years. Pickup trucks continue to be made in Fort Wayne, which in 1949 was called by *Look*, the former national bi-weekly picture magazine, "America's happiest town."[5] Though both plants have been closed for several years now, both BorgWarner and GM made transmissions in Muncie, Indiana. The silver-plated BorgWarner trophy given to the winner of the Indianapolis 500-Mile Race each year comes from this heritage. Muncie was the town described in the landmark 1929 best-selling book *Middletown: A Study in Contemporary American Culture* and the 1937 *Middletown in Transition: A Study in Cultural Conflicts*, both groundbreaking anthropological studies by Robert and Helen Lynd that were funded by the Rockefeller Institute of Social and Religious Research. It was the middle class prosperity engendered by several manufacturing industries that led the sociologists to Muncie.

South Bend is best known today as home to the University of Notre Dame and its photogenic "golden dome," but well into the 1960s innovative Studebaker cars were made there by a company that started in the nineteenth century making horse-drawn wooden farm wagons. Bloomington, home to the main campus of Indiana University, a place where Nobel Prize–winning geneticist James D. Watson did his graduate school research on the double helix, did not have a car industry, but for years made General Electric refrigerators and RCA picture tubes right in town. A downsized GE is still there; RCA is gone. Bloomington also was home to the important Showers Brothers Furniture Factory, once one of the largest employers in the state. They planed, turned, joined, and finished oak and walnut that loggers felled in nearby old-growth hardwood stands. Remnants of the factory and its characteristic, repeating wedge roof have been cleverly restored and now serve as Bloomington's city hall.

Visteon, a Ford Motor Company parts supplier, closed a major plant in Connersville in east-central Indiana in 2007, idling 900 employees. Indianapolis had a major Chrysler "gray iron" foundry, a Ford assembly plant, and a GM metal-stamping plant for many years, though as a percentage of population these auto factories were not as singularly important as in the smaller and midsize Indiana towns. The Chrysler foundry closed several years ago; the GM stamping plant, on the other side of the White River from downtown Indianapolis, was slated for closure even before the recent auto industry crisis.

GM continued to maintain an aluminum casting plant in Bedford, Indiana, but the factory's 425 workers were biting their nails throughout 2009. The plant, which dates to 1943, once employed 1,200. About a half hour south of Bloomington, Bedford is deep in the Hoosier Hills and supports a good forest products trade, with veneer exports going to China and Germany. It's also the self-styled "limestone capital of the world" (the Empire State Building was built with limestone from a nearby Bedford quarry). But it's the city's percentage of auto industry jobs that has historically been very high — the town's population is only 13,000.

"This is a hardworking community that has a history of making things," said Bedford mayor Shawna Girgis. "If we were to lose that plant . . . we would either have to go somewhere else to find work or recreate ourselves, which is what I would push for. I'm not going to be happy being a mayor of a city that is dying."[6]

Marion, Indiana, was long one of the more important manufacturing towns in the state. For years it relied on both an RCA television factory and a General Motors metal-stamping plant for thousands of jobs. The RCA facility, later purchased by French-owned Thomson Consumer Electronics, closed in 2004, but the metal-stamping plant was still in operation well into 2009. Wayne Seybold was elected mayor in 2003. His priority since the RCA collapse has been diversification, he said.

"I think the community at large was just waiting for the day that [RCA] would go," Seybold said. "Really, I would say it was probably a blessing when it did go because as long as it was here and you always had that cloud over your head that it would go, people weren't ready to move on." It's a bit of spin, of course, but in recent years Seybold has promoted the expansion of Indiana Wesleyan University, which is based in Marion, as well as the establishment of two large retail distribution centers for Dollar General stores and Walmart, respectively. But he didn't intend to ignore the GM plant, which still employed nearly 1,000. Seybold was exploring every possible tax break and incentive he could muster to make sure the metal-stamping plant stayed open, even if GM were to eventually file for bankruptcy protection.

Anderson had been the focal point for GM anxiety in Indiana in the recent past, but Kokomo was now the epicenter of Chrysler anxiety in the state. John Morris, a retired Chrysler autoworker in Kokomo who settled in Daytona Beach, Florida, recalled the looming failure of Chrysler a generation earlier, in the dark days of 1979 when both union leaders and company president Lee Iacocca went hat in hand to Congress for an earlier bailout package. "I can remember the Union Bank in Kokomo, which no longer exists, but they came around putting brass tags on all the machines in Kokomo and we asked what's going on, and they said, 'Well, we own these machines and we're putting these numbers on them.' I'd say that's when we knew our jobs were in jeopardy. That's when we started talking, 'Well, if we go under what are you going to do?' and all that. Union Bank was going to sell it for pennies on the dollar."

Morris says prospects were so bleak then that neither Sears nor J. C. Penney would sell you a washer or dryer on revolving credit if they thought you were an autoworker. Thousands of workers were laid off that year.

Jeff Shrock, just a boy in 1979, also remembers those grim times. "My dad was an electrician in the auto plant," he said. "I remember my mom and dad having conversations whether Chrysler was going to survive and whether Dad was going to go to work tomorrow. You'd hear stories about guys getting their checks and rushing to the bank to cash them. There were a lot of people around Kokomo at that time who lost their jobs. Times were tight at home. We didn't go out a lot to eat. We'd have soup at home and we didn't have a lot of new things, but we were always provided for as kids."

Susan Perry, fifty-one, has worked at Chrysler most of her adult life. She went straight to work out of high school, then after studying part-time for years completed a bachelor's degree in labor studies in 2005 at Indiana University–Kokomo. Perry started in the factory at age twenty, then was laid off several months later, just before the first Chrysler auto bailout in 1979. She wasn't called back to work for ten years. By then she and her husband, also an autoworker, had a three-year-old son. "Seniority was so high I had to stay second shift for fourteen years," Perry said. "My husband worked days. We'd meet in the parking lot and hand off the kids. It was hard on a marriage and a lot of marriages didn't survive."

Perry remembers the bad times in the late 1970s and early 1980s, as all old-timers in Kokomo do. "From 1978 to 1984 Kokomo was devastated," she said. "Stores were closed. People didn't have money. They didn't shop. Kokomo Mall was a giant indoor flea market."

It might as well have been the Great Depression. Things didn't really pick up until the early 1990s, when soccer moms drove those Chrysler Corporation minivans, and real men drove Jeeps and Dodge Ram trucks. Plus, easy credit and short-term leases on new cars moved a lot of product off dealer lots then. A new car payment might be $400 a month, but a 36-month lease might only be $199 a month. Whatever the reasons, Chrysler prospered in the early 1990s, which is partly what caused Daimler to buy it in 1998, and workers inside the factories to cheer at the time. "One year we received $4,000 profit sharing," Perry said. "It was a boom time."

But things were changing in the American workforce. Apart from the vicissitudes of the automobile industry itself, union membership has long been in decline. By 2008 the vast majority of Americans didn't belong to a union at all. Union membership in absolute numbers peaked in 1979 at 21 million; by percent of employed Americans it peaked in 1954 at 28 percent. By 2003 only 11.5 percent of all Americans were unionized, however, and the only growth was in the public employee sector, not the spirited, militant industrial sector of the old Walter Reuther days.[7] The trends should have sounded alarm bells inside the auto plants and the UAW halls, but they didn't. The job market might be different in the technology-based information society of the future, but manufacturing jobs would always be there, they must have felt. At least, that's how people in Kokomo and auto plants everywhere in North America saw things.

That was the way Tom LaSorda saw things, too. A fresh-faced, middle-aged Canadian engineer, LaSorda was vice-chairman of DaimlerChrysler under the company's German ownership. He had earned his reputation in the industry during a twenty-three-year career at General Motors building state-of-the-art car assembly plants around the world when DaimlerChrysler hired him in 2000 as head of manufacturing. He quickly rose through the ranks and became CEO of the company. LaSorda knew all about strikes and hardships. His father was an autoworker paid by the hour who had raised eight children in a 900-square-foot house in Windsor, Ontario. By the time LaSorda reached the top of DaimlerChrysler his straightforward management style was widely appreciated throughout the company. "Tom's the kind of guy people like to do stuff for," said Frank Faga, director of advanced manufacturing engineering for Chrysler. "He's friendly and smart, and he's good with people."[8]

Good with people or not, when Daimler sold the majority control of Chrysler to New York–based private equity firm Cerberus Capital Management in 2007, LaSorda was pushed down a rung on the corporate ladder in favor of Robert Nardelli, a former Home Depot executive that the investment firm hired for the top job. The new management regime furloughed 32,000 employees and eliminated a third of Chrysler's production capacity and a dozen shifts in various plants. But LaSorda in particular was ever the optimist, looking ahead to a partnership with upstart Chinese carmaker Chery. Unable to field its own small car that might look good, sip gas, *and* turn a profit, Chrysler figured Chery's low-cost labor and processes in China could help it put a competitive car on American roads with a Chrysler nameplate on the front grille. "We researched the world and found they were the best," LaSorda said. "With us or without us, they're going to grow. So the question is, 'Are you going to go with a winner?'"

Then the subprime mortgage crisis erupted, credit markets shrank, and Chrysler's deal with Chery skidded into the ditch. Cerberus began exploring a Chrysler merger with GM in early 2008, but that fell through, too. By the fall, Chrysler was in desperate straits. So was GM. So was Ford, which now carried a mountain of debt and faced falling sales just like the other Detroit-based companies, but wasn't as close to bankruptcy.

Yet cautious optimism prevailed, naively so or not. When the Detroit Three auto executives went to Washington to seek a bailout in the autumn of 2008, no one figured Congress could turn down an industry so vital to the nation. Just in case some lawmakers were uninformed, Nardelli spelled out why a bailout mattered during Senate hearings in November. "Immediate financial assistance will serve the country and the economy directly in two key ways," Nardelli intoned. "First, the lifeblood of the U.S. economy will continue to flow. The industry will be able to continue to pay at its current levels $22 billion in annual wages to our employees, $13 billion in annual pensions to our retirees and surviving spouses, and meet our current commitment of $102 billion in health care costs to employees. We will continue to pay $156 billion annually to our suppliers and work to keep them strong by providing significant additional financial relief for distressed suppliers fighting to stay in business."9

It was a lot of money that two of the Detroit Three were requesting, but LaSorda later echoed Nardelli, saying that a bailout was better than a bankruptcy. A bankruptcy could force Chrysler's auto-parts suppliers into bankruptcy, too, a true snowball effect that would quickly lead to an avalanche of bad news and dire consequences. Ninety of Chrysler's 100 top suppliers also did business with Ford and General Motors, which meant that if one of those companies failed, all the interrelated companies would suffer, as well.

Then-GM chief Richard Wagoner and UAW president Ron Gettelfinger, a native of Indiana, also vigorously supported the bailout and opposed a bankruptcy, arguing that no one would buy a car from a bankrupt company. That hypothesis was to be tested in time.

The congressional leaders listened and wailed and beat their breasts and finally insisted that in order to qualify for a bailout (sometimes called a bridge loan), the automakers must show them a plan to become viable. Congress especially wanted to see progress in bringing more fuel-efficient products to market. Nardelli had a response. In 2009 alone, he claimed, fleet fuel economy for the brand would improve dramatically, new models would be engineered, and there would be a true EV (electric vehicle), as well, a Jeep driven solely by an electric motor feeding off a battery. Even the once mighty Dodge Ram, the star of the early 1990s but now considered a fat cow by the marketplace, would finally have a fuel-efficient hybrid option in 2010, Nardelli promised.

GM, which had a better research and development program than Chrysler, also touted its upcoming products, including the Volt, a plug-in electric vehicle. GM had long experimented with alternative and electric vehicles, including the ill-fated EV1 in the

1990s, as well as odorless, emissions-free hydrogen fuel cell technology. If GM really were to have a future, it might be in electric vehicles and fuel cells. Spokespeople for Ford also trumpeted new models and new hybrids in front of the Washington legislators.

Back in Detroit, all the auto industry executives figured the Democrats in the House of Representatives would go for the deal. LaSorda was uneasy about prospects in the Senate, however, particularly among Republicans from Southern states traditionally hostile toward labor unions. "This isn't about Joe the Plumber. This is about Joe and Josephine, the autoworker," he told a town hall meeting at the Chrysler Jeep complex in Toledo, Ohio, referring to the Ohio plumber made famous during the Obama-McCain presidential campaign that year. "A strong U.S.-based automotive industry also is the backbone of the nation's economy."

LaSorda's hunch about the United States Senate proved to be right. A week after the Senate failed to approve the bailout plan in December 2008, LaSorda announced the company would idle 29 plants for a month, virtually shutting down all its manufacturing capability in North America. It was the sharpest, most desperate reaction to the crisis by any of the Detroit Three automakers. New car and truck sales were down for all major domestic and import brand manufacturers in 2008, but Chrysler was hit the hardest of all: its sales nose-dived fifty-three percent in December 2008 compared to the previous year's sales for the same month. Furthermore, independent industry analysts doubted that Chrysler could bring many, if any, of the products Nardelli had announced to market in a timely fashion with such poor cash flow.

Many workers in Kokomo felt that German automaker Daimler was to blame for Chrysler's woes. Daimler purchased Chrysler in 1998 in the so-called merger of equals, paying $36 billion for what it believed was the hottest, most innovative American car company going at the time. Less than a decade later newspapers were to use words like "dumped" and "unloaded" to describe Daimler's sale of the new venture, which had been named

DaimlerChrysler, to Cerberus. Daimler received only $7.4 billion for giving an eighty percent stake in the company to Cerberus; it kept a twenty percent stake for itself. Even at that, Daimler effectively gave most of the sale price back to Chrysler's loan arm, Chrysler Financial, to cover outstanding debts, restructuring charges, and to recapitalize the brand's balance sheet.[10] Daimler was, however, able to transfer an $18 billion pension liability to Cerberus, which many observers felt was key to the deal. When business analysts compare domestic auto manufacturing costs to those of import brands and speak of "legacy costs" for the Detroit Three, it is mostly pension and retiree health care costs they're referring to.

The 2007 Daimler retreat was universally popular with autoworkers in Kokomo, even though Cerberus had no automobile manufacturing history. The big complaints about Daimler? The Germans were blamed for: the continued emphasis on big trucks and SUVs, even as the market was softening for such products; losing the edge in the minivan segment to Honda; and especially abandoning the subcompact car market. After production of the subcompact Neon ceased in 2005 (a popular ad campaign for the car in the mid-1990s began "Say hello to Neon" and featured a humanlike front view of the car with cute ovoid headlamps), the company was alone among all mass marketers in not having a true entry-level or budget model in its lineup.

"In my entire life in the plant the membership has always questioned the strategic decisions of management, especially the small car going back to the Horizon and Dodge Omni, and then Neon," said union leader Jeff Shrock. "When the Neon was stopped people were asking why in the world would Chrysler put itself in the position of only being in the big car market? You'd talk at break time and things like that, and Chrysler's vision and attitude toward middle-class people was always a topic of discussion. The topic was always on Chrysler's focus on large trucks."

The clean-edged Omni and Horizon hatchbacks were the first front-wheel drive small cars mass-produced in America. They were good sellers for more than a decade after their introduction in 1978 — just in time for the Iranian Revolution, the 1979 energy crisis, and the subsequent worldwide recession. The basic design for the cars came from a Chrysler subsidiary in Europe. In 1986 alone, the Chrysler final assembly plant in Belvidere, Illinois, turned out 335,000 Horizons, Omnis, and sporty two-door versions of the cars. In 1995, the plant would churn out 247,000 Neons, the best year ever for that model. Yet subcompact production ceased when Chrysler decided to make "mini-sport utes," also known as small SUVs or "tall station wagons," at Belvidere instead. These were the Dodge Caliber, Jeep Compass, and Jeep Patriot, which are essentially the same vehicles underneath their skins. The first year of production, 2007, saw a combined output of 335,000, which was good, but sales plummeted the following year with the global recession and talk of an industry collapse. Of course, Chrysler hadn't intended to abandon the small car market at all. Profit margins were just too small and legacy costs too high to bother with subcompact car production in America. The company had loved minivans, Jeep Cherokees, and Dodge Rams for one reason only — profit margins were much larger on such vehicles. But Chrysler would re-enter the small car market. It was going to help engineer such cars in China with Chery — that is, until the deal collapsed in 2008.

Alas, Chrysler and GM received their reprieve. If the Senate wouldn't provide an aid package, then-President George Bush would. He announced on December 19, 2008, that he would dip into the $700 billion Troubled Asset Relief Program (TARP) funds that Congress had approved earlier in the year for financial institutions. GM and Chrysler would receive a combined total of $17.4 billion in loans in order to keep operating through March 31, 2009, at which time the companies' progress in gaining concessions from workers, suppliers, dealers, and other stakeholders would be reviewed. The agreement also gave the federal government non-voting stock warrants in the two companies.

In Kokomo, Mayor Greg Goodnight was relieved at the bridge loan, as he preferred to call it, but not surprised. If he had sweated during the nervous days in early December he didn't show it much. He figured someone would call the Senate's bluff. He even figured it might be the radical laissez-faire Republican George Bush who would ante up. No president would want to be seen as the one who lost any of the Detroit Three on his watch, Goodnight figured. "I wasn't totally discouraged that nothing would happen," he said.

Still, events were being determined over his head and that bothered Mayor Goodnight greatly. He could offer no incentives himself to Chrysler; restrictive laws only allowed tax breaks for new development, not just for a company to stay put. All he knew was that the city had received a ninety-day extension just like the car company had. But if Chrysler ultimately failed it would be his city that paid the greatest price because of the number of townspeople relying on the company for employment. Goodnight, like the rest of America, could only look to Washington, Detroit, and New York to see what fate had in store.

---

1. Monica Davey, "For Indiana Voters, Talk of Change May Fall Flat," *New York Times*, April 24, 2008, http://www.nytimes.com/2008/04/24/us/politics/24indiana.html?scp=1&sq=Greg%20Goodnight&st=cse.

2. Newsmaker Interview transcript, "UAW Chief Gettelfinger Defends Position on Wage Cuts," PBS Online News Hour, December 12, 2008, http://www.pbs.org/newshour/bb/business/july-dec08/autouaw_12-12.html.

3. Deborah Bonnet and Robert Hoke, "2007 Needs Assessment for Howard County, Indiana" (Indianapolis: DBonnet Associates), 4 (http://www.unitedwayhoco.org/needs/Full_Report07.pdf).

4. Ted Evanoff, "Anderson Looks for New Ventures as it Loses Its Automotive Past," *Indianapolis Star*, October 19, 2006, News-1.

5. Kevin Leininger, "Not the Brightest Bulb in the Box," *News-Sentinel* (Fort Wayne, IN), January 12, 2005, A1.

6. Josh Duke, "Bedford Hopes Its GM Plant Isn't Casualty of Expected Bankruptcy," *Indianapolis Star*, May 31, 2009, http://www.indystar.com/apps/pbcs.dll/article?AID=2009905310389.

7. Gerald Mayer, "Union Membership Trends in the United States" (Washington, D.C.: Congressional Research Service, Library of Congress, 2004), 3 (http://digitalcommons.ilr.cornell.edu/cgi/viewcontent.cgi?article=1176&context=key_workplace).

8. Sharon Silke Carty, "New CEO at Chrysler Has Cars in His Veins, LaSorda Received His Values From His Dad," *USA Today*, October 24, 2005, http://www.usatoday.com/educate/college/careers/CEOs/10-24-05.htm.

9. Robert Nardelli, "Testimony of Robert Nardelli to the U.S. Senate," November 18, 2008.

10. Gail Edmondson, "Why Daimler Gave Chrysler to Cerberus," *Business Week*, May 15, 2007, www.msnbc.com/id/18680299/.

CHAPTER 2

Dogs at the Gate

IN THE FIRST WEEKS OF 2009, the American automobile industry was reeling. Chrysler clearly was in the worst shape of the traditional Big Three. The company needed a partner to prop it up and keep it alive. Many doubted the swashbuckling New York investors in control of Chrysler were up to the challenge of managing a car business, particularly in light of the controversial figure they had put at the head of the car company.[1]

Robert Nardelli had walked away from the Home Depot hardware chain with a reputed $210 million severance package and moved into the chairman's suite at Chrysler in 2007. Yet he had no automotive experience and had never led a complex enterprise like Chrysler. The company — headquartered in a sleek fifteen-story tower in the Detroit suburb of Auburn Hills — employed 66,000 people and typically took in more than $60 billion in annual sales, although weak entries in the small, midsize, and family sedan markets had dragged down profits for a decade.

The New York investor, Cerberus Capital Management, had acquired control of Chrysler from German auto giant Daimler for $7.4 billion in 2007 and acted like the old manufacturer needed simply to cut costs and polish its brand image to remain competitive. But by the end of 2008 Chrysler was on the verge of bankruptcy. Indeed, the entire auto industry was suffering. Nardelli found himself in the procession of auto, bank, and Wall Street executives calling on Washington for bailouts.

The country had been mugged by a sudden recession whose ferocity stunned Americans. *Wall Street Journal* columnist Peggy

Noonan, who had been a speechwriter for President Ronald Reagan, captured America's mood, writing: "People are not feeling passing anger or disappointment, they're feeling truly frightened. . . . [It's] systemic collapse. It's not just here, it's global."[2]

Yet a solution to the crisis could be found, oddly enough, in the old industrial cities where tens of thousands of skilled citizens knew how to design, engineer, and fabricate products. In the world of think tanks and economic strategists, there was a sense that America could manufacture and export its way back to prosperity.[3] If so, this actually presented an opportunity for three of the nation's largest manufacturers — Chrysler, General Motors, and Ford Motor Company — the very companies hammered by the recession. Their futures would be insured if only they would engineer a new fleet of fuel-efficient vehicles to power sales and help ease the nation's reliance on imported oil. They had the know-how and the manufacturing capacity. But they were in a tailspin.

Ford was hanging on, having lined up huge loans before the economy soured, but Chrysler and General Motors were nearly bankrupt and looking to the federal government for a cash infusion. GM's reception in the capital was slightly better than Chrysler's. Some lawmakers openly wondered why taxpayers should back Chrysler, a private company owned by investors whose identities were not even public record. Other lawmakers insisted Chrysler find a partner to lean on so it didn't collapse in ruin and squander the bailout loans. That was one reason Nardelli was searching for a partner for Chrysler. The other reason was his boss. Making money in the car business was not as easy as plucking ripe fruit from the tree. Cerberus was scorched by its short adventure in the car business and now was eager to get out.

Cerberus was an upstart investment firm on Park Avenue in Manhattan run by secretive billionaire Stephen Feinberg. Essentially a banker unschooled in the relentless booms and busts of the manufacturing business cycle, Feinberg's entire career had been lived in Wall Street's golden age.[4] Reaganomics and a new American attitude toward debt — once sinful, now good — had unleashed a massive updraft of the stock market.[5] Wall Street traded debt, and bought and sold companies like a grand game of Monopoly. By the middle of the 2000 decade, an unprecedented wave of buyouts was reshaping corporate America.[6]

So it did not seem odd at all for private investors to buy 80.1 percent of Chrysler in early 2007 from German owner Daimler-Chrysler. Indeed, the transaction looked like another winning hand for Feinberg, enhancing his reputation on Wall Street as a shrewd judge of distressed assets. "We believe we bought the company very cheaply, and we do not need to be heroes to earn a good return on the investment," says a note he and a partner sent to Chrysler investors in January 2008. "Even though we have higher hopes of deeply and fundamentally improving Chrysler, solid blocking and tackling and reasonable execution should be enough to earn a good return."[7]

In a meteoric Wall Street career, Feinberg had quickly embraced a lesson dear to the wealthy traders he saw around him — buy cheap, cut costs, resell the business fast as possible. The son of a steel salesman, young Feinberg had captained Princeton University's varsity tennis team in 1982.[8] Rather than go on to a tony Manhattan address, he latched his star to the second-tier investment firm of Drexel Burnham Lambert. Drexel, now out of business, enjoyed a brief fling as a Wall Street wonder until one of its notorious junk bond salesmen, Michael Milken, served a prison sentence in the late 1980s.

By 1992, Feinberg had launched his own business, teaming with investor Bill Richter. The pair amassed $10 million — a modest sum on Wall Street even then — and set up Cerberus.[9] Taken from Greek mythology, the name was that of the three-headed dog guarding the gates of Hades. The intimidating moniker was fitting for a vulture fund whose business was buying the cheap debt of troubled public companies and betting on their recovery. If the company failed, Cerberus could liquidate the assets and pocket the proceeds. If the company succeeded, Cerberus's holdings rose in value.

Feinberg soon developed a reputation in finance circles for razor-edge tactics. Real-estate mogul Sam Zell saw the dealings firsthand in the 2000 bankruptcy of Coram Healthcare of Denver, Colorado. Coram's top executives proposed a bankruptcy restructuring that would hand Cerberus and other bond holders full control of the company, but cancel out any financial gains for regular investors, including Zell. Unknown to Zell, Cerberus was secretly paying Coram's chief executive officer $1 million per year in addition to his regular salary. When the secret pay came to light, Cerberus insisted nothing was errant, although a federal bankruptcy judge ruled a conflict of interest existed. The *New York Times* reported that in 2003 "Cerberus and two other investors agreed to pay $56 million to Coram, partially to settle the conflict-of-interest claims."[10]

In the rough-and-tumble world of distressed asset investing, Cerberus's Coram dealings were considered par for the course. "When you play in the distressed arena, you develop sharp elbows," Joel Simon, a principal in the financial advisory firm XRoads, told the *Times*. "They have a reputation as tough negotiators who avoid public attention."[11] Despite a penchant for secrecy, Cerberus's aggressive image traveled beyond Wall Street. A study of distressed asset firms by Moody's Investors Service confirmed Cerberus was one of the fastest at pulling cash out of a new acquisition and putting the money in its own pocket.[12] The fast-buck reputation proved a hindrance in the deal for Air Canada, the leading air carrier in Canada. Cerberus was derided as "American piranhas" by protestors who turned to a white knight investor (Trinity Time, an investment firm headed by billionaire Victor Li) to fend off Cerberus. After labor unions sidelined the white knight, Cerberus was back at the table, this time with the aid of Brian Mulroney, the former Canadian prime minister. Cerberus had hired him as a special advisor to see the deal carried out to fruition in 2004.[13]

In 2009 with its run-and-gun reputation, Cerberus most likely would have expected a skeptical Washington reception when it dispatched Nardelli in search of taxpayer bailout dollars. But in what would prove to be a stroke of good fortune for Cerberus, Feinberg had set out to redo the image not long after the deal for Air Canada was completed. By then, he wanted Cerberus positioned as a more traditional investment firm to enhance its ability to take over high-profile businesses.

Rehabbing the image was partly a necessity driven by a budding concern about the new tide of buyout artists on Wall Street. All over Manhattan, investment houses hired publicity firms and turned to Washington insiders to help temper any push back. Contemplating the trend, Wall Street sage Felix Rohatyn speculated about the amount of transparency the wheelers and dealers would tolerate. "The public wants to know who is buying up corporate America," Rohatyn said. "It will be interesting to see how far those at the top are willing to pull back the veil."[14]

Cerberus never revealed enough of itself to become a household name. But in 2006 it disclosed control of forty-five companies employing 250,000 people and running up $50 billion in annual revenue. The car rental chains Alamo and National were in the fold, along with retailers Mervyns and Albertsons, Aozora Bank of Japan and IAP Worldwide Services, one of the larger contractors to the United States government in Iraq.[15]

So much money was flowing into Cerberus it was not unheard of for Feinberg himself to take home $75 million in total compensation in a year.[16] The tide of money helped attract prominent investors and deal makers whose star quality opened doors for Feinberg and smoothed out the firm's reputation. Former Vice President Dan Quayle and ex–U.S. Treasury Secretary John Snow, who had been chairman of the board at CSX, a major railroad once known as the Chesapeake & Ohio, signed on as partners in Cerberus.[17] Both had been in President George H. W. Bush's administration. Also onboard was car executive Jacques Nasser, whom the Ford family had ousted from the top of Ford Motor Company in 2001.

Quayle (a former senator from Indiana before becoming Bush's vice-president) and Snow were attached to the firm's

Washington office with former Louisiana senator John B. Breaux and Billy J. Cooper, who had been a partner in the influential Washington lobbying firm Patton Boggs. Cerberus also hired government specialists. Their knowledge would prove useful when it was time to seek financial assistance from the government. These included Arnold I. Havens, who had been general counsel in the United States Treasury; David Hobbs, who had been President Bush's congressional affairs aide; and Christopher A. Smith, former Treasury chief of staff.[18]

The powerful names helped attract wealthy investors including J. Ezra Merkin, a financier in the upper crust of New York's social elite. He advanced $79 million for the Chrysler deal and another $66 million for Cerberus's purchase of half the stock in GM's finance company, General Motors Acceptance Corporation. For his efforts, Merkin was appointed chairman of GMAC, though he resigned from the finance company in 2009 after the high-profile collapse of Bernard Madoff's $50 billion investment fund caught him in the blowback. The New York attorney general's office launched a separate probe into Merkin's investments on behalf of universities and charities.[19]

Surrounded with a new cadre of prominent deal makers, Feinberg forged ahead in 2007. Seeing a lucrative opportunity to cheaply pick up Chrysler, Cerberus ignored the warning signs flashing around the old automaker. Daimler had dreamed Chrysler would be a reliable cash engine when it paid shareholders $36 billion in 1998 for the American icon. Instead, the Germans watched Chrysler skid and slide: first when the senior American executives departed, then when cash reserves dried up, and later as a price war with GM broke out. Weary of the nettlesome company, Daimler essentially gave away the American brand.

The German industrial group gave Cerberus $700 million as a sweet inducement to take over Chrysler. Then, according to *Business Week* magazine's Gail Edmondson, Daimler injected $7.4 billion into the American car company and its consumer loan arm, Chrysler Financial, to cover outstanding debts and restructuring charges, and recapitalize the ailing automaker's balance sheet.[20] Closing the deal in August 2007, the investment firm quickly appointed Robert Nardelli chairman of Chrysler. Nardelli had no more seniority in the auto business than Feinberg. But the square-jawed Pennsylvanian had a knack for bagging big jobs, even when he had worn out his welcome at other leading corporations.

As the head of Home Depot, Nardelli had angered investors when he refused to answer questions about the hardware chain's weak stock price in 2006. He went on to anger corporate reformers jarred by CEO pay when he reportedly took home $38 million in 2006 income, then allegedly received a $210 million golden parachute in severance and stock when he was finally pushed out the door in January 2007.[21]

Earlier in his career, Nardelli had come up the ladder at General Electric, at one point managing GE's Canadian retail appliance division. Disgruntled, he left GE when he was passed over to succeed the legendary Jack Welch, who retired in 2001 as GE chairman. Feinberg had articulated an idea that he wanted Cerberus to some day be like General Electric — a stable of different companies in a wide range of fields, each fine-tuned to make money. So it made sense for Feinberg to bring in a former GE exec to run the biggest company in the stable.

Meeting with Chrysler's Canadian autoworkers in 2007, Feinberg had assured them he had no intention of quickly selling off the car company for a fast buck. Though he may have been sincere, Chrysler's problem was actually designing a new fleet of autos for an era when consumers were clamoring for high-mileage automobiles like the Toyota Prius hybrid-electric sedan. Under Daimler's nine-year reign, Chrysler designers had brought out only a single head-turning vehicle, the masculine, rear-drive Chrysler 300 midsize sedan. There was, of course, its Dodge sibling, the Charger, plus perhaps the Dodge Caliber mini-sport ute, which sold well for a short time.

Nardelli, who was accustomed to the fast pace of mass-market retailing, had no difficulty reaching decisions. Taking control at Chrysler, he jettisoned 32,000 employees, including talented engineers, in a cost-cutting move.[22] He began pressing the designers. He wanted customers to like what they saw. He ordered 400 changes at a cost of $1.5 billion to get rid of cheap-looking materials inside the cars. While the changes were necessary, many were on the surface. What was really needed was a retooled Chrysler fleet.

As late as 2007, Chrysler was all about high-testosterone pickup trucks and rugged sport-utility vehicles for affluent sub-urbanites. Pickups, sport-utilities, and minivans accounted for almost three of every four vehicles sold by Chrysler, making its reliance on trucks more complete than any automaker in the world. But the market was about to shift, stunning Detroit and catching Feinberg and Nardelli unprepared.

In the summer of 2008, crude oil surged to $145 a barrel, and consumers snubbed the heavy trucks and SUVs that had long delivered profits for Chrysler, Ford, and GM. By the end of the year, the recession was charging ahead full bore. Forecasts called for sales in 2009 of only 10.5 million new autos in the United States, compared to 16.1 million vehicles two years earlier. In an open U.S. market that had come to be crowded with seventeen foreign automakers — there had been only a handful in the country a generation earlier — almost no car company was making money. But the downturn was decisively brutal on the Detroit Three because of their high operating costs, as well as the outlays that went to support more than 1 million pensioners and their spouses retired from the domestic industry.

Just when the American automobile industry needed stable and visionary leaders, it was confounded by uncertainty. The timing was unfortunate. Clyde V. Prestowitz Jr., who had been a trade advisor in the Reagan administration, was by the end of 2008 arguing that the United States had to consume less from abroad and sharply step up its own exports. "But the good news is that, at least for the United States, we're going to have a man-ufacturing renaissance," Prestowitz said in an interview that aired on public television's *NewsHour with Jim Lehrer* the day before Christmas. "Jobs in production are going to come back to the U.S. because the only way for the U.S. to achieve sustainable, long-term growth is for the U.S. to produce more here, export more, relatively, while Asia imports more relatively. So I see this as the beginning of a long-needed shift in the base of the U.S. economy."[23]

Prestowitz, president of Economic Strategy Institute, a conservative think tank in Washington, D.C., had put his finger on what could revive the industrial belt. Early in 2009 in Washington and Detroit, however, there was little talk about breathing life into the fading industrial sector. Manufacturing accounted for only about ten percent of the U.S. economy, half the size it had been a generation earlier, while financial services had become twenty-two percent of the economy before the Wall Street meltdown triggered by the collapse of the housing market. Instead of forging a new industry, though, Chrysler and GM were living on slender financial lifelines fronted the month before by President George W. Bush. No one was sure Chrysler could survive. No one was certain GM and Ford could avoid bankruptcy protection, either — a process the auto executives argued would scare away car buyers and sink the companies.

Speaking at an automotive conference in Detroit, Ron Gettelfinger, the president of the United Auto Workers union, had called on the industry to stand up and jointly shoulder responsibility for rebuilding the car companies. "We've got to put partisan differences aside, and look for real solutions. . . . We know that additional sacrifices may be required to get these companies back on track," Gettelfinger said.[24] Everyone imagined more job losses, plant closings, wage concessions, and mergers. Although the union president pointed out sacrifices ought to be equal among the various constituents — labor, management, dealers, lenders, investors — it looked increasingly as if Cerberus was going to skate along free while the union workers and the taxpayers shouldered Chrysler.

Nardelli, after all, was angling for a partner in part to persuade skeptical legislators Chrysler would not melt down and squander the $3 billion in further assistance wanted from Congress on top of the $4 billion infusion in December. Cerberus itself was deemed stingy. Although Feinberg's firm had put into Chrysler the $7 billion handed over by Daimler, Cerberus's commitment to Chrysler was still in question. "Why isn't the parent company stepping up? In reality, they should," said Maurice "Mo" Davison, a Gettelfinger lieutenant in charge of UAW Region 3, which coordinates UAW activities in Indiana and Kentucky. Just as skeptical was congressman Elijah E. Cummings, a Maryland Democrat. "Chrysler should come back to Congress and say, 'This is what we've asked Cerberus for, and this was their response.' I think the public is due that," Cummings said.[25]

If Cerberus was hesitant about sowing more cash in Chrysler, it wasn't afraid of wielding its well-connected insiders in Washington. In December, Snow and Quayle had lobbied members of Congress for financial aid. Snow had called on his successor at the United States Treasury, Henry Paulson, himself a wealthy former Wall Street executive. Feinberg also had shown up in Washington, at one point visiting Bob Corker, the senator from Tennessee dubious about propping up Chrysler with federal loans. With the economy falling apart, and truck sales sinking, the automaker was on pace to lose $8 billion in 2008. "I really did feel badly for these guys," Corker told the *New York Times*.[26]

What many politicians wanted to see was a Chrysler–General Motors merger. It would deflect criticism of helping out private investors. Nardelli had explored just that possibility earlier in 2008. But by autumn, GM Chairman Richard Wagoner Jr. had lost interest, fearing his company was in dire condition as auto sales bottomed out. He decided the discussions with Chrysler were merely a distraction from what was key — landing a federal bailout for General Motors.

With the merger off the table, and a growing awareness that Chrysler and GM really were on the ropes, union leaders in Indiana struggled with their response to the crisis, as well as their badly tarnished image. Mo Davison can watch the traffic flow by on Interstate 465 from the picture window in his large office on the west side of Indianapolis, just across from the city's international airport. Most of the cars Davison sees in Indiana, unlike in New York City or Washington, D.C., still are American-made, which to him really means UAW-made. A bulky-looking, aging baby boomer who grew up not a mile from where he now works, Davison started his career in the auto industry at the old gray iron Chrysler foundry in Indianapolis.

"It was poorly lit. There was sand and silica dust in the air. You couldn't leave without taking a shower before you went home," Davison recalled. "You'd breathe that black smoke and cough for hours after you'd leave your shift. My dad worked there for twenty-five years and died of lung cancer. Most of the fellows who retired out of that plant didn't live for very long. They mostly died of breathing problems."

The foundry made the engine blocks for motors all Chrysler and "MoPar" fans loved — the 383 cubic inch motor, which was in the fancifully named Plymouth Road Runner, and the more mundane 318 cubic inch V-8, which powered legions of vinyl-roof Chrysler Fifth Avenue sedans, among others. Over the years Occupational Safety & Health Administration (OSHA) regulations improved air quality and noise issues, but the foundry closed in 2005, idling the last remaining 900 workers there.

If Mo Davison were the leader of a Third World country, he'd be what you call a moderate, or at least a pragmatist. Even though his dad was a lifelong autoworker, Davison started his career as a janitor in Indianapolis at Eli Lilly and Company. He wanted to be a pharmacist. Then he tested for an apprentice electrician's job with Chrysler. He later worked in management for Chrysler, but went back into production because he wanted to be active in the union movement.

Davison said no one worried about layoffs in the old days, even before sweet UAW contracts guaranteed so-called supplemental benefits, meaning the auto companies would have to make up most of the difference between state unemployment benefits and the laid-off worker's regular pay while he or she was on unemployment.[27] "I was never out of work for a day," Davison said. "When I first got laid off I got a job at Link-Belt. They had a place on Rockville Road then. I could have sat around and drawn unemployment, but it was easy to get a job then."

Over the years Davison came to represent unionized workers at GM's Guide plant in Anderson, Navistar truck engineers in Indianapolis, Delco auto radio workers in Kokomo, and workers in more than twenty other factories in Indiana and Kentucky. Most are closed now. Today, Davison's all for concessions, as long as all other stakeholders make concessions, too. He's said good-bye to the much maligned Job Bank, which guaranteed jobs for some laid-off workers at full pay, including for such dubious volunteer efforts as one laid-off Michigan worker who continued to pull down a forty-hour-per-week paycheck because, he claimed, he pushed a disabled Vietnam War vet around in a wheelchair all day. Davison says no more than 3,400 auto-workers at any one time ever qualified for the Job Bank, but it was one of the sacrifices he said the union was willing to make to keep the auto companies solvent. Davison also pointed out that in the last UAW contract negotiated in 2007 the autoworkers agreed that a portion of their annual cost-of-living adjustments would go to fund the autoworkers' health care plans. More significantly, the UAW had already accepted a two-tier hourly wage schedule, meaning many new hires would be paid significantly less than more senior employees, basically at a rate comparable to what is common in the non-organized "transplant" factories in America. Davison believes these have all been big concessions, and said the union will make more in the future.

"We don't want businesses to fold. We want them to be successful," Davison said. "That's our top priority."

Danny Hiatt also is a moderate, or at least a realist. Shop chairman of UAW Local 292, which represents Delphi workers in Kokomo, Hiatt says he is struggling to help get the former GM electronics and radio division out of bankruptcy while holding on to the loyalty of union members. Delphi has taken big hits in the last several years. GM spun off the division in 1999, giving GM shareholders twenty percent of their stock in the new company and reducing their GM holdings accordingly. Delphi would have to bid on new contracts with GM, but was also free to bid on contracts with any other auto company. The idea was to make traditional American suppliers more competitive overall. GM maintained the pension liability for workers in the spin-off, however, a major concession. Based in Troy, Michigan, Delphi employment had been as high as 52,000 workers, but the company has been shedding jobs in recent years. Delphi's gross revenues topped $35 billion in 1995, but fell to just over $28 billion in 2000, its first year as a fully independent company. By 2005 Delphi was in Chapter 11 bankruptcy and most production workers, such as those in Kokomo, saw their UAW contract wages cut almost in half, from about $28 per hour to $15. A major reason critics of the auto industry bailout argued to let the car companies reorganize under bankruptcy protection was because that would, in fact, be a way to get out from under onerous collective bargaining agreements — the union contracts — and cut wages dramatically. It's what happened at Delphi, after all. But the Delphi bankruptcy eliminated 12,500 jobs nationally and cost American workers and taxpayers at least $9.2 billion, while costing Canadians an additional $800 million.[28]

Hiatt, fifty-four, is a Purdue University dropout who once toured the upper Midwest as part of a musical duo that performed anything from Broadway show tunes to country standards by Buck Owens and Waylon Jennings in hotel lounges, Native American–owned casinos, and the like. But with a wife and young child on the way he gave it up to come back home and begin a career in the auto plants. He says he covets his union leadership role because he enjoys being a leader, but also because he believes in the cause. "I think the unions were very important in creating a substantial middle class in America," he said. "That may sound a little socialistic but when the unions began there were unsafe work conditions, unlivable wages, and no hope of a reasonable retirement."

Hiatt said worker pay and benefits had crested as far back as

1986 when Delco, the earlier name for Delphi, went on strike and shut down GM nationwide. Delco workers could do that because they made most of the electronics for GM cars. As in most strikes, union stewards and officers trod to the different work stations inside the plants and told employees it was time to leave — usually a hand gesture or a nod of the head would be enough of a signal, but sometimes reluctant employees would need to hear a short lecture on union solidarity and collective bargaining before they would "down tools" and go. These always were tense moments inside a factory and management tended to stay off the shop floor during such walkouts. The 1986 strike was settled in short order, but the plant manager later got hold of Hiatt and told him something he would not forget. "He said this would never happen again. At that time that was just the start of the movement to Mexico," Hiatt recalled. "He also made the statement that Kokomo would be a research and development facility with less than 1,500 people. At that time we were just shy of 10,000 people. We thought that would never happen because we had always been a moneymaker for GM. I guess we were kind of spoiled."

Also in Kokomo, a watchful Jeff Everett waited out Nardelli's month-long shutdown of all Chrysler plants in North America by going into the plant almost every day during the winter of 2008–09 to tend to paperwork and check on the small group of workers maintaining the machines. He remembered it as a depressing period. Everett was the elected president of United Auto Workers Local 1166, which represented 800 workers at Chrysler's casting plant, a low-slung building that covered an entire city block. Transmission housings, engine blocks, and other power train parts were formed out of molten aluminum. Inside the plant, everyone was worried. Everyone griped. Only three months earlier, Congress had turned over $700 billion to the United States Treasury to rescue Wall Street and the banks, but it seemed no one in power gave a hoot about a car company employing 75,000 people. Or so it seemed to Everett.

Everett went home at night and said little about the situation in the plant to his family, but he thought to himself that Cerberus was the wrong owner at the wrong time. Chrysler needed passionate fighters, not Manhattan financiers. "They're not in it to make cars. They're in it just for the money," Everett said. "They thought they would slap some paint on it and sell it. They didn't see the economy was going to turn around on them."

Everett, age forty-nine, a burly man with a friendly smile and thick mustache, had grown up an hour away in a little town. Until he graduated high school, home had been his parents' small three-room house. The bathroom was an outdoor privy. Since then, the autoworker and his wife had raised five children, bought a nice house on ten wooded acres near the broad Wabash River. Two sons were enrolled in Ball State University, not far away in Muncie, Indiana. In some years, Everett had made $100,000 with overtime. But now he wasn't so sure the good times would last.

In early January 2009, the vast bulk of Chrysler production workers in Canada, Mexico, and the United States were on a month-long layoff imposed by Nardelli to conserve cash. Even so, Everett feared the company would rip through the $4 billion fronted by the White House and wind up bankrupt. Finally on January 20, the long shutdown ended. On that very day, Nardelli dropped his bombshell. An email from the chairman to plant and union officials revealed Fiat S.p.A., the Italian industrial giant, was keen on a deal with Chrysler. From the message, Everett couldn't tell if a linkup was good for Kokomo, but he liked the idea of Fiat car executives at the helm. "I think it gives us a glimmer of hope," Everett said.

Chrysler and Fiat had entered what the companies called a "non-binding term sheet to establish a global strategic partnership."[29] It meant the companies would share assets. Fiat could use Chrysler's network of auto dealers to sell Fiat cars, and perhaps assemble Fiats in North America in Chrysler plants. Chrysler, in turn, could rebadge small Fiats and sell the high-mileage cars as Chryslers. The alliance carried a certain logic. Cerberus would avoid spending billions of dollars necessary to engineer and tool its own fleet of fuel-efficient cars. Fiat would tap a network of 3,300 Chrysler dealers in North America. And the deal promised an exit strategy for Cerberus to unwind its stake in Chrysler.

Of course, Cerberus controlled 80.1 percent of Chrysler, and the remainder was Daimler's. Cerberus was so eager to be rid of Chrysler its deal would hand Fiat thirty-five percent of the American automaker essentially for free. Fiat could buy another twenty percent of Chrysler sometime in the future for as little as $25 million.[30]

Unwilling to gloat in the press about the budding American-Italian-German alliance, the head of Fiat was careful to hedge his opinion of the American entity. "Chrysler has all the prerequisites to survive," Fiat Chief Executive Officer Sergio Marchionne said. "But the bigger issue is, 'What does it look like two or three years from now?' It's not as if Fiat is going to show up and Cinderella is going to be magically turned into something else."[31] Marchionne easily could have said the same about his company. Fiat had not sold cars in America since the early 1990s, when it pulled out amid a wave of complaints about quality (pundits derisively said Fiat stood for "Fix it again, Tony"). Now the Italian automaker was stymied by intense competition in Europe. Marchionne saw the huge American auto market as a lifeline. Fiat made true economy cars, but it also had the Alfa Romeo, Ferrari, and other luxury brands. Fiat was eager to put up the sleek cars against Mercedes and BMWs in the wildly lucrative American luxury market.

For Chrysler, the notion that it could sell small Fiat cars seemed like a lifesaver. The engineering corps in Auburn Hills, Michigan, headquarters was being hollowed out at precisely the time Chrysler needed a home run in the design studios. When the 2009 Detroit auto show opened in early January, Chrysler had no new production models to show the 5,000 international journalists who frequent the annual automotive bonanza, in spite of Robert Nardelli's earlier boasts to Congress. It was an ominous sign. Hybrids and electric cars were thought to be the future of the business. Yet Chrysler had nothing even under wraps to show it could compete in this new world, just the 200C EV, a plug-in electric vehicle concept car with an appealing muscle car body style, but no evidence it ever would be built.

There was one downside to the partnership. Fiat, the largest industrial company in Italy, had nearly run out of money itself in 2004. Five years later it was stronger, but Fiat was still no financial powerhouse. Only a few years earlier it had sought an alliance with General Motors but was unable to salvage any profits from the venture and backed out of the deal. Now it needed a partner as much as Chrysler did, which meant there was no cash in Italy for the American company. Instead, Chrysler would have to lean again on taxpayers for more bailout cash. That would be no easy task. Corker, the Tennessee senator who sat on the influential banking committee, pointed out the Italian company itself was an obstacle. "In essence the U.S. taxpayers have written a check to get a foreign entity to take over a U.S. automaker . . ." Corker said. "Hopefully the jobs will be saved. Hopefully the brand will be empowered. But at the end of the day, it poses quite a dilemma for U.S. taxpayers."[32]

Founded in 1899 as the Fabbrica Italiana Automobili Torino — Fiat is formed from the first letter of each word — the company fueled Italy's powerful Agnelli family. As late as 1990, Fiat was Italy's undisputed automotive leader, accounting for about sixty percent of the new autos sold in the country.

As trade barriers fell, and lean production techniques took hold, Japanese automakers stepped into Europe and riddled Fiat with many of the same competitive issues the Detroit Three faced from foreign rivals. In the 1990s, Fiat's market share shrank to thirty-nine percent, and patriarch Gianni Agnelli decided to look abroad for new profits. He turned to General Motors for help.[33] In 2000, GM paid $2.4 billion for twenty percent of Fiat with a right to buy the company outright. More important, the automakers agreed to share engine production, purchasing, and financing operations in Europe and South America. Just as Daimler had acquired Chrysler, Ford had taken on Volvo and Land Rover, and Renault merged with Nissan, GM and Fiat saw global economies of scale that could flatten production costs. What looked like a turning point, though, soon turned into a dead end. Unable to win over customers Fiat was losing $1.9 billion per year by 2004. The desperate Agnellis brought in Marchionne, an intense lawyer and accountant who had successfully rebuilt the ailing Swiss company SGS Group, to right their empire.

Marchionne focused on General Motors. He let GM out of a stipulation that it must buy Fiat outright. In return, GM paid the Italian automaker a tidy $1.99 billion.[34] The Italian press hailed Marchionne, first for keeping the Fiat empire out of GM hands, second for prying the cash out of GM, and then achieving a real turnaround. By 2006, Fiat was breaking even financially and getting welcome accolades for new cars such as the Alfa Romeo 159.

Three years later, Fiat was still no financial powerhouse, but Marchionne had managed to stabilize the business. And when Nardelli came knocking, the Fiat boss realized America offered him a fresh market for Fiat luxury models, while Fiat had the fleet of small cars Chrysler needed to remain viable in the American market. But in a new world where the key to survival was federal bailout money, forging an alliance was no simple matter. Key lawmakers had insisted, as a condition for implementing Round Two of a federal bailout, that Chrysler present a preliminary blueprint for survival by February 17, 2009, to be followed by the full document on March 31. Nardelli had to lay out plans to fully repay the federal loans and show how Chrysler could achieve a positive net present value on their books; GM faced the same accounting challenge.[35] What both companies presented in February was an eye-opening insight into the difficulties of staying afloat amid a devastating recession. Chrysler, which in December had requested $3 billion for Round Two, now set its sights on $5 billion. GM pushed its demand to $30 billion, up from $18 billion, and discouraged any discussion of entering bankruptcy as a way of getting out of its debt and union obligations. A bankruptcy, GM President Frederick A. Henderson claimed, would require the federal government to ante up as much as $100 billion in financing necessary to pull the company out of a Chapter 11.[36]

Both companies pledged thousands of more job cuts, plant closings, and the elimination of models, including the weak-selling Dodge Durango and GM's outlandish Hummer H2. Rumors remained rife that GM also would do away with the Pontiac and Saturn brands altogether within three years — both companies mostly sold other GM cars that simply were rebadged. Under the threat of losing the federal lifeline, both automakers had embarked on a slash-and-burn strategy that would sharply reduce their production capacity and operating costs. In one sense, this was a retrenchment strategy not unlike what the once world-leading British motorcycle industry followed in the 1960s and 1970s, closing inefficient factories, abandoning market segments, consolidating product lines in an effort to compete with Japanese and German motorcycle manufacturers, and ultimately asking for British taxpayer subsidies. It didn't work for the British, but maybe it would work for GM and Chrysler, with Ford watching closely from the sidelines.[37]

Nardelli played the hardest hard ball of all, however, asserting that Chrysler would liquidate and go out of business if the federal loans were not forthcoming. Throughout the factory cities of the industrial Midwest, the anxiety was palpable. The next step was up to President Obama. He had to decide if the country would back General Motors financially as well as the odd American-German-Italian hybrid that Feinberg and Cerberus had concocted with Fiat.

Back in Kokomo, Mayor Greg Goodnight wrangled with smaller sums, but issues no less vital to the survival of his city. He had slashed up to six percent of the city's bloated payroll, but that was only the beginning. The firefighters in particular were proving to be his nemesis, collectively speaking. Members of Firefighters Local 396, with 121 members in Kokomo, earned $58,000 per year, on average, plus benefits, when Goodnight took office on January 1, 2008. The wage scale and benefits closely matched what autoworkers in town received, and were far in excess of what firefighters in comparably sized towns elsewhere in Indiana received. Amazingly, and in spite of recession everywhere, the firefighters wanted more. Both the city and union leaders agreed in 2008 to non-binding arbitration to settle the wage dispute, with the unspoken understanding that the city council likely would vote a pay raise if that's what the arbitrator proposed. This is what happened in January 2009; an arbitrator recommended a 1.5 percent raise, and the Kokomo Common Council, as it is known, rubber-stamped the plan.

Goodnight, the former steelworkers' union local president, fought back. He said he would have to put up to four firefighters on indefinite layoff to find the money for the raise; the four already were on temporary layoff. The firefighters immediately filed a grievance through their union, Local 396 of the International Association of Fire Fighters. It was very small potatoes compared to possibly losing thousands of jobs at the auto plants and millions of dollars in tax revenues, but Goodnight was learning to cut costs and count pennies where he could. In fact, he raised the stakes by threatening to eliminate the fire department's ambulance runs if he was forced both to hire back the four laid-off employees and pay all the firefighters a higher wage.

It was the stuff of small-town newspapers, and the battle was duly covered by the daily, *Kokomo Tribune*. "With the looming economic conditions going forward to the 2010 budget, we're not leaving any stone unturned that could possibly save the taxpayers money," city director of operations and Goodnight aide Randy Morris told the local press. The city had twelve emergency medical technicians (EMTs) and others on the fire department payroll assigned to ambulance service, but the city also had two hospitals, each with their own ambulance service. Moreover, the hospitals offered advanced life support services, known as ALS; the fire department only offered basic life support, known as BLS. All in all, it was small-town politics at its best, or at its worst.

With the two largest private employers in town in or near

bankruptcy, Goodnight was frustrated that he couldn't even convince some of the highest paid municipal employees in the state that they were not immune from making sacrifices themselves. Firefighters are popular fellows in any town; their extended families can sway elections in small towns like Kokomo, too. Yet here Goodnight was, having to stand up to a union in much the same way his former steel company employer had tried to stand up to him, and as trucking companies had tried to stand up to his father before him. It was beginning to dawn on the mayor that there was something bigger than worker solidarity at stake — it was the future of his beloved city itself. The smoldering battle with the firefighters was months away from resolution.

---

1. Micheline Maynard, "Once Tainted, Now Handed Chrysler Keys," *New York Times*, August 7, 2007, A1.
2. Peggy Noonan, "Remembering the Dawn of the Age of Abundance," *Wall Street Journal*, February 21, 2009, A11.
3. *The NewsHour with Jim Lehrer*, December 24, 2008, transcript found at www.pbs.org/newshour/bb/asia/july-dec08/globaleconomy_12-24.html.
4. Todd Spangler, Justin Hyde, John Gallagher, "The Force Behind Cerberus: Competitive Feinberg Comes Off as a Man of His Word – Not to Gut Chrysler," *Detroit Free Press*, May 20, 2007, A1.
5. Richard Duncan, *The Dollar Crisis: Causes Consequences Cures* (Singapore: John Wiley & Sons, 2003).
6. Charles Duhigg, "Can Private Equity Build a Public Face?" *New York Times*, December 24, 2006, sec. 3, 1.
7. Justin Hyde, "Letter to Investors Says Cheap Chrysler Deal Will Pay Off," *Detroit Free Press*, February 16, 2008, Business sec., 10.
8. Spangler.
9. Spangler.
10. Duhigg.
11. Duhigg.
12. Louise Story, "Chrysler's Friends in High Places," *New York Times*, December 6, 2008, B1.
13. Duhigg.
14. Duhigg.
15. Duhigg.
16. Duhigg.
17. Story.
18. Story.
19. Leslie Wayne, "An Investor with Madoff Faces Inquiry," *New York Times*, January 16, 2009, B1.
20. Gail Edmondson, "Daimler Gave Chrysler to Cerberus," *Business Week*, May 14, 2007, http://www.businessweek.com/autos/content/may2007/bw20070514_849359.htm.
21. Katie Benner, "Robert Nardelli Named CEO of Chrysler," *Fortune*, August 6, 2007, http://money.cnn.com/2007/08/05/news/companies/chryslernardelli.fortune/index.htm.
22. Snyder.
23. *The NewsHour with Jim Lehrer*.
24. "Remarks of UAW President Ronald Gettlefinger to World Automotive Congress, Jan. 21, 2009," http://www.uaw.org/news/speeches/vw_fst2.cfm?fstId=66.

25. Story.

26. Story.

27. This is why auto plants often call for volunteers for so-called temporary layoffs, and get them, too. Employees can sit at home for a while, maybe work on a project, and still receive nearly full pay.

28. Patrick L. Anderson, "Likely Impact of Delphi Bankruptcy," AEG Anderson Economic Group (East Lansing, Michigan, USA), AEG Working Paper 2005-10, October 31, 2005, undated press release, http://www.andersoneconomicgroup.com/Portals/0/upload/AEG_delphi_Oct05.pdf.

29. Joshua Duval, "Fiat to Buy 35 Percent Stake in Chrysler," *Automobile*, January 20, 2009, http://rumors.automobilemag.com/6425263/news/fiat-to-buy-35-percent-stake-in-chrysler/index.html.

30. Warren Brown, "GM, Chrysler Need to Think Change – Big Change," *Washington Post*, February 15, 2009, G2.

31. Bill Vlasic, "Chrysler's New Ally Takes a Pragmatic Approach," *New York Times*, February 3, 2009, B1.

32. Steven Mufson, Peter Whoriskey, "Chrysler and Fiat Strike an Alliance," *Washington Post*, January 21, 2009, D1.

33. Richard Boudreaux, "GM, Fiat Agree to $2.4-Billion Alliance for Cutting Costs," *Los Angeles Times*, March 14, 2000, C1.

34. Gabriel Kahn, Lee Hawkins Jr., "GM Agrees to Pay Fiat $1.99 Billion to Settle Dispute," *Wall Street Journal*, February 14, 2005, A1.

35. Jewel Gopwani, Justin Hyde, Brent Snavely, "A Fiat Deal May Risk Chrysler Loans; But It Also Could Mean a Comeback," *Detroit Free Press*, February 1, 2009, 1.

36. Bill Vlasic, Nick Bunkley, "Automakers Seek $14 Billion More, Vowing Deep Cuts," *New York Times*, February 8, 2009, 1.

37. From the 1930s through at least the 1950s the British motorcycle industry was believed to be the largest producer of full-size motorcycles in the world. Famous brands included BSA, Triumph, Matchless, Norton, Velocette and others. Truly, Birmingham, England, was the Detroit of the motorcycle world. For more information on the collapse of the British motorcycle industry see Abe Aamidor, *Shooting Star: The Rise and Fall of the British Motorcycle Industry* (Toronto: ECW Press, 2009) and Boston Consulting Group, "Strategy Alternatives for the British Motorcycle Industry: A Report Prepared for the Secretary of State for Industry" (London: Her Majesty's Stationery Office, 1975).

CHAPTER 3

Their Year of Decision

THE KOKOMO WASTE WATER TREATMENT facility, bound by a rural two-lane highway in front and a small creek winding its way around the back, is essentially a sprawling pole barn with painted aluminum exterior and a high chain-link fence for security. Sewer lines carry soiled water in; treated water pours into the creek. It's what municipal water treatment facilities everywhere do. But the rambling Kokomo facility, rarely seen by ordinary citizens or on their minds, received a new commission in early February 2009. It would be home to K-Fuel, just one of Mayor Greg Goodnight's disparate projects aimed at salvation in the here and now, irrespective of what might happen to Chrysler and Delphi in the future.

K-Fuel, named for the city, is biodiesel. The city of Kokomo aimed to market it far and wide the way that Hugo Chavez aims to sell his nation's oil across the globe. A partnership between the city and twelve area restaurants, K-Fuel began to collect used cooking oil and convert it for use in the city's diesel truck fleet. Goodnight unveiled the program on a cold but clear morning, just a dusting of snow on the ground outside. Approximately 100 community and business leaders, city council members, and local environmentalists gathered inside the facility. He personally greeted the guests and exchanged small talk as people found their places in a crowded corner. Normally a casual dresser, Goodnight wore a suit and tie for the occasion. "I have to get it back before noon," he joked with a newspaper reporter.

Then Goodnight took a position behind a lectern. He stood almost shoulder to shoulder with the tanks that would convert the cooking oil to biodiesel; they looked a lot like distillery tanks in a brewery. Goodnight spoke energetically, even effusively, about his city's new initiative, which he said was the first municipal-owned biodiesel plant in the country, while a projector showed schemata of the chemical processes involved overhead.

"We call this initiative Kokomo's Renewable Energy Partnership, and it's about sustainable development," Goodnight told the audience. "This program will eliminate about a half million pounds of carbon dioxide and several hundred pounds of diesel ash from our atmosphere every year."

One small step for the planet, but one giant step for Kokomo, you might say. K-Fuel would save the city money. It would create jobs. It would show that Kokomo was not waiting to be rescued. Although only twelve businesses participated in the program at first, and although projected savings to the city would be a mere $25,000 in the first year of operation (or just one-half the cost of one full-time employee on the municipal payroll), Goodnight said he hoped to collect all used cooking oil from the city's homeowners and renters in time, plus oil from more restaurants and other institutions such as hospitals and schools throughout the region. He got the idea for the project from a local firefighter who mixed processed cooking oil in his own truck and told the mayor it worked fine.

Goodnight, the high-school graduate and former factory hand, had taken a lead in helping local citizens find their way out of the morass caused not only by the terrible slump in the auto industry worldwide, but plummeting housing prices and diminished value in stock portfolios for investors big and small. Worst of all was the skyrocketing unemployment in the area. Unemployment had averaged 5.4 percent in the Kokomo Metro Area in 2007. By December 2008 it had zoomed to 9.9 percent. By February 2009 it was 17 percent.[1]

Goodnight was not alone in the battle to save his city, of course. Local business and government leaders had long spoken about the need for diversification of the local economy. "'We need to diversify.' After hearing that for over thirty years I think

Kokomo finally will," said John Wiles who retired as managing editor of the *Kokomo Tribune* following thirty years in the business. "I see the auto industry being a smaller part of our community in the future. We'll have more small businesses. It used to be that when GM hiccupped we all got sick. GM had 16,000 employees here at one time."

The car industry was king in Kokomo. Chrysler employment in town once had been 13,000, but it was down to 5,300 in early 2009, still significant in a town with a population of about 46,000. Only a little over two decades before, the city had also lost one other giant employer. The Continental Steel Corp., which once employed 1,200 people, was shuttered for good in 1986. Community and business leaders touted the need for diversification back then, but everybody went back to business as usual, perhaps waiting for someone else to actually solve the problem, or else just waiting for the inevitable. Continental Steel made sheet metal, roofing, and culvert stock that was sold all over the country, plus rebar, wire, rods and nails, and chain-link fencing. For years the workers had been offered shares in the company in return for concessions on wages and benefits, but it didn't save jobs or the company in the long run. Some workers claimed that profits from the local mill were expropriated by management to cover losses at other companies belonging to the corporate owner in other states.

"Many families went broke while trying to find work," recalled Ray Day, who transitioned successfully from the steel factory to a retail sales job with Sears, Roebuck and Co., another American icon that would later see hard times. "Many got bad sick because they couldn't accept what happened. Many went back home to the South after spending most of their family life here in Kokomo, Indiana."[2]

The Continental mill stood empty for years — a relic of a declining civilization as much as an eyesore — yet city officials and local business leaders still could not find a way to truly diversify their economy. Nor could they after the Delphi bankruptcy in 2005, or after witnessing the steady erosion of Chrysler jobs over the years. The auto crisis of 2008 and 2009 was not merely another wake-up call, but the last alarm that would be sounded, they knew.

Wiles now is head of the Downtown Kokomo Association, a nonprofit dedicated to quality of life issues and historic preservation as much as to business development. The association shares space with other businesses in a refurbished downtown office building; Wiles's cluttered office at street level features a huge picture window that directly faces passersby on the sidewalk outside. Clients from a nearby mental health outpatient center sometime stop and press their noses to the glass, or knock on it to get his attention, a sign that downtown revitalization has a way to go. Wiles doesn't just fault the corporate giants or city leaders for his town's decline, however. "Kokomo was the second wealthiest community in Indiana for a long time," he noted. "But [the workers] didn't take that money and invest it in quality of life issues in the local community. They'd buy a vacation home in Florida."

As recently as 2003 Kokomo ranked first among metropolitan areas in the state in real earnings per job. According to the Indiana Business Research Center, the figure was $53,378 per job, or twenty-three percent better than second place metro Indianapolis's $43,620 per job.[3] But much of that money never stayed in Kokomo or Howard County. Many retired autoworkers are believed to have spent their extra income on big recreational vehicles or vacation homes in Tennessee or Florida, but not on community assets, just like Wiles asserts, and many mid-level managers, executives, and engineers at Delphi and Chrysler never lived in the city or county anyway. The latter were much more likely to have lived closer to Indianapolis, or perhaps in Carmel in well-to-do Hamilton County about thirty miles immediately south of Kokomo and nearer Indianapolis's north side. The leading private school in the state, the very pricey Park Tudor School, and the leading Catholic school in Central Indiana, Brébeuf Jesuit Preparatory School, are on the far north side of Indianapolis, virtually requiring that any upper income families move close by if they want their children to attend either school. For years General Motors had a program to guarantee buyback of homes for executives who were transferred by the company; several sources claim GM always hooked up these executives with real-estate agents who would only show them homes in Hamilton County because they were just better investments. The parallel to "redlining" (in which banks and real-estate agents allegedly don't want anything to do with black neighborhoods) is striking, albeit without any racial overtones in this instance. Here it was not the ghetto being redlined. It was Kokomo itself.

Nearby the Downtown Kokomo Association is the United Brotherhood of Carpenters Local 615 with offices right on the courthouse square. The walls inside the union hall are lined with certificates and news clippings attesting to Local 615's contributions to various causes: the Make-A-Wish Foundation for terminally ill children, a Helmets to Hard Hats program for returning war veterans needing work, a rally for unemployment benefits at the statehouse in Indianapolis, and more. Jerry Santen, a college dropout who always wanted to work with his hands, is president of Local 615.

"For years Chrysler was one of the biggest employers indirectly for our members," said Santen. "We had many, many contracts to go into the factories for both Delphi and Chrysler . . . the casting plant in particular. This is where they pour the molten aluminum to make the transmissions."

Working in the factories was almost like hazard duty for the carpenters. "The lubricants from the machinery form a fine mist," Santen noted. "It gets in your hair. It gets in your clothes. When you get home you can actually taste it in your mouth."

Union carpenters who perform many complex building trades, not just fabricate kitchen cabinets and the like, earn $24 an hour in Kokomo, but only when they're actually working. They don't get "SUB-pay," or supplemental unemployment benefits from their employers like UAW workers do. When UAW workers are laid off this SUB-pay makes up for eighty-five percent of their regular salaries. However, union carpenters have long had a de facto two-tier pay scale — apprentices make only sixty percent of what journeymen earn, but the beginners do become journeymen eventually.

In the old days, not only were the auto factories a prime source for commercial work for the carpenters, but prosperous, confident autoworkers would hire union carpenters to do room additions to their homes, build decks, and make other improvements to their homes. Santen admits that the carpenters would often cut a deal on their usual labor rate with the autoworkers; in return, the autoworkers would only hire union contractors and carpenters. It was an arrangement that worked well for years. With the auto industry crisis of 2008–09 both large commercial contracts and those kinds of small jobs have largely dried up.

Santen is a member of Greater Kokomo Economic Development Alliance, working alongside business leaders, government officials, and nonprofit administrators — anyone, really, who knows diversification is a must. "Kokomo is going to have to change its mindset and change its total reliance on the auto industry," Santen said. "You have a city government that's extremely receptive to doing this, and you have a county government that's also receptive."

But the leader of any survival plan for Kokomo today is Greg Goodnight. He had warned of tough times ahead in his first State of the City address, promising to reduce the city payroll and annex unincorporated areas that received city benefits, but didn't pay their fair share of taxes. He repeated that mantra in his second State of the City speech in early 2009. In just over fourteen months in office he had reduced city payroll — including in the contentious fire department — by about ten percent, and had negotiated a pay freeze with the police department. But revenues were lagging, and as Chrysler continued to face an uncertain future Goodnight wondered if the company would even pay its spring property taxes.

Little Kokomo had begun to capture much of the world's attention in 2009. The British Broadcasting Corporation, CNN, the *Wall Street Journal*, and the *New York Times* all did lead stories on the town, and the *Washington Post* was diligent in reporting from town every few weeks, virtually making Kokomo one of its beats. Predictably, many stories originated from local bars or restaurants, easy places to find the common man with a gripe, and were dry economic tomes filled with hand-wringing and platitudes about the future. But whether out of mere curiosity about life in the hinterlands or a more profound understanding of what the loss of an industrial base really would mean to all of America, the journalists came to Kokomo to follow the story. The content of their stories and broadcasts followed certain themes: unemployment is high, retail is down, and the workers always feel betrayed.

Kokomo even came to the attention of Yale University. On February 23, 2009, a business professor hosted two special guests from Indiana. One was Maurice "Mo" Davison, director of UAW Region 3 (based in Indianapolis but covering all of Kentucky and Indiana). The other was Goodnight. The men were guests of the university; they had to transfer planes three times to arrive at their destination, turning the appearance into an arduous journey, but all expenses were paid and the men were glad for the attention — someone cared. The two men spoke to about 180 students in three different graduate management classes. Goodnight also personally met with a former Kokomo High School valedictorian who was an undergraduate at Yale on scholarship; there are not many kids from Kokomo at Yale.

Both Davison and Goodnight said the graduate business students had read up on Kokomo's automobile heritage and even knew what the unemployment rate was. They saw no discernable evidence that the students looked down on hayseeds from the Midwest, perhaps unlike the big city reporters, or that they thought what happened in the heartland didn't matter to them. Nor were the students willing to make the Detroit Three executives the exclusive scapegoats or whipping boys, as Michael Moore had done in his 1989 movie about General Motors, *Roger & Me*. These students especially knew all about the legacy costs for retired UAW workers, which added between $1,000 and

$1,500 to the cost of every vehicle Detroit made. They knew about company-paid health care costs, including retirees, which are just not an issue for companies making cars in Japan.

"I went there anticipating the possibility of a hostile audience," said Davison. "It was not like that at all. They seemed to understand the working man. They're very big on green. They were excited about Mayor Goodnight's biodiesel program."

Doug Rae, an Indiana native and the Yale professor who invited Goodnight to New Haven, lauded the mayor's appearance. "He's got a wide angle of vision — of conservation and environment, transportation, and administration and contractual relationships, along with an unusually realistic vision of the economic risks [Kokomo] faces," Rae said.[4]

Upon his return from New Haven, Goodnight said he'd had a good visit. Still, it was only a class exercise for the graduate students, not unlike medical students who have to do a real autopsy now and then. Perhaps Kokomo was just a specimen they were examining. If so, Goodnight wasn't buying the notion that his town was effectively dead. Goodnight also said that in spite of his support for diversification and going green, he really wasn't giving up on cars.

"I don't think looking at having an auto industry in America is looking backward," Goodnight stated one Saturday morning over breakfast at his favorite local restaurant, Frittatas, in between waving at constituents and trying to down his scrambled eggs. "The steel industry went through a major restructuring, but still plays a major role in northern Indiana and in Pennsylvania, and even parts of Ohio. I don't think Delphi is going to have 13,000 employees again, but they have 3,000 employees [in Kokomo] and that's a substantial number."

K-Fuel is one initiative in the city to move away from a direct or total dependence on the auto industry. The city also had offered many of its municipal rooftops gratis to the local power company, Duke Energy, so that it could install solar panels and split the energy produced with the city. The city would use the electricity generated to power the affected building, and the power company would get the rest. Duke said no, however, and Goodnight and his sustainability adviser, David Galvin, are still trying to find out why.

Another hope for the future is the Inventrek Technology Park, an incubator for small businesses opened several years ago and supported by various public and private sector agencies plus modest rent receipts from businessmen who occupy offices in the building and share expenses and secretarial help. Inventrek is housed in the former Delco Electronics headquarters building, which Delphi donated in 2003 to a local economic development corporation. The most successful venture there today is Neupath. Ironically, Delphi's reduction in manpower led to a surfeit of engineers in the area, which has benefited Neupath greatly. The company is a contract engineering firm, sort of a "have gun, will travel" venture, but rather than real six-shooters it's comprised of people with higher level computer and technical skills.

Another success story is AndyMark, Inc., named for its co-owners, Andy Baker and Mark Koors, both engineers who formerly worked at Delphi. AndyMark specializes in transmissions and other technical parts for small robotics projects, but has been branching out into parts and designs for the burgeoning mobility-scooter market in America. AndyMark employs five and one-half "full time equivalents," including the two co-owners, though both men worked on the business for several years without compensation while maintaining their jobs at Delphi. Even today, each draws only a small salary. Baker, forty, was earning $75,000 per year when he left Delphi in 2007. Koors, fifty-four, earned $120,000 when he retired in 2008 and now receives a pension from Delphi in addition to his salary at AndyMark.

Both men said they felt like small cogs in a very big machine at Delphi. "The last thing that I worked on there that went nowhere was a new belt tension sensor system," said Koors, a bookish-looking man with thin hair on top and narrow eye-glasses. "It cut costs to about ten percent of what they were before but it went nowhere. Nobody told me why. It represented a $10 million savings."

Baker and Koors moved into the Inventrek Technology Park in 2007, but their company has existed since 2001. Small business incubators do not necessarily spawn new businesses, but help in other ways, including growth. Besides sharing business expenses, the rent typically is below market rates, and creative and risk-taking people get to talk to other creative and risk-taking people every day.

Some of the small parts assembly at AndyMark is done right in the main office. Bins filled with nuts, washers, and small screws look like they came right out of an Ace Hardware store. More complex jobs are farmed out to local machine shops, often one-man businesses where the owner is the skilled tradesman performing the work himself. Baker says he was recently approached by a Chinese manufacturer that wanted to create a mold and the parts that the mold would produce that AndyMark needed for one of its mobility products. The Chinese company was stunned to learn that its bid price was no cheaper than what a Howard County machine shop had put in. "The Chinese said that had never happened to them before," Baker recalled. "They were very apologetic."

Across Indiana, other small towns that had been highly dependent on the American auto industry and other manufacturing jobs also were scrambling for a way out of recession. The state had seen the demise of many (but not all) of Gary's steel mills; Fort Wayne's International Harvester, which made farm implements; Indianapolis's Western Electric, which made telephone handsets; Muncie's Chevrolet division; Marion's Thomson and RCA television picture tube plant; every one of Anderson's GM, Guide, and Remy plants (about twenty overall); and Richmond's Dana Weatherhead. In 1969, Indiana had 741,000 industrial jobs, but by September 2005 that number was down to 571,000 and in a free fall.[5] Early in 2009, the number would drop to 483,000, the first time it was below the 500,000 level since the country was emerging from the Great Depression in 1941.

Now, local leaders were really rolling up their sleeves to save jobs, save their tax base, and save their towns. Besides Good-night, there was Wayne Seybold, the Republican mayor of Marion; Kris Ockomon, a former police detective recently elected mayor of Anderson; and Shawna Girgis, a former medical social worker and Independent mayor of Bedford in southern Indiana.

Seybold, one-half of the pairs figure ice skating team with his sister Kim that represented the United States in the 1988 Calgary Olympics, grew up in a mobile home park on the south edge of Marion, which is about seventy miles northeast of Indianapolis. The actual trailer where he grew up still is there, inhabited by the same woman his parents sold it to some thirty years ago. The Idyl Wyld, the same roller rink with hardwood floor and barrel vault ceiling near the entrance to the trailer park where he first learned to skate, still is open. Seybold says he was "trailer trash" to some growing up, yet was welcomed back as a hero when he returned to Marion in the mid-1990s even though by then there was plenty of middle-age spread on his short frame. He had always loved Marion as a youth. He'd play catch in a small field in the middle of the trailer park, which is otherwise heavily wooded with a few small patches of meadow, or he'd watch the trains that ran by either side of the trailer park. He'd ride his bicycle all the way downtown, often seeing double features at the Indiana Theater on Saturday afternoons.

Seybold left town to compete internationally (he and Kim were silver medal winners twice in the U.S. ice-skating champi-onships in the 1980s) and later produced ice-skating shows. Living in southern California and New York he discovered that a lot of people don't respect the Midwest. "There is a feeling that the Midwest isn't as advanced as we are," he said from his glass-paneled office in downtown Marion. "I would call it a little bit of arrogance more than anything. I think the media is a little skewed that way, too."

Marion has always been a boom-or-bust town. Natural gas fields were discovered in the 1880s (one nearby town still is named Gas City) and attracted a wave of foundries, paper, wire, and glass factories. At one point, four long-haul railroads crossed the city. General Motors built its mammoth metal-stamping plant there in 1955. For many years the largest employer was Thomson Consumer Electronics, the French company that bought the old RCA television business in America. As recently as 1993 more than 11,000 people were employed at all manufacturing plants combined in Marion, including Thomson, GM, and smaller industries that fed these two giants.[6] That was a huge number for a town with a population of only 35,000. But Thomson pulled the plug in 2004, triggering a major recession locally years before it hit other parts of the country. The final 1,000 employees at the picture tube factory lost their jobs, though Thomson had employed 3,000 at the facility as recently as 1999. Contemporary news reports say the Thomson plant was stripped of all its machine tools and automation, which were packed into 100 tractor-trailers and ocean cargo containers and shipped to both Mexico and China. The high cost of labor, the rapacious appetite for quarterly profits, the vice grip of environmental regulations, and the local tax structure were all factors in driving Thomson offshore. "There was no notice," Seybold recalled. "They had been talking about things for a while. We had been talking to them for two weeks on what we could do to help them, abatements and things. I don't think they knew what they wanted. The plant manager was trying to position the plant so that it could stay open [vis à vis other Thomson plants]."

Seybold says the Thomson closing was the wake-up call Marion needed. The town had hit rock bottom and the only way was up. Besides the GM stamping plant, which makes body panels for trucks and cars, the largest employers today are Indiana Wesleyan University, Marion General Hospital, the public schools, and city and county government. Marion is the seat of Grant County; in general county seats always have an advantage over other small towns because of the government jobs and law offices present. Good jobs stimulate local retail development, increase property values, and improve the quality of life for all. Yet most of the aforementioned jobs either are tax supported, meaning without payment transfers they would not exist, or they are based on insurance payments or student loans. Seybold is proud to have these enterprises in his backyard in the interests of diversification, but he also knows the belief that the public sector and/or nonprofit institutions in and of themselves can drive the economy for long simply is a chimera. That's why he's pushing for new industry, as well as working hard to keep what he's got.

An expert in economic incentives, Seybold notes that new businesses always have an advantage over established business in terms of incentives or tax abatements. By law, he cannot reduce the tax burden on established companies. If he — or any local leader — started cutting property taxes for one established factory or business, then every other similar entity in town would rightfully demand the same perks. Decades ago, incentives weren't much of an issue. If a company wanted to go out into the country and build a plant, it often paid for new roads to its site and sewer and water connections itself. But the game changed over time. Local and state governments began incentivizing company expansion and development to attract new businesses. In 1984 General Motors received $26.4 million in incentives for infrastructure work at its new pickup truck assembly plant in Fort Wayne, for example. Only five years later Fuji Heavy Industries landed $94 million for roads and utility extensions at a Subaru-Isuzu joint venture in Lafayette, Indiana. In 1995 Toyota's truck works in Princeton, Indiana, in the southwest corner of the state, received $75 million, while Honda's new Civic car plant at Greensburg wangled $85.5 million in incentives in 2006. The Detroit Three could have continued to win such incentives if they were expanding — local and state governments were not discriminating against them — but the 1990s and 2000s collectively was an era of foreign automakers ramping up truck and car plants in the United States while the domestic manufacturers were entering a period of outsourcing production and increasing layoffs, in spite of the pickup truck and SUV boom.

"The problem with incentives is they're all performance based," explained Seybold, meaning you can give help to move forward, expand, and build new, but never an incentive to just stay where you're at. Why? "Those tax revenues already are committed, and if you give help to one, they'll all ask for help," he said.

Marion has won new investment in recent years. Veriana Networks, a technology-based company that settled there in 2007, projects 280 full-time employees by 2012. The company specializes in technology, media, and risk management for the entertainment industry. Co-founders Rob Swagger and R. Ross Cooper said they selected Marion in part because of various state and local incentives, but also because the low cost of utilities in the city, availability of fiber optics, and Marion's city-wide Wi-Fi capability, plus the proximity to Purdue University in West Lafayette, seventy-three miles away. Purdue is the state's technology university.

In late 2008, the city landed another company — TriEnda — which produces plastic pallets for industry. Based in Wisconsin, the company announced that when at full capacity it would employ up to 345 people in part of the old Thomson TV tube factory, including machine operators, finishers, warehouse technicians, automation specialists, supervisors, and office help. Literally hundreds of residents, local leaders, city officials, and even Republican Governor Mitch Daniels turned out for the TriEnda opening. Company spokespeople said they chose expansion in Marion over their corporate headquarters in Portage, Wisconsin, because the old Thomson factory was empty and cheap, but also because lots of skilled workers were at hand. Incentives also helped. They totaled $2.3 million, including $1.85 million in tax credits, $325,000 for the city to run a rail spur to the factory site, and $130,000 in worker training grants.[7]

The main tool Marion has used since Seybold was elected mayor in 2003 has been the Community Revitalization Enhancement District tax credit, euphemistically known as CRE(e)D and pronounced as if it has the double E. The state program allows the taxpayer to take a credit against state and local taxes as long as the money is used for qualifying improvements to businesses and property. The old Thomson plant, for example, qualified. So have retail businesses in an older in-town shopping center, which has spurred revitalization of that commercial district. In recent years both Walmart and Dollar General opened major distribution centers on the edge of town, too, taking advantage of the city's proximity to Interstate 69, the main link between Detroit and Indianapolis. Each facility employs in the low hundreds. Much of the downtown revitalization centers on the new YMCA, a planned riverfront plaza, and the Cardinal Greenway — a rails-to-trails bicycle path that connects much of northeast Indiana, including Muncie and Marion. The city simply gave the Y the historic municipal coliseum it owned, a beautiful early twentieth-century gymnasium with huge brick arches and slender limestone trim in the front façade. It was a facility that seated 5,000 but had sat empty for years. The Y rehabilitated the gym, then added on new program facilities. STAR Financial gave a reported $500,000 to the project and earned naming rights to the building — unusual but cost-effective to the nonprofit and to the city.

Between 2004 and 2009 the city also used general fund revenues to tear down nearly 700 dilapidated homes and commercial properties at a cost of $2,000 to $8,000 each. The city recoups most of the expense by putting a lien on the parcels of land when they are sold. Other major eyesores included the remnants of the old Marion Malleable site, once the largest iron foundry in the world. In 2009 the owners finally tore up the old concrete floor that was all that remained of the foundry, their first improvement on the property in the thirty years they had owned it. Threats of legal action from the city were one driver, but an optimistic picture of Marion recovering was the real force. Overall, assessed property value in Marion, Indiana, increased by $63 million in 2008, according to the mayor, with projections for a similar increase in 2009.

But there's still a long way to go. While the Indiana Wesleyan campus is as attractive and well manicured as any private college in the country, complete with its own innovative, European-style pedestrian mall and student-run businesses inside, and downtown is looking vibrant again with the addition of that new

YMCA and the riverfront park, the south side of the city remains problematic. On the still leafy side streets near the old Thomson plant there are many run-down single-family homes. Covered in the original aluminum siding from the 1940s or 1950s, their shiny white enamel paint is now a dingy matte gray. Empty storefronts with murky plate-glass windows dot the through streets. A water park was built in the neighborhood a few years ago — it seems to be the major amenity in the area.

Andy Lowden has lived in Marion since his family moved here from Fort Wayne while he was in the fourth grade. When he was just twenty-four, the tall, burly young man did something almost no native-born Americans do anymore — he started his own business. It's not a franchise that requires large amounts of capital up front, nor a turnkey operation that requires no real skill on the investor's part, but an independently owned and operated business. Lowden Jewelers is the kind where the owner is in the store, just like the old days. "I was twenty-four. I didn't have a lot to lose," said Lowden who has owned his jewelry store on the edge of Marion for the last nineteen years. "I had been in the business a couple of years when a couple of jewelry stores were going out of business and I saw an opportunity."

Lowden, now forty-three, was recruited to work in a different jewelry store while on Christmas break from college one year. He liked it so much he soon dropped out of school and started in the business full time. Later, when the town's only jewelry repair specialist announced she was retiring, she offered to teach Lowden the trade. He learned at her table. Later, he bought out a jewelry store, but continued to do repairs for all the other jewelry stores in town. He didn't pay himself a salary for two years. Eventually he moved out of rented quarters and bought his own free-standing building, which he calls his retirement insurance. The small red-brick building he now owns had sat vacant for years and previously housed a flower shop.

The 2008–09 credit and auto industry crises hurt all types of business badly, Lowden said. He fired none of his eight employees, but put them all on three-day work weeks to spread the pain evenly. "All last year [2008] was slow but I wasn't that concerned," Lowden said from the corner of his small store. He was taking a break from a meeting with two Citizen Watch salesmen, who were organizing a display case for him. "But last Christmas we had a forty percent drop in business. That's a lot, especially for December."

Normally, Lowden would spend about $5,000 on billboard ads in December, but he bought none during the Christmas 2008 shopping season. He cut his radio advertising by nearly half, as well. And his charitable contributions have mostly gone by the wayside — the most he could offer several local nonprofit fundraisers in the past year were a couple of those Citizen watches, not diamond jewelry as he had given previously. This is all part of the ripple effect that economists talk about when a major employer goes belly up.

Today, Lowden runs the last independent jewelry store in town. His only competition is a national chain jewelry store inside a nearby mall, and he says he wouldn't survive if it wasn't for the repair work he continues to solicit. Yet he believes the country looks down on people who work with their hands, whether it's in the auto factories, the building trades, or people like him. "I think so," Lowden said, speaking in a very plain but confident voice, without any rancor or bitterness at all, but a tinge of disappointment quite apparent. "I don't know why that is so. I look at [what I do] as an art form. But they push everybody toward college. I don't know why. College is not for everybody. I know there are good trades out there."

Like other businesspeople in town, Lowden says he's had to weather other recessions, especially after the RCA television plant closed, but also after a large glass manufacturing company, Foster-Forbes Glass Co., later Ball Foster, closed in 2000. It employed 750 people throughout most of the 1990s. But the current recession is the worst he's ever seen it. "Pretty much everybody I talk to, things are slow," he said. "I have a friend who owns a carpet store, things are very slow. Another friend owns a paint store. Things are slow there."

The major industrial employer in Marion is GM. Nearly 1,000 people continued to work at the giant metal-stamping plant on West Second Street on the edge of town. With sixty-four acres under one roof, dozens of football fields could fit inside. Running on forty tons of pressure giant dies stamp out sheet-metal panels, while milling machines cut and shape other parts. Some of the behemoth machine tools are older Danly USA models made in Chicago, but newer ones come from Germany. Often lost in the discussion over the fate of the American automobile industry is the fate of the machine tool industry — these are the machines that make other machines and are the tools that only the leading industrial countries make. Much of the machine tool industry in the United States has closed down in the face of lower-priced imported machine tools.

When running at full capacity, the plant is loud. Earplugs are available like candy at stands everywhere in the factory, but otherwise it is a surprisingly clean and well-lit place. In an effort to keep the plant open Mayor Seybold led a local task force that met repeatedly with GM executives throughout the winter of 2008–09, including offering to create a TIF district (Tax Increment Financing) that would allow GM tax credits if it made capital improvements and brought in new dies and presses to the plant. "If you're only going to have one stamping plant in the United States, we'd like it to be Marion," he told the GM executives.

The importance of the metal-stamping plant, both to the local economy and to ordinary working-class Americans, cannot be overstated. Mike Hayden, fifty-seven, has been working in the auto industry for forty years. He began two months after graduating from high school in Yorktown, a hamlet partway between Marion and Indianapolis. During all those years this is only the fourth factory he's worked in. He could have taken his "thirty and out" pension years ago, but he likes his job and makes more money by actually coming to work. For a production worker he earns top scale at $28 per hour plus benefits (skilled trades make more, an important distinction), and still has that pension in his pocket.

"My dad worked in the auto industry," said Hayden, a slight, plain-speaking man. "I've got two brothers that worked for GM. When they came around in eighth or ninth grade and asked what would you like to do, I said I'd like to work in an auto factory."

The factory is highly automated, which is what leads, in part, to claims that American workers are the most productive in the world. You simply divide the output by number of employees, and come up with a productivity score. But it is the machines doing most of the work. Claims that American automobile manufacturers did not reinvest in their companies simply are not true. Much of the automation had to do with catching the Japanese in quality, scrap rate, defects, and manufacturability. GM alone spent more than $40 billion building new assembly lines in the '80s precisely to counter the Japanese use of robotics, according to various accounts.

But what if GM were to close the Marion plant? "A lot of people in my party don't like what I'm doing," said Mayor Seybold, a Republican who believes strongly in so-called tax breaks to attract business, something that runs counter to the ethos of more doctrinaire Republicans. "They say why should we save these companies. But they don't have 1,000 people in their district who work for one of them."

In the spring of 2009 Seybold was cautiously optimistic that even if GM was destined for major restructuring the Marion stamping plant would remain. Its quality and efficiency ratings were just too high within the corporation, and as a Republican mayor he was fighting hard to make sure the economic environment was favorable to doing business there. "If GM closes down, we lose not only the plant, but twelve to fifteen businesses in Marion that are connected to the plant," Seybold said. "Now we're in a financial disaster because we have to cut thirty to forty percent out of budget, and we've got a lot of federal and state mandates saying you've got to have this and this, [mandates] that you can't fund now."

Across Indiana it was much the same story — create incentives for business, or face financial ruin. Fort Wayne had 2,600 employees in its GM pickup truck facility through 2009. It was one of the newer GM final assembly plants in the country, but full-size pickup truck sales were plummeting. One trick city officials there allegedly used in 2008 to try to keep GM happy was simply to lower the pickup truck factory's assessed value from $101 million to $75.6 million. Because the city and county could not really do this as a kind of disguised tax incentive for an existing business, they simply argued the plant was worth less in these troubled times.[8] Maybe they were right. The city in northeast Indiana, named for Revolutionary War hero Anthony "Mad Anthony" Wayne who led the fight against the British in the Northwest Territories, had already lost its giant International Harvester plant in 1982. At its peak that company employed 10,000; the company made farm implements, but also the Jeep-like four-wheel-drive Scout. Fort Wayne's Tokheim, which long made the iconic gas pumps beloved of auto memorabilia collectors and 1950s diner-style movie sets, went bankrupt in 2002. The brand now is part of a Paris, France–based conglomerate. Unemployment in the Fort Wayne area hovered at around ten percent through the spring of 2009.[9]

Bedford, Indiana, struggled to hold on to its GM aluminum casting plant, but in 2008 it had already lost a Visteon auto-parts plant that built fuel modules for Ford cars. Visteon employed 600, a significant number in a town with a population of only 13,000. The empty factory shell was purchased late in 2008 by investors who renamed the 340,000 square foot facility the East Gate Business and Technology Center. The marketing plan for the property included vacant lots for development, as well as space for office, laboratory, manufacturing, distribution, and warehousing. Local government leaders all were behind the redevelopment, of course. "I think these kinds of events either make you or break you," said Bedford's mayor, Shawna Girgis. "Because things are changing I think people have to look at things and ask themselves what do I have to do to stay ahead of the curve? I hope that because of things that are happening people will look at education and training. It used to be you didn't have to do that because you 'could get a good job at Visteon or GM."

In the meantime, Girgis said she is relying on a host of economic development tools to assist companies that may want to relocate in town, including property tax abatement and tax credits through a Bedford Urban Enterprise Zone. The unemployment rate for Bedford and surrounding Lawrence County stood at 13.5 percent in the spring of 2009, which was half again as high as the national average of 8.6 percent at the time.[10]

The queen city of American automobile manufacturing in Indiana for many years was Anderson, a town of about 57,000 some forty miles northeast of Indianapolis. At one time Anderson had twenty auto industry–related factories, almost all of them owned by General Motors. As recently as 1999 GM plants in Anderson and surrounding Madison County directly and indirectly accounted for $10.5 billion in annual wages, $43.5 billion in industrial output, and $156 million in tax revenue, according to Charles Staley, president of the Flagship Enterprise Center, based in Anderson. What towns like Kokomo and Marion now face, Anderson has already experienced.

Downtown Anderson looks almost like a ghost town today. Empty storefronts and light or nonexistent foot traffic add a melancholy atmosphere to the disparate architecture, including a Romanesque-style county courthouse completed in 1885, squarish commercial brick buildings from early in the twentieth century, and an artless, pre-stressed concrete mid-rise from the middle twentieth century. One small restaurant started by two former autoworkers touts a local newspaper article about its recent opening in the front window, but the restaurant looks run-down on the inside and nobody is dining there on this particular winter morning. Anderson's population is down nearly twenty-five percent from 1970. At that time it was 70,000, a vital city with a real, vibrant downtown.

Jerry Rubenstein has helped run Allan's Jewelry & Loan in downtown Anderson since 1978. It's a family-owned business. "My dad, I thought he was nuts to think about buying a pawn shop," said Rubenstein, a sixty-year-old man of average build and short, tightly curled hair. "I didn't know anything about it except that the previous owner got shot."

Indeed, the store, then known as the S & S Pawn Shop, was burglarized and the owner murdered before the Rubensteins bought it. The business was moved to a larger, more brightly lit store with its own parking lot on the edge of downtown in 1979. Over the years autoworkers were a mainstay — buying too much in the good times, pawning too much during economic downturns. The store features the usual musical instruments, drums and amplifiers, as well as jewelry, power tools, and a large array of rifles and hunting equipment. The cash and better merchandise reside in a walk-in safe in back, but there is no banker's style teller cage separating the customers from the staff as in most Hollywood depictions and some real life pawn shops. Foot traffic was brisk in 2009; actual sales a little less so, Rubenstein said. One couple — a middle-aged man with mutton chop sideburns and a bushy mustache and his much younger, very pregnant wife who was dressed in Army fatigues — came to pawn a professional-looking spotting scope and a Jim Bowie–type hunting knife. Rubenstein did not want the spotting scope.

"Your knife, if you sold it to us, would be worth ten dollars," he said almost apologetically. "It's a nice knife but that's all I can give you." The couple eagerly accepted the money.

Rubenstein later said he could monitor recessions via his business. The "default rate" on loans was pretty steady at eighteen percent, he said, meaning eighteen percent of people consistently never paid back loans on merchandise they left with him, but the number of people pawning merchandise was up, while buying was down, creating a cash flow problem for him. "Right now, we're seeing an increase in people who are pawning for the first time," he said. "We've got a teacher that I don't remember doing business with before. We've had a couple of auto salesmen, obviously."

Anderson is hurting. For decades, the town has been home to the second largest high-school gymnasium in the country, affectionately known as the Wigwam because of the high school nickname, the Indians. The Wigwam seats 8,996 guests, more than most college gymnasiums, yet in early 2009 the local school district held public meetings on whether to close the storied facility for good. The venue didn't sell out anymore and the utility bill alone was $350,000 a year. "If they close the Wigwam, this town is done," long-time resident Kenny Reed told a newspaper reporter.[11]

The school board apparently agreed with Reed. On March 10, 2009, an evening that saw lashing rain and high winds throughout central Indiana, a well-attended public hearing was covered by all the local TV stations and area newspapers because of the historic nature of the gym. The board voted to close three elementary and middle schools instead and move a vocational center to offices inside the Wigwam. The gym was saved in a narrow vote, but were the long-term interests of students and families really served? Parents affected by the school closings soon began their own series of protests and threatened a lawsuit.

On one level the reasons for Anderson's troubles are simple — the local manufacturing industry was in a historic decline for decades and finally collapsed in the late 1990s and early part of this century. Brown fields surround Anderson where giant auto industry plants were simply demolished. Eventually they'll return to farmland, or to woodlands, which is what the land was before white settlers began clearing away the trees in the early nineteenth century. The Guide Corporation plant was the largest factory in town by far, with 3 million square feet. One original structure, a building dating to 1908, lasted the entire life of the business. The last addition was in the 1980s. But it was all demolished shortly after production was moved offshore. One former GM factory, Plant 18, a low but sprawling building with light blue exterior on a country road just south and east of town, stands empty. It was sold in late 2008 for $450,000 and part of it will be used for light manufacturing. Plant 19, a newer building, sat empty for five years before a local entrepreneur bought it in 2001. It is now occupied by a magnesium alloy company that employs twenty-six workers with an average salary of $14.50 per hour.

Since the late 1970s Anderson has lost 24,000 auto-related jobs overall, maybe more, said Anderson community affairs spokeswoman Tammy Bowman. That's more than one-third the current population of the city, though many of the employees commuted to work from surrounding communities. Nevertheless, imagine if Chicago or Los Angeles lost 1.5 million manufacturing jobs each in less than thirty years.

Yet, in a sense, all that auto industry history and human capital are part of what is making Anderson potentially viable again. For example, the utility infrastructure — including the electrical power grid and water supply, both features that were required by GM's massive presence here over the years — has helped lure Nestlé, the Swiss-based chocolate and food processing company, to town. The new Nestlé chocolate and coffee creamer plant needed access to the one million gallons of water per day that Anderson could provide, says Bowman, as well as easy access to Interstate 69 and to Indianapolis, which often styles itself as "the crossroads of America." In 2008 Nestlé built an entirely new facility just off the interstate with the help of $1.325 million in state tax credits, a commitment by the state to improve a nearby interstate interchange, a ten-year sliding scale property tax abatement, and other incentives. In return, Nestlé invested $359 million in the manufacturing and distribution center and put about 300 citizens to work in 2009 at wages between $16 and $24 per hour, with plans to hire 135 more in a factory expansion scheduled for 2011.[12]

Another major coup for the city, albeit a mixed blessing from some points of view, was the Hoosier Park horse racing track and casino. The racetrack opened in 1994 and a new, attached casino opened in 2008. The "racino," as it's sometimes called, employs about 800 people. Whether gambling revenues make for good tax policy on the state level is debated by economists (most think it is not good policy), but it does create jobs. Yet Jerry Rubenstein says the business of people pawning merchandise picked up almost immediately after the Hoosier Lottery began operating in 1990, and surged again both when the Hoosier Park racetrack opened, and when the casino opened. He says plenty of customers have admitted to him that gambling debts have forced them to sell off prized possessions.

The real future of the city may lie with its engineering heritage and projects such as those being encouraged at the Flagship Enterprise Center. Economic development corporations and state-run workforce development offices often have a bad name — bureaucracies are created, funds are allocated, promises are made, yet not much really happens. But the Flagship Enterprise Center has been different, the organization's president, Charles Staley, claims. Funding for the multimillion dollar, four-building complex came from several sources: indirectly from the city, which bought land for the center; locally based Anderson University, which owns the main building the center uses; and a $1.6 million federal Economic Development Administration grant. Then there was one very surprising source: General Motors itself, which donated $3 million from the sale of one of its buildings when it left town.

Just off Interstate 69, the center, which opened its incubator facility in 2005, helps business start-ups in the area and provides classroom space for the private, Christian-based Anderson University and the state-run Purdue University. Staley says the center's first "graduate," as it was touted at the time, was Continental Quality Engineering, which does re-inspection of imported manufactured parts for various companies. Now part of Continental, Inc., the company employs about 125 people in various divisions and is growing. Altair Nanotechnologies, with corporate headquarters in Reno, Nevada, develops high-tech rechargeable battery systems. Altair currently rents 70,000 square feet from the Flagship Enterprise Center. Another major technology partner, iPower, co-founded by Mike Hudson, former head of the Rolls-Royce gas turbine engine division in Indianapolis, makes distributive electrical products that help companies sell back energy to their local power grid. Staley says the center "launched" 700 jobs overall locally from 2005 through 2008 and brought in another 500 through recruiting established businesses to Anderson. Most jobs were technology related.

"From my perspective we fare very well in electrical engineering [compared to] Palo Alto and San Jose and elsewhere," said Staley. "There is a much higher percentage of electrical engineers here than in other parts of the country. There are a lot of bright people that came out of the automobile industry."

At one time Anderson had 3,000 to 4,000 engineers and managers, including a bevy of engineers at Delco Remy. The old GM division pioneered the electric car, beating Toyota to market in 1993 with the EV1 electric car. Much of the electronics work for the EV1 was carried out in Indiana, leaving a legacy of talented engineers. A few former Remy engineers, including John Waters (CEO and president of Bright Automotive and integrative design team leader at the Rocky Mountain Institute) and William Wylam (president of International Energy LLC and former corporate director of technology, Remy International), have become entrepreneurs and are trying to innovate a new electric car, tapping federal funds advanced for designing new propulsion systems able to reduce the reliance on oil.

The Flagship Enterprise Center taking credit for Continental's success is a bit of a stretch, though. Continental dates to 1985; it was founded by Bill and Judy Nagengast shortly after Bill was transferred by General Motors to town. Bill was not happy with how GM was doing business, nor were many other engineers who worked at Guide, owned by GM at the time, according to Judy, who is now the chief operating officer of the company she and her husband jointly operate. GM had plenty of engineers on staff, but the company either did not give them enough work to do or didn't listen to their suggestions — it was all about bean counters and marketing studies in those days, not necessarily better engineering ideas. The Nagengasts simply hired away other disaffected engineers for their company. Today the small parent company owns a 38,000-square-foot former Remy Corporation building that's been converted into office space. Continental has indeed done quality control and evaluation of imported parts in recent years, as well as some assembly of its own. A growing portion of its business is in staffing — Continental hires skilled and semi-skilled laborers, then farms them out to regional businesses on a "temp to hire" basis. The employers promise to hire anyone still working for them after a year, but working through companies like Continental allows them to give prospective employees an extended try-out with no real obligation first.

"We see a lot of people coming in willing to work for eight dollars, ten dollars, twelve dollars an hour," said Judy Nagengast, a former homemaker and avid amateur bicyclist who likes to ride some of the "rails to trails" conversions sprouting in central Indiana. "We don't see people coming in expecting to get twenty-five dollars an hour and good benefits."

The Detroit Three automakers have a reputation for abandoning communities where they did business for decades — witness filmmaker Michael Moore's *Roger & Me*, the 1989 documentary assault on General Motors' role in Flint, Michigan. Moore's allegations were unfair, though — the well-paid hourly rate workers themselves began abandoning Flint as far back as the 1950s by chasing the American dream right into the suburbs, as did millions of other Americans. In any case, GM treated Anderson well during its retreat, current mayor Kris Ockomon says. As far back as the late 1990s GM funded an independent study on how Anderson could diversify its economy and survive a GM pull-out. Recommendations included expanding the city's logistics (shipping) industry and seeking high-tech industries because of the plethora of highly trained engineers the auto industry would leave behind. Another recommendation? Go after food processing plants, in part because of the electrical and water capacity in Anderson, and also because the food industry is considered relatively recession-proof. That's how Anderson got Nestlé. "When Nestlé came through we knew that was ours for the taking," Tammy Bowman said.

GM's collegiality, even far-sightedness, was not entirely selfless. By law, GM would have had to pay massive property taxes on buildings it owned, even if idled. As it was, the company had to pay demolition costs for some buildings, but it donated several to the city's economic development arm, which then put them up for sale.

A major hurdle to overcome with prospective investors has been Anderson's strong union heritage. Ockomon — a former police detective whose parents worked in the auto plants for decades and whose wife is a teachers' union member — says flatly that no prospective employer or investor wants to do business in a union environment. "They don't want any part of it, obviously," Ockomon said. "We have that reputation because of all the years that GM was here, but I think we've outlived that."

One of the first successful sit-down strikes in automobile history was at the Guide plant in Anderson, which in part led to GM recognition for the union. Yet the city has gone so far from being a union town as to now trumpet a recent failure by the Teamsters to organize a nearby warehouse and distribution center. The employees, many twentysomething and thirtysomething children of veteran UAW autoworkers, voted down the union handily.

Still, the city administration was losing money throughout 2009. Ockomon, newly elected in 2008, inherited 715 full-time employees or equivalents, and was forced to begin a strong layoff program in 2009, one he predicted would continue into 2010. Some workers were to be put on seasonal employee status, while others had their jobs reclassified, meaning they would be paid less. Some positions would be eliminated by attrition. But other employees would just be terminated. The budget shortfall for 2009 was put at $2.3 million, with a projected shortfall of $4.5 million in 2010. To pay the bills Ockomon would need to see a lot more Nestlé chocolate consumption, and a lot more gambling.

Back in Kokomo in early 2009, Greg Goodnight was making his second State of the City speech. One of Goodnight's beliefs is that in order to make his city attractive to prospective employers, and to keep talented workers grounded, he has to deal with quality of life issues. That's why he promised to allocate money for beautification projects and the arts as well as good, old-fashioned items such as sidewalk repair. The city several years ago unveiled a major public sculpture to honor a former Miami Indian chief, and in 2008 local craftsmen created a 12-foot-tall, space age–like piece of modern sculpture made from rare alloys donated by Haynes International, the mayor's former employer. Nevertheless, Goodnight said his immediate task remained balancing the city budget. To that end he got rid of one of the city's five "trash packers" and arranged with most citizens to voluntarily put out their trash on only one side of the alley or street on pickup days, so the remaining trash packers would have to make one pass only. (Trash packers have mechanical arms that pick up purpose-built trash containers and can only work one side of a street at a time.) These moves alone would save the city $150,000 per year, Goodnight said.

The city also was down to 481 municipal employees by March 2009, thirty fewer than just a year earlier. Goodnight had renegotiated contracts with about 100 city employees who were members of the American Federation of State, County and Municipal Employees (AFSCME), and managed to get the police department to agree to a pay freeze. He successfully shifted a higher proportion of health care costs to virtually all city employees, too, though he is still concerned that remaining health insurance liabilities for the city will go up anyway. Later that spring, he did the unthinkable — he indefinitely laid off twelve additional firefighters, bringing the department's total down to 100 from 121 when he took office. Firefighters in Kokomo average $58,000 per annum, plus benefits. The pay scale effectively had been linked to all those high-paying auto industry jobs.

The reaction from the firefighters was predictably strong. They launched a door-to-door handbill campaign denouncing the mayor's move as a threat to public safety; they also opined that they never were offered a "no layoff" clause in their last contract similar to what the AFSCME and police collective bargaining agreements contained. Local press reports at the time said the firefighters were being disingenuous on that point, however — they had been offered a no layoff clause in one draft contract, but pressed for additional pay instead.

The total fire department budget for 2009 in Kokomo was nearly $11 million, much higher than in Muncie, Bloomington, and Anderson, even though those cities have larger populations by twenty percent or more each. The mayor was not backing down — he said there might even be more layoffs in the future. It was quite a stance for a former union president to take, yet Goodnight was not asking anyone to make sacrifices he wasn't willing to make himself. He had turned down two annual pay raises in a row in his first two years in office.

Privately, Goodnight wondered where the money would come from to balance the budget and still pay for needed services. He rejected raising trash collection fees because, he said, you can't collect taxes from unemployed people. He also resisted calls to raid a $3 million Economic Development Income Tax (EDIT) distribution from the state and transfer the money to the city's General Fund to cover ordinary operating expenses, such as paying those firefighters. The EDIT money, as it was called, was for future growth and economic development, he noted. All the contentiousness over just who would make what sacrifices may have been emblematic of a deeper cultural phenomenon, however. Some people in Middle America strived hard to serve the common good and save their towns, while others constantly shifted responsibility or played the game of "You first," when it came to making real sacrifices.

David Galvin, Kokomo's sustainability manager, expressed deep pessimism about the public's understanding of the financial challenges facing the city, state, or country. "I actually read that some ridiculously large proportion of the population thinks they will win the lottery to pay off their debt," said Galvin, a blue-collar guy who joined the navy after graduating high school in 1991, then later went to Purdue University. "Where do they come up with this stuff? This is not an economic problem. This is an educational problem."

---

1. Stats Indiana, Kokomo Metro Area http://www.stats.indiana.edu/profiles/prmetro29020.html.
2. Ray Day, "Continental Steel Not Forgotten," *Kokomo Tribune*, February 22, 2008, www.ktonline.com/columns/local_story_053015755.html.
3. Ted Evanoff, "Battle for Prosperity," *Indianapolis Star*, November 13, 2005, Business 1D.
4. Scott Smith, "Yalies Take Note of Mayor Goodnight," *Kokomo Tribune*, March 3, 2009, http://www.kokomotribune.com/archivesearch/local_story_062234510.html.

5. Evanoff.

6. Ted Buck, "Marion," *Indiana Business Magazine*, March 1, 1993, www.allbusiness.com/north-america/united-states-indiana/357296-1.html.

7. Ted Evanoff, "Marion Lands TriEnda Jobs," *Indianapolis Star*, October 31, 2008, Business 1.

8. Kevin Leininger, "GM Plant Assessment 25 Percent Lower," *(Fort Wayne) News-Sentinel*, March 17, 2009, www.news-sentinel.com/apps/pbcs.dll/article?AID=/SE/20090317/NEWS/903170329.

9. Stats Indiana, http://www.stats.indiana.edu/profiles/prmetro23060.html.

10. Stats Indiana, http://www.stats.indiana.edu/profiles/pr18093.html.

11. Will Higgins, "Is Storied Wigwam History?" *Indianapolis Star*, March 9, 2009, A6.

12. Nestlé USA press release, March 11, 2009, http://www.insideindianabusiness.com/newsitem.asp?ID=34303.

CHAPTER 4

Government Motors

THE DETROIT THREE OCCUPIED a pivotal place in the economy. With nearly half a trillion dollars in annual sales between them, GM, Ford, and Chrysler typically spent about $10 billion on research and development each year, accounting for a large share of America's corporate R&D.[1] Even so, Detroit could tout few technical breakthroughs of note in recent decades.[2] Nor had the city developed car models regarded as clearly superior in the public mind to Japanese or German brands. That was a reason Detroit sold only forty-three percent of the new automobiles in the United States in the winter of 2009, while the market share of foreign brands reached fifty-seven percent.[3] Since 1990, Detroit had ceded nearly twenty-five percentage points of market share, causing it to forego billions of dollars in profits, making the recession of 2009 doubly difficult to survive.

Yet, when Richard Wagoner arrived in Washington, D.C., on March 27, 2009, to meet with the members of President Barack Obama's automotive advisory task force, the GM executive seemed neither selfish, nor out of touch, nor incompetent. It was a Friday, the kind of day when business consultants and contract salesmen leave the nation's capital, and upper-level government bureaucrats head out to their comfortable vacation homes or other retreats. Wagoner was the chairman and chief executive officer of General Motors. A tall, rawboned Virginian with a Harvard MBA, he spoke calmly, much like a pragmatic conciliator in an Episcopal rectory. Fifty-five years old, he had been employed for thirty-one years by General Motors. For the last seventeen years he had helped orchestrate a continual overhaul of the company, expanding in Eastern Europe, South America, and China while scaling back at home. In the United States, GM had shed tens of thousands of jobs, closed dozens of plants, sold entire divisions. The company was shaking off bulk added in the 1980s — a misguided effort to fend off the Asian automakers that were then becoming formidable rivals.

Now, as Wagoner arrived in Washington on a chilly day in March, General Motors was staggered by a deep recession and questions as to whether high gasoline costs finally had staved in the lucrative market for pickup trucks and sport-utility vehicles, a market that long had kept GM alive. No automaker — not the Koreans, the Germans, the Japanese, or the Americans — was making money in this deep recession. But of the twenty carmakers selling into the American market, Chrysler and GM appeared the worst off, having drained their cash reserves to keep plants running as sales dried up.

In four days, Wagoner was due to make the final pitch for $16.6 billion in federal bailout loans, on top of the $13.4 billion already received. The March 31 deadline had been set in December by President George W. Bush's administration. Bush had since left office, but the deadline remained. GM executives had worked out the framework of a restructuring plan required by the Bush officials and insisted on by President Barack Obama's automotive task force. But when Wagoner arrived in Washington, he lacked two crucial pieces of the restructuring plan. No concessions were in hand from two sparring groups — the UAW and bondholders. The latter had loaned GM about $28.5 billion and insisted the UAW accept larger concessions, while the union contended it had given enough. Two weeks earlier, Ron Gettelfinger, the president of the UAW, had agreed to modify the 2007 labor contract with Ford Motor Company, making concessions worth billions of dollars, a package widely expected to be the template for Chrysler and General Motors. Ford was not in the desperate condition of its Detroit rivals, having borrowed billions of dollars just before the financial crisis dried up sources of loans. But knowing GM and Chrysler would seek concessions, Ford pushed for them, too, and worked out a favorable deal with the union.

UAW leaders agreed that Ford could change the way skilled trade work was done at certain factories, and it accepted shorter breaks as well overtime changes. This would let the company schedule four ten-hour days without overtime. The UAW also suspended the Jobs Bank, which paid laid-off workers their base wage while performing certain other duties, including community-based volunteer work. The biggest change was in the retiree health care plan, which the union already had agreed to take over during the 2007 contract talks with Ford, Chrysler, and GM. In the new concession package, the UAW let Ford cut in half its cash contribution to the health fund, called the Voluntary Employees' Beneficiary Association, and make up the difference with Ford stock, beginning in 2010.[4] Ford executives believed the concessions would bring the company's hourly payroll cost (including all benefits and deferred payments) to about $55 an hour, close to the payroll of the Japanese auto plants in the United States. Union leaders described the concessions as significant, and balked when the bondholders demanded more give backs. "We feel like we're already on third base giving significant concessions," said Alan Reuther, UAW legislative director, suggesting bondholders now "need to step forward."[5]

Heading to Washington, Wagoner had hoped he could assure government officials that GM had made progress on its restructuring even if the final plan was not fully ironed out. Obama had different ideas — much different than Wagoner's. The White House had summoned the executive to town not to explore GM's survival, but to tell the CEO his career had ended. Obama was ready to intervene directly in General Motors, committing the government to the extraordinary task of steering an industrial company. Not since President Harry Truman nationalized the steel industry during the Korean War had the government actually taken over an industry. It had come close in Detroit in the early days of the Second World War when Ford was in disarray under its aging founder. Henry Ford II replaced his grandfather, Henry Ford, and put the company on a sound course. Now, in the recession year of 2009, the government was ready to reach inside General Motors. "We cannot, we must not, and we will not simply let our auto industry vanish," Obama said in public comments.[6]

First, the White House wanted Wagoner and most of the board of directors at the top of the company moved aside. For Obama, Wagoner was a symbol of staid, ineffective leadership. If the government was going to control the destiny of General Motors, the White House needed to oust the CEO and press home among American taxpayers the point that the president of the United States was not simply cozying up to GM. "This is Obama, and symbols of change are important," an insider told the *Wall Street Journal*.[7]

Wagoner's fate had been determined in the White House during meetings Obama had with his auto industry advisors. On March 26, Obama and his team met in the Roosevelt Room in the West Wing of the White House. They agreed the GM and Chrysler restructuring plans were insufficient. GM had pledged to chop away another 47,000 jobs, close five assembly plants, discard four brands, shed 1,500 dealers, and reduce its supply chain by thirty percent.[8] It was a sizeable cutback intended to eliminate billions in dollars in costs. But in the White House, officials were not sure spending was being slashed enough, and feared GM and Chrysler would return for more federal aid. "We're not going to put these companies on some kind of indefinite intravenous drip feed of money," said Steven Rattner, Obama's chief advisor on automotive issues. "We need to come out of this with something that makes sense."[9]

One tension point was the prospect of bankruptcy. White House officials favored what they called a surgical, prepackaged bankruptcy, and knew political support in Washington was likely. Many members of Congress, especially legislators from anti-union Southern states where foreign automakers had located assembly plants, viewed bankruptcy reorganization as a sure way to break the high-wage UAW contracts. Lawmakers doubted citizens across the country would object. In early 2009 only eighteen percent of the American public favored a full government bailout of Detroit, a point pressed home by Nancy Pelosi, an important Democrat in the House of Representatives. Pelosi, a Californian elected Speaker of the House, echoed Rattner in saying a bankruptcy could shear costs and keep Detroit off perpetual life support. "In a prepackaged [bankruptcy], you would bring all the stakeholders — the management, the bondholders, the shareholders, the workers, the union, the dealers, the suppliers — everybody to the table and say, 'What is the market?'" Pelosi said. "This has to be salvageable. This has to be fair: Workers shouldn't be the only ones who have to bite the bullet."[10]

Both Wagoner and UAW leaders opposed bankruptcy. Companies that reorganized under the United States Bankruptcy Code typically stayed in business while they devised a plan to repay debts. Union members, however, knew a bankruptcy judge easily could side with GM and bondholders in court, scuttle the labor contracts, and gut the pensions and medical plans covering 800,000 GM retirees and their spouses. The newspapers had been full of accounts of other companies tossing their own pension obligations to the Pension Benefit Guaranty Corporation (PBGC), a quasi-government entity in Washington that assumes pension liabilities of failed companies. An important Obama advisor on the auto task force, former Wall Street investment banker Ronald Bloom had seen firsthand how a company could jettison its heavy pension costs and become profitable again. Bloom had been financial counselor to the United Steelworkers, advising the union during the restructuring of bankrupt steelmaker LTV in 2003. With the steel union's blessing, LTV cut 4,000 of 7,000 jobs and handed its pension fund, then underfunded by $2.3 billion, to the PBGC. It also eliminated health care insurance for retirees.[11] Wall Street investment banker Wilbur Ross picked up the bankrupt steelmaker for $300 million, then took over Bethlehem Steel, paying $1.4 billion for that bankrupt mill operator, which had pushed its own pension fund onto PBGC and canceled retiree health care benefits.[12] Ross paired LTV and Bethlehem with three other steel companies, forming a new entity, International Steel Group. Shorn of its costly pension obligations and streamlined for higher output with fewer workers, the company was ready to produce profits. International Steel was sold for $4.5 billion in 2005 to Indian industrialist Lakshmi Mittal.[13] For his efforts, Ross garnered $267 million in cash and Mittal Steel stock and won the praise of ex-Bethlehem CEO Steve Miller, who had sold the steelmaker to Ross.

"I had two objectives," Miller, in a speech at the Detroit Economic Club, said of the Bethlehem sale. "One was to put the plants in safe hands. The other was to do the best I could for the retirees. The second, I didn't achieve. I was disappointed for the retirees. But there was no way to generate the millions needed to take on the legacy costs."[14] Miller went on in 2005 to become CEO of automotive supplier Delphi. He promptly led the former auto-parts arm of General Motors in its bankruptcy reorganization. While GM agreed to take over responsibility for some Delphi pension obligations, in early 2009 the bankrupt supplier persuaded a judge to let it cancel medical coverage for 15,000 salaried retirees. Delphi later dialed back and stashed about $9 million in a medical trust fund set up to help pay for the retirees' health insurance.

While the union members at Chrysler and General Motors feared for their pay and benefits, Wagoner feared for the company. He thought car shoppers would avoid GM dealers out of concern a bankrupt automaker might fail to honor warranty claims. Already, GM and Chrysler dealers had seen signs that bankruptcy talk had taken a toll on sales.[15] Wagoner also warned the costs could be high to the federal government. If GM entered bankruptcy and sales crumbled, no banker would risk lending the money GM would need to pull itself out of bankruptcy. Then, Wagoner told the White House, the United States government might have to loan the company as much as $100 billion to keep it open and operating. Wagoner had shared the estimate with the White House advisors, Bloom and Rattner, but they were resolute. Bankruptcy — or at least the prospect of bankruptcy —

could bring the UAW and the bondholders quickly to heel and relieve GM of its burdensome obligations.

Interestingly, Obama's leading automotive advisors were investment bankers from Wall Street. It was the very place whose irresponsible practices with derivatives and mortgage-backed securities had set off the global credit crisis that withered lending in 2008 among corporations worldwide. The credit crunch spawned the subsequent recession. No longer able to borrow cash inexpensively, GM and Chrysler drained their cash reserves, which had exceeded $30 billion between the two of them. But as the recession set in late in 2007 and dragged into 2008, auto sales volume receded — especially in the autumn of 2008 after Henry Paulson, the United States Treasury secretary, astonished the country with a desperate plea. He insisted Congress mount a massive taxpayer bailout of Wall Street firms mired in a financial crisis spawned by risky mortgage loans going bad in huge numbers. As lawmakers quickly committed $700 billion to what was called the Troubled Asset Relief Program (TARP), the ordinary citizens finally got it: America really was in a major recession. Consumer spending dried up. By December, auto sales slumped thirty-six percent industry-wide.[16]

Short on money late in 2008, GM and Chrysler turned to the White House for loans from the TARP fund to keep the plants operating. What Chrysler and GM execs found in Washington, though, was a government reluctant to simply plow cash into Detroit. Ironically, GM in particular had recently made serious strides in terms of efficiency in the plants and the engineering of vehicles. That winter, the Detroit Three produced three of the nation's top seven selling vehicles.[17] GM's 2008 Chevrolet Malibu was rated better on quality than the Honda Accord by market researcher J.D. Power and Associates. And Power's dependability studies graded GM's 2009 Buick brand ahead of Toyota's top-shelf Lexus. But in the court of public opinion, Detroit was widely regarded as inept. The White House hewed to this view.

Obama, shortly after taking office in January, had assembled a handful of banking experts to advise him on the automotive bailouts. None of the experts had any manufacturing experience, though they did have solid Democratic Party credentials. The team was led by Ronald Bloom, the former investment banker at Lazard Frères & Co., and Steven Rattner, a former reporter at the *New York Times* who went to work at Lazard Frères and then helped found the investment firm Quadrangle Group. Rattner's wife, Maureen White, had headed fundraising for the Democratic National Committee, a role that interested Rattner.[18] He became a financial advisor for Michael Bloomberg, then-mayor of New York, and a money man on the national political front, raising $100,000 for the unsuccessful 2008 presidential bid of New York Senator Hillary Clinton. Obama brought her into his cabinet as Secretary of State.

On the auto task force, the two bankers gathered more than two dozen analysts, including figures drawn from the Boston Consulting Group and Rothschild Inc., a Wall Street investment firm where Wilbur Ross had been for twenty-four years before he made his mark buying LTV and Bethlehem Steel.[19] In late February, the auto team began poring over the financial status of GM and Chrysler. As they went to work, Bloom and Rattner were peppered by admonitions from an ad hoc committee representing GM bondholders. Bonds are a kind of loan. In this case, bondholders had loaned the automaker $28.5 billion, some of it to help GM fund a new medical trust it had created for retired autoworkers. When GM went to the White House for a bailout late in 2008, President Bush's administration had decreed GM should repay only $9 billion of the debt. The bondholders could make the difference by taking shares of stock from the company free of charge — a move that essentially would hand the bondholders control of GM. But the bondholders insisted the stock was almost worthless and would lose all value in a bankruptcy. Taking on the stock meant the lenders had "been asked to make deeper cuts than other stakeholders," especially the UAW, the ad hoc committee told Obama's advisors in a letter sent late in March. The letter went above Rattner and Bloom and was sent directly to their immediate boss, United States Treasury Secretary Timothy F. Geithner, a former executive in the Federal Reserve Bank of New York. If bondholders irked at the UAW indeed rejected the proposed debt-for-stock swap, the committee told Geithner, the result could tip General Motors into "a bankruptcy that would have dire consequences for the company."[20]

Geithner never replied publicly. Rattner shrugged off the contentions. It was no wonder. In the White House, officials considered bankruptcy good medicine, a point soon impressed on Wagoner. That Friday in late March when Wagoner arrived in Washington he was accompanied by Frederick A. Henderson ("Fritz" Henderson), GM's chief financial officer. They went straightaway to Rattner's office in the Treasury building. Rattner had Wagoner come into his office alone. Rattner explained the government's new direction. Wagoner was out. Henderson would be the new CEO, at least temporarily. And in another slight to Wagoner, at least six members of General Motors' board of directors would have to step down, as well.[21] A CEO often brings in capable directors for advice and as a sounding board. In American corporations, directors hire and fire the chairman and CEO, and approve broad strategy. Intended to safeguard the interests of the shareholders who own the company by virtue of controlling the stock, directors usually serve part-time and often are outsiders selected by the chairman and CEO from the ranks of other corporations. Now, Obama was intervening directly in the management of a corporation, and heeding GM bondholders and industry insiders. They earlier had told Rattner and Bloom that GM's directors seemed "a collection of failed CEOs."[22] By Sunday, word trickled out indicating Wagoner's departure. The next day, GM confirmed the changes in a short report that included Wagoner's terse comment: "On Friday, I was in Washington for a meeting with administration officials. In the course of that meeting, they requested that I 'step aside' as CEO of GM, and so I have."[23]

If Wagoner opposed bankruptcy, Henderson soon adopted the government view. On Monday, he announced he was prepared to do anything to right the company, including taking GM into bankruptcy.[24] It was not immediately clear in the factory cities of the Midwest, or even in the seventy-one-story tower on the Detroit River that is GM world headquarters, what the new CEO might actually do, or how deeply the Obama team would insert itself in the affairs of General Motors. But it was clearly a quick and stunning change that seemed to have no sense of the culture inherent in a century-old corporation. Wagoner had been a GM man — part of a long succession of self-effacing executives drawn in particular from the Ivy League and the rich land-grant universities of the Midwest. The execs considered loud boasts or rash and unstudied actions distasteful for people who, in fact, led what had for decades been the world's largest corporation. They were sober and cautious. Their conservative public face hid from the outside world the painful battle going on inside General Motors. The executives had put on iron gloves, and had wielded them relentlessly against the UAW, ever since the extraordinary boardroom coup of 1992.

Riled as losses mounted in the 1991 recession, GM board member John Smale, the retired chairman of consumer products giant Procter & Gamble, led the ouster of senior executives and brought in John "Jack" Smith, Wagoner's mentor, to remake the company. For the next seventeen years — until that meeting in Rattner's office — GM largely had held to the course set by Smith, who himself was trying to reverse the bulk up of GM presided over by a prior CEO named Roger Smith. Lampooned in the 1989 film *Roger & Me* for neglecting the urban decline of Flint, Michigan, a manufacturing bastion where GM then had 60,000 employees, Roger Smith actually made his mark in GM for an intensely ambitious plant-building and technology spree that would surpass $40 billion in capital spending.[25] Meant to diminish the Japanese automakers' presence in the United States, Roger Smith put up robot-filled new plants, created the Saturn small-car division, and overhauled an array of old plants in Flint into something called Buick City — a direct counter to Toyota City in Japan. To moviegoers who saw the cheeky film by Michael Moore, Roger Smith was an imperious and distant executive little concerned for the blue-collar citizens of Flint laid off by GM. Although the film introduced GM culture to thousands of Americans for the first time, and pressed home the notion that here was another American edifice unworthy of its status, there was more to the city and the company than Moore let on.

Flint, located seventy miles north of Detroit, was where GM was founded in 1908 around the Buick motorcar. A leafy old wagon-making town, Flint became the second largest Michigan city after Detroit, growing up around the more than two dozen GM plants and offices, including the headquarters and engineering centers for the Buick and Chevrolet divisions. Flint residents in Moore's film seemed at once unlikeable, uncouth, and uneducated. Moore was wide of the mark, however. Flint was America, the industrialized Midwestern America. When the film was made, the city and adjacent Genesee County were home to more than 400,000 people. Tens of thousands of them traced their lineage to parents, grandparents, and great grandparents who had come to the city in a great migration from the American South, other Upper Great Lakes states, and a vast swath of Europe. Flint was an American cultural chowder that endured. When rioters burned parts of Detroit in 1967 over allegations of police irregularities toward African-Americans, the U.S. Army's 82nd Airborne division entered Detroit to put down the violence, while Flint remained calm and peaceful. Paid one of the highest industrial wages on earth, thousands of GM employees in Flint moved to the new suburbs, beginning in the 1960s, using the new interstate highways to commute to the warren of factories near the center city. By the time Moore, who himself was reared in suburban Flint, made his movie, the old brick stores of the downtown shopping district were largely abandoned, a point that came through in the film. That wasn't because of Roger Smith, though. Following the middle class to the suburbs, merchants had relocated to the new shopping malls.

In the film it was hard to understand what Roger Smith actually was doing for GM, if anything. In reality, he was doing quite a lot. Intent on cutting costs, Smith ended the GM historic organization of independent fiefdoms, restructuring the Buick, Cadillac, Chevrolet, GMC, Oldsmobile, and Pontiac divisions into two units. He harnessed GM to new technology, acquiring Electronic Data Systems in Texas and Hughes Aerospace in California. He ordered GM's first front-wheel-drive cars and formed a joint venture with Toyota to assemble small cars in Fremont, California. Although Smith was trying hard to respond to the foreign automakers then flowing into the United States, the response was ineffective in the view of Maryann Keller, a stock analyst who began studying GM in the early 1970s on Wall Street. "Roger [Smith] represents a huge turning point for GM. It was Roger who really destroyed the balance sheet" of the company, Keller said. Smith squandered money, investing in robots, opening new plants, forming Saturn from scratch, all of which cost billions of dollars, but made little profit. Keller said this left GM poorly prepared to take on the leaner Ford and Chrysler and the incoming tide of Asian automakers. "What we're seeing, it's a problem of forty years in the making. You really have to go back to the fact that GM and most of the [Detroit] auto industry really has been run by people who didn't understand cars and didn't understand car companies," said Keller, author of the 1993 book *Collision: GM, Toyota, Volkswagen and the Race to Own the 21st Century.*[26]

Roger Smith, like Wagoner years later, came up on the financial side of GM, figuring out how to raise cash for operations and invest and borrow. Faced with the new flood of imports in the 1970s, Keller believes Smith should have more deeply retrenched GM like its two Detroit rivals. Buffeted by imports, Ford and Chrysler closed plants in the early 1980s, shedding thousands of workers. Smith went the other way. He meant to wrest American baby boomers out of their Japanese cars, but the mission lost traction after he retired. Saturn became a niche car, largely neglected by GM execs as profits suddenly piled up in Detroit on the sale of SUVs and pickup trucks to those same boomers. Rather than cut back jobs quickly in the plants, Robert Stempel, Roger Smith's successor, slowly moved on plans to shed 75,000 positions and restore GM to its size of 1985. When the recession of 1991 riddled profits, GM's board ousted Stempel and turned to Jack Smith, a native of Worcester, Massachusetts, who had been president of GM's extensive European operations. He immediately set out to wage war on the UAW. Under his leadership in the 1990s, GM endured eighteen major strikes, but largely accomplished the mission set down by the board of directors.[27] GM whittled away the labor force, moving tens of thousands of workers from the payroll onto the pension plan in retirement, and in turn started to copy Toyota's lean manufacturing processes to produce more vehicles with fewer workers. The most jobs were shed in auto parts divisions centered largely in Indiana, Michigan, New York, Ohio, and Mexico. GM sold the Remy and Guide divisions to Wall Street investment firms and cast off Delphi auto parts as a standalone business. Free of GM, Delphi sold shares on the stock market in 1999 for the first time. GM's corporate success was demonstrable. By 1999, $20 billion filled short-term cash accounts. GM's stock traded for $90 a share. Engineering reports began to favorably compare the efficiency of its assembly lines with Honda, Nissan, and Toyota. It was a remarkable turnaround lost on Washington in the winter of 2009.

Step into a GM, Ford, or Chrysler assembly plant of 1975 and it might have 5,000 to 10,000 workers. Twenty-five years later, the same plant could get by with 2,500. The difference was in the design of the vehicle. Bumpers on pickup trucks, for example, were redesigned so two workers could mount them on the vehicle instead of four workers. And more components were assembled in distant plants by lower-wage workers outside the UAW and shipped to the final assembly point ready to be mounted on the car or truck. Using these lean production techniques in the mid-1990s, Japan's three largest automakers could assemble a vehicle twice as quickly as their rivals in Detroit. That saved the Japanese as much as $1,000 per vehicle compared to the costs of the Detroit Three. It was a lesson Detroit grasped and set out to mimic.

One of the biggest disciples of lean manufacturing was Tom LaSorda, a top Chrysler executive whose career had begun at

GM. LaSorda was the son of a Chrysler line worker in Windsor, a well-kept Canadian industrial city across the border from Detroit. Graduating from the University of Windsor with an engineering degree, the young LaSorda was hired by General Motors at a pivotal time. Roger Smith, then chairman of GM, was sure the Japanese automakers' prowess for quality traced to robots and other new technologies. To find out for sure, GM sought out Toyota, Japan's largest automobile manufacturer. Toyota agreed to participate, fearing political backlash from Washington over imports. In 1984, the companies created a joint venture to make cars together known as New United Motor Manufacturing Inc.[28] It brought together General Motors production workers and Toyota engineers in an old GM plant in the San Francisco suburb of Fremont. Retooled with Toyota machinery, paying GM's UAW autoworkers full union wages, the venture soon became a GM center for hands-on manufacturing technology. Called NUMMI, it schooled a who's who of notable GM engineers including LaSorda. It was still operating in 2009, making the well-regarded Pontiac Vibe small wagon (though Toyota ultimately decided later in the year to close it down).

The California venture dismissed doubts that critics had voiced about the UAW's ability to assemble well-made cars. And it laid to rest Roger Smith's notion of the robot as the key source of manufacturing quality. What GM learned at NUMMI was that Toyota executives demanded meticulous measurement of critical functions on the shop floor. Toyota, which had opened in 1919 as the Toyoda Loom textile machinery company, was short on cash after the Second World War and embraced a simple measure it called "lean production" to do more with less. Henry Ford had pioneered the whole notion and put it in practice in the 1920s, but the idea had been lost in Detroit during the wartime boom. Lean production called for keeping only enough inventory in the plant for a few hours of production, cutting down on warehousing costs, and it came with a Japanese emphasis on *kaizen*, or continuous improvement. If a batch of newly made door handles, for example, arrived in the assembly plant and didn't fit on the car precisely as intended, the scrap rate showed up immediately in the metrics kept by engineers. They quickly investigated and tweaked the production process to cut the scrap rate on door handles. Do this enough times and *then* you have a production process that is nearly flawless.

Not long after his stint at NUMMI, LaSorda went abroad, a North American expatriate putting up General Motors assembly plants across the globe. One after another, GM opened plants in Hungary, Poland, and elsewhere. LaSorda's continuous improvement lessons were put to work. With each new facility, LaSorda learned to scale back, reduce costs, shrink the footprint. By the late 1990s, he was on a team that had designed a GM car plant in Lansing, Michigan, which could be built and equipped for about $500 million — half the price for the typical vehicle assembly plant. The savings put the Canadian engineer in a rare limelight. In 2000, Chrysler hired him to help improve its production processes. Spurred on by lean techniques, Chrysler, Ford, and GM narrowed the productivity gap. In 2008, the annual Harbour Report, an engineering study widely read in the auto industry, ranked Chrysler and Toyota equal in productivity. Both could assemble a vehicle in 30.37 hours. Just behind them were Honda (31.33 hours), GM (32.39 hours), Nissan (32.96 hours), Ford (33.88 hours), and Hyundai (35.10 hours).[29]

As the lean techniques took hold at GM, Jack Smith promoted Wagoner from chief financial officer of the company in 1993, making him head of GM's North American operations. By 1998, Wagoner was president of the entire company. In 2000, he became CEO, and in 2003 succeeded Jack Smith as chairman. By then, Wagoner was widely seen on Wall Street as the most capable replacement in GM for Jack Smith. Viewed as a calm hand after the UAW uproar caused by Smith's attrition policy, Wagoner had critics in and out of the industry who faulted him for failing to continue to quickly retrench GM. What many critics failed to observe, however, was that Wagoner continued the attrition as fervently as Smith, but avoided the din of the 1990s by steering clear of strikes, and instead offering the thousands of graying workers still in the plants retirement buyouts. Sean McAlinden, chief economist at the Center for Automotive Research, a think tank in the Detroit suburb of Ann Arbor, called the downsizing perhaps the most humane ever conducted by any major American corporation.[30]

What was happening was the continued retrenching of GM's auto-parts manufacturing empire. GM was doing more than introducing lean production into its plants. It was trying to become more like Chrysler, a company that relied on outside suppliers to make the bulk of the 5,000 auto parts that went into a vehicle. In the 1910s and 1920s, GM had grown up quickly by buying its supply chain. Looking for reliable auto parts and economies of scale, GM acquired dozens of manufacturers including Dayton Engineering and Packard Electric in Ohio, Harrison Radiator and Mott Axle in New York, Allison Engineering and Remy Electric in Indiana, and Champion Spark Plugs and Fisher Body in Michigan. By the time Wagoner was hired on at GM as a financial analyst in 1977, General Motors employed 600,000 people throughout the world, almost a fifth of them in auto-parts plants concentrated in Flint, Michigan; Dayton, Ohio; and Anderson, Indiana. For decades, the economies of scale had worked to GM's advantage, allowing it to outmuscle rivals.

But by the 1970s, the UAW was using its leverage over the Big Three to protect remaining employees and secure even greater wages and benefits. To do this, the union wielded the strike threat. The UAW would target one of the Detroit Three first, threatening a walkout there and forcing it to accept a contract for fear of enduring a strike that would shut its plants, all the while allowing cross-town rivals a leg up on sales. That contract would then become the pattern, setting the standard for labor contracts with the other two companies. Critics believed the pattern contract was extortion, or like taking hostages. For the UAW, however, it was a winning strategy, securing gains even as the Detroit Three's share of the auto market declined.

Just as UAW wages were climbing, however, Japanese automakers were becoming formidable rivals, benefiting both from lower wages prevailing in Asia as well as Japan's pioneering efforts in lean manufacturing. As Japanese imports came into the United States at markedly lower prices, Americans took notice. The Datsun B210 became one of the most popular subcompacts of the era, selling new for about $4,500 in 1980, while the mid-size Buick Regal went for about $6,100. The Datsun got better gas mileage, too, always a concern after the 1973–74 Arab oil boycott and the 1979 Islamic Revolution in Iran. Throughout the United States, incomes had stagnated in the 1970s, especially in blue-collar and middle-class families, as inflation spawned by the Vietnam War and the oil shocks pushed living costs higher. The lower priced Hondas, Toyotas, and Datsuns (a brand name later changed to Nissan) of the 1970s and 1980s not only could travel more miles on a gallon of gasoline than a typical Chevrolet, Dodge, or Ford, but many consumers became certain the Japanese cars broke down less often. And for baby boomers steeped in the self expression that went with coming of age in the Me Decade, driving small imports set them apart from stodgy adults in their big Detroit cars. It was not long after this that GM had to resort to its famous, or infamous, "Not your father's Oldsmobile" ad campaign. (Oldsmobile later went so far as to introduce a new luxury model, the Aurora, without the Oldsmobile nameplate on the vehicle at all.)

The American companies still had a substantial lead in terms of raw performance because of their typically larger engines — witness the old saw that "there's no replacement for displacement" — but even this advantage began to disappear as the government began mandating low emissions and clean air standards for cars. Detroit responded to the clean air challenge mostly by detuning their cars and adding restrictive devices rather than just making the engines more efficient. Yet the Japanese and Europeans knew that you could get both better fuel economy and more horsepower out of efficient engines — efficiency and better engineering were the replacement for displacement. The performance gap simply was closed in time, especially by the Japanese — a current four-cylinder Japanese midsize car engine produces almost as much horsepower as a V-8 Ford Mustang motor mid-1980s vintage.

Worried they trailed the Japanese on price and quality, GM execs turned first to automation in the factories, particularly at Saturn and in Buick City. When they continued to fall behind, GM then looked for ways to shed parts factories in order to secure components from cheaper and usually non-union suppliers, often based in Europe and Asia. In the mid-1990s, GM created a new unit called Delphi and folded into it an array of businesses. The largest was GM Delco, the modern name for what had been Dayton Engineering Laboratories Co. (It was a founded by Charles Kettering, a famed engineer who became a ranking GM executive and whose name now graces the private Kettering University in Flint, which had originated as General Motors Institute, GM's own West Point for engineering.) Along with Delco, Delphi took in Champion, Harrison, Packard, parts of Remy, and other GM supply plants. In 1999, GM cast off Delphi as a standalone company employing slightly more than 200,000 workers worldwide. The next year Wagoner was promoted to CEO of General Motors, heading a global business employing 401,000 people. By the spring of 2009, Wagoner had ratcheted GM's employment level down to 244,000 worldwide.

On March 27, 2009, Wagoner arrived in Washington committed to chopping away another 47,000 jobs worldwide. It was a staggering turn of events. General Motors would have eliminated 400,000 jobs during Wagoner's thirty-two years at the company. He must have thought that the prospect of additional job cuts gave him leverage in Washington, though one has to ask if such employees were truly expendable, why were they there in the first place? Either Wagoner was admitting that GM would not have enough work for them in the future, or that the company planned to outsource their jobs, or that it would load up with lower-paid replacements in the future, when and if business improved. In any case, cutting out jobs was a better course than putting the company in bankruptcy, or at least Wagoner thought it was. Obama's auto task force thought differently. On the

Monday that Wagoner stepped aside, Rattner gave Henderson sixty days to complete the revival plan. Chrysler got thirty days to hitch up with Fiat.

From the outside, Obama looked the part of the hero, the strong leader who finally had tamed Detroit and its errant executives and union leaders. That picture would be as superficial as a photo op for the president, however. From the inside, it was clear there was not much left for Henderson to do other than follow Wagoner's template — lop off 47,000 more jobs — while heeding White House's call to more quickly secure the necessary concessions from the UAW and the bondholders, if at all possible. The threat of bankruptcy — a government-sanctioned bankruptcy this time — might move those stakeholders to action and give Henderson a kind of stick to wave at them. Independent observers figured the bondholders would take the biggest hit. It was hard to believe a Democratic president who counted on labor unions as one of his biggest backers would impose more severe cuts on the UAW. But the threat of bankruptcy might squeeze further concessions from labor while allowing the administration to say it was not the Democrats, but the bankruptcy judge, who was mandating them. That is, if it came down to a real bankruptcy.

The union in 2007 *had* agreed to major concessions that went a long way toward wiping out the cost disadvantage for the Detroit Three compared to the Japanese carmakers. The union would take responsibility from the Detroit Three for medical trust funds that covered the health care costs for the retirees. Although the trusts were to be filled with money from the auto companies, the Detroit Three would be relieved of perpetually funding the health accounts. This alone would help erase most of the $1,500 cost disadvantage on Detroit cars relative to the foreign makes — in time. And the UAW had agreed to a two-tier wage scale. Once the economy rebounded and auto sales took off, the Detroit Three would have to restaff the empty factories with thousands of newly hired workers. Many would come in at less than $15 an hour, far less than the $26 average hourly wage in the Honda and Toyota plants, or the prevailing $29 base wage in the Detroit Three labor contracts.

While the Detroit automakers could sense relief once the economy turned the corner, one nagging concern remained. None of the companies had a fleet of head turners on the drawing boards, no cars considered clearly superior to rival brands. Indeed, the automakers had been hollowing out the Detroit engineering corps for years in an effort to cut costs. The model seemed to be Dell Computer — a business that designs, assembles, and markets products under its name, but relies on its suppliers for the parts and innovation.

While Obama and his task force had stunned Detroit with the removal of Wagoner, the government leaders had done little to actually bring government policy to bear on issues of vital importance to GM and, indeed, almost every manufacturer in the nation. Health care coverage absorbed employers' profits and pushed down workers' wages in the absence of a national medical insurance system. Imports, especially from Asia, cost jobs at domestic manufacturers, despite increasingly strident claims from Middle America of Asian currency manipulation to maintain low prices on exports. "We know many Asian currencies are undervalued," said Clyde V. Prestowitz Jr., president of the Economic Strategy Institute in Washington, and a former United States trade negotiator in the 1980s.[31] And while Americans favored better air quality, there was not yet any cogent policy emanating from Washington to move the automakers quickly to electric cars or another alternative to gasoline.

Indeed, GM's former Delco Remy engineers around Indianapolis were buzzing with talk about reconstituting the EV1, an electric car GM produced to comply with California's emission laws in the 1990s, but pulled off the market in 2003 before gasoline prices doubled and tripled. In the early 1990s, GM Delco Remy had engineered the electrical heart of the EV1 in Indianapolis, a project that spurred Toyota into developing hybrid-electric cars such as the Prius. A legacy of the EV1 project remained in Indianapolis in the form of EnerDel, a manufacturer of lithium-ion batteries still looking for a customer for its high-tech electrical storage units in the winter of 2009. Many of the engineers who had since left the auto companies were looking for the new Obama administration to launch a clear-cut push for a new electric car complete with federal funding. But the White House remained vague on its plans through early 2009.

Conservative pundits bristled that Obama's auto bailout was merely meddling superficially with Detroit. "Better than trying to rewrite GM's business relationships," opined Holman W. Jenkins Jr. in the *Wall Street Journal*, the president ought to "try giving the country a coherent auto policy for a change" that might "impose a $5 gasoline tax so at least customers would have a reason to buy the cars Washington is forcing Detroit to build. None of this will happen. Mr. Obama will instead be content with incoherent policies that poll well — which means GM, Chrysler, and eventually Ford will need taxpayer subsidies as far as the eye can see. . . ."[32]

Whether the columnist was correct in the spring of 2009, it was certain the domestic auto industry was shriveling. That was clearly the case at Chrysler, where the bailout left the company mired in questions about whether it could even survive the year. In early 2009 President Bush had poured $4 billion in Chrysler to keep it alive. By the end of March, Obama's team was willing to commit another $6 billion, but only if Chrysler worked out a merger with Fiat within thirty days. The bailout promised a small measure of relief for Cerberus Capital Management. The Wall Street firm, headed by billionaire investor Stephen Feinberg, had bought 80.1 percent of Chrysler from Germany's Daimler in early 2007. The subsequent recession and credit crisis forestalled any hopes Feinberg had of polishing the stricken automaker and handing it off to another buyer. Much to the relief of Cerberus, Fiat had stepped up as a potential partner for Chrysler early in 2009. Just as the White House intervened in General Motors, though, the Obama team decided the provisions of the preliminary Chrysler-Fiat proposal would have to be reworked.

The original deal called for no cash infusion from money-strapped Fiat but handed the Italian automaker ownership in thirty-five percent of Chrysler with the prospect of eventually owning fifty-five percent, leaving twenty-five percent to Cerberus and twenty percent to Daimler. By the end of March, the Obama auto team had decided Fiat would take a controlling stake and Cerberus could walk away from Chrysler and give up its ownership claim to Fiat. In turn, the White House would inject $6 billion in Chrysler if Robert Nardelli and Sergio Marchionne could pull together the terms of a new deal by the end of April. It meant Fiat could marry an American industrial icon for no money down and receive a $6 billion dowry courtesy of American taxpayers. Even so, Marchionne was measured in his remarks. Calling the Obama auto task force "tough but fair," Marchionne said he believed the reworked deal would give Fiat and Chrysler a "credible future"[33]

One problem tempering the deal was Chrysler's heavy appetite for borrowed cash. Once in the hands of Cerberus, Chrysler had mortgaged plants and machinery to the hilt. The $9 billion worth of secured debts were still in place in the recession, chiefly in the hands of the New York banks J.P. Morgan Chase, Citibank, and Goldman Sachs. Secured debts gave the bankers the right to claim money from the company before anyone else if it went into bankruptcy. Obama's team insisted the debt burden far exceeded what Chrysler could handle even after partnering with Fiat. The recession was in full fury. Sales of cars and trucks sagged more than forty percent compared to the previous year, a decline heightened by other entities Cerberus had bought, Chrysler Financial and General Motors Acceptance Corporation. The finance companies had scaled back auto loans to consumers. By the spring of 2009, Chrysler was again starved for cash, after spending most of the $4 billion in federal bailout loans provided in December. Obama's auto team told Nardelli and Feinberg to get rid of most of the debt. It was a troubling order for Chrysler and the industrial cities where parts and vehicles were assembled. If the bankers wouldn't restructure or write off the loans, Chrysler could land in bankruptcy court. There, the bankers would most likely take control of the company. They could demand steep union concessions and in turn sell Chrysler in pieces, maybe spin off the iconic Jeep brand and vehicles assembled in Toledo and Detroit, sell the Ontario minivan plant, and close some or all of the transmission works in Kokomo, Indiana.

Greg Goodnight followed the news from Washington, Detroit, and Italy as closely as any stock analyst or auto insider. On April 14, 2009, the Kokomo mayor sent an open letter to Fiat chief Marchionne. In it he touted Kokomo's available skilled labor force; low cost of doing business; and good rail, air, and highway connections, all of which was true. "As we both know, these days every city — and every company — is talking about renewable energy and green initiatives," Goodnight wrote. "However, we have gone beyond talk, implementing innovative ideas such as our Kokomo fuel program. Through this program, the city part-ners with local businesses and residents to convert used cooking oil into biodiesel for our municipal vehicles. Similar sustainability programs are also being contemplated by my administration. With our city's combination of comprehensive manufacturing experience and innovative entrepreneurship, we are extremely well-positioned to be a regional, national, and global leader in the economy of tomorrow." There was no immediate response from Marchionne, however.

---

1. Anthony Howard, "Global Market Review of Automotive 4WD transmissions," *Just Auto*, March 2009, 11.

2. Thomas Klier, James Rubenstein, *Who Really Made Your Car?* (Kalamazoo, MI: W.E. Upjohn Institute for Employment Research, 2008), 26.

3. Automotive market share compiled by market researcher Morgan & Co., West Olive, Michigan, for the *Indianapolis Star*.

4. Louis Aguilar, "UAW, Ford Agree on New Pact," *Detroit News*, March 10, 2009, 1B.

5. Robert Snell, "GM Races Deadline for Deals," *Detroit News*, February 13, 2009, 1C.

6. Jeffrey McCracken, John D. Stoll, Neil King Jr., "US Considers Bankruptcy for GM, Chrysler," *Wall Street Journal*, March 31, 2009, A1.

7. Monica Langley, Neal E. Boudette, "CEO's Fate Sealed in West Wing," *Wall Street Journal*, March 31, 2009, A1.

8. "GM, Chrysler Updating Plans," *Detroit Free Press*, March 27, 2009, 8.

9. Langley.

10. David Shepardson, "Pelosi Offers Tough Critique of Automakers," *Detroit News*, April 4, 2009, A1.
11. Christopher Snowbeck, "Retired Steelworkers Face Health Care Crisis," *Pittsburgh Post-Gazette*, May 30, 2006, A7.
12. "Steel Rival Makes Deal to Acquire Bethlehem," *New York Times*, February 6, 2003, C5.
13. Heather Timmins, "Mergers Show Steel Industry Is Still Worthy of Big Deals," *New York Times*, October 26, 2004, C1.
14. Gregg Shotwell, Live Bait & Ammo, Issue 75, http://www.soldiersofsolidarity.com/files/livebaitammo/lba75.html.
15. Ted Evanoff, "Uncertainty Still Shrouds GM and Chrysler," *Indianapolis Star*, March 29, 2009, D1.
16. Automotive market share, Morgan & Co.
17. Automotive market share, Morgan & Co.
18. Louise Story, "Obama's Top Auto Industry Troubleshooter," *New York Times*, April 6, 2009, B1.
19. Allison Leigh Cowan, "Hilary Geary and Wilbur Ross Jr.," *New York Times*, October 17, 2004, 9-13.
20. Neil King Jr., John D. Stoll, "Auto Task Force Set to Back More Loans – With Strings," *Wall Street Journal*, March 26, 2009, A1.
21. King.
22. Jeffrey McCracken, John D. Stoll, Neil King Jr., "U.S. Considers Bankruptcy for GM, Chrysler," *Wall Street Journal*, March 31, 2009, A1.
23. Monica Langley, Neal E. Boudette, "CEO's Fate Sealed in West Wing," *Wall Street Journal*, March 31, 2009, A1.
24. John D. Stoll, Monica Langley, "New GM Chief Bends to U.S. Pressure," *Wall Street Journal*, April 1, 2009, 1A.
25. Reginald Stuart, "Few New Car Plants For South," *New York Times*, September 21, 1981, D1.
26. Mary Ann Keller interviewed by Ted Evanoff, March 26, 2008, and earlier interviews.
27. Ted Evanoff, "GM-UAW Deal Shows Peace: More Plants Are Signing Operating Agreements," *Detroit Free Press*, October 18, 1999, 1C.
28. James Mateja, "Rivalry Lively Between GM, Toyota," *Chicago Tribune*, February 14, 1985, 4.
29. Anthony Howard, "Global Market Review of Automotive 4WD transmissions," *Just Auto*, March 2009, 11.
30. Sean McAlinden interviewed by Ted Evanoff and comments at automotive trade conference in Detroit on November 3, 2003, sponsored by the Federal Reserve Bank of Chicago.
31. Clyde V. Prestowitz Jr. interviewed by Ted Evanoff on April 2, 2009.
32. Holman Jenkins Jr., "GM Bankruptcy? Tell Me Another," *Wall Street Journal*, April 1, 2009, A21.
33. Kate Linbaugh, Jeff Bennett, Neil King Jr., John D. Stoll, "Chrysler Plan Trims Fiat Stake, Cuts Out Cerberus," *Wall Street Journal*, March 31, 2009, A6.

CHAPTER 5

UAW

FRANCIS CALL IS A "SAGINOID." That's a contraction of Saginaw — a faded factory town 100 miles north of Detroit — and hemorrhoid. The derisive name wasn't given to him by strangers, nor by his longtime employer, General Motors Corporation. His union brothers and sisters in the United Auto Workers tagged him with that label and they meant it. It made no difference that Call was a lifelong dues payer, committed activist, and a terrific repository of information on UAW contracts past and present. Here's why his union family was so angry at Francis Call and other autoworkers like him.

Less than a year out of high school, Call began his auto industry career at GM's Saginaw metal casting plant on April 1, 1971. He remembers the date like his birth date, as all UAW workers do, because of its implications both for retirement benefits and plant seniority. He helped make engine blocks, cylinder heads, brake rotors, water pumps, and just about any other part that needed to be cast in a gray iron foundry that traced its origins to a 1917 building. "It was dirty, it was dark, we were pouring metal at 3,200 degrees Fahrenheit," said Call. The work was so unappealing that GM would let employees retire with full pension benefits after twenty-five years instead of the usual thirty — and this was called "credited service," not unlike hazardous pay for soldiers in combat.

Yet in the early 1980s recession Call was laid off for two years, one of the perennial hazards of the cyclical car business. He transferred to GM's Danville, Illinois, foundry, just off Interstate

74 near the Indiana state line. General Motors is largely thought to be centered in Detroit, but in fact many of its component operations were located in relatively out-of-the-way locations like Saginaw, an old lumber mill town near Lake Huron, or Danville, a community of 34,000 where GM opened a foundry in 1943 to tap the supply of local farm hands for the defense effort during the Second World War. Actor Gene Hackman, comedians Dick and Jerry Van Dyke, and jazz musician Bobby Short all hailed from Danville — it's not the obscure place one might think.

Call was one of 185 workers who made what he terms an "exodus" from Michigan to Danville in 1986. The Illinois foundry employed about 1,200 workers at the time. The move was related to "Paragraph 96," a key rule in the UAW-GM contract that stipulated the union could negotiate the transfer of laid-off workers to other GM plants, and guaranteed the transferees would keep all accumulated plant seniority.[1] Intended to let GM close worn-out facilities while preserving jobs and benefits for union members at the same time, Paragraph 96 had disastrous unintended consequences.

"It created some bad feelings," said Call. "They felt we came in and took away their jobs."

That's exactly what the Michigan boys did, though it was hardly their intention to do so. A worker who had, say, fifteen years experience at Saginaw Metal could transfer to Danville with his or her fifteen years seniority intact. Preserving the seniority was far-sighted and humane for the workers in transit, but it riled many Danville workers with less seniority. They had to give up not only choice assignments to "Saginoids" with more seniority, but in some cases, even lost their jobs as the recent arrivals with greater seniority would always be called back from future layoffs before local men and women with less seniority.

"We were called Saginoids," said Call. "We were like hemorrhoids, a pain in the ass."

Call said several of the transferees hadn't really wanted to come to rural Illinois, but were in fact fleeing the law, sometimes because of court-ordered alimony and child support payments. In one incident a sheriff's deputy arrested a "Saginoid" right inside the Danville foundry lunchroom. A native local employee stood up and tossed his car keys to the deputy. "Hey, Charlie," the man allegedly said to the deputy, "take my van and arrest ten more of the sons of bitches so maybe my son will be called back." Other Illinois employees cheered, Call remembered, saying that only calmer heads prevented a riot.

When the Danville foundry closed several years later, Call moved again, this time to Kokomo, Indiana, home to GM's Delco electronics complex that at the time employed 7,000 workers. He worked in the complex for years, even after Delco was spun off in 1999 by GM as part of Delphi. Yet by 2005, Delphi had filed for bankruptcy and it began to eliminate nearly 4,000 jobs in the Kokomo plants. Call had all his accumulated seniority, though, so he was relatively safe.

Seniority is one of the lynchpins of union solidarity and collective bargaining agreements. You commit to a company and the company guarantees you priority in employment over anyone who came after you — it's as simple as that. Seniority is one of the things that's right about unions and their historic movement to protect working men and women, but seniority is also part of their downfall, although it did not look like that at the beginning. The intention was to help all workers, not pit one against the other.

The United Auto Workers union, founded in 1935, always was as much a social movement as a force to balance corporate power and greed with worker rights. Its most important leader was Walter Reuther, president from 1946 until his untimely death in a small commuter airplane crash in 1970 near Detroit. Reuther and his brother, Victor, traveled through Europe during the Great Depression, working two years in a Russian car factory in Gorky during the Stalinist era. Walter Reuther quickly abandoned his Marxist idealizations of the proletariat and the inevitability of the demise of capitalism and became a staunch anti-Communist after the Second World War. As well he became a big supporter of America's military might, a kind of Henry "Scoop" Jackson, the liberal Democratic senator from Washington State who died in 1983.

The Reuther brothers had taken jobs in the auto industry in and around Detroit upon their return from Russia, even as the Great Depression set in and pushed the United States unemployment rate over twenty-five percent. The brothers were able communicators with the unschooled migrants from Europe and the American South who filled the auto factories. Angered by lost wages and job insecurity, autoworkers launched strikes in factories in Cleveland and Toledo, Ohio; Kansas City; Atlanta, Georgia; and Anderson, Indiana. The most notable action was a sit-down strike in 1937 in Flint, Michigan, in which workers locked themselves inside a GM Fisher Body stamping plant to prevent authorities from hauling them out and restaffing the production lines with fresh hires. In what union historians call the "Battle of the Running Bulls" (bulls being a derogatory reference to police[2]), Flint police and private security forces attacked strikers, wounding thirteen, while the workers hurled metal objects from inside the seized factory buildings. Unable to eject the Fisher Body strikers after forty-four days, GM Chairman Alfred Sloan gave in and signed an agreement with the UAW, the first labor contract ever for an American automaker.

As the UAW organized one factory and automaker after another, benefiting from the pro-union policies of the Roosevelt administration and the subsequent boom in industrial output brought on by the Second World War, Walter Reuther's thinking evolved. He abandoned his Communist sympathies, but cherished one leftist ideal. A lifelong social reformer, Reuther believed only the union movement could and would bring justice to the working class — not just UAW members, but everyone who worked for an hourly wage. It was this kind of thinking that galvanized unions in the twentieth century and brought about a host of social improvements Americans take for granted today. Forty-hour weeks, paid vacation and holidays, health insurance, seniority rights, company-paid pensions, maternity leave, even the 1960s Civil Rights movement — all trace to notions of social justice that crystallized in America with the union movement in the 1930s, though many salaried and "white collar" employees already enjoyed some of these benefits.

Walter Reuther saw the UAW as a vanguard for social change. At his election as president of the Detroit-based UAW in 1946, he called for "a labor movement whose philosophy demands that it fight for the welfare of the public at large. . . . We won the war. The task now is to win the peace."[3] His words stirred Americans, in part because Reuther was an eloquent statesman speaking for the average working man and woman, and in part because he *was* an average American. Born in 1907 in Wheeling, West Virgina, a gritty steel town in a mountain gorge on the Ohio River, young Reuther was enthralled when he heard a speech in his hometown by radical labor leader Eugene V. Debs, an Indiana railroad worker and United States presidential candidate who was a founder of the Industrial Workers of the World, then a prominent American union. It's said that Deb's speech turned Reuther to socialism. He dropped out of high school at age sixteen and became an apprentice tool and die maker. Resettled in booming Detroit, Reuther completed high school at night and attended Detroit City College, where he helped organize a student socialist committee and protested against the United States Army's Reserve Officers Training Corps. Despite his early pacifist leanings he later urged the automakers at the start of the Second World War to convert production to the war effort, calling for tanks and planes, not automobiles, and he served on several government boards during the war.[4]

Reuther's anti-Communism appears sincere. He was a founding member in 1947 of the Americans for Democratic Action, a group often pegged as Left-leaning, but which also was anti-Stalinist. And it was during his tenure as head of both the UAW and the broader Congress of Industrial Organizations (CIO) that as many as eleven affiliates in the late 1940s and early 1950s suspected of being Communist-led were expelled, even though this represented about seventeen percent of CIO membership.[5] His position vis à vis the House Committee on Un-American

Activities (generally known as HUAC) and the so-called Army-McCarthy Hearings in the 1950s was a bit more ambiguous as he advised union leaders to cooperate while simultaneously condemning the anti-Communist crusades.[6]

To this day the UAW echoes a strong position on social justice and the rights of the workingman and workingwoman — help for everyone, not just union members, belying the idea of an insular, even indifferent labor movement. "We are a social movement, but you don't see that in the papers," said Reuther disciple and UAW Region 3 director Maurice "Mo" Davison, the highest ranking UAW official in Indiana and Kentucky. "You'll hear about us day after day if we strike someone."

The UAW website touts the same themes. "From our earliest days, the UAW has been a leader in the struggle to secure economic and social justice for all people," it reads. "The UAW has been actively involved in every civil rights legislative battle since the 1950s, including the campaigns to pass the Civil Rights Act of 1964, the Voting Rights Act of 1965, the Fair Housing Act, the Civil Rights Restoration Act of 1988, and legislation to prohibit discrimination against women, the elderly, and people with disabilities. The UAW also has played a vital role in passing such landmark legislation as Medicare and Medicaid, the Occupational Safety and Health Act, the Employee Retirement Act, and the Family and Medical Leave Act."[7] Indeed, it was the UAW that funded the Reverend Dr. Martin Luther King's March on Washington and "I have a dream" speech in 1963. Walter Reuther himself was one of the few white men standing near the civil rights leader on the rostrum.

Sylvester Stafford is part of the Reuther brothers' legacy. When some other unions shunned blacks, the UAW opened the door. A big, burly, deep-voiced die maker, Stafford is a fifty-three-year-old African-American from Muncie, Indiana. He's worked at the same GM plant his entire career, a sprawling metal-stamping plant on West Second Street in Marion, Indiana, which makes body panels for trucks, sedans, and the resurrected Camaro sporty coupe. GM Marion is itself a success story amid the American auto industry crisis. In spite of the terrible down-turn in the North American auto industry, more than 950 employees in Marion were working two full shifts in the spring of 2009. The employment level is down from more than 2,000 in the late 1980s and 1990s, but is still a success. In a sign that GM executives favored Marion in 2009, the plant's sterling metrics on productivity had helped attract a massive high-tech transfer press from a GM stamping facility shutting down at Grand Rapids, Michigan.

Stafford's first job in the Marion factory was "conveyor atten-dant," but he later tested for an apprenticeship in a skilled trade and did well. GM paid for all his training, including math and engineering classes at Ivy Tech Community College. Stafford has since worked as a "troubleshooter" and currently is a die maker. Like all those in the skilled trades, he works with his mind as much as his hands, a result of the production technology con-stantly flowing into the plants. Stafford reads engineering drawings and uses "white light" technology to precisely gauge dies that will be used to form car and truck body panels. He proudly shows off a smoothly contoured sample hood panel like a sculptor might unveil a new *Venus de Milo*. Stafford considers himself a skilled craftsman, though when he started out some racial animosity was directed at him, he says, usually based on a belief that he was hired and promoted only because he was black.

It was a sign of white hostility to affirmative action programs as much as to racial differences, and the animosity was fed in part by managerial indiscretions over the years, he believes. Stafford accuses a number of supervisors of "Bwana syndrome," meaning they didn't think an African-American could do any-thing beyond simple tasks so they challenged every suggestion he made. An example? When he was a troubleshooter, he said, one employee kept running panels "off gauge" by inserting them slightly off-center in a conveyor. Doing so meant they would be stamped incorrectly and would not fit properly. Stafford says it was done to make him — as troubleshooter — look bad if the parts got through and were installed on a vehicle. When Stafford pointed out to a supervisor that the production employee was actually sabotaging the panels, the supervisor did not believe him at first, but later checked for himself. The delinquent employee was disciplined, but not fired, Stafford said.

Although the work in the plant takes stamina, Stafford is by no means the oldest employee in the Marion plant. Go into an auto assembly plant run by Toyota or another foreign automaker, though, and the labor force generally looks like it is ready to celebrate its tenth or fifteenth anniversary since graduating high school. Step into GM Marion, or any other GM plant, and there are many aging baby boomers. Even though he's only fifty-three, Stafford is eligible for a pension, but has chosen not to take it yet. In an auto plant run by a foreign automaker, the company can pressure older employees into leaving, but that's more difficult under the web of rules enshrined in hoary UAW labor contracts with the Detroit Three. One key rule, known as "thirty-and-out," actually was a job security provision won by the UAW in a long strike in 1970 against General Motors. It assures employees they will have three decades of employment before going out the door. Now it's mostly viewed as easy money for workers who get to retire too early, if they so choose. The formula for the UAW-GM "thirty-and-out" pension is complicated, but the pension is worth at least $32,000 per year for retirees who have not yet qualified for Social Security benefits. Once a retiree does qualify for Social Security, the pension benefit drops, but still is worth at least $18,500.[8]

Another coveted benefit guaranteed under UAW contracts is health insurance. Again, it's part of the union movement's effort to assure workingmen and workingwomen a decent life. For decades, the Detroit automakers have paid virtually all health care costs for hourly employees and retirees, even while workers in most other industries were forced to shoulder larger portions of their own health and retirement tabs as time went by. From the outside, it made those Detroit auto industry workers look like the smug beneficiaries of a corporate welfare state. Other employers and industries exposed to competition from imports, or the movement of work to lower-wage states and nations like Mexico, were forced to cut payroll costs by providing less generous health benefits, but the UAW was staunch in maintaining this costly benefit for its members. The union was able to tap into the profits rolled up by the automakers in Detroit, who had seemed immune to foreign competition for decades.

The milestone for health and pension benefits dates to the five-year contract between GM and the UAW in 1950, called by one pundit "the Treaty of Detroit." The union won unprecedented pension and health benefits that year, "as favorable as, and probably more liberal than, those previously negotiated in the basic industries,"[9] wrote one scholar at the time. The union also moved much closer to winning a closed union shop (meaning all workers had to join), as well as a guarantee that wages would increase with increased productivity in the plants, and that such productivity would be based on technological and capital improvements, not merely production line speed-ups or other disguised piece-work rates. In exchange for these major corporate concessions the union signed a five-year contract, which guaranteed peace for the company. Health care costs were not yet so great in the 1950s, of course, and paying out pensions was a long way off, so management may have felt it was a fair trade-off at the time.

Six decades later, Sylvester Stafford was still benefiting from "the Treaty of Detroit." During his years at GM, pension and health care benefits had steadily increased, not only for him but all autoworkers employed by the Detroit Three. The companies were able to pass on the costs in the form of higher vehicle prices — again, a major advantage in not having much foreign competition or any non-union competition. This went on for decades even though, in time, the Detroit Three were to face daunting challenges from international manufacturers and non-unionized transplant auto factories in the United States itself. Union leaders, who viewed pay raises as the rank and file's share of the profits, routinely got what they wanted by targeting one manufacturer at a time in contract talks. This, of course, was the infamous "pattern contract." Ford, for example, might fear that if it fought the union's demand for, say, a four percent pay raise, the subsequent strike would shut down production and starve Ford dealers of cars, giving a market share boost to GM and Chrysler that Ford would be hard-pressed to gain back later. The UAW could pressure any one of the Detroit Three to accede to its demands, then move on to the next company, a kind of divide and conquer approach that corporations themselves love when they seek to reduce organized workers to the level of independent contractors. It's a tactic that works.

The pattern contract and the concessions came as regular as the change of seasons. But the executives knew, indeed all of Detroit knew, that a day of reckoning would come. Foreign competition was increasing. Non-union parts suppliers were emerging. Market share was slipping. The companies no longer would be able to bear the rapidly increasing "legacy costs," as they came to be known. But that day always seemed to slide into the future on a tide of good fortune: the 1960s economic boom, the pent-up demand for new autos following the 1981–82 recession, America's truck and SUV craze of the 1990s.

Finally, as the average price of a new automobile rose from $18,000 in the 1980s to $20,000 in 1990 and $28,000 by the end of the decade, Detroit executives *had* to react. First, they hammered their regular auto parts suppliers on cost, then they embraced Toyota's lean production methods, allowing Detroit to design vehicles for assembly by fewer workers. That allowed the companies to use buyouts to move workers off the payroll and into retirement, in a sense abrogating the job security that "thirty-and-out" was meant to guarantee. GM alone had moved 100,000 workers since the late 1990s from the factory floor into retirement — that saved payroll costs, but only exacerbated the legacy issue, which really was a kind of "heads you lose, tails you lose" situation for the companies. GM was sized to produce more than seven million vehicles per year in North America at the turn of the century, a capacity that equaled nearly half the market for new autos and light trucks, but as it lost market share it had fewer active employees in effect subsidizing more and more retired workers. It was, and is, a dilemma very much like that facing the government's Social Security Administration — fewer workers supporting more retirees in the country's nationalized pension program.

In time General Motors concluded that Toyota could make a car for $2,500 less than GM, in part because of legacy costs, but for other reasons as well. For years GM hacked away at the $2,500 imbalance and finally in negotiations in 2007 achieved a breakthrough. The UAW agreed to take over responsibility for health insurance for the 600,000-plus retirees and their spouses at, ultimately, the three Detroit companies by establishing the Voluntary Employees' Beneficiary Association (VEBA) to administer health care plans. Taking control of the retiree medical trust fund was seen as a major concession by the union because it meant the big companies would no longer have to shore up the health fund if it ever ran low on money. Still, the fund would not start out empty. GM alone agreed to pour $35.3 billion in cash into the VEBA. In exchange, it could wipe out a $51 billion commitment for future retiree health care payments.[10]

By 2008, however, the Detroit Three were wracked by staggering losses. Car sales had slid to the lowest level in decades. The union made deeper concessions in early 2009, allowing the companies first to delay some VEBA payments, then to fund fifty percent of the commitments with shares of GM, Ford, and Chrysler stock rather than entirely in cash. Because the car market was so weak, union members knew the stock was almost worthless. In Detroit, UAW leaders decided to face up to the new realities. The day of reckoning had dawned.

Interestingly, autoworkers in Canada faced fewer problems on this front because of their nationalized health insurance. It would have been a capstone for Walter Reuther in his career to have made national health insurance a standard feature for all Americans. But subsequent UAW leaders were noncommittal on this point. Reuther himself early on supported a national health insurance plan, but after he passed away the idea found little serious backing inside UAW head offices. Robert Finch, author of *Solidarity for Sale: How Corruption Destroyed the Labor Movement and Undermined America's Promise*, claims the UAW in particular balked at a single-payer plan because it would end a long sweetheart arrangement in which it got to pick providers for its employees. They'd lose their allegedly cushy deals in a single-payer system, which typically is a government-run plan that takes in all the money and pays all the bills. It was a sign that the UAW was willing to shelve the broader national good in favor of its narrower interests, though the UAW may not have been alone in betraying a historic ideal. According to Finch, the broader American Federation of Labor (AFL) also voted not to support a single-payer health insurance plan in 1991, albeit in a close executive vote. Finch writes that "the deciding vote against such a plan was cast by Robert Georgine, chief executive of ULLICO, a huge insurance provider created by the unions." Georgine, who was paid $3 million per year by ULLICO, a decade later was the subject of a fraud investigation into insider stock trading that extended to several members of ULLICO's board of directors, all heads of major AFL-CIO unions. Georgine agreed to pay back $13 million to the company and several directors resigned after the federal probe.[11]

A single-payer national health insurance scheme was widely perceived as a cornerstone of making American business more competitive for no longer would companies have to build the cost of their employee health insurance premiums into the cost of products they made and sold. Yet the kind of health care reform debated in America in 2009 had nothing to do with a single-payer scheme. Indeed, President Obama and other Democratic leaders had backpedaled so far from this ideal that businesses were being warned that they would not be able to drop their company-provided insurance plans; if so, heath insurance reform would do businesses no good at all. Part of the dilemma facing the president was that he had campaigned against taxing health insurance benefits; a single-payer health insurance system by definition is paid for out of tax revenues.

Though generally known as the United Auto Workers, the full, correct name today is The International Union, United Automobile, Aerospace and Agricultural Implement Workers of America. The Canadian Auto Workers, originally a unit of the UAW, broke away in December 1984 after several years of conflict with the Detroit-based international over concessions in pay and work rules the Canadians were not willing to make. The Canadians thought the union should focus on wage gains and back away from the talk of a partnership with management that was occurring in the 1980s. The Canadians also claimed that the American leadership was too bureaucratic and remote.[12]

Although the UAW made efforts to help Detroit executives beginning in the 1980s (in part because of the 1979 Chrysler crisis, which had a bracing effect on union leader attitudes, if not yet the rank and file), the Detroit Three still lost market share and the union lost members. In 1978 UAW membership peaked at about 1.5 million. By 2008, the UAW had 513,000 active members and 575,000 retired members who received various benefits, but could not vote on contracts, in the United States, Puerto Rico, and Canada. As of 2008, the CAW had about 225,000 members, but only about 30,000 were directly employed by the three Detroit auto companies. An obvious source of new members for the union were the foreign auto plants — the so-called transplants — opening in the north in Ohio and Indiana, but largely in the non-union Southern states of Alabama, Kentucky, and Tennessee. As far back as 1986 the UAW had tried to organize workers at the transplants, including Honda's first plant in Marysville, Ohio. But the union had no success. Automakers from Germany, Japan, and South Korea kept wages and benefits high enough to discourage union activism. By the 2000s, the average transplant's wage paid about $26 per hour, just below Detroit's $29. In 2007 some dissident Honda workers in Lincoln, Alabama, invited the UAW to launch an organizing campaign but it hasn't succeeded as yet in the 4,500-employee plant, which produces the Pilot sport utility vehicle and the Odyssey minivan. The UAW also maintained a small office several miles from the massive Toyota complex at Georgetown, Kentucky, home of the Camry sedan. But the union has not organized any workers there, either. Indeed, only foreign plants affiliated with the Detroit Three — such as the Mazda-Ford plant south of Detroit at Flat Rock, Michigan — have a union. None of the stand-alone foreign auto plants in America has been successfully organized, even though industry analysts figure the transplants stand to surpass the Detroit Three in production capacity in the next several years.

Rather than bring the transplant payrolls up to Detroit's level, the UAW has accepted some concessions demanded by GM, Ford, and Chrysler in an effort to cut costs to the level of the foreign automakers. In 2007, two-tier pay scales came online, allowing some new hires in a Detroit Three plant to earn about half the prevailing UAW wage of $29 per hour. Writing in the left-leaning *The Nation* in 2007, Max Fraser decried two-tier pay scales as an assault on worker solidarity, and pointedly said Toyota instead of the UAW now sets the standard for prevailing wages in the auto industry.[13] Many union leaders agree with the latter point; furthermore, they fear that once UAW wages come down overall to Toyota levels, Toyota will then start clamoring for prevailing wages based on an average of all manufacturing jobs in America, not just auto industry jobs. Such a wage scale would be much lower yet.

Not everyone in the UAW likes this slippery slope of more and more concessions, of course. Lana Puterbaugh, fifty-nine, a zone committee representative committeeman (like a shop steward) for Local 292 in Kokomo, remembers the good old days when the union won concessions, not made them. She once was sent by her employer to train replacement workers in Mexico to make auto radios — they were all women, all looked to be teenagers or not much older, and all were happy to be earning about $1.50 per hour, she said. Puterbaugh says she was ashamed of what she was doing and asked not to be sent there again. She has better memories of August 1970 when she and thousands of other workers struck Delco for three months. "That was the thirty-and-out

strike," she recalled. "The union was strong. We had signs out —
'thirty and out.' Management didn't like that, but we got it."

Despite reverses in recent years, labor leaders say unions are
not obsolescent. The mere threat of unionization is widely
believed to be an incentive for management at non-union shops
to treat workers fairly and pay a decent wage. But some labor
historians date the beginning of the end of the UAW to the
Chrysler bailout in 1979, less than a decade after Walter
Reuther's death. The bailout included $1.5 billion in loan guar-
antees from the United States government (all later repaid), as
well as $2 billion in concessions from various stakeholders in the
company, including the UAW. Legislation authorizing the bailout
was largely written by Indiana Senator Richard Lugar (Republican) and Massachusetts Senator Paul Tsongas (Democrat). Newly
appointed Chrysler chairman Lee Iacocca and then–Detroit
mayor Coleman Young often are credited with "selling" the deal
to Congress and to the American public.[14]

Just what were the concessions the stakeholders made,
though? Creditors at the time accepted thirty cents on the dollar
for the $600 million in paper they held, while an additional
$700 million in debt was converted into stock. Labor's concessions,
both direct and indirect, are harder to calculate, but included a
$2 per hour decrease in pay as compared to GM and Ford
workers plus an estimated $220 million in deferred pension fund
contributions. Thousands of hourly rate (i.e. union) workers
were permanently laid off in the following years, anyway.[15]

At the time more militant union leaders said labor's concessions
were not just a temporary setback for the movement, but a reversal
of policy. The Canadians in particular had argued that instead of
protecting employees, the union leadership allegedly cared more
about the health of the employer. Indeed, some of the first Chrysler
bailout concessions were rolled back in late 1982 after a threatened strike by the UAW and an actual strike by the Canadian wing,
which in part led to the establishment of the separate Canadian
Auto Workers two years later. Nevertheless, it was an odd criticism the militants made, accusing fellow union leaders of *not*

wanting to kill the goose that laid the golden egg.

Perhaps that kind of thinking is a reflection of the cultural, even cosmic, battle between labor and management in the auto industry, a perceived zero-sum game in which the only goal is to make sure the other guy doesn't screw you before you screw him. Mo Davison denies this is the case. "We don't want businesses to fail. We want them to be successful," he said. "That's our top priority." Even so, the militants' argument reverberated with a vocal minority of autoworkers, especially those who regarded the union as a social movement. What good was the union if it couldn't wrest a good share of the profits for the workers and protect their long-term interests?

Instead of the hated word concession, it became common for both management and UAW leaders to speak of a partnership between the two entities. The one great experiment was GM's Saturn auto plant in Spring Hill, Tennessee. Saturn was to be an "import fighter" more interested in "conquest sales" than raw numbers, meaning how many buyers could the new enterprise take away from Honda and Toyota and the like. Saturn cars went on sale in 1991 with a single subcompact model that received good reviews in the motoring press and consistently high reliability ratings from the closely read *Consumer Reports* for many years. The much vaunted partnership allowed GM to pay UAW workers there a base wage that was twenty percent lower than at its other plants, but with the promise of greater bonuses, and the UAW looked the other way as GM outsourced many parts for the cars, including to Japan. Outsourcing parts when you have your own suppliers, as GM did at the time, always is problematic. If you buy parts from yourself then the profits go back to you, even if those parts are more expensive than what you can get from other suppliers. But if you pay too much for the parts, then the price of the finished product — the car — will be too high and sales will suffer.

Things fell apart in 1998 with an August strike authorization vote by the overwhelming majority of Saturn's 7,200-plus workers. Where Saturn workers previously had been shown smiling and speaking proudly of their partnership with management in countless TV and print ads, they now complained that some of their work was about to be shifted to other GM plants, claimed they were being cheated on bonuses (a dispute about how overtime was credited, really), and they complained of a speed-up at the factory itself. Some Saturn workers went on TV news shows and said how bad labor-management relations really were and how foremen allegedly ordered production workers to push through defective parts and assemblies, suggesting they might not buy a Saturn car themselves. It was just crushingly bad publicity for the brand. The Saturn factory, which leaned heavily on "just in time" low inventory policies, closed temporarily after problems later that summer at several other GM plants that supplied it with parts.

"They're walking all over us," autoworker Luis Gonzales said at the time. "It's time to show some muscle."[16] It was the us-versus-them mentality at its worst, a kind of internecine war inside the American automobile industry that could only force some buyers to look elsewhere, namely Europe and Japan, for their car choices.

Saturn workers were not the only ones in a surly mood that year. In Flint, a strike broke out at a GM stamping plant that dragged on fifty-four days and effectively shut down all of GM production in North America for much of the summer of 1998, including at Saturn, costing the company more than $3 billion. Largely considered a standoff, the strike exhausted autoworkers financially. Then, in 1999, GM finally spun off its Delphi unit, the 200,000-employee global auto-parts empire made up of the old suppliers such as Delco electronics, Harrison Radiator, and Rochester Carburetor acquired early in the century. Although Delphi went out the door as a stand-alone company, then the fifty-sixth largest corporation based in the United States, the UAW continued to represent Delphi workers with contracts that matched GM's. And the union, during the 1999 labor contract negotiations, won a plant-closing moratorium that barred the Detroit Three from shutting or selling more plants.

Muscle, of course, had long been on the mind of UAW rank-and-file workers. In the old union hotbed of Flint, a dissident UAW group sprang up in the mid-1980s around David Yettaw, then-president of UAW Local 599 at the massive Buick City manufacturing complex. Calling the group New Directions, the dissidents railed against UAW leadership as GM outsourced ever more work to Mexico, embraced Toyota lean production techniques, and pressed Flint and Michigan for tax breaks on the new machinery displacing jobs. The Buick complex by then had lost nearly 16,000 of the 20,000 jobs in place two decades earlier. "[Yettaw] really believed in Walter Reuther and I think he tried, in his own way, to emulate him, to look to his principles," said Bob Roth, director of UAW Region 1C in Michigan.[17]

In the 1990s, UAW President Stephen Yokich managed to largely quash New Directions, but the advent of the fax and the Internet opened new ways for dissidents to reach the rank and file. Gregg Shotwell, a GM employee in southwest Michigan whose plant was spun off as part of Delphi, hewed to a Reuther-like spirit. Shotwell launched his own newsletter, calling it "Live Bait & Ammo" — ammo harked to the Reuthers' own newsletter decades earlier, which was called "Ammunition." In one missive in 2009, Shotwell contended UAW President Ron Gettelfinger "thinks the name of the game is concessions. He informed assembled local UAW reps that he will unilaterally concede the Job Bank without a ratification vote of the membership" although Shotwell contended that the bank is "the lynch pin of our national job security agreement." The Job Bank was meant to encourage workers to feel they had a job for life, and it assured the company that when it was ready to crank up production a ready workforce was available. It applied in four instances — plant closure, completion of a temporary assignment, loss of market share, or acts of God that altered the work flow. If there was not enough work in the factories, a worker in the Job Bank might do office work, or even volunteer work in their communities.

Gettelfinger, an Indiana native, has headed the United Auto Workers since 2002. A thoughtful United States Marine veteran and devout Catholic, Gettelfinger was remarkable within the UAW in the ways he differed from labor leaders before him. He was the first UAW president with a college education, and the first not to come out of a Michigan plant. But it was his true pragmatism that was different. "An ardent, lifelong trade unionist, Ron Gettelfinger (sixty-one), has presided over an era of unprecedented concessions to the Detroit automakers, telling his members that the alternative is for the companies and the union to go down together," wrote the *Washington Post* in 2006.

"The companies know that whatever lies before them is vastly worse if something happens to Gettelfinger," said Michigan's Democrat Representative John D. Dingell, the industry's champion in Congress. "They're all teetering at the precipice together."[18]

Gettelfinger is considered modest in dress, appearance, and lifestyle, hardly the stereotype of the cigar-chomping, barrel-chested union boss who might like big, expensive cars as much as the corporate bosses allegedly do. Press reports like to tout that he does not drink, smoke, gamble, or kiss women, even on the cheek, other than his wife Judy, and he even tried but failed to have a UAW convention moved from the gambling Mecca of Las Vegas. His sometimes fiery rhetoric, delivered in a characteristic southern Indiana twang (he reportedly pronounces Washington as "Warshington"), can cut deep. "Our union does not want to strike, but when employers act as if collective bargaining is a one-way street and not a two-way street, we will do what we have to do," Gettelfinger told cheering delegates at the union's 2007 convention in Detroit.

Two years later, however, after saying he was not "stupid" and would not accept potentially worthless company stock to fund legacy costs, he did just that. "We're willing to take an extra step here," Gettelfinger said. The truth is, Gettelfinger the pragmatist always was willing to take that extra step.

Gettelfinger was born in 1942, the son of an Indiana farmer and one of twelve children. He hired in as a chassis line repairman in 1964 at Ford's massive plant in Louisville, known at company headquarters as "Lousyville" because of poor quality control on the flagship Crown Victoria sedans made there at the time. (The plant later made Ford Ranger pickup trucks that for years had a stellar reputation for quality.) Gettelfinger picked up an accounting degree in 1976 after studying part-time for years at a branch campus of Indiana University across the Ohio River from Louisville. He came of age when the union was at its peak, representing nearly 1.5 million members in the United States and Canada. In 1970, when the UAW walked out against General Motors, the fifty-eight-day work stoppage tipped the United States into a recession.

When Gettelfinger took the reins of the union in 2002 it was a different story, a different ball game, however. Traditional American car brands (meaning UAW- or CAW-built cars and trucks) were about to go under fifty percent market share in domestic sales (and already were far below the fifty percent threshold not counting light trucks). That cold reality, along with the staggering size of legacy costs, was finally sinking in everywhere. Indeed, GM announced in its 2008 annual report that funding its legacy costs from 1993 to 2007 had totaled a seemingly unbelievable $103 billion.[19]

UAW wage increases, when adjusted for inflation, peaked in the 1970s by some estimates. But the legacy costs, the notorious Job Bank, the costly "supplemental unemployment benefit" referred to as "SUB-pay," and guaranteed buyouts for permanent reductions-in-force were proving to be an impossible burden for the companies. SUB-pay in particular is little understood outside the auto industry. Under this provision, the companies have long had to make up most of the difference between a state's unemployment benefit and an autoworker's regular wage for any laid-off employee while he or she qualified for unemployment. According to union leaders, the provision was not meant to milk the companies, though it had that effect, but instead was meant to discourage the Detroit Three from laying off people in the first place. The companies would have an incentive to keep production lines up and running because they were going to have to pay the workers anyway. The SUB-pay provision partly explains why Ford, for example, would continue building the old Taurus model even after it introduced its replacement, the short-lived Five Hundred, in 2005.

Although the Job Bank has received far more scorn in the press, truly informed observers of the auto industry know that SUB-pay is a far bigger problem than the Job Bank just because so many more people have qualified for it over the years. SUB-pay, which was still in force even as the Chrysler bankruptcy was announced on April 30, 2009, guarantees laid-off workers approximately eighty-five percent of the normal take-home pay. In fact, SUB-pay is so generous that historically autoworkers would eagerly volunteer for temporary layoffs (known casually as TLO) during slowdowns in production.

Outside UAW Local 685 in Kokomo, Indiana, on May 1, 2009, the day after the Chrysler bankruptcy was announced, current and previously laid-off workers milled about and talked out their frustrations. One of the top topics was what would happen to their SUB-pay. Scott Johnson, thirty-three, was laid off at a Chrysler transmission plant in Kokomo in 2008, but had been collecting SUB-pay right through April 30, 2009. His wife, Pat, another autoworker, still had her job at the time of the bankruptcy. Between the two of them the Johnsons continued to pull down more than $100,000 per annum. The Johnsons had come to the union hall because of rumors that paper SUB-pay checks were not being honored at area merchants and banks. Union leaders like to say that labor represents only about eleven percent of an average car's cost, but that claim can only be valid when all employees actually are working. How does one calculate the percentage cost of labor in a car when workers are paid to stay home?

When elected, Gettelfinger presided over a union that still had nearly 800,000 members, yet it was roiling in controversy. Its record at organizing any of the dozen foreign auto plants that had opened in Indiana, Ohio, and the South was dismal. Indeed, as the Detroit Three lost market share to foreign rivals, Americans in large numbers held the UAW responsible for crippling the auto companies with high wages, allegedly poor workmanship, and those hardball bargaining tactics. Yet militants inside the labor halls reviled the leadership for accepting concessions going back to the near bankruptcy of Chrysler in 1979.

Scottish-born high school dropout Doug Fraser headed the union then. With a mischievous smile and gregarious manner, Fraser was popular with the union's rank and file. Once, in the recession of 1982, a United States Department of Commerce official in the Reagan administration had come to Detroit to argue that laid-off autoworkers didn't really have it so bad — after all, they received SUB-pay on top of state unemployment benefits and many American households had two-incomes by then, too. In response, Fraser arranged an impromptu press conference where he was flanked by two African-American autoworkers whose benefits had in fact run out altogether, then he told a cheering crowd that he'd personally call the secretary of commerce and ask that the errant official be "let out of his cage" more often so that he might visit other union towns where autoworkers had been laid off by the thousands.[20] Yet it was Fraser who had agreed to wage-and-benefit concessions, not only at Chrysler but some concessions at GM and Ford in the 1982 recession.

Even as the UAW wage gains moved autoworkers into the middle class, the union lost its positive grip on the popular imagination of Americans. Outside the auto industry, wages for blue-collar workers had been stagnant for years, but labor historian Neil Lichtenstein contended by the 1980s few ordinary working people thought they could enlist the UAW to help them turn the tide. Why join a union that had presided over plant closings, pay cuts, and dead-end strikes? As early as 1989, management professor Peter Drucker argued unions were irrelevant unless they could rethink their role and work with executives on productivity and quality, and perhaps adopt the Japanese style of lifetime employment to help quell labor unrest.[21]

Deciding to mimic Toyota and Honda, in 1987 GM had agreed

to a job security provision that kept idled autoworkers on full payroll in the Job Bank. But abuses were clear, over and above the costliness of the venture. Whereas Japanese workers really had to do useful work, and generally for the company, not the community at large, rules for the Job Bank were far looser. Early in 2008 PBS economics correspondent Paul Solman interviewed such a worker on camera who claimed he pushed a disabled Vietnam War veteran around town forty hours per week as his Job Bank service — Solman was visibly incredulous. The man was interviewed as part of a segment on Michigan-based UAW workers who were *celebrating* the closure of their factory at a Friday afternoon party — they knew they were going to get paid handsome sums under various contract provisions anyway. The thought that their children and children's children would have nothing to celebrate apparently was lost on them. Other cultures flourish because the current generation is willing to make sacrifices for future generations, but the opposite was happening here. Celebrating the death of their industry and the short-term gain they might experience, they seemed not to realize that it was their children's futures being cannibalized. The Job Bank remained a fixture at the Detroit Three until it was singled out in 2008 by Southern Republicans as a reason the automakers were uncompetitive. Gettelfinger soon eliminated the feature to help the auto companies win bailout loans.

But the problem wasn't the Job Bank alone. By 2008, GM had only 74,000 hourly workers in the United States, compared to 511,000 three decades earlier. That same year about 3,500 GM, Chrysler, and Ford workers were in the Job Bank. The bigger problem remained those legacy costs that tacked $1,500 on to the cost of every car any of them made.

Autoworkers were unwilling to take the blame, however. They said the problems were not SUB-pay, the Job Bank, or any quality issues relating to the workers themselves. Many thought the problems lay with national industrial and health care policy. Opined autoworker Gregg Shotwell, publisher of the dissident UAW newsletter "Live Bait & Ammo": "Manufacturing in the

U.S. doesn't suffer from a lack of skill or productivity. It suffers from a pandemic patchwork of lame excuses for health insurance. Our major competitors were never burdened with an albatross that compares to the private insurance rackets strangling American business. The notion that a federal subsidy for the Detroit Three can waylay the reckoning is naive."

The health insurance component of the legacy costs — on this point there actually was no disagreement between the UAW leadership, the rank and file, or the dissidents within the union. Walter Reuther had been perhaps the leading proponent of a national insurance plan going back at least to the first post-war election in 1948, when Harry Truman also supported such a proposal. Oddly, though, there was a case of unintended consequences at play here. America's triumphalism after the Second World War allowed corporations to cover the cost of health insurance for most non-union and union employees. This meant that relatively few Americans were forced to care about the issue of national health insurance as compared to citizens in Europe and elsewhere. Then, Americans became spoiled by choice. The lack of choice or control over one's own health destiny is part of the price for single-payer health insurance, historically derided in American politics as "socialized medicine." Then there is the issue of Americans' notoriously unhealthy lifestyles, most notably seen in massive levels of obesity that is linked to hypertension, diabetes, arthritis, and more, but also heavy levels of smoking, including among autoworkers and other so-called blue collar workers, plus sexually transmitted diseases, drug and alcohol problems, gun violence, and more. Some Americans don't think they should be taxed to pay for the unhealthy lifestyles of others, an issue completely suppressed in the great health insurance reform debate of 2009 in the United States. Last, but not least, is the propensity to medicalize every behavior that is not liked, most notably behavioral issues that many Americans continue to believe are really character flaws. In truth, single-payer (or national, or "socialized") health insurance in America likely would cost much more here than in other countries, and America is no longer the richest country on earth. In the meantime, the corporations have had to bear the burden of health care costs, making them less competitive in an increasingly global economy.

On Wednesday, April 29, 2009, hundreds of hourly wage Chrysler workers — meaning UAW members — converged on Local 685 headquarters near downtown Kokomo to vote on the new, emergency contract that their leaders had hammered out with Chrysler management over the previous weekend. They knew they would have to approve the deal in a last-ditch effort to avoid bankruptcy, and to keep Italian carmaker Fiat in the mix of a new Chrysler, as well. They voted in three shifts. Linda Taylor, fifty-three, a quality control specialist for Chrysler since 1996, was there.

"It was packed," said Taylor. "I had to park two blocks away. There was standing room only. It let out after a couple of hours. There were a few naysayers, but pretty much everyone knew we had to take it. I think the theme was live to fight another day."

Chrysler workers overwhelmingly approved the deal in votes across the country that Wednesday, yet the very next day on national television President Barack Obama announced a Chrysler bankruptcy anyway. All stakeholders except some hedge fund managers had voluntarily agreed to a restructuring plan. Yet the hedge funds held secured loans against Chrysler and their claims would come first in a court-supervised bankruptcy, something the Obama plan did not offer them, so they had the most to lose by agreeing to the president's terms. The UAW, which represented only 26,800 autoworkers at Chrysler by the spring of 2009, was primed to come out least scathed. While bondholders would voluntarily forego billions of dollars in claims, and hundreds of dealerships would be closed, the UAW made no concessions on the $29-per-hour base wage for veteran autoworkers; the two-tier pay scale for some new hires already had been negotiated in 2007. Instead of saying the UAW won this game of chicken, it might be fairer to say that veteran UAW workers came out best, something younger workers and union dissidents clearly understood and resented.

Scott Johnson, the laid-off Chrysler worker who was living off unemployment benefits and SUB-pay, supported the new Chrysler deal, even though it meant he'd probably never be called back to work in Kokomo. He had the option of transferring to another Chrysler plant — if work were available, but even there some seniority protections of Paragraph 96 would be lost. Besides, his wife still had a job with Chrysler in Kokomo and they were not going to split up the family. "I'll probably end up taking the buyout," said the burly autoworker. That buyout itself was worth $75,000 in a lump sum payment, plus a $25,000 voucher good toward the purchase of a new Chrysler. It would be a one-time charge to Chrysler, but multiplied by thousands of buyouts it really was huge.

Delphi workers in Kokomo already had been through a bankruptcy of their own. UAW Local 292, which represents most of the 1,500 remaining Delphi autoworkers in town, holds its monthly meetings on third Thursdays in the union hall multipurpose room. At one meeting in the spring of 2009 banquet tables and folding chairs were neatly set up on the floor, as was the rostrum for the speakers. Several ladies sold bright yellow, red, or blue all-cotton T-shirts emblazoned with the UAW logo for the wholesale cost of $7 each. Impressively, the T-shirts were both union-made and made in the USA, which does raise questions as to whether so many American jobs really have to be shipped offshore. About thirty union members showed up for the noon meeting; in the good old days hundreds would come to every meeting.

Bruce Young, the only non-UAW employee in the building, is an African-American who has worked maintenance at Local 292 for thirty-three years. There used to be five non-UAW workers at the hall, but due to dwindling revenues from UAW worker dues they were all laid off save for Young. Young, a part-time minister who does all the gardening, maintenance, and janitorial duties himself now, was asked to lead the invocation prior to the opening gavel. He told the gathering that he wasn't better than anyone else, that no one is better than anyone else, in fact, and that he prayed for everyone's welfare. The workers in attendance all bowed their heads and prayed with him. The meeting itself was closed to outsiders.

Later, Young said he was mostly worried about the young people in his hometown. They don't have much of a future because of the dwindling manufacturing base in America; it is just foolish to think everyone can go to college and get a high-paying professional or white collar job, Young says, concurring with a common UAW theme. "One fellow said he'd like to be a marine," Young noted. "I told him he better be sure before he finds himself somewhere under fire. Then it's too late to change your mind."

Jim Main, forty-five, is a sandy-haired man with a trim beard who often dresses in dark blue jeans and a light blue chambray shirt. A skilled laborer who does facilities maintenance, he's also an outspoken union activist who twice ran for city council in Kokomo, losing each time. He comes regularly to the Local 292 meetings like going to church. Yet he is not naive about union misdeeds in the past. "You've got two sides of it," Main said. "Some people say, 'The unions have done this for us, if it wasn't for the unions we wouldn't have had this,' and they volunteer, and they're for the unions. And then you have the other side of the coin, the only thing they were taught about unions was this — 'If you work the system right, you can take six months off and still get paid, so here's how you work the system.' A lot of those people worried about how can I get out of work today. But now they know if they don't work they might not have a job tomorrow."

All Delphi production workers, regardless of hire date, accepted pay cuts that brought their hourly wage down to a maximum of $18.50 per hour in 2007 from the $27-per-hour level in 2005 when the company filed for bankruptcy protection. Main was protected because he is a skilled laborer (his training was paid by Delphi in a partnership with the state of Indiana). But he rejects further pay cuts, any differential pay scales, or any kind of downward spiral in wages, which is what many observers believe will be a long-term outcome of the current crisis.

"The two- and three-tier pay scales are what make me the most argumentative," Main said. "When the companies do get their liquidity back, are they going to reward the employee, or are they going to give themselves $5 million in bonuses, like Delphi [already] has done since they've been in bankruptcy?"

He has a reputation as a militant, but with Jim Main it's the fairness angle that keeps coming up. If somebody else is getting rich off his labor, he wants to share in that bounty as well. And if workers are asked to make sacrifices, then everyone else has to make sacrifices, too. It is not possible to understand the union movement without at least appreciating this attitude, whatever other flaws and faults unions may have.

This feeling of a double standard in terms of sacrifices required is nearly universal in the union movement. Bruce Raynor, general president of UNITE HERE, a union representing 465,000 apparel, textile, laundry, hotel, gaming, and other workers, summed it up in a guest editorial for the *Los Angeles Times*. "When one compares how the auto industry and the financial sector are being treated by Congress, the double standard is staggering," Raynor wrote. "In the financial sector, employee compensation makes up a huge percentage of costs. According to the New York state comptroller, it accounted for more than sixty percent of 2007 revenues for the seven largest financial firms in New York. At Goldman Sachs, for example, employee compensation made up seventy-one percent of total operating expenses in 2007. In the auto industry, by contrast, autoworker compensation makes up less than ten percent of the cost of manufacturing a car. Hundreds of billions were given to the financial-services industry with barely a question about compensation. . . ."[22]

Yet even here Raynor is comparing apples and oranges, which weakens his argument. Manufacturing still is labor-intensive, in spite of years of automation and streamlining. And basic service industries are far less productive in terms of productivity per worker compared to high-flying financial services, which is why brokers and deal-makers and the like earn so much money.

Meanwhile, in the spring of 2009, union leaders like Ron Gettelfinger and Canadian Auto Workers national president Ken Lewenza had to wrestle with big decisions. Ed Hardesty worked with Gettelfinger at the Louisville Ford plant in the 1960s. He described the attitude well in a newspaper interview a few years ago. "They treated us like dogs," Hardesty told the *Washington Post* in describing his and Gettelfinger's days in Louisville. "And you would think: How could I get back at them?"[23] Yet in recent years Gettelfinger had shown that he was ready to deal. Would the CAW consider further concessions? Lewenza was asked over the winter of everyone's discontent in December 2008. He noted that in the last few years the union had accepted changes to local agreements at GM in Oshawa, Chrysler in Brampton, and Ford in Oakville, which altered work rules and pay schemes. This was on top of a freeze in wages for three years at GM Canada, as well as suspension of a cost of living increase for almost two years and other cuts to benefits. This was a far cry from earlier Canadian leaders who had belittled their Detroit cousins for making too many concessions to Chrysler in the early 1980s.

"We have always shown a willingness to help and there are different ways of doing that," Lewenza had said in late 2008. "It doesn't mean we have to reopen contracts every time and cut wages and benefits.[24]" But, of course, that's exactly what "a willingness to help" did mean.

Labor leaders had finally learned what a pyrrhic victory was all about, so named after King Pyrrhus of Epirus, whose army defeated the Romans at Heraclea in 280 B.C. and Asculum a year later, but suffered irreparable harm to themselves in doing so. Ever since that time the term "pyrrhic victory" has been a derisive term for a victory that harms the victor as much as the vanquished. The term has often been applied to religious and ideological feuds in the past, but it could well describe some historic UAW attitudes toward management. There is a kind of contentiousness between labor and management in the auto industry that dates back to the early organizing days in the 1930s, with labor often acting like management is always trying to cheat them out of something, while their goal is primarily to pry everything they can from the greedy clutches of those managers. It's the cosmic battle between good and evil, the zero sum game, in other words. But union leadership finally was catching on — a pyrrhic victory was no victory at all. Did the rank and file understand, however? It was not a growing gulf between labor leaders and corporate executives, but between labor leaders and their own membership, that was simply not understood by pundits who followed the tense auto industry negotiations between the rival stakeholders and government officials in early 2009.

The tears and bittersweet memories were everywhere in Kokomo in the spring of 2009. Susan Perry, the fifty-one-year-old Chrysler transmission worker who earned a degree by going to school nights for years, just like Gettelfinger had done, said that if she were younger she'd take one of the buyouts, too, and put her auto industry career behind her. "The last couple of years, every time there's a buyout package, [people] take it," she said. "We had 500 buyouts recently. If they have anything else going they'll take the buyout. If I was in my thirties I'd be gone, too."

And John Morris, the retired Chrysler transmission plant worker and former Local president who retired to Daytona Beach, Florida, could only look back at his career tearfully. He had begun on October 13, 1964 — again, autoworkers always remember that date like they know their birthday, or the day they were married, or when inducted into the military. It was a cool but sunny fall day in Indiana, which has autumns as colorful as any in New England, he recalled. The foreman gave Morris a little tour of his new work area, showed him how to process his time card, and wished him luck. It was a hopeful time. The work itself turned out not to be so pleasant, but Morris still liked what he was doing, liked that he was an autoworker. "I can remember working a form broach [a machine tool], it was probably fifteen to twenty feet in the air," he said. "I was working second shift then and the air quality was so poor, it was so hot, and I was up there in the air fifteen, twenty feet in the air, and in those days we got twelve-minute breaks and fifteen-minute lunches and I can remember coming off those, and I remember taking off my shoes, and pouring water out of them, and taking off my socks, and wringing the water out of them. People say we're lazy, but we paid our dues. It's not like we walked inside the plant and walked outside the other door and got our pensions."

Morris paints a picture of earnest, hardworking, self-reliant Americans. That's one picture, an honest picture, a true picture. But it's not the only picture. Before turning to journalism, Bloomberg News reporter John Lippert spent eight years at several GM factories in the 1970s, including its aging Fleetwood plant in Detroit. He is a rare nexus between the white-collar and professional classes that populate one America, and the blue-collar workers that populate this other America. Academics talk about race and gender a lot, yet they have all but forgotten class. Lippert is proud to have been an autoworker, but he does not look at the past through rose-colored glasses. He says the militancy of his days on the production line were informed by Vietnam War protestors, the drug culture, and an anti-establishment fervor that would have impressed both the black nationalist militant Stokely Carmichael and the white radical Bill Ayers of the same general era. Workers smoked dope in their cars during lunch breaks or took uppers to just stay awake, Lippert wrote. In 2007 he recalled a nasty auto strike thirty years earlier for readers of the *Toronto Star*.

"The news rippled along the assembly line," he began. "'The man says we goin' at seven,' a worker nicknamed Bird said as he trotted through Fleetwood, a General Motors Corporation plant in southwest Detroit that spanned eight city blocks. We were going on strike to protest our bosses' insistence that we do more work. In one case, GM had cut the number of two-person teams installing vinyl tops to thirty-five from forty. Already that day, GM had suspended two United Auto Workers leaders for balking at the company's 'speedup.'

"At 7 p.m., hundreds of us poured into the street in the kind of wildcat work stoppage that was rocking Detroit almost every year. About 600 of us started drinking beer. The line would stay shut for a day and a half. We called that a victory. It was August 26, 1976 — and another skirmish had erupted between what were then the world's biggest automaker and the most-powerful American union. We the employees won that one. Management won others. In the end, we all lost."[25]

---

1. Agreement between General Motors Corporation and the UAW, September 28, 1999, excerpt, "(96) When there is a transfer of major operations between plants, the case may be presented to the Corporation and, after investigation, it will be reviewed with the International Union in an effort to negotiate an equitable solution, in accordance with the principles set forth in the previous paragraph. Any transfer of employees resulting from this review shall be on the basis that such employees are transferred with full seniority, except as the parties may otherwise mutually agree. [See App. K III(C)15] [See Doc. 104]," www.uawndm.org/library/contract/91-100.htm.

2. Patricia Sullivan, "Victor Reuther, Labor Leader and UAW Pioneer, Dies," *Washington Post*, June 5, 2004, B-06. Victor Reuther also survived an assassination attempt after WWII that left him blind in one eye. Third brother Roy Reuther also was a leader in the UAW after the war.

3. Irving Bluestone, "The Time 100: Walter Reuther," www.time.com/time/time100/builder/profile/reuther.html, 2.

4. Some information for this biographical sketch comes from the AFL-CIO and was found at www.aflcio.org/aboutus/history/history/reuther.cfm.

5. Eric Amesen, ed., *Encyclopedia of US Labor and Working-Class History* (Boca Raton, FL: CRC Press, 2006) 297.

6. Nelson Lichtenstein, *Walter Reuther: The Most Dangerous Man in Detroit* (Champaign, IL: University of Illinois Press, 1997), 326–328.

7. http://www.uaw.org/about/uawmembership.cfm.

8. The scale of the looming crisis for the automakers, including pre-bankruptcy parts makers Delphi and Visteon, was clear at this time as even the UAW was touting that about half of its 302,500 specifically auto industry members would be eligible for retirement within the next five years. For more details see www.chryslerretiree.com/docs/Retiree_SMM.pdf, www.uaw.org/barg/03/barg05.cfm and www.uaw.org/contracts/07/chrysler/hrly/chry_hr08.php.

9. Frederick H. Harbison, "The General Motors-United Auto Workers Agreement of 1950," *The Journal of Political Economy*, Vol. 58, No. 5, October 1950 (Chicago: University of Chicago Press), 405. Though the UAW won health care benefits for the autoworker, social reformer Reuther urged company executives to go to Washington with him to demand a national health care program, but they allegedly refused for ideological reasons even though a national health insurance program would have relieved them of this dangerous obligation.

10. David Barkholz and Jamie LaReau, "UAW Deal Puts GM on Toyota's Heels; Agreement Pares Labor Gap to $800 per Vehicle," *Automotive News*, October 1, 2007, 1.

11. Robert Finch, "Big Labor's Big Secret," *New York Times*, December 28, 2005, A19. This editorial is a preview of his 2006 book.

12. Sam Gindin, "Breaking Away: The Formation of the Canadian Auto Workers," CWA-TCA Canada, www.caw.ca/en/3276.htm. This is a lengthy article that references the 1979 Chrysler bailout and a major strike against GM in 1984, among other issues, yet is filled with nationalist pride without

acknowledging that this might have a been a factor in the split.

13. Max Fraser, "UAW R.I.P?" *The Nation*, November 5, 2007, www.thenation.com/doc/20071105/fraser.

14. "1979 Chrysler Bailout Holds Lessons," Associated Press, November 24, 2008, www.washingtontimes.com/news/2008/nov/24/1979-chrysler-bailout-holds-lessons.

15. James K. Hickel, "The Chrysler Bail-out Bust," *Backgrounder #276*, July 13, 1983, www.heritage.org/research/regulation/bg276.cfm.

16. Micheline Maynard, "Saturn Strike Authorized," *USA Today*, July 20, 1998, 1A.

17. Todd Seibt, "UAW Activist Dave Yettaw Dies Suddenly," *Flint Journal*, April 15, 2005, A03.

18. Dale Russakoff, "United Auto Workers' Gettelfinger Navigates Job Cuts, Concessions," *Washington Post*, May 15, 2006, A01.

19. Roger Lowenstein, "Siphoning GM's Future," *New York Times*, July 10, 2008, 21.

20. Kathy Sawyer, "Fraser Nears Retirement As UAW Grapples with Detroit's Downturn," *Washington Post*, September 5, 1982, A2.

21. Peter F. Drucker, *The New Realities* (New York: Harper & Row Publishers Inc., 1989), 191.

22. Bruce Raynor, "Union Busting, Southern Style," *Los Angeles Times*, December 18, 2008, A31.

23. Russakoff.

24. Tony Van Alphen, "Detroit 3 Leaning on CAW," *Toronto Star*, December 4, 2008, B01.

25. John Lippert, "Still Paying for Yesterday's Errors," *Toronto Star*, September 26, 2007, B06.

CHAPTER 6

Ciao!

AMERICAN PRESIDENTS USUALLY BREAK into network television programming to announce that war or some other national emergency is at hand. Barack Obama had an entirely different message when he appeared live on national television on the morning of April 30, 2009. Dressed in a conservative, dark gray suit and diagonally striped tie, he stood behind a lectern emblazoned with the Seal of the President of the United States to announce the fate of Chrysler, one of the legendary Detroit Three automakers. The process that had allowed both Chrysler and General Motors to tap into federal bailouts and bridge loans several months earlier to avoid bankruptcy had suddenly taken a sobering turn. The White House and the government of Canada together had pledged as much as $90 billion in total to both automakers. With most of the bailout cash coming out of Washington, Obama and the previous George Bush administration had set strict conditions for the auto companies. GM, because it was the far larger company, had a deadline of May 31, 2009, to come up with a final restructuring plan. This day — April 30 — was Chrysler's deadline.

Obama, speaking without a script, calmly explained that Chrysler had successfully wrested concessions from major stakeholders, including the United Auto Workers, and that the company was prepared to close more factories and slash hundreds of dealerships, but he singled out a small group of unnamed investment firms and "hedge funds" for obstructing a final deal. He failed to mention that these lenders held secured loans against the company and had no real incentive to make deep concessions. Nevertheless, the reluctance of the hedge funds meant Chrysler was unable to go forward with a White House–sanctioned bailout plan. Obama announced the result of those failed negotiations. Chrysler was declaring bankruptcy after all.

Obama had served in the White House only since January 20, but he swiftly had taken on the new mantle of automaker-in-chief, laying down the rules for Chrysler and General Motors. Between them, the pair still employed nearly 150,000 people in North America, though the recession had tried their old empires severely. Auto sales had collapsed worldwide, a crisis magnified by a global credit crunch that denied many loans for well-heeled corporations and would-be car buyers alike. When executives presented their reorganization plans in late March in a bid for yet more bailout cash, Obama turned thumbs down, figuring both revival plans were too weak to make either company good bets for more taxpayer dollars. They must cut deeper: pare even more jobs, reduce debt even further, get rid of underperforming brands, eliminate excess manufacturing capacity, and more. Plus, Detroit would have to finally commit to more fuel-efficient and environmentally friendly hybrid-electric cars. "Year after year, decade after decade, we've seen problems papered over and tough choices kicked down the road, even as foreign competitors outpaced us," Obama had said of the earlier deadline. "Well, we have reached the end of that road."[1]

Standing in that road, guarding it really, was an investment banker named Steven Rattner. In Manhattan he was a well-known fundraiser for the Democratic Party. Only a few years earlier Rattner had devoted as much as $1 million of his own money to an investment pool set up by Cerberus Capital Management, the private equity firm that controlled Chrysler, to buy auto parts firms.[2] Now, Rattner headed a band of Wall Street veterans recruited by Washington to run Obama's new automotive advisory task force. By late spring of 2009, Rattner's team had ousted General Motors' chairman, called on six members of GM's board of directors to step down, and agreed the United States

Treasury would own up to seventy percent of GM — or Government Motors, as some now scoffed. For Chrysler, Obama's auto team pledged $6 billion more from American taxpayers, on top of $4 billion already advanced, if the company could come out of bankruptcy quickly with an alliance in hand with Italian automaker Fiat. A merger was viewed as a fast way to move the American company off the public dole. In return for the $6 billion in U.S. cash, Obama demanded Chrysler win concessions from the United Auto Workers union, which represented most of Chrysler's 26,000 hourly workers in the United States, and the Canadian Auto Workers, representing 9,000 Chrysler workers.

Obama had ruled out making a single official (such as Rattner) or a cabinet secretary solely responsible for handling the situation in Detroit inherited from the outgoing Bush administration. Instead, he created an auto team housed in the United States Treasury Department — a place where it could dip into the $800 billion Troubled Asset Relief Program created by Congress in the previous autumn to assist Wall Street. Rattner likened the auto task force to any investment banking house that used its business acumen to win favorable deals for their clients, which in this case was American taxpayers. "We're making an investment decision," Rattner said in early April. "We're not running these auto companies. We are helping them restructure and reposition themselves for the future."[3]

He was being disingenuous. The White House team obviously was more than an impartial bystander dispensing advice. It was the ringmaster. Behind the scenes, and not at all well hidden, was Obama himself. He gave the team wide scope, but made his own sorties into public view when he deemed it necessary to act on a matter. On March 31, Obama gave Robert Nardelli, Chrysler's chairman, thirty days to complete negotiations in the three separate deals with the UAW, CAW, and Fiat. It was a tough chore on a short deadline for the former Home Depot hardware executive, but the most compelling player in the action was the president himself.

What Obama and his administration really had done was

stare down the bankers who were poised to take over the automaker. Gathering the lenders and Chrysler and Fiat executives in a United States Treasury office in Washington on April 12, Obama's team laid out their plan, *the* plan. The task force would reach into the Troubled Asset Relief Program fund and use the taxpayer cash to repay the Chrysler bondholders $1 billion — or fifteen percent — of the $6.9 billion in bond debt they held. The lenders bristled. They thought they deserved more. They had not merely loaned Chrysler money, they had loaned it in a special form known as a bond. And as bondholders they were the senior lenders, entitled to good repayment terms. Or, at the least, they should be able to trade their debt for ownership in the company once it was in bankruptcy. That was how the American legal system long had worked. Stockholders, workers, regular lenders, and vendors suffered the big losses when a company went into bankruptcy, while bondholders were treated like the fair-haired children, a principle enshrined in bankruptcy law as the absolute priority rule.[4] Now, the White House was in negotiations with a private company's bondholders; indeed, it was in command by virtue of being the single institution ready and willing to put heavy volumes of cash in Chrysler. Yet the administration was jettisoning the absolute priority rule. Surprised bondholders learned they would get neither good repayment terms nor an owners' stake. "Whether it's a bankruptcy or a restructuring, you would wipe out the senior lenders group last," a banker complained to the *Washington Post*. "We all realize that some pain is going to have to be shed. But sacrificing eighty-five percent at the top of the capital structure just doesn't make sense."[5] Knowing that legal principle favored their side, the bankers angled for better terms from Obama.

Chrysler owed the $6.9 billion to forty-six banks, investment firms, and hedge funds, most of them centered in New York, although pension funds in California, Indiana, and Michigan, were among the lenders. Chrysler had taken on the debt in 2007 at the insistence of owner Cerberus. Selling bonds was a tried and true method of borrowing money from lenders. Ford had taken the same route in 2006, mortgaging its plants to raise more than $20 billion, cash it was spending in 2009 to avoid having to tap the White House for aid. Chrysler executives intended to use their bond money for the design of a much-needed fleet of new cars and trucks. But the company had run through the cash, spending it to stay in business after the economy tanked in the autumn of 2008. Within a few months, conditions were dire. On March 30, 2009, the government of Canada rushed $250 million ($201 million in U.S. dollars) to Chrysler's Canadian operations, which accounted for a quarter of the company's production output. "Very clearly if the money had not been forwarded today, they would not have been able to make payroll," Tony Clement, Canada's minister for industry, told the nation. "That was the stark choice we were faced with."[6]

As Chrysler's finances worsened, bondholders dug in. Chrysler had pledged factories and equipment as collateral for the bonds, putting the bondholders in position to send Chrysler into a free-wheeling bankruptcy where the assets could be auctioned off and the subsequent cash from the sale turned over to them — the bondholders. On April 20, lenders led by the New York banks J.P. Morgan Chase and Citigroup rejected the White House offer of fifteen cents on the dollar in bond repayments. It was a delicate rebuff, considering both banks and several other lenders were, like Chrysler, beholden to the White House for massive infusions of taxpayer aid after Wall Street's collapse a few months earlier. Even if they were like quasi wards of the state, lenders reasoned, they were entitled to a better deal under the absolute priority rule. Figuring the Bankruptcy Code was on their side, the banks pitched their own offer. They suggested selling off Chrysler's Jeep brand and other assets in bankruptcy, and handing bondholders a forty-percent ownership stake in the streamlined post-bankruptcy Chrysler. Following this strategy could raise as much as $4.5 billion, or sixty-five cents on the dollar, though at least one banker warned that a free-wheeling bankruptcy "would be very messy and everyone would lose — those of us who carry the debt, and those in the government who are trying to save jobs."[7]

Lenders knew they stood to gain more money in a bankruptcy than the government was offering. But investment bankers on the White House auto team refused the counter offer to break up Chrysler, a stand that drew staunch support from Midwestern lawmakers including Jim Peters, a Democrat from Michigan in the United States House of Representatives. Autoworkers feared bondholders, if in charge of Chrysler, might push the underfunded pension of workers onto the Pension Benefit Guaranty Corporation, forcing the thousands of retirees and their dependents to take the smaller stipends paid out by the quasi-government PBGC. Retired workers might get as little as $20,000 per year in pension payments under PBGC compared to about $30,000 under Chrysler. What's more, Peters saw real irony in the banks turning a cold shoulder on Chrysler after the government bailout of Wall Street already had poured $45 billion in new capital in Citigroup and $25 billion in J.P. Morgan Chase, all of it coming from American taxpayers. "It is extremely disappointing that while other stakeholders have agreed to work with President Obama to advance Chrysler's restructuring, financial institutions that have already taken billions of dollars in taxpayer support are refusing to do the same," Peters said.[8]

Obama himself said little in public about the matter, but officials very close to him did comment. They took news reporters aside, said they were speaking off the record, and explained things from their point of view. The anonymous sources were widely thought to be: Rattner; a reporter for the *New York Times* who, in 1979, had written about the near bankruptcy of Chrysler; and members of the auto task force in the United States Treasury. "It is neither in the interest of Chrysler's senior lenders nor the country for them to advance a proposal that would yield them an unjustified return," an anonymous official in the Obama administration told the *New York Times*. "Our hope and expectation is that these lenders take a more constructive position in the coming days that reflects the actual situation that they and the company face."[9]

Of course, the actual situation was that Chrysler could sink into bankruptcy without a federal lifeline held in place by the

White House. This alarmed government officials more than the lenders. In fact, some lenders were said to be delighted at the prospect. As negotiations went on with the Obama administration, details leaked out about the bankers casting for ideas to put Chrysler in bankruptcy and reduce their losses. Other lenders asserted Fiat ought to put cash in the deal rather than simply get a windfall stake in Chrysler for free. Fiat insisted it did not have the money to put into Chrysler, but it would transfer small car technology to any new, merged company and, of course, would operate it. And the bankers suggested the UAW cut wages — not just the two-tier system for new hires, already agreed to in the 2007 contract, but actual pay cuts for veteran employees. Bankers figured lower wages could partly offset pension costs for retired autoworkers. Under the Detroit Three's labor contracts with the UAW, hourly employees could retire after thirty years on the job. That meant a worker hired on at eighteen could retire at age forty-eight and draw about $30,000 per year until his Social Security kicked in. Even then, the company pensions would still make up the difference between what Social Security offered and what the companies promised.

Although the bankers rattled on about wage concessions, union leaders opined that they had already given enough. After all, they had agreed to the two-tier pay system for wages in 2007 (a move that was seen as a betrayal of the union ideal by the few remaining radicals within the UAW). And they had made additional concessions on work rules, days off, and cost of living adjustments. They jettisoned the Job Bank, too, but kept the far more lucrative SUB-pay provision, or supplemental unemployment benefit, which came on top of a state's unemployment benefit. The one really big union concession had to do with a retiree health plan. UAW employees and retirees have long had virtually free health insurance. But the union agreed Chrysler could fund half of the retirees' medical trust fund with its own stock rather than completely in cash, a move that obviously was risky for the trust fund but would save the company about $5 billion in payments. The trust fund, called a VEBA, short for

Voluntary Employees' Beneficiary Association, would pay nearly 100 percent of the health insurance premiums for Chrysler retirees and their dependents in the future. Each of the Detroit Three had created VEBAS in 2007 for hourly retirees and had begun to fund the trusts. This was very expensive to do up front, but each company viewed the medical trust as a long-term benefit that would eventually shift the cost of health care off the company's books. With the recession, however, the companies did not have the money to keep operating *and* develop new models *and* put cash into massively expensive trust funds. Taking shares that might be worthless was indeed a union concession, though on the upside it was true that if all the talk out of the White House in the winter of 2009 about nationalized health insurance came to be, the risk would ease for the UAW retiree health fund. In that kind of scenario the corporate welfare state simply would be replaced by the real welfare state. The issue of VEBAS didn't exist in Canada, of course.

While the union dug in its heels over further modifications to its labor contracts, the bondholders created their own informal steering committee to help spar with the union and government. The steering committee was led by bankers from J.P. Morgan, Citigroup, Morgan Stanley, and Goldman Sachs, the hedge fund Elliott Management, and a trio of investment firms named Oppenheimer, Perella Weinberg Partners, and Stairway Capital Management. Among the lenders, a bankruptcy was welcomed especially by several hedge fund managers, latecomers to the deal who had repurchased the Chrysler bonds cheaply from the original lenders. Bankruptcy promised a payday because the hedge funds had used the derivatives market to fully insure the bonds in case Chrysler defaulted on its debt.

Obama, sensitive to the union, turned down the lenders' ideas about bigger UAW concessions. However, the government sweetened the offer to lenders on April 22. Bondholders could recover $1.5 billion of the $6.9 billion in debt, or twenty-two cents on the dollar, and get a five percent ownership stake in Chrysler. Bondholders again stalled. Then the government offered $2 billion and no ownership. On April 30, J.P. Morgan accepted. So did most of the big banks, while some smaller lenders — notably Oppenheimer and Stairway Capital — refused the deal, saying the big banks had caved to government pressure rather than stand by their rights as bondholders. "Treasury is using a strong-arm negotiating tactic to convince lenders they should take thirty cents on the dollar," a Washington lawyer told the *Wall Street Journal*.[10] Finance experts warned that the White House had trampled the Bankruptcy Code's absolute priority rule, which could cloud future bond sales for weak companies like General Motors. But for the time being, Obama's auto task force could claim it had a workable plan to salvage most of Chrysler.

The deal promised a vast shift in the ownership of the company, marked by the exodus of Cerberus Capital Management and Daimler, the German conglomerate behind Mercedes-Benz luxury cars. Daimler had given up everyday control of Chrysler in 2007 when it unloaded the bulk of the American company at a loss to Cerberus. Now, Cerberus head Stephen Feinberg and Daimler both were eager to be completely rid of the ailing carmaker. A new Chrysler would emerge from bankruptcy owned chiefly by the UAW. Details peppered the proposal.

The UAW held firm on wages, averaging $29 per hour in base pay, but Chrysler autoworkers conceded two paid holidays, Christmas and performance bonuses, and two additional benefits. Workers gave up an automatic pay escalator that kept inflation from deeply eroding wages. Retirees gave up vision and dental benefits.

In turn, the UAW's retiree medical trust would own fifty-five percent of Chrysler while Fiat would get twenty percent, the United States government eight percent and the governments of Canada and Ontario two percent between them. Fiat could gain another fifteen percent of Chrysler, but that was on the condition it put a car on American roads capable of traveling forty miles on a gallon of gasoline, and assemble fuel-efficient engines in the United States, as well as re-pay the bridge loans. Bond-holders would own nothing in Chrysler.

Although the union would have the largest block of stock in the new Chrysler, it would not have a commanding voice in management. Chrysler's board of directors, the group responsible for hiring and firing senior executives and setting broad policy, would disband. In its place, the United States government would name four new directors while Fiat named three members, the UAW one, and the governments of Ontario and Canada one. Fiat would put no cash in Chrysler, though Fiat executives insisted the Italian cars and technology bound for America were worth $10 billion. Analysts assumed Sergio Marchionne, the Canadian-Italian in charge of Fiat, would oversee the merged entity. Robert Nardelli, Chrysler's chairman, and Tom LaSorda, Chrysler's manufacturing star and number two executive, each said they would resign.

Cerberus would stay in the auto business, but on the banking side. Chrysler Financial, a struggling business separate from the carmaker, would fold its loans into General Motors Acceptance Corporation. GMAC would make consumer loans for Chrysler and GM dealers. Earlier Cerberus had bought Chrysler Financial from Daimler and had purchased half of GMAC from General Motors. Meanwhile, Daimler would contribute $600 million to the pension fund of hourly Chrysler workers, and forgive its earlier loans to Chrysler.

That was the deal — neat, tidy, and yet very incomplete. Twenty or so hedge funds, investment firms and, in what was a great surprise, Indiana State Treasurer Richard Mourdock, continued to rebuff the White House, reminding all once again that the Chrysler bonds were legal contracts. As senior lenders, they insisted they should not be dealt a lesser hand by the White House than the union or Fiat, each of whom would wind up with ownership stakes in Chrysler, while the bondholders would lose the bulk of their Chrysler investment.

For Obama, the way to force the investors to accept the terms was to prevail on a bankruptcy court and have the White House's Chrysler deal presented to the judge for the final verdict that would put it in action. On the morning of April 30, the president strode to the grand foyer of the White House to tell the world that Chrysler was filing for bankruptcy. It was here he publicly rebuked those hedge funds in his remarks.

"While many stakeholders made sacrifices and worked constructively, I have to tell you some did not," said Obama who was surrounded by a bevy of top-ranking Treasury Department and auto task force advisers. "In particular, a group of investment firms and hedge funds decided to hold out for the prospect of an unjustified taxpayer-funded bailout. They were hoping that everybody else would make sacrifices, and they would have to make none. Some demanded twice the return that other lenders were getting. I don't stand with them. I stand with Chrysler's employees and their families and communities. I stand with Chrysler's management, its dealers, and its suppliers. I stand with the millions of Americans who own and want to buy Chrysler cars. I don't stand with those who held out when everybody else is making sacrifices. And that's why I'm supporting Chrysler's plans to use our bankruptcy laws to clear away its remaining obligations so the company can get back on its feet and onto a path of success."[11]

White House officials believed the bankruptcy court would quickly dispatch the recalcitrant lenders and usher forth a new and improved Chrysler. They expected Chrysler would emerge from bankruptcy by the end of July in the arms of Fiat.

Would the plan work? None of the experts and pundits really knew. Analysts at the credit rating agency Standard & Poor's warned the bondholders could prevail and break up Chrysler in bankruptcy. Other experts suggested the bankruptcy court would simply dismiss the hedge funds' concerns and rubber-stamp the White House plan. Jesse Toprak, senior industry analyst for automotive market researcher Edmunds.com, said that Fiat-Chrysler alliance at least gave the American company a fighting chance. "Fiat will be able to bring new products into the United States at a dramatically lower cost compared to Chrysler having to come up with vehicles on its own from scratch," Toprak said. "If done well, it's plausible to come up with a line of vehicles that can cater to any income level."[12]

Yet, as Rattner and the Wall Street veterans on the Obama team wrapped up the talks with the bondholders, then put Chrysler in bankruptcy, it was as if the *deal* with Fiat and Chrysler was paramount, but not the products. It was as if the investment bankers had forgotten about the manufacturing side. Little was said in public by the government about what would come *after* the merger of a pair of worn industrial icons in Detroit and Turin.

For Chrysler, the problem was time and money. Certifying Fiat's cars for federal highway standards in the United States and restyling the models as Chryslers would delay their entry until 2011, most analysts reckoned. And the barren product pipeline Daimler left Chrysler would bring forth nothing of note until the remodeled Jeep Grand Cherokee sport-utility appeared — late in 2010 as a 2011 model. The question was whether Chrysler could survive even two more years. Fiat insisted its cash reserve was too tight to spare on a new partner. Deep-pocketed Cerberus was walking away without investing another dime. Chrysler had cut 32,000 jobs since Cerberus, under Nardelli's leadership, took over and closed production capacity for 1.2 million vehicles, but even pared down it was on pace in the spring of 2009 to spend billions of dollars per year. While the budget was less than in its robust years, Chrysler still was living beyond its means. The $4 billion government infusion in the winter plus the $6 billion promised by Obama if it tied the knot with Fiat could hardly carry the company into 2011. Chrysler had to learn to scrimp by.

As he chided the hedge funds in his April 30 Chrysler speech, Obama appeared to be urbane, composed, and intellectual. The country liked the confident new president. His approval rating in polls of American citizens was sixty-two percent after three months in office. His handling of the situation in Detroit did him no political harm except, perhaps, with some auto industry insiders and financial experts. The soft-spoken publisher of the authoritative Detroit trade journal *Automotive News*, Keith Crain, looked at the abrupt ouster of GM Chairman Richard

Wagoner and wondered what had Obama done to Detroit. In an editorial, Crain wrote: "I am troubled by the heavy-handed manner in which the president of the United States fired the chairman of GM; appointed the new CEO, Fritz Henderson; appointed the new interim nonexecutive chairman; and had plans to replace most of the board. Meanwhile, the president proclaimed to the world that he has no interest in running GM. Give me a break. I find the entire episode rather disconcerting and a bit scary. I'm not sure who Henderson works for, but it appears that he doesn't work for the shareholders or the board anymore. Those days are gone forever for GM."[13]

The fast work by the Obama administration also bothered newspaper columnist Peggy Noonan, once a speechwriter for conservative President Ronald Reagan. Writing in the *Wall Street Journal* about the tenor of the country in May 2009, Noonan described a reckless confidence in both the president and his most recent predecessor in the White House. "I continue to be astounded by how much Mr. Obama reminds me in his first few months of George W. Bush in his first few years. There is a sense with both men that they pushed too hard, were always revolutionizing and doing 'the work of generations,' as Mr. Bush put it. They appear to share an insensitivity to the delicacy of even so great a nation as ours, an inability to imagine how quickly things can turn south, go bad, a strange reluctance to see limits, and to know at a certain point that what you do with a nation becomes what you do to it."[14]

Noonan was dwelling on Obama reforms planned for the United States health care industry, but she as easily could have written on the government's intervention in the auto industry, or the other high issues on Obama's agenda. As spring turned into summer, the president pressed hard. There was the $787 billion economic stimulus package; the relentless credit crunch; and the $700 billion Troubled Asset Relief Program to shore up Wall Street and the big banks, which still faced $1 trillion of losses over the next two years. And there was the war to manage in Afghanistan, and the withdrawal from Iraq, and the nuclear build-up in Iran. And there was energy. Obama was going to have the country rely for its power needs less on imported oil and more on the sun, wind, and coal — though the latter plans seemed largely stagnant, almost forgotten, and this by a president who had said during his campaign that he didn't blame Americans for being cynical about energy independence because politicians had been talking about it for at least thirty years.

Bill Wylam, a retired General Motors engineer in Indianapolis, was wary. He had been a key figure on GM's electric car program in the 1990s, when GM Delco Remy had pioneered the electrical systems in Indianapolis for the EV1 electric car sold briefly in California. Now he was dismayed by the sudden turmoil in Detroit. "I don't know where we're going with this," Wylam said.

In the industrial Midwest an array of companies were vying for $25 billion advanced by Congress to pay for environmentally friendly vehicle technology. The money was to be doled out by the United States Department of Energy. With the credit crisis in full bore, promising tech ventures shut out by traditional banks were hungry for the Department of Energy (DOE) loans and grants. But in the late spring of 2009, no money had been forwarded to any company, even entrepreneurial ventures such as Bright Automotive, a GM protégé in Anderson, Indiana, that was ready to go forward with an electric work van powered by a battery, or EnerDel, a 100-employee venture in Indianapolis that traced its roots to the old GM Delco Remy. EnerDel was ready to make lithium-ion batteries for electric cars and had requested $450 million in DOE loans in 2008 to build a plant. Seven months later, no loan had come through. Executives would not publicly complain about the slow work by the energy department officials for fear of alienating the White House. Finally, Senator Evan Bayh, a Democrat from Indiana, sent top officials in the energy department a terse note, pointing out China was moving faster to develop green cars than the United States.[15]

Department of Energy officials insisted the sheer mass of loan applications was slowing down the approval process, not the ministrations of the Obama White House. Nevertheless, the reluctance to chastise the White House was visible to Richard Mourdock, the elected state treasurer of Indiana. Mourdock was the only high public official in the nation to challenge the White House's Chrysler bailout plan. Mourdock, who himself drove a gray 2004 Dodge Ram pickup with 129,000 miles on the odometer, said he had to act under state law that required the treasurer intervene when wrongful actions diminished the value of investment funds overseen by his office. Mourdock said public pension funds in California and Michigan also held Chrysler bonds, but officials there were vying for more stimulus money from the White House, and so they were reluctant to object to the bailout of the Detroit automaker. "It's unbelievable that in the United States of America this kind of stuff is happening," Mourdock said.

Mourdock had been a relatively unknown Republican from a distant corner of Indiana on the Ohio River when he was elected to the office in 2006. A former coal and oil geologist, he was still an obscure public official in 2009 when recalcitrant hedge funds and other investors in Chrysler bonds resisting the Obama bailout decided not to stand in the way of the president after all. Mourdock alone stood firm. He chalked it up to principle. "They want to take money from Hoosier retirees," Mourdock said in reference to the nickname for Indiana residents, "to help this foreign company take over twenty percent of Chrysler."

Arguing the matter for the Indiana treasurer's office was the law firm White & Case. The white-shoe Miami firm had been preparing a legal argument for the other investors. When they backed down, Mourdock's office alone retained the Miami firm, which filed a lawsuit in U.S. District in New York in May on behalf of the Indiana treasurer. The lawsuit attacked the Chrysler bailout as illegal on two main points. By diverting money to Chrysler from the Troubled Asset Relief Program, the White House was violating a measure established by Congress solely to aid Wall Street. Moreover, by neglecting the Bankruptcy Code's absolute priority rule, the White House plan for Chrysler was unfair to the senior lenders, undermining more than 150 years of bankruptcy law.

Chrysler execs slammed Mourdock, issuing a news statement that questioned whether he was grandstanding for political gain by opposing the bailout. Chrysler's statement pointed out that if Mourdock prevailed Chrysler could be broken up in bankruptcy, costing the state millions in tax revenue and thousands of jobs. Mourdock shrugged off the attack. A thoughtful middle-aged man given to prayer and contemplation, he had been seen in the Indiana Statehouse's fourth-floor chapel, where he spent nearly forty minutes one afternoon just after the lawsuit was filed. He insisted the law gave him no choice. If a wrongful act depleted public investment funds, the treasurer had to take action to preserve the funds, no matter how small was the loss.

Mourdock's treasury office oversaw a pair of police and teacher pension funds as well as a state construction fund that among them held more than $10 billion in total assets, including $42.5 million worth of Chrysler bonds, or less than one-half of one percent of the total. In August 2008 a private money manager hired by the office had purchased the bonds on behalf of the Indiana State Police Pension Fund, the Teachers' Retirement Fund, and the Major Moves Construction Fund from another bondholder for the discounted price of $20 million. The money manager, Reams Asset Management of Columbus, Indiana, had purchased the Chrysler bonds as part of a pool of investments on behalf of the state. The bonds were sold at a discount because Chrysler sales already were reeling due to its limited product line and the price of gasoline, which was more than $4 a gallon that summer. But with oil prices starting to ease late in the summer, the money manager figured the bonds could be a sure winner for the state's investment funds. Once the bailout plan was hashed out by the White House, however, it assured the Indiana Investment Fund would get no more than twenty-nine cents on the dollar — or about $5.6 million for the Chrysler bonds, a loss of $14.4 million off the discounted $20 million price the state had paid. Chrysler executives insisted that the state of Indiana and any other bondholders were lucky to get twenty-nine cents on the dollar for their investments. Mourdock demurred. Holdings of the Indiana funds would be reduced in value while the union and Fiat were rewarded with large ownership stakes that simply flew in the face of established bankruptcy procedure.[16]

For his actions, Mourdock quickly became public enemy number one in Kokomo. "The legal action recently initiated by the state treasurer, if successful, would lead to the liquidation of Chrysler's assets," said Democratic Joe Donnelly, a congressman in the House of Representatives whose district represents part of Kokomo. "Simply put, if the state treasurer gets his way, more than 5,000 good-paying jobs in Kokomo and around the state will disappear."

Richie Boruff, a gravelly voiced ex–amateur boxer, was far less diplomatic. The Kokomo-based UAW Local 685 president smelled a conspiracy, saying Republican Governor Mitch Daniels was actually orchestrating the treasurer's moves. Daniels himself was being touted in Republican circles as a possible contender for the White House in 2012. Mourdock rebutted any hint of conspiracy, saying he had conferred with the governor and did have the governor's backing, but was not trying to attack Obama and sidetrack the Chrysler bailout for Daniels' political gain. Republican insiders concurred, calling Mourdock a "straight arrow" who was acting solely on principle. But Boruff thought the price to be paid was too high. "Kokomo, Indiana, has the largest Chrysler workforce in one location in the country, and we're the only state throwing a monkey wrench in the works," fumed Boruff. "It's a shame that people think this is what Indiana is about. I think he should just shut up."

As the treasurer's fight against the bailout moved through the courts in May and June of 2009, there was little public discussion about a companion issue and its bearing on the future of Chrysler. The White House had brought out rules requiring auto-makers to sharply raise the fuel economy standards of cars and trucks by 2015. The last time something like this had happened was in 1976, and it had been particularly nettlesome for Chrysler.

It was one of the reasons the automaker nearly went bankrupt in 1979 and survived only with federal loan guarantees back then. Now it was a problem again. Chrysler was still behind the curve on new engine technology. Fiat would bring economy cars and compact sedans from Europe. These cars could help Chrysler meet the stricter federal mileage standards, but not bring its fleet fully in compliance. Buyers of new autos in the United States were usually in the upper third of the income strata, and for more than a quarter-century had consistently shown a marked preference for Asian or European cars over those from domestic manufacturer. When they bought "American" it was more likely to be pickup trucks, sport-utility vehicles, and minivans, but none of these got superior gas mileage. Ford had a winner in the small car market with the popular, good-handling Focus, and GM had done the same with its competent if uninspired Chevrolet Cobalt, but even here many international competitors had multiple entries in the small car market while Ford and GM really had only one each. (GM ultimately rebadged the Cobalt as a Pontiac G5, but it was the same car.) The domestically built Saturn Ion had been abandoned in favor of a German-built hatchback, a rebadged Opel, which was a good car that sold well in Europe but was a huge sales flop in America. Chrysler? It had inexplicably dropped its once popular Neon subcompact in 2005.

Chrysler's Dodge Ram full-size pickup was its best-selling vehicle, whether car or truck. Its minivans were long the best-selling in America, though they had recently lost that mantle to the Honda Odyssey. Fiat's small cars could help Chrysler, but only if American consumers decided the Fiat-Chryslers matched the high quality of Honda, Nissan, and Toyota cars, or at least that of the GM and Ford models. Not just Chrysler, but all the Detroit Three were in a bind — they couldn't sell as many trucks and SUVs anymore, yet they couldn't easily compete in the small-car market. Consumer preference wasn't the only issue. The Detroit Three could hide those disastrous legacy costs negotiated in various UAW contracts over the years in high-profit, high-volume big vehicles, but profit margins were much, much thinner in the highly competitive small-car market. They just could not afford to absorb $1,500 of legacy costs in a car with a starting price of only $14,000 or $15,000. Back in November 2008 executives from all the Detroit manufacturers had come before Congress and had fallen on the sword, apologizing for not building the right kind of cars for today's economy. But how do you fault companies for wanting to make profitable vehicles and avoiding products with little or no profit potential?

Of course, it was not trucks that Fiat wanted in a merger with Chrysler. Fiat's executives and the owners of the company, the powerful Agnelli family, wanted their cars reintroduced to North America in heavy volumes. One of the least costly ways was to piggyback on the Chrysler network of 1,600 dealers and put the Italian cars in front of the American and Canadian public rebadged as Chryslers. Sergio Marchionne, the chief executive of the Italian automaker, saw the vast American market as Fiat's stepping stone to the top rung of global automakers — Honda, Toyota, and Nissan in Japan; GM and Ford in the United States; and Volkswagen in Europe. What each had was a large global market to spread development costs over millions of vehicles. If Fiat could sell 5 million cars per year worldwide instead of its current 2 million, the economies of scale would keep prices down for consumers; bring in the profits that kept the Agnellis happy; and afford the expensive research and technology required to keep up with the world leaders in the auto business.

Germany's Daimler had based its takeover of Chrysler a decade earlier on virtually the same economies of scale argument. The strategy had failed Daimler and left Chrysler an empty pipeline for new designs. Now, the American company faced an expensive tab to ready its truck fleet for the new fuel mileage rules. Seventy percent of the assembly capacity in Chrysler plants was allocated to Dodge and Jeep truck production. What the automaker did not have was a surefire technology in hand to boost the fuel economy in those trucks the way GM and Ford were getting ready to do with a new generation of electric-hybrid systems. Ford was buying elements of its system from Toyota. General Motors had much of the technology already on the shelf, a legacy of its $1 billion EV1 electric vehicle program developed for California in the 1990s and canceled in 2003. Chrysler had not had the money to tinker with that kind of technology even when it was part of Daimler, which had handled the bulk of the R&D chores. By the spring of 2009, Chrysler had asked the United States Energy Department for $8.5 billion to develop electric systems, but it was far behind its rivals. When next-generation car technology dominated the Detroit auto show in early 2009, Ford touted electric cars and its impressive Fusion hybrid sedan as the wave of the future. GM showed the Chevrolet Volt, a plug-in hybrid electric car expected to debut in 2010. Chrysler pledged new hybrid vehicles, but showed nothing new.

Fiat felt the same pressure. Marchionne saw a windfall for Fiat in the $8.5 billion that Chrysler was angling for from the United States Energy Department for new technology develop-ment, which was separate from the bailout money. Automotive R&D was expensive, and Fiat had little money available on its own for the next-generation technology that the larger VW, Toyota, or GM Opel could use to squash it in Europe. Mar-chionne, born in Italy, had grown up in Canada and was educated as an accountant. He had lived for a time in Windsor, an industrial city across the border from Detroit, but had never before worked in the auto industry. He was running a Swiss com-pany in 2004 when John Elkann, the young great great-grandson of Fiat founder Giovanni Agnelli, recruited the brash executive to revive the sagging car company at the heart of the Agnelli family fortune. Since then, Fiat had begun making money again but was still struggling for market share in Europe, and still dogged by quality problems in some of its models. Though an auto industry newcomer, Marchionne understood strategy. He publicly warned that he thought the worldwide recession would grind down the global auto industry to a half dozen big survivors by 2012. Unless Fiat doubled in size, the Agnellis could lose their golden goose.[17]

Elkann, the vice chairman of Fiat, showed up as a panelist at a Swiss industrial conference in early May of 2009. He outlined an audacious plan hatched with Marchionne. The Agnellis would spin off much of their Fiat holdings. The new Fiat would merge with Chrysler and hopefully take over a pair of respected GM brands up for sale, Opel in Germany and Saab in Sweden. The scale of the new Fiat, along with the $8.5 billion Chrysler was seeking from the American government for technology, would help bring the revenue necessary to plunge into next-generation technology. "It's financial pressure triggered by technological change," London banker Klaus Flum told the *Financial Times* about the Agnelli strategy. "They know they can't finance the technology themselves."

Hardly anyone was surprised by the banker's analysis. Carmakers were hurting in an industry rife with overcapacity. GM had lost more than $80 billion in three years. In 2009 German conglomerate Daimler, despite its Mercedes profits, sold a $2.7 billion stake to Aabar Investments, a financial arm of the government of oil-rich Abu Dhabi. Aabar and Daimler announced they would work on electric cars together. Toyota, the world's largest automaker, had lost more than $7 billion in 2008, its first loss in nearly six decades. Toyota's close straits prompted the family to send in Akio Toyoda, grandson of the founder, to take over as head in early 2009 and regroup the company. While no one came right out and said so directly, it sure looked like days were numbered for Chrysler, at least the flashy, big-horsepower Chrysler the country had long known.

Just what would come in its place was uncertain. Chrysler had faced hard years before, but it had always had cunning managers or creative engineers able to bring the company a fresh new model that turned heads on the roads. In the 1980s its K-cars were Detroit's first mass-produced mid-size front-wheel drive cars. Its minivans brought a host of imitators. Its manly looking, rear-drive Dodge Charger and Chrysler 300 were daring moves in the twenty-first century, even if sales proved somewhat disappointing. Now, with manufacturing chief Tom LaSorda stepping down at Chrysler as Marchionne prepared to take over control, the company was clearly bereft of a veteran Chrysler man at the top of the business. Not since Walter P. Chrysler had come on the scene had this ever happened.

Chrysler the car maker had emerged out of the cacophony of 258 automobile companies in the United States in the first decade of the last century to become one of Detroit's Big Three. It had succeeded in the earliest years by virtue of luck and acquisition, and finally by hiring boy genius Walter P. Chrysler. The son of a Kansas railroad train conductor, he had started out not in cars but in railroads, then the largest industry in America. His rigorous streamlining of rail house operations in Pittsburgh brought him a small fortune in salary and bonuses and the attention of wealthy railroad financier James Storrow, who was also seated on General Motors' board of directors. In 1912, Storrow convinced Walter Chrysler to move to Flint, Michigan, and take charge of production at Buick, then GM's biggest car line. Under Chrysler, Buick ushered out the craftsman approach in which a small team of workers would assemble an entire car. Like Henry Ford Sr. in Detroit, Chrysler also created an assembly line. A worker stayed in position. He performed the same task as a conveyor line slowly brought a parade of cars past his work station. Buick output more than quadrupled to 200 cars a day, but after repeated clashes with company founder Billy Durant, Walter Chrysler left General Motors in 1922 to take the top position at Detroit rival Maxwell Motors. Maxwell traced to Maxwell-Briscoe, a well-heeled Detroit carmaker. Financed early on in part by legendary New York banker J.P. Morgan, Maxwell-Briscoe put up what then was the world's largest auto plant in New Castle, Indiana, in 1904. By 1922, Maxwell was wrung out by the post–World War recession and stumbling against the top four automakers, Ford Motor, General Motors, Dodge Brothers, and Hudson, a line of cars founded by a Detroit department store magnate of the same name. Maxwell lured Chrysler, offering a salary of $100,000 per year — or about $2 million in today's U.S. dollars — along with five percent of the profits and an open hand to run the company.

Chrysler brought with him a welter of ideas, some incremental, some advanced. He meshed them in a new sedan, the 1924 Chrysler Light Six, an innovative car Maxwell touted as comfortable as a Buick but lighter, faster, and more maneuverable. The new Maxwell featured a high-compression engine, hydraulic brakes, and balloon tires. Light Six sales boomed. As car shoppers bypassed other, stodgier Maxwells, Walter Chrysler dropped the Maxwell brand and in 1925 renamed the company Chrysler Corporation. Three years later, Chrysler bought Dodge for $170 million in stock, a merger then regarded as one of the largest in American history. With Dodge cars in the lineup, Chrysler surpassed Hudson in total auto sales in 1928, joining GM and Ford to become Detroit's Big Three, a phrase coined that year by an automotive trade journal. The trio accounted for seventy-five percent of the new cars sold in the United States.

Walter Chrysler became a household name. The news magazine *Time* featured him as its Man of the Year in 1928. By then, Henry Ford Sr. was considered distant and autocratic, and he was tainted by profoundly anti-Semitic articles published throughout most of the 1920s in a widely read newspaper he owned, the *Dearborn Independent*. The articles condemned not individual Jews, but cast Jews as a people bent on controlling the world, both by capitalistic and Communist means. Reactions to Ford's anti-Semitism and to his personality touched off ruthless power struggles in the fiefdoms of Ford Motor. Far more polished was Alfred Sloan, the chairman of General Motors, an intelligent executive who became famous as the mastermind of GM's decentralized, impersonal, and coldly efficient do-it-by-the-numbers approach to making and selling cars. Chrysler himself was regarded as a strong leader who set great store in individual enterprise among the people around him. For the next several decades, that was the hallmark of Chrysler Corporation — capable leaders and enterprising managers. Tear-shaped cars able to flow through the wind like airplanes came out of the Chrysler studios along with quiet engines mounted on rubber pads, an innovative feat before mid-century. Yet by the 1950s company fortunes began to flag, outflanked by the inventive genius of GM's design studios, as well as highly competent engine and transmission laboratories. But the company always managed to come back with a winning model, often with a powerful V-8 engine under the hood. "Chrysler really has understood how Americans identified with and wanted the muscle cars from the 1960s," said automobile historian John Wolconowicz.[18]

By the 1970s, the inrush of fuel-efficient Japanese cars smashed the muscle car and caught Chrysler and Detroit unawares. Just as the United States later would later be blindsided, first as oil surpassed $50 a barrel in 2005, then the meltdown of Wall Street and corporate finance in 2008, the oil shocks of 1973 and 1979 stunned Americans. Detroit had few models able to drive far on a few gallons of gas. Compact cars from the early '60s such as the Chevrolet Corvair, Dodge Lancer, and Ford Falcon all were gone. In the early 1970s GM *had* created the four-cylinder Chevrolet Vega that was fitted with an aluminum engine (forward thinking for its time), but the car earned a very poor reputation for reliability and soon disappeared. Meanwhile, sales of little coupes and sedans designed for the congested streets of Tokyo continued to climb in America. The Detroit Three didn't have competitive small cars in the marketplace again until the late 1970s, namely in the form of the rear-drive Chevrolet Chevette, a surprising best-seller for several years, along with the Ford Escort, and the Chrysler twins, the Dodge Omni and Plymouth Horizon. At the same time, the rapid rise in gasoline and energy prices touched off an astounding inflation rate. The Federal Reserve responded by sharply raising interest rates in 1981 and 1982 to tame inflation. Car loan rates soared to more than fifteen percent. Chrysler had turned to the United States government for loan guarantees in 1979 to help tide it over. The bailout saved Chrysler, but when it rains it pours — a deep recession followed a few years later that hurt the entire auto industry. In its exuberance to fend off inflation, the Federal Reserve had cranked interest rates higher than needed, provoking the devastating recession. By late 1982, the unemployment rate in the United States had risen above ten percent for the first time since the end of the Great Depression. Chrysler shed thousands of workers, sold component lines, and closed plants. Its designers also began quietly grooming a vehicle designed for suburban families, the minivan, as well as the four-wheel-drive Jeep Cherokee, the first SUV to sell in high volume. Neither was a muscle car, but both were bigger and more powerful than the sedans dictated by the U.S. fuel economy rules. But because they were each classified as trucks under federal rules, they did not have to meet the more stringent mileage standards required of cars. Armed with profits from the minivans and the Cherokee, Chrysler brought out the hugely popular Grand Cherokee, then the fabulously redesigned 2004 Ram pickup. Chrysler had so much cash it was able to do something no one in the depths of 1979 could have contemplated. It committed to a $3 billion capital plan, putting up new drivetrain plants in Detroit and Kokomo, Indiana.

By 2009, it was all ancient history. The White House insisted Detroit had to revamp its fleet to meet the stricter mileage rules of the times. Chrysler announced it would scrap several truck models, including the luxury Chrysler Aspen and rugged Dodge Durango sport-utility vehicles, as it went ahead with a Fiat alliance. Although the old factory town of Kokomo would be a supposed beneficiary of the government largesse, autoworkers there were increasingly disillusioned. Todd Gibson had been a Hawk missile electrician in the U.S. Army's 7th Armored Cavalry in Germany, where he grew to appreciate that country's solid blue-collar craftsmanship in the metal- and wood-working trades and on the farms. Returning home to Kokomo after the Cold War ended, Gibson hired in at Chrysler in 1993 and worked through the truck boom and into the 2000s decade, until he was "downsized" in March 2009. Gibson was dismayed at the willingness of the government to shower taxpayer money on Wall Street and what he described as brain-dead automobile companies, because it was hard to understand how all that money ever could be recouped by ordinary citizens.

"I don't think Chrysler is going to make it," said the lean forty-year-old former forklift driver. "We're already in a downward spiral. I think we're in the process of a rapid removal of the blue-collar class from this whole country. You have the coast lines, where the money is, and those people don't live paycheck to paycheck like we do. They don't care about us, but without the blue-collar class, you have only two classes, rich and poor. And when you have just two classes, people without options are going to make bad choices. We're going to see more crime, more drugs, more breakdown."

Over at the flat-roof Local 685 union headquarters on East Hoffer Street in a residential part of Kokomo, Richie Boruff also sweated the future. When Chrysler finally declared bankruptcy on May 1, 2009, and laid off virtually all its North American employees, Boruff, too, had to lay off his office staff. Signs at every entrance to the union hall said "Closed," but it didn't stop people from coming in or calling the union leader on the phone incessantly. Slumped in his chair, alternating between his cell phone and landline, he took one call after another while an assistant counseled laid-off workers at a small table in the middle of the office and other workers stood in the hallway outside. Had there not been this beehive of activity one might have mistaken the office for a private den or family room — it was filled with boxing posters, photographs, and gloves on display. "The number one question people have is why their unemployment claims were denied, that and when are they going to be called back to work," the wary union president said.

The first question was easy to answer: you have to reactivate your claim as long as you've worked any period of time between now and your last layoff, he told his fellow union members. He repeated the same message over and over and over.

He was not the person to address the second question, however. That would be up to Chrysler, Fiat, and the bankruptcy court, he said.

The Chrysler transfer to Fiat looked all but certain on May 5, 2009, after a bankruptcy court judge approved the rapid sale of Chrysler's assets to the Italian automaker, overturning objections from many of the company's lenders. The sale was reaffirmed by a New York appeals court, but that court gave opponents of the deal until 4 p.m. on Monday, June 8, to object to the deal, or forever hold their peace. While others dropped out, Indiana treasurer Richard Mourdock decided to continue the battle, appealing to the United States Supreme Court on Sunday, June 7, to stop the sale. This was in spite of the fact that Mourdock controlled less than one percent of all Chrysler's outstanding debt, nominally valued at $6.9 billion. Judge Ruth Bader Ginsburg, acting on behalf of the full court because she had oversight of the New York appeals court, heard the appeal and ordered the sale "stayed pending further order."

Ginsburg's declaration sent shudders through the various stakeholders in Chrysler. But what did "further order" really mean in this context? Ginsburg had not imposed a deadline on herself or the court. Some observers were alarmed by the open-ended nature of the declaration, while others argued that she and the full court just needed more time to decide if it really wanted to hear the full appeal. On June 7, 2009, no one knew what was on her mind. The bankruptcy was turning into a soap opera.

Back in Indiana, Richard Mourdock was taking heat for his bold action. "I'm getting emails from people in Kokomo and at Chrysler now that say that I'm trying to cover up a bad investment," Mourdock told a newspaper columnist on June 8. "Wait a minute — we invested in you."[19]

The fallout was quick. Dire warnings soon followed that Fiat could pull out of the deal on June 15 if the sale were not consummated by then. The date was significant: should the full Supreme Court agree to hear the case then surely it would need more than a few days to study the matter and actually issue a ruling. Fiat would — not could — walk away from the deal and Chrysler would have to liquidate, many observers fretted. And even if Fiat did not exercise its right to back out of the deal, Chrysler still was losing money during the bankruptcy itself. All its North American plants were idled, but there still were skeleton crews that had to maintain the factories, property taxes to pay, and other ongoing expenses. And if liquidation really were to happen then billions of dollars in bridge loans would never be repaid. Parts suppliers would go bankrupt, too. The UAW pensions would not be fully funded. Everybody would lose.

Disillusioned Chrysler dealers across the country who were set to lose their franchises on June 9 were about the only people who didn't care what happened to the company anymore. With or without the bankruptcy, Chrysler already had announced it was cancelling franchises with 789 dealers on that date. This was said to be a cost-cutting move for the ailing corporation, even though dealers are independently owned businesses that pay about ninety-five percent of their own expenses, including borrowing money to buy inventory from the manufacturer that was now showing them the door. Fort Wayne, Indiana, and environs were particularly hard hit — five Chrysler and Dodge dealers in the area lost their franchises on what to them would be Black Tuesday forever. Several spoke of betrayal, or said losing long-time customers who bought a new car every three or four years was like losing family. They also blamed the new sheriff in town, so to speak, which was the president.

"This is being forced through by the government," said Toby Sorg, president of Sorg South Chrysler-Dodge-Jeep in Warsaw, a small community near Fort Wayne. Sorg, like others, would stay in business as a used car dealer and service center. Any remaining Chrysler vehicles would have to be sold at a discount to franchised dealers because he could no longer offer factory incentives to customers interested in buying the cars directly.[20]

But other stakeholders watched and waited as the hours counted down that Tuesday, waiting for the Supreme Court to tip its hand. Uncertainty continued well into the afternoon, though Fiat's Sergio Marchionne provided some cushion when he announced on that day that the June 15 date was not really a deadline, but rather a goal. "We would never walk away," Marchionne said. "Never."[21]

In truth, Marchionne wanted Chrysler as much as Chrysler needed him.

Late on the evening of June 9, the Supreme Court issued its definitive statement — it would not hear a full appeal by opponents to the sale. Those opponents had to convince at least four of the court's nine justices that the issues raised were serious enough to warrant hearing a full appeal. "The applicants have not carried that burden," the court said.[22]

The sale would go forward. Daimler and Cerberus were free of Chrysler, and vice versa. Previously announced terms of the deal would hold: bondholders would get a total of $2 billion, or twenty-nine cents on the dollar, for their $6.9 billion in secured loans, but no equity in the new company. The Voluntary Employees' Beneficiary Association, or union health care trust fund, would get a fifty-five percent stake in the company; Fiat would get twenty percent with an escalator clause to grab a larger stake if the new company were to introduce fuel-efficient cars made in America and pay off the bridge loans; and the American, Canadian, and provincial Ontario governments divvied up the rest. Marchionne would head the new Chrysler, as expected. Bob Nardelli, who President Obama had singled out for praise as the man who had guided Chrysler through its reorganization, was out.

It would be an exaggeration to say there was relief in Chrysler factories and towns across the country, but not by much. One obstacle had been cleared; there would be more. In Kokomo, Mayor Goodnight could only shake his head at the turn of events. He had stood helplessly by as actors in Detroit, Washington, and New York — and Italy — determined the fate of his city. He voiced his greatest frustration at Mourdock, though, whose actions he called "questionable."

"I cannot believe that a liquidation of Chrysler's assets would prove to be more financially beneficial to the state than protecting thousands of jobs for working Hoosiers," said Goodnight.

He was right — for the time being.

1. Sheryl Gay Stolberg, Bill Vlasic, "President Gives U.S. Automakers a Short Lifeline," *New York Times*, March 31, 2009, A1.

2. Louise Story, "Auto Advisor to Obama Had Ties to Industry Fund," *New York Times*, May 28, 2009, B5.

3. Louise Story, "Obama's Top Auto Industry Trouble Shooter," *New York Times*, April 6, 2009, B1.

4. Todd J. Zywicki, "Chrysler and the Rule of Law," *Wall Street Journal*, May 13, 2009, A19.

5. Kendra Marr, Tomoeh Murakami Tse, "Chrysler Creditors Disagree on U.S. Plan to Cut Carmaker's Debt," *Washington Post*, April 11, 2009, A09.

6. Ian Austen, "Canada Paints a Stark Picture of Chrysler," *New York Times*, March 31, 2009.

7. Bill Vlasic, David E. Sanger, "Debtholders vs. U.S. Over Chrysler Deal," *New York Times*, April 22, 2009, B1.

8. Vlasic.

9. Vlasic.

10. Serena Ng, Annelena Lobb, "Many Lenders Say Partial Payback Is a Raw Deal," *Wall Street Journal*, May 1, 2009, A13.

11. President Barack Obama, "On Chrysler and the Autos," April 30, 2009, http://www.whitehouse.gov/video/On-Chrysler-and-the-Autos.

12. Jesse Toprak, senior industry analyst for automotive market researcher Edmunds.com, was interviewed by Ted Evanoff on March 23, 2009.

13. Keith Crain, "GM Is Now Government Motors," *Automotive News*, April 6, 2009, 12.

14. Peggy Noonan, "What's Elevated, Health-Care Provider?" *Wall Street Journal*, May 16, 2009, A11.

15. Ted Evanoff, "Hybrid Spotlight Shines on Bright," *Indianapolis Star*, April 21, 2009, 6A.

16. Ted Evanoff, "Indiana's Appeal Puts Chrysler Deal on Hold," *Indianapolis Star*, June 4, 2009, A1.

17. John Reed, "Out on a Family Drive," *Financial Times*, May 8, 2009, 7.

18. John Wolconowicz, an automotive analyst at IHS Global Insight in Lexington, MA, was interviewed by Ted Evanoff on several occasions in 2008 and 2009.

19. John Ketzenberger, "Treasurer Explains Why State Sued," *Indianapolis Star*, June 9, 2009, C1.

20. Marty Schladen, "Dropped Area Dealers Feel Betrayed," *(Fort Wayne) Journal Gazette*, June 10, 2009, http://www.journalgazette.net/article/20090610/BIZ13/306109940.

21. Luca Ciferri, "Fiat's Marchionne Says He Won't Walk Away from Chrysler Deal," *Automotive News*, June 9, 2009, http://www.autoweek.com/article/20090609/CARNEWS/906099997.

22. Tomoeh Murakami Tse, Robert Barnes, "Supreme Court Clears the Way for Chrysler Sale," *Washington Post*, June 10, 2009, A1.

Kokomo mayor Greg Goodnight (standing) and Ed Montgomery (seated, glasses). [*Indianapolis Star*]

Former Obama administration "auto czar" Steve Rattner. [AP Photo/J. David Ake]

Indiana native Ron Gettelfinger is president of the United Auto Workers. [Courtesy UAW]

Long-term Chrysler employee Susan Perry refused buyout offers in 2009.
[Courtesy Susan Perry]

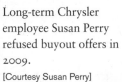

Bedford's GM casting plant survived the 2009 closures.
[Courtesy UAW Local 440]

Shawna Girgis is the first-term Independent mayor of Bedford, Indiana.
[Courtesy City of Bedford]

Reclusive Stephen Feinberg is CEO of Cerberus Capital Management.
[AP Photo/Haraz N. Ghanbari]

Die-maker Sylvester Stafford is a long-term Marion GM stamping plant employee. [Courtesy Steven Wright, GM Quality Network Representative]

GM Chairman and CEO Rick Wagoner was forced out in 2009 bankruptcy.
[Indianapolis Star]

Former U.S. Olympic figure skater Wayne Seybold is mayor of Marion, Indiana.
[Indianapolis Star]

Figure-skating siblings Kim and Wayne Seybold competed in the 1988 Calgary Olympics. [Indianapolis Star]

Sergio Marchionne is head of both Fiat and the new Chrysler. [*Indianapolis Star*]

Former Chrysler employee Benjamin Stine took a big buyout, hopes to record in Nashville. [*Indianapolis Star*]

Scott Moore is president of UAW Local 440 in Bedford, Indiana. [Courtesy UAW Local 440]

Danny Hiatt is shop chairman of UAW Local 292 in Kokomo, Indiana, representing Delphi hourly workers. [Courtesy UAW Local 292]

Former GM executives Rick Wagoner and Jack Smith in happier days. [*Indianapolis Star*]

Canadian Tom LaSorda was pushed down the ladder at Chrysler when Cerberus Capital Management bought it in 2007. [*Indianapolis Star*]

Former police detective Kris Ockomon is mayor of Anderson, Indiana. [*Indianapolis Star*]

Ken Lewenza is president of the Canadian Auto Workers. [Courtesy CAW]

UAW Local 292 President Ginny McMillin. [Courtesy UAW Local 292]

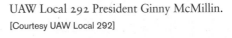

Gray iron Chrysler foundry in Indianapolis closed in 2005. [*Indianapolis Star*]

Maurice "Mo" Davison is Director of UAW Region 3 representing Kentucky and Indiana. [Courtesy UAW Region 3]

CHAPTER 7

What's Good
for General Motors . . .

WHAT HAD ONCE BEEN UNTHINKABLE, then inevitable, became reality. General Motors followed Chrysler into bankruptcy, filing on June 1, 2009. Some of GM's brands would remain, of course, but it was clear to all that a new General Motors would be trimmed back greatly. Just how much, though, was not understood beyond a handful of insiders in Detroit and the White House. Someone who *did* sense the enormity of the task was Albert Koch; he understood because he was to have a hand in performing radical surgery on what until recently had been the world's largest automaker. Laboring in conference rooms on the thirty-eighth floor of the Renaissance Center, the Detroit skyscraper that housed the offices of GM's senior executives, were dozens of Koch's employees, all financial analysts poring through nearly 500,000 contracts General Motors had in place with thousands of vendors.[1] Koch was vice chairman of AlixPartners, a suburban Detroit consulting firm hired by GM for its wise counsel. While the White House was committed to a quick sixty- to ninety-day bankruptcy for General Motors, Koch's analysts were focused on what would be done once the bankruptcy process itself was over.

Koch and his team knew that GM would have to strip away unwanted assets like so much ballast in order that this hoped-for phoenix rising might have a fighting chance of success. Once the bankruptcy was filed, GM could obtain court permission to abandon billions of dollars worth of factories, machinery, offices, and real estate throughout North America. Identifying the unwanted assets and possibly finding buyers for some of them was the task of Koch's team. That he lived in an upscale Detroit suburb heartened many in the community, as if Koch could spare the Motor City, if not other parts of the country, from a spate of plant closings. "He's from Bloomfield Hills and he'll advocate for Michigan," a school district administrator gushed to a local newspaper.[2] In truth, there was so much to discard and dispose of, not only in Motown but throughout North America, that Koch measured the enormity of the task before him in years. The sixty-six-year-old accountant figured he might turn seventy-one before the chore was completed. "GM is a very, very complicated company," he explained. "The magnitude of understanding the company, what needs to be done, the number of people you need to work with is very, very striking."[3]

GM was complicated, all right. Until quite recently, the company had employed nearly 600,000 people, almost half of them outside North America, and amassed sales of about $210 billion per year. Between the end of 2004 and the spring of 2009, GM automobile plants located on five continents assembled nearly 36,000,000 new vehicles. Yet, despite the outpouring from the factories, GM profits were nil. Over those same months GM collected $730 billion in revenue, about 55 percent of it on sales outside the United States, but still lost $82 billion, which amounted to $2,296 in red ink for each vehicle made. The executives in the Renaissance Center and the United Auto Workers officials a short way up Jefferson Avenue in the union's Solidarity House headquarters had tried to stave off disaster, especially with a landmark 2007 contract that allowed GM, Chrysler, and Ford to shift their retiree health care benefits to a trust fund under union control and bring in new hires at sharply reduced wages. But time had run out on GM, as with Chrysler just a month earlier. Lawyers for General Motors filed papers in New York, claiming debts of nearly $173 billion. It was the largest industrial bankruptcy in American history. The United States Treasury prepared to take a sixty percent stake in the company. "Working with my auto task force, GM and its stakeholders have produced a viable, achievable plan that will give this iconic American company a chance to rise again," President Obama said at the time. "It's a plan tailored to the realities of today's auto market, a plan that positions GM to move toward profitability even if it takes longer than expected for our economy to fully recover."[4]

Throughout the Midwest, the meaning of Obama's message gradually sank in. Tailoring for market "realities" meant the old leviathan would shrink, and when it did, GM would cast away factories and suppress spending on steel, polymers, glass, sensors, aluminum, chemicals, carpet, fabric, rubber, and the 5,000 individual parts purchased from 1,500 manufacturing companies that in turn were supplied by a second tier of 2,000 to 3,000 companies. "GM will be trimmed down in almost every respect," said Michael Robinet, vice president of CSM Worldwide, an automotive research firm in suburban Detroit. "And they're not using scissors. They're using a hatchet."[5] Obama's auto task force, led by Wall Street investment banker Steven Rattner, had insisted only a lean automaker could weather the dire recession. To ensure the hatchet was used, the White House summoned a friend of Rattner's to replace Richard Wagoner as chairman. He was Edward Whitacre Jr., a member of ExxonMobil's board of directors and former chairman of telephone giant AT&T Corporation, where he had just collected a $158.5 million retirement package, the second largest ever doled out in corporate America. Whitacre, long known as "Big Ed" in the phone business, admitted, "I don't know anything about cars. A business is a business and I can learn about cars. I'm not that old and I think the business principles are the same."[6] The sixty-seven-year-old Texan quickly set out to find new members for GM's board as Rattner's team named Al Koch the chief restructuring officer.

Obama and Rattner spoke of change ahead for General Motors, though their choice for CEO was no radical outsider. Fritz Henderson, who would oversee the daily operations of General Motors, had distinguished himself a decade earlier as one of the youngest people ever selected as a GM vice president.[7] Insiders long had believed he was destined for the thirty-ninth floor executive suite. Just like Wagoner, the fifty-year-old Henderson had worked his entire career for the company, though he had a reputation for being decisive where Wagoner was more deliberate and, some said, prone to bury himself in details. "Fritz is more hands-on in enforcing decisions than Rick was," Koch, who had worked with both execs, told *Business Week* magazine.[8] Henderson's career path paralleled Wagoner's. Although the deposed boss had received his bachelor's from Duke University and Henderson's came from the University of Michigan, both had been college athletes, Wagoner playing basketball, Henderson pitching for the baseball team. Both earned MBAS from Harvard University. Both landed in the GM Treasurer's office in New York. Both got on the fast track with assignments in South America. Both were then routinely transferred from country to country, GM's method of acquainting rising stars with the far-flung empire. On the day he was promoted to vice president in 1997, Henderson was also named head of GM in Brazil. He was thirty-nine. Within four years, he would head GM production and sales throughout Latin America, Africa, and the Middle East, and then get a prized assignment running the growing China operations. Finally, he went to the last grooming post, heading GM Europe. In 2005, Henderson was named chief financial officer of the entire corporation, the same position held by Wagoner before his rise to head GM a decade earlier. Although the new CEO was one of GM's bright young execs, doubts persisted outside the company. Could he, could anyone, right so complex an organization? "Fritz might be twenty percent better than Wagoner, or maybe fifty percent better," said investor Jerome York, a former GM director. "But the question is, is that good enough?"[9]

Henderson quickly set out to show his mettle. He began dismantling the management structure favored by Wagoner and his predecessor in the chairman's seat, Jack Smith, another finance man. Henderson started with GM's hidebound culture. He pared the ranks of senior execs, offering 4,100 managers buyouts, a move that would eradicate fifteen percent of the managerial corps, then announced more cuts to achieve a three percent reduction worldwide. He eliminated the executive strategy board that Wagoner had relied on to help guide the company. Figuring the board's sixteen execs as a group were too cautious and consensus-minded to quickly reach decisions, Henderson turned to small teams of middle-rung managers. He urged them to move fast. Old habits were deeply ingrained. GM, for example, relied on consumer clinics. The clinics included everyday citizens called on from outside the company to look at future models and explain their likes and dislikes. In the spring of 2009, product planners in the GM design studios wanted a clinic to weigh in on a sporty Buick styled by GM designers in China, a car that was being considered for the North American market. Henderson opposed the clinic. Focus groups could stretch car projects for weeks at a cost of millions of dollars while the data were evaluated, a cost GM no longer could afford. Despite the chief exec's verdict, the planners scheduled the clinic anyway, knowing the data would help back their recommendation on the car.[10] Ginning up a clinic was GM conservatism on display. While the focus group might have some useful insight, the mountain of data culled from the clinic could give the designers political cover in case their car turned out truly awful in the market. Realizing the GM culture was iron clad, Henderson hired Booz & Company consultant Jon Katzenbach to coach the managerial corps. The consultant, *Business Week* magazine explained, was ordered to "make GM's middle managers less risk-averse and more willing to make decisions" on their own.[11]

While he tackled the corporate culture, Henderson also set out to scale back the company. Decades earlier, GM had bought its supply chain and its brands, such as the Oakland Motor Company, later renamed Pontiac. Now, that policy made it a bit easier for Henderson to parcel out the old empire in chunks. GM announced it simply was retiring the Pontiac brand and canceling its franchise agreements with Pontiac dealers. It also found a Chinese buyer for Hummer, subject to Chinese government approval, and it negotiated the sale of Saab to a Swedish group, though that deal, in time, was to fall apart. More significantly, the corporation promised the heart of GM Europe — Adam Opel and Vauxhall — to Magna, a big Canadian auto-parts company that was buying it in tandem with Russia's state-owned Sberbank, which would pass a share of Opel to Russian automaker GAZ. Lastly, GM peddled the Saturn brand and retail arm, considering a sale to Detroit auto dealer Roger Penske, a wealthy former race car driver who once owned engine maker Detroit Diesel. These steps may have looked breathtaking from the outside in their sweep and scope, yet were just first steps in GM's transformation.

To weather the recession, Henderson had to vastly scale back the manufacturing footprint, as well, not just get rid of brands. It should have come as no secret, but many consumers did not realize that their Pontiac G6 sedan, for example, did not originate in a Pontiac factory. There were no Pontiac factories. Nor were there Chevrolet, Buick, Pontiac, GMC, or Cadillac factories. GM had split the manufacturing functions from the car divisions in the 1980s in a consolidation meant to cut costs. Buick or Cadillac, Chevy or GMC truck, models of similar size were designed on the same computer screens in the design studios and produced on common assembly lines run by GM's manufacturing department. Now, Henderson had to do away not only with the seventeen percent of assembly capacity taken by Pontiac and Saturn. He had to slash production capacity available to the surviving brands. Sixteen of the forty-nine auto-parts and vehicle assembly plants in North America, or a third of capacity, were selected for permanent shut down and disposal. GM would be reduced to its size in the 1920s. "This is a remarkable opportunity for us," a chipper Henderson said in early June, putting a brave face on GM's radical surgery. "This allows us to permanently address problems that we have not been able to address before today."[12]

Although the CEO was, arguably, GM's most capable executive, he was not the single guiding intellect behind the restructuring. Obama's task force was filled with advisors, including a thirty-one-year-old Yale University law school dropout named Brian

Deese. The son of a Boston College professor, Deese had left Yale to work for Hillary Clinton's 2008 presidential campaign, where his smart take on politics had come to the attention of Lawrence Summers, the former president of Harvard who had been a prominent figure in President Bill Clinton's White House. In 2009, Obama named Summers director of the National Economic Council, a position that gave the former United States Treasury secretary heavy influence on Obama's automotive task force. Summers hired Deese and asked him to study whether the government should aid Chrysler or let it fail. Deese concluded a Chrysler liquidation would trigger massive Medicare and unemployment insurance payments, and bankrupt Rust Belt cities.[13]

Armed with Deese's study, Summers deflected the rival argument in Washington posed by Austan Goolsbee, a former University of Chicago economist who insisted GM would be better off if Chrysler failed. Goolsbee, an Obama colleague, also served on the National Economics Council. His logic had merit. GM could pick up Chrysler customers, people who presumably were going to "buy American" no matter what, and consequently face less pressure to scale back quite so drastically in bankruptcy. Summers stormed out of one meeting, livid with Goolsbee. Summers eventually made sure Goolsbee was not involved in the White House sessions discussing the Fiat takeover of Chrysler, though Summers did show Obama the Goolsbee memos objecting to federal aid for Chrysler. In the end, the argument was won by Summers, as well as Timothy Geithner, the United States Treasury secretary, who concurred with him on this point. Chrysler would be saved, and GM would in turn probably be smaller than if Chrysler had not been saved. "My judgment, and Tim's judgment, was that given all the equities involved, and given the potentially traumatic effects on confidence, that it was much better to try to save Chrysler if a reasonable merger agreement could be reached," Summers told the *New York Times*.[14]

Even as the president's auto task force debated the fate of Chrysler, Henderson began to recast GM as a sliver of its old self. Henderson ushered 24,000 autoworkers into retirement, reducing the hourly (as opposed to salaried) head count in North America to 38,000, compared to the peak of 511,000 in the United States three decades earlier (a total that included the massive Delphi auto-parts division that later was spun off from the corporation). Another 4,000 salaried workers were retired out of jobs, reducing their American ranks to 23,000. At the same time, the White House commitment had reached $50 billion in taxpayer loans to secure the 61,000 remaining American jobs at General Motors, or $819,000 per job. As the magnitude of the government largesse sank in, a puzzled reaction followed. "It's a very strange predicament," mused college professor Robert Reich who had been United States labor secretary in Clinton's White House. "Is the goal to preserve and protect automobile jobs or is it to create a new, lean-and-mean, slimmed-down, and debt-free GM?"[15] Clearly, being lean and mean trumped job preservation in the calculus of the bankers on Obama's auto team. A smaller GM could withstand the recession and survive to, hopefully, repay the government loans one day. Debtless trumped all.

The White House strategy quickly drew criticism, especially in the industrial Midwest, where lots of jobs would be lost. John Ketzenberger, a business columnist at the *Indianapolis Star*, assailed GM for new television spots extolling the "rebirth of the American car" at a time when GM had no trailblazing models to tout. He understood the company was scaling back rather than truly going forward. "The government whizzes calling the shots on behalf of shareholder taxpayers don't engender much confidence, either," the columnist wrote. "Lee Iacocca is right to warn his successors at Chrysler and GM to get the government out of their businesses sooner rather than later."[16]

Another damning objection came from Alan Tonelson, an economist in Washington, D.C. Noting that some new hires in the surviving GM plants would start at $15 per hour, little more than half the wage of the retiring workers, the thoughtful conservative insisted Obama had squandered the opportunity to look far ahead and fashion industrial and trade policies designed to resurrect high-wage factory work. "Washington had no interest in thinking this through and asking what does an industry require to remain a viable high-wage industry in the United States," said Tonelson, senior economist at the United States Business and Industry Council, a trade group that claimed 1,500 family-owned manufacturing firms as members. "Steve Rattner and Larry Summers have decided the reason the American auto segment can't compete is wages are too damn high. This group regards cars as it regards steel and it regards the entire manufacturing sector. They think manufacturing is something high-wage countries shouldn't be doing — it's Third World work."[17]

In public, Obama himself stayed above the fray. Indeed, there was little reason for him to answer critics. Washington and the entire apparatus of government was largely mute on the issue of Detroit. Instead of holding hearings, Congress looked away from General Motors restructuring. And there was virtually no discussion of forming a national industrial policy, despite the loss of 4 million manufacturing jobs in the United States during the 2000s and a steady outflow of cash for imports from abroad. Instead, the buzz during the spring and summer of 2009, when it came to GM, was largely lawyer talk: who would own how much of the automaker?

On that matter, the United States Treasury reigned, controlling GM by virtue of the lifeline in bailout loans. But just as Chrysler bondholders wanted a bigger slice of Chrysler, GM's bondholders wanted a bigger slice of the to-be-remodeled GM. Obama's team was willing to bargain, having learned a lesson in May's Chrysler deal. Then, government edict forced big losses on Chrysler bondholders, some of whom, like the Indiana state treasurer, fought the deal in court.

Although the U.S. Supreme Court ultimately declined to hear Indiana's case on Chrysler, Obama's team tried to ease the concerns of GM bondholders by handing them a stake in the GM ownership group. Bonds are a kind of loan repaid over time to the investors who fronted the money. For GM's bondholders, the task force agreed the lenders could exchange the bonds for a ten-percent ownership stake in the "new" GM coming out of bankruptcy. Lenders would lose the billions of dollars still owed on the loans, but they would hold stock in the new GM, stock that could rise in value if GM made money again. It was risky. GM's success wasn't assured. Some analysts pointed out a second bankruptcy might come along in a year or two and erase all value in the "new" GM stock.

Even so, fifty-four percent of the bondholders had accepted the deal by late May, including most of the big banks and pension funds. That wasn't the ninety percent that the auto task force wanted to see in a bankruptcy procedure — ninety percent hinted of a calm courtroom free of challenges by recalcitrant bond investors. Even so, Obama noticeably stood silent rather than chastise GM bondholders as he had chided certain lenders in the Chrysler episode. Chrysler went into bankruptcy in part to bring those lenders to heel. So did General Motors.

GM's filing landed in the Manhattan courtroom of United States Bankruptcy Judge Robert Gerber in the summer of 2009. By then, Henderson already was scaling back GM and sending franchise closure notices to 1,100 auto dealers located in every state and province. Henderson and Koch were acting as if the bankruptcy court was certain to give them a free hand. What they were doing was legal, but the quick 90-day bankruptcy sought by the auto task force was no foregone conclusion. Despite the Obama team's willingness to enlist the bond investors as stakeholders, opponents abounded. One group, calling itself the Unofficial Committee of Family & Dissident GM Bondholders, had hired the prominent Washington, D.C., law firm Patton Boggs to oppose the new ownership plan for GM. Dozens of the dissidents had acquired the bonds as personal investments, including income for retirement. In total, Patton's clients owned about ten percent of GM's $28.5 billion in bonds.

Just as the Chrysler bondholders had argued the UAW would own more than its fair share of Chrysler, the family dissidents made the same point before Gerber, saying the union concessions did not equal the losses faced by the bond investors. Under the plan devised by the auto task force, all the unwanted assets would be retained by the "old" GM in bankruptcy, while the remaining assets went to Vehicle Acquisition Holdings LLC, a new entity to be funded by the United States Treasury. Every share of original stock in "old" GM would lose all value, which is common in bankruptcy. Vehicle Acquisition would send forth a new company, also called General Motors, and issue new shares of ownership. Sixty percent of the new stock would go to the United States Treasury, 17.5 percent to the UAW retirees' medical trust fund, 11.7 percent to the governments of Canada and Ontario, and the remainder to bondholders and others owed money by GM.

The dissidents did not oppose Canada's stake. Leaders in Ottawa had pledged $9 billion (U.S.) in bailout loans to GM Canada, which promised to retain nineteen percent of GM's North American production capacity in the country. But when it came to the UAW, the dissidents argued the deal treated the Detroit-based union better than the bondholders, in violation of longstanding Bankruptcy Code procedures that gave bondholders favored status. Few expected the dissidents would prevail, and they didn't. After all, the Supreme Court had spurned the Indiana state treasurer's similar complaint in the Chrysler case.

Yet, the Patton Boggs' strategy was watched closely by investors outside the family dissident group. The lawyers maintained that the quick bankruptcy sought by the Obama team, known as a Section 363 procedure under the Bankruptcy Code, was a rush job inappropriate for a complicated corporation like GM. More fitting, they said, was a Chapter 11 reorganization, which could last months, even years, and permit the deliberate reordering of the company. Dozens of bondholders outside the family group concurred, not because they wanted to see a deliberate restructuring of GM, but because many were rooting for GM's failure.

In the peculiar world of Wall Street, speculators could buy bonds from the original investors and in turn buy insurance policies that reimbursed them if the borrower went bankrupt or stopped loan payments. Known as credit-default swaps, the insurance had quietly become a pillar of Wall Street since J.P. Morgan & Co. launched the policies in the mid-1990s. Between 2000 and 2008, the value of credit swaps had soared from $900 billion to $42 trillion, a surge that eventually factored into the worldwide credit crisis at the root of the global recession. In any event, a major chunk of the GM bonds were in the hands of investors set to receive as much as $2.3 billion in insurance payments if GM defaulted, reported the Depository Trust & Clearing Corporation.[18]

As the issue simmered in Gerber's courtroom during the summer of 2009, complaints arose from other fields. A group of product liability attorneys took aim of the UAW's large slice in the new GM. The lawyers claimed clients in car accidents owed billions of dollars after judgments against the automaker would be shorted by getting only a small piece of stock in the new GM. Attorneys general from ten states also joined the fray, weighing in on one of the most visible aspects of the GM restructuring to people in the community — the closing of the auto dealerships.

In May, GM had identified 1,100 car lots that missed the mark due to poor sales, low profits, or inadequate investment in the buildings and equipment. This was separate from closing down the Pontiac brand; in truth, most Pontiac dealers also sold other GM products, such as Buick or GMC trucks. They would lose the Pontiacs, but they would keep the other brands. For days, newspapers throughout the country filled pages with articles about local dealers getting letters from GM via FedEx disclosing the company would sever the franchise agreement in 2011. Car dealers advertised extensively in newspapers and on television. In many cities, the dealers were prominent household names. Giving to charity and special civic causes, the dealers often were among the last wealthy hometown merchants on retail strips filled by national chain stores. GM held firm. Executives in Detroit long had wanted to trim dealer numbers to the smaller number of Toyota and Honda. GM's dealer network traced to the 1920s when Chevy competed with Pontiac and both took on Oldsmobile and Buick. As the years wore on, Chevy dealers came to compete with other Chevy dealers, much to the chagrin of the execs in Detroit, who realized the rivalry drove down the price for customers and in turn cut Chevy profits. Honda and Toyota commanded higher vehicle prices in part because they assigned fewer dealers to a territory so competition was minimal between Toyota dealers. To winnow down its dealer network required GM go to court and fight each dealer it wanted to eliminate, a process made lengthy by state franchise laws that tended to favor dealers. Once in bankruptcy court, however, the company could simply ask the judge's consent to sever the franchises at once, eliminating expensive wrangling with each dealer protected by state franchise laws. In all, GM planned to eliminate 2,600 dealerships, starting with the 1,100 identified in May.

Shortly after the bankruptcy filing, Judge Gerber heard from attorneys general protesting in Connecticut, Kentucky, Maryland, Minnesota, Missouri, Nebraska, North Dakota, Ohio, Vermont, and West Virginia. They argued GM was trying to circumvent state laws protecting dealers. The National Automobile Dealers Association, a trade group, vigorously supported the banished dealers, saying GM needed as many outlets as possible to recover lost sales. In Washington, congressmen who had refrained from public comment on the dismantling of GM or the infusion of taxpayer money suddenly weighed in on behalf of the dealers. In spite of such arguments, the White House prevailed and bankruptcy went forward.

But the Obama administration was playing both sides of the fence on the dealership issue. In spite of supporting plans at both Chrysler and GM to cut the number of dealerships, the government had made the grand gesture of announcing it would guarantee up to $4 billion in floor plan loans to surviving dealerships that needed the money to acquire vehicles from the automakers. Worried that auto sales were plummeting in part because banks were refusing to make loans, the government was put in the position of financing auto dealers *and* dealers of recreation vehicles notorious for poor gas mileage. The loan program was announced in

Kokomo, Indiana, in May as the White House put on a special effort to show it was heading off disaster in the industrial Midwest. Dispatched to Kokomo by the administration were Karen Mills, head of the Small Business Administration, and Ed Montgomery, the special envoy to small towns in America hit hardest by the auto industry crisis. Democratic Senator Evan Bayh of Indiana, Mayor Greg Goodnight, and other elected officials also were on hand in the hard-hit town for the press conference. "Countless small businesses, including dealerships, across the country are facing significant challenges as a result of the uncertainty in the auto industry," Mills said. "[We] can offer some dealerships the opportunity to get through these tough economic times by allowing them to keep their inventory and cash flow intact, as well as save the jobs these small businesses provide."

Having the president's emissaries personally disburse aid to recreation vehicle manufacturers and dealers may have struck anyone in Boston or Los Angeles as odd and unusual. No one ever had regarded RV production as an economic engine for America. Sales of new RVs neared 248,000 in 2008, down from the pre-recession level of 390,000 units two years earlier.[19] Yet, in a certain pocket of the country, such as northern Indiana, RV plants were crucial employers. Elkhart, Indiana, was the heart of the industry, the veritable Detroit of RVs. For decades, Elkhart led Indiana as the city with the highest income per job, even though most RV plants were not unionized. Number two in the state in income per job was the UAW bastion of Kokomo with its warren of Chrysler and Delphi plants. Obama, in his campaign leading to the 2008 presidential elections and once in the White House, had visited Elkhart and fixated on the industry as a worthy cause. Yet when it came time to announce dealer aid, it was Kokomo with its concentration of unionized autoworkers that drew the brass from Washington. In terms of national importance, positioning Karen Mills in Kokomo was a blip, but it gave car and RV dealers as well as the UAW a sense someone in Washington was doing something to try to get Americans out into the stores again. For much of the country, the image emanating from the Midwest, at least when it came to the Detroit bailout, had been acrimony and finger pointing.

As dealers, the state attorneys general, and the bondholders argued in bankruptcy court, GM tapped into the $30 billion in new loans dispensed by the Treasury early that summer. In all, the government had committed $50 billion for GM and another $17 billion for General Motors Acceptance Corporation, the car-loan arm now half owned by Cerberus Capital Management, the former owner of Chrysler. With $67 billion flowing to GM and GMAC, and $10 billion in total going to Chrysler, the $77 billion in United States Treasury loans was five and a half times greater than the $14 billion in the Detroit bailout bill spurned by the United States Senate the previous December. Although President George Bush had opened the spigot in 2008 with limited aid for GM and Chrysler, Republican leaders in Washington who were silent in 2008 chortled at Obama's largesse. "No matter how much the president spins GM's bankruptcy as good for the economy, it is nothing more than another government grab of a private company and another handout to the union cronies who helped bankroll his presidential campaign," contended Republican National Committee Chairman Michael Steele.[20]

Obama conceded the government's actions "may give some Americans pause."[21] But the president described the streamlining of GM as an absolute necessity, saying the company was now approaching "the beginning of a new GM, a new GM that can produce the high-quality, safe and fuel-efficient cars of tomorrow . . . [that will] out-compete automakers around the world. . . . And when that happens we can truly say that what is good for General Motors and all who work there is good for the United States of America."[22]

Not long after Obama spoke, the United States Department of Energy finally began to release some of the $25 billion allocated by Congress to retool the American auto industry for fuel-efficient cars; this money was separate from the bailout funds. The first recipients included Tesla, a minor California producer of $109,000 electric cars, and Nissan, Japan's second-largest automaker. A staunch rival of Detroit, Nissan received $1.6 billion, and promised to produce 100,000 electric cars per year at its complex in Smyrna, Tennessee. Money for GM and Chrysler was withheld until each could show they were a viable business. Being viable was a criterion established as a condition for the loans and in the case of GM was an irony. The giant automaker had pioneered the EV1 in the 1990s and had promised to roll out its descendant, the all new, stylish Chevy Volt plug-in hybrid electric car, by 2011.

In Detroit, insiders sensed that even if GM got a green-car loan, its engineering clout had faded. If the future rested on innovative cars, then GM needed to quickly scale up electric car technology, but the old technical know-how was drying up. "People like GM simply can't afford to do research and development anymore," opined Ken Baker, the retired GM vice president for global R&D.[23] Electric car research and battery technology, however, had hardly been a primary goal of the United States government, GM, Ford, or Chrysler. By the end of the first decade in the 2000s, innovations in batteries were coming out of Seoul and Tokyo, the new intellectual centers of battery technology, and lately China. Outposts of the technology were scattered across the United States and Canada. But the question was whether a shrunken GM could muster the resources to reorganize the suppliers and muscle up an advanced technology car before Asian companies took an insurmountable lead in the field. One point was clear: GM would be smaller.

In the spring of 2009, CSM Worldwide released an extraordinary forecast. CSM, a research firm in suburban Detroit, estimates future car sales by model for clients, which include engineers in auto-parts companies trying to decide how much production capacity to allocate for certain model lines. CSM's new report showed that in 2011 the trio of Detroit automakers would assemble fewer vehicles in North American than the thirteen foreign rivals producing cars and trucks on the continent.[24] That never had happened before. Detroit always had produced more than half the vehicles in its home market. But as much as a third of the production capacity would vanish as Chrysler and GM reorganized. By 2012, the Detroit Three together would make only 6 million vehicles, and perhaps 6.5 million by 2015, CSM estimated. Number two Toyota could surpass GM in assembly capacity in its home market. The once undisputed king of the car industry worldwide would assemble only half the number of vehicles it had made a few years earlier.

The report in one respect signaled Detroit's defeat in the car wars. The battle traced to 1983 when a free-trade minded government led by President Ronald Reagan opened the way for the wave of foreign automakers setting up assembly plants in North America. Many would say it was better for Japan Inc. to make cars in North America and employ people here rather than import all its cars from its home country. Nevertheless, an exhausted GM was in retreat by 2009. Tonelson, the conservative economist, suggested trade reform at the national level could aid Detroit if only we would crack down on nations that essentially barred U.S. companies from selling in their countries. Among Americans and members of Congress, however, the will for reform was weak, meaning GM, as well as the other two Detroit-based manufacturers, would be perpetually challenged, fighting to retain sales in their home market while being at a distinct disadvantage in foreign markets. In the years ahead, the North American auto market would resemble Europe's, suggested Jim Gillette, a CSM research analyst. There, a bevy of automakers slug it out. Other than Volkswagen, none is clearly dominant. None has much more market share than its rivals. And none, including Volkswagen, has the profits that pay for a clear edge in exciting technology.

It was a staggering turn of events for GM. Henderson was trying to galvanize the managerial corps, using consultants, stressing urgency. The stricken automaker clearly needed game-changing technology to make its autos stand out. But at the beginning of the twenty-first century, no breakthroughs were at hand. When it came to GM culture, what's clear was Henderson was not dealing with a broken culture. It was *the* culture. For decades, GM prized volume — stamping out 300,000 of this model, 500,000 of that model. There was even a common phrase among insiders — "moving Detroit iron" — as if sheer volume mattered most. Exceptional technical achievements had come along — the automatic transmission and Oldsmobile's Rocket 88 engine in the 1940s, Chevrolet's small-block V-8 in the 1960s, the catalytic converter for exhaust emissions in the 1970s (an invention adopted by every automaker in the world), the EV1 electric car in the 1990s. Since the 1950s, though, innovation had hardly been the cornerstone of the company.

General Motors had gotten so big so fast, surpassing Ford as the number one automaker in 1927, that its executives were less concerned with innovation over the years than keeping White House trust busters from coming after them. By the 1950s, the thinking in GM executive offices was that any amazing technical achievement that led drivers to abandon Ford or Chrysler, and pushed bankruptcy on one of those competitors, could engulf General Motors in an anti-trust probe by a U.S. government intent on warding off monopoly in the nation's single largest industry. "So caution made sense. GM hardly wanted to innovate its way to corporate dismemberment," explained the manufacturing scholars who wrote *The Machine That Changed the World*, a 1990 study by researchers at the Massachusetts Institute of Technology.[25]

Alfred P. Sloan, the legendary CEO who remade GM into *the* model of the modern corporation, had himself pointed out that "it was not necessary to lead in technical design or run the risk of untried experiments [provided that] our cars were at least equal in design to the best of our competitors in a grade."[26] Of course, when those words were written in the 1960s, the company was huge and prosperous, put there by a Sloan managerial style that had helped GM elude bankruptcy in the 1920s and move past Ford to become the world's largest corporation. Yet by the early twenty-first century, in an industry known for its overcapacity worldwide, it clearly was not good enough to merely be "equal" to one's competitors.

Overwhelming General Motors by 2009 was a recession and

ruinous competition in the auto industry. Oddly enough, GM's roots trace to a similar rivalry, the fierce capitalism of the nineteenth century. Weary of the laissez-faire system that touched off numerous bankruptcies in the Panic of 1893, the name for the deep recession then, wealthy industrialists urged the United States government to stand down on enforcing the Sherman Anti-Trust Act. Trusts referred then to what are today called holding companies that control raw materials, factories, and distribution of the finished goods to consumers. When the U.S. Supreme Court ruled an 1895 sugar trust was not necessarily a commercial monopoly in the sugar business, American moguls sensed they were safe from anti-trust crusaders venting on about monopolies.[27] New York banker John Pierpont Morgan led the way, buying small competing steel mills and rolling them into one giant new entity in 1901 he named the United States Steel Corporation. It was the first company capitalized with more than $1 billion. It was not his last. The banker financed a slew of trusts including General Electric, International Harvester, and American Telephone & Telegraph. "A little competition he did not mind, Morgan said, but 'ruinous' competition he believed, in concord with his fellow industrialists, ought to be ended," sociologist Robert Conot pointed out in his history of Detroit, *American Odyssey*.[28]

Following Morgan's lead, Americans went on an acquisition spree. William Durant, an owner of the Durant-Dort Carriage Co., had become a millionaire making horse-drawn wagons north of Detroit in Flint. Durant sensed that just as Morgan dominated steel, he could monopolize automobiles. In 1904, Durant bought the struggling car business of Detroit plumber David D. Buick, who had invented a fast and innovative gasoline engine. Durant, the grandson of a wealthy New England lumberman, moved the business to Flint and poured $1.5 million into Buick Motor Car, the equivalent of about $35 million in 2009 dollars. His success was spectacular. By 1908, nearly 70 car companies operated in Detroit alone, fueled by the city's specialties. Railroad and lumber profits seeded new car ventures. And engineers and machinists were abundantly available to set up plants and make cars, an abundance tracing to the Detroit shops making engines for railroad trains and Great Lakes steamships. Powered by a fast engine, Buick outsold every rival in Detroit, running up profits of nearly $9 million in 1908. Rumors were rife. Conot notes Durant was thought to be angling to roll into one trust the Big Four — Buick, Ford, Oldsmobile offshoot R.E.O., and Chrysler predecessor Maxwell-Briscoe.

Unable to entice Henry Ford to sell — Ford wanted more than Durant was willing to pay — Durant bought Olds Motor Company in 1908 and quickly created General Motors as a holding company, adding Cadillac Motor Corporation in 1909. Durant's dream of an automobile monopoly never came to be, though he built the foundation for a gigantic enterprise. The key to getting big fast was a sure supply of the 10,000 pieces that comprised the early car. Henry Ford was creating a vast complex of shops to turn out auto parts, a business model called vertical integration, while Durant set out to rapidly expand by acquisition. He bought a supply chain that assured reliable sources of auto parts. Within two years, Durant had acquired twenty more companies for GM, primarily manufacturers of auto parts, including Hyatt Roller Bearing, a New Jersey firm run by M.I.T. graduate Alfred P. Sloan. Short on cash after the buying spree, Durant borrowed heavily from Lee Higginson & Co., a Boston investment bank where railroad financier James J. Storrow figured prominently. Storrow decided Durant was incapable of managing the huge company he had created. The banker quickly forced out Durant as president of General Motors. (Storrow also sent to Flint to run Buick a gifted supervisor from a Pennsylvania railroad yard, Walter Chrysler, who later took control of Maxwell, renaming it Chrysler Corporation.)

Even after he was pushed out of GM, Durant did not give up. Long an avid gambler, Durant plowed stock market winnings into a fledgling car business of Louis Chevrolet, a French car racer drawn to the new Indianapolis 500 race track. Durant also used his winnings to quietly buy shares in General Motors, amassing enough stock by 1915 to wrest back control of the company. Two years later, GM and the Chevrolet business were merged, but the recession following the First World War exposed Durant's wild speculation on the stock market. He'd pledged $20 million worth of General Motors shares owned by GM as collateral on loans along with $14 million of his own money — $34 million in total, or about $680 million in current dollars, all of it used to buy stocks. When the recession flattened the stock market, and Henry Ford launched a price war in 1920, GM's own stock price plunged. Creditors demanded Durant repay the loans. Unable to come up with so much cash, Durant turned to Sloan and chemical maker Pierre Du Pont, a GM board member made rich on war contracts for explosives. Du Pont ousted Durant, installed himself as president of GM, and arranged a new issue of GM stock to help pay the entrepreneur's debts. J. Pierpont Morgan, Du Pont, and a company in Great Britain called Explosive Trades Limited bought the bulk of the new stock.[29]

With Durant out of the way, Du Pont tempered General Motors' empire building. He put Sloan in charge of daily operations with orders to restore the corporation's financial footing. General Motors was a passive owner of independent car companies run by seasoned and determined managers who often competed for the same customers. A legacy of their determination was the proliferation of dealerships in almost every town and city. Sloan, an engineer by training, quickly adopted Du Pont's mode of managing his East Coast chemical works. It became the basis for the modern American corporation, not markedly different in concept from the modern GM where Obama had just sacked Richard Wagoner. Under Sloan, a central office handled finances and made broad policy decisions. Executives in the central office split into committees to oversee the operations. They need not know precisely how to design, engineer, assemble, advertise, or sell cars. Hired experts handled those chores in the car divisions. What the executives had to understand was finance. GM was the first large company to funnel all the financial decisions into one central office. Managers there were aided by a new forecasting system that reached into dealerships to assess future vehicle sales. Power moved from the entrepreneurs in the car divisions to the central office. If a Buick superintendent came to the office for cash to design a new engine, the money was doled out if the finance committee judged the investment sound. "Decisions were made by committee," Conot explained. "Faceless bureaucracy was carried to the ultimate, and humanity was submerged within *the system*."[30] Sloan assigned each division a specific market segment. Cadillac, a luxury make since its inception, took the top price tier, Chevrolet the bottom, while Buick, Oldsmobile, and Pontiac were arrayed across the middle. The idea was a young man would start with a Chevy, then graduate to Pontiac or a powerful Oldsmobile, and later, in their prime earning years, depending on their taste, turn to a respectable Buick or the flashier Cadillac. Each model was priced to provide precisely a fifteen percent return on investment. With each brand hewing to a single price bracket, no longer would GM's sticker prices fluctuate with the pulse of the economy, a common occurrence in the 1910s and 1920s. "General Motors was separating itself from the competitive operations of the marketplace . . ." Conot wrote. "The concept of 'administered prices' was being substituted for laissez-faire."[31]

While the company was never the monopoly envisioned by Durant, it was the next best thing under Sloan, a trust so large, so efficient, the worst vicissitudes of the market were sundered like an ocean liner parting the waves. When Henry Ford idled his plants in 1927 to retool for the Model A, successor to the legendary Model T, GM surpassed Ford as the country's largest car maker. That year, GM ranked among the ten American corporations valued at more than $1 billion. Smaller automakers, unable to compete with GM, went out of business. Aided by Morgan and Du Pont money, Sloan steered GM through the Great Depression, the Second World War, and into the rich consumer era created in the post-war prosperity. Nearly everyone in America had believed the memorable line delivered in the late 1950s by ex–GM president Charles "Engine Charley" Wilson, later the United States

Secretary of Defense, when he said: "What's good for the country is good for General Motors, and what's good for General Motors is good for the country." Other than the United States government, and the military armadas created for the 1940s' war, Durant's brainchild was arguably the largest and perhaps the most complicated enterprise ever assembled in the history of the world. One division, Chevrolet, was nearly as large as all of Ford Motor Company. The prime edict became to never idle the vehicle assembly lines. Embedded in GM culture, that edict eventually shaped labor relations with the United Auto Workers and led to the unsustainable legacy costs for each of the Detroit Three, as well as made innovation redundant so long as factories were humming and sales were good. In time, this culture led Obama and Rattner, and Henderson and Koch, to begin the dismantling of General Motors.

What they were tearing down, of course, was an industrial empire. Bill Wylam had seen it at its peak. And he had seen first hand the roots of its decline. The Purdue University graduate was a young engineer in the 1960s and 1970s at the sprawling GM Delco Remy complex in Anderson, Indiana. The city was then home to more than 20,000 GM autoworkers, the second-largest concentration of GM employees after Flint, Michigan. Delco Remy traced to two companies purchased in the empire-building era by Durant. Like GM itself, Delco Remy had quickly swelled. Engine Charley Wilson himself had run the division when it was considered a kind of West Point for GM electrical engineers. Starters, alternators, and other critical electrical components used on every GM engine and car poured out of the Anderson works for delivery to the car assembly lines located throughout North America. "You couldn't let anything happen on a Delco Remy line. If something happened it could lead to the shutdown of General Motors," Wylam remembered. "The cardinal sin was shutting down any GM assembly line."[32]

UAW officials in Anderson fully appreciated their magnificent bargaining chip. Executives in GM's Detroit central office were reluctant to take on the UAW if a strike would curtail production.

Deprived of inventory, GM dealers could lose customers to Ford, Chrysler, and the old American Motors, a Detroit company created in the 1954 merger of automakers Hudson and Nash. Less costly for GM in the short term was to simply accede to the union rather than wage a fight for market share after a strike ended. A union official, Wylam remembers, once demanded that a friend discharged for sexually assaulting a woman in an Anderson plant be reinstated, and the friend was back on the job. Union officials could insist no electrician should have to pick up a pipe — that was the pipefitter's job — and it was written into the contract. "We'd be told, 'Settle that right now and get that contract signed,'" Wylam said. "It resulted in some really insane agreements."

There was one knock-down fight, the bitter strike of 1970, which the union won, gaining the retirement provision that guaranteed a pension after thirty years of service, as well as annual raises to keep up with inflation. Yet serious strikes were few in the post-war prosperity. GM became known as "Generous Motors." For the most part, the union got what it wanted without strikes while the company quietly trickled jobs to Mexico from Ohio, Michigan, and Indiana. As long as Detroit's automakers competed only among themselves, the companies could afford ever larger benefits. Rising costs simply were passed on to consumers, leaving the companies prosperous. Spearheaded by imaginative design, GM controlled nearly half the vehicle market in the United States into the 1970s. For the young and upwardly mobile — say a law school graduate buying that first nice automobile — muscle cars like the Pontiac GTO or Oldsmobile Cutlass 442 were the car of choice. For the slightly older male swinger (and the cars were heavily marketed to males) there was the Buick Wildcat or Pontiac Bonneville. The trend-setting 1965 Ford Mustang spawned other so-called pony cars such as the Chevrolet Camaro and Dodge Challenger and remained a class leader for decades. With an unprecedented economic boom under way in the post–Second World War era, fueled by the massive stimulus spending for the space program, the material going into the Vietnam War, and even the construction of the interstate highway system, the last thing the executives in Detroit wanted was a strike. Between 1960 and 1970, UAW hourly wages rose from $19.53 to $24.63, expressed in 2004 dollars, reaching $30.58 by 1980, also in inflation-adjusted dollars. And there were accumulating gains in those legacy costs — the retiree health care benefits and the pensions — that were to prove even more significant down the road.

Despite the wage and benefit gains, America's new focus on individuality bred a defiant generation of young autoworkers at a time of social upheaval. In the 1960s, nearly every social current that swirled through the country came through Detroit — from the great migration of Southerners to the North, to the bluesy new sound of rock and roll, the tolerance for drugs, the anti-establishment attitude embellished by middle-class youths opposed to the Vietnam draft. While its popular image was blue-collar, Detroit was indeed a great and sophisticated industrial city. Home to one of the largest concentrations of engineers in the country, and one of the very largest middle-class black populations on earth, Detroit ranked fifth in population among American cities with 1.7 million residents. It was, as Conot explained in *American Odyssey*, a success — a testament to America's ability to bring together people of all colors and walks of life and find a way to move forward. This was the odyssey in his title. He meant that if a place like Detroit moved ahead, America prospered. Yet, by the mid-1960s, Detroit clearly was breaking down. On the blocks around GM's head office, muggings, shootings, and street violence were so common that disc jockeys at rock-and-roll radio station CKLW, located just across the Detroit River in Windsor, Ontario, routinely referred to themselves on the air as broadcasting from the murder capital of the world. Detroit's massive riot, set off in 1967 by a police raid of an after-hours bar, went unsuppressed until combat units of the U.S. Army's 82nd Airborne division reinforced the Michigan National Guard. No one ever linked the riots to unrest in the plants, though the book *Detroit: I Do Mind Dying* contended a nascent urban revolution rooted in the riots was festering in the plants among disgruntled autoworkers. "Their rebellion is expressed in extraordinary absenteeism, particularly on Mondays and Fridays, in chronic lateness, in the open use of drugs, in poor workmanship, in repeated demands for earlier retirement, in sabotage, and in the wildcat strike."[33] It was not quite as if Karl Marx had arrived in Detroit, but the whiff of socialist dreaming embedded in the book caught the tenor of a 1970s generation that came to abhor the manufacturing jobs of the industrial Midwest. "The capitalistic work ethic has been discredited," *I Do Mind Dying* proclaimed in 1975. "Men and women no longer wish to spend forty to fifty years performing dull, monotonous, and uncreative work."

While the United Auto Workers and GM had been preoccupied with dividing the profits of an ever expanding American market, unnoticed was the hard work in Japan. In Tokyo, Nissan engineers in particular were impressed with the sporty BMW 1600 small sedan made in Germany. By 1968, Nissan engineer Yutaka Katayama had adapted several of the 1600's features, including four-wheel independent suspension on a rear-drive platform and sporty dual carburetors in the Datsun 510, a vehicle designed for export to the United States. In Japan, few consumers could afford such a car, but it would fit precisely in the American subcompact market, showing that Nissan "was capable of not just improving its small, durable little cars, but of going ahead, giving the low-end customer something that had never been available before, an inexpensive, sporty, mass-produced sedan," says David Halberstam's book on the Nissan-Ford rivalry, *The Reckoning*. "The 510 marked the beginning of the end of the small car in America as a clumsy, flimsy econobox. It was a fulfillment . . . of Katayama's vision, of taking the best of modern European engineering and marrying it to Japanese manufacturing expertise to produce an inexpensive, small, rugged car that was also high-performing."[34]

Small cars from Japan and Europe cars had steadily gained acceptance with American drivers throughout the 1960s. Imports accounted for about twenty percent of the United States' car market in the early 1970s, a not insignificant sum. But what finally hammered home the notion of imports as a competitive threat was a political crisis in the Middle East. The 1973 Arab oil embargo doubled gasoline prices overnight at American gas stations, a problem later magnified when the United States government botched fuel allocation procedures. Small cars suddenly were prized for their fuel economy, catching Detroit off guard. Ford eventually flirted with bankruptcy, while only the promise of $1 billion in federal loan guarantees saved Chrysler. General Motors, far larger than its rivals, had deeper pockets and avoided financial trouble then. It also had what looked to be a ready solution in the Chevrolet Vega, a subcompact designed to fend off the refined little imports like the Datsun 510 streaming into North America.

Before the Vega, compact cars from Detroit such as the Ford Falcon or Dodge Lancer had really been only slightly smaller versions of the same basic platforms and engineering designs Detroit had been building for years, though the Chevrolet Corvair had been a notable exception. It copied a Porsche and Volkswagen rear-engine layout with horizontally opposed cylinders and also featured four-wheel independent suspension. The Corvair's popularity quickly waned after crusading anti-corporate lawyer Ralph Nader attacked it in his 1965 book, *Unsafe at Any Speed: The Designed-In Dangers of the American Automobile*. The second generation Corvair, introduced in 1965, was a very good handling car, but the damage to its reputation had already been done and the car was discontinued in 1969. That left the Vega to take on the challenge of standing out from Detroit's lackluster line up of compacts, which in any case had started to grow in physical dimensions and size of their power plants. The Vega was small, sleek, modern, and light with great gas mileage. GM even put in a new, automated assembly line built at Lordstown, Ohio, just for the Vega, but labor strife there soon erupted and quickly colored America's perception of the import fighter. The strife in part traced to the anti-trust sentiment taking hold in Washington at the end of the 1960s. Executives created a new unit called

General Motors Assembly Division with the single idea of casting it off as an independent company if the administration of President Richard Nixon ever tried to break up General Motors on anti-trust grounds. Among the plants taken over from Chevrolet by General Motors Assembly was the Vega factory. With the change in control came a new management team that decided Chevrolet had overstaffed Lordstown. When jobs were cut away, the UAW cried "speed-up" and walked out. Even when they returned, labor strife continued in what came to be known as "Lordstown syndrome" — a plant so modern in its automation the workers were bored, numbed, and unusually destructive. According to a retrospective in the respected trade newspaper *Automotive News*, conflict at the Lordstown complex hit a peak in 1971 and 1972, just as the Vietnam War protests spread beyond elite college campuses, where many students had learned to evade the draft, to a wide array of state colleges and into the working classes itself, where young people had not. As the popular culture took a decidedly anti-corporate bent, Lordstown workers put foreign objects in engines and gas tanks, intentionally left parts off vehicles, slashed upholstery, scratched paint, set fires, took drugs and drank alcohol at the plant, staged illegal walkouts, and frequently failed to show up for work at all, the trade newspaper reported. It was "working-class resistance to work itself," said the report, quoting Socialist writer Ken Weller.[35]

Only a skirmish in the car wars that would come, the Vega episode proved pivotal for GM. Once the Vega failed to catch on with motorists, imported cars poured into the United States. In a new era fond of open American markets, the massive Detroit auto industry ushered in by the late nineteenth-century barons began to unravel. Nevertheless, GM fought back. The leader who emerged to take on the imports in the 1980s was Roger Smith, a diminutive finance man enamored of technology. Smith poured resources into new plants and mimicked the Japanese, deploying painting and welding robots and reconfiguring GM's small and midsize fleets to the front-wheel drive systems popular on

Japanese cars, spending more than $40 billion on the endeavors. Not only was the change over in transmissions required by a switch from rear-drive to front-drive a hugely expensive engineering chore, GM was at a decided disadvantage. Chrysler and Ford, both on the edge of bankruptcy, closed dozens of auto-parts plants or sold them to suppliers who did not have top-of-the-scale wage agreements with the UAW. Hanging on to the supply companies purchased in the Durant era, GM became the most expensive producer in Detroit.

Rather than shed plants, or go "lean and mean" early, GM restructured in a way that merged divisions but both dispirited and disoriented the engineering corps. Smith's reorganization merged many aspects of the car divisions — keeping them separate in name only for the most part — and accelerated the trend of look-alike cars from the GM divisions. At the bottom of the lineup was the Chevrolet Chevette, introduced in America for the 1976 model year as a hurry-up replacement for the Vega. A similar car had been sold by GM elsewhere in the world, including in Brazil, for several years. Though technologically inferior to the Vega, it actually was more reliable than its predecessor, if not competing imports, and remained one of the best-selling cars in America for several years. With Smith's restructuring in the 1980s, though, models coming out of the GM studios started to look alike as the engineering and design jobs in the various divisions were meshed to cut costs. What was worse, the new front-wheel drive cars in the heart of GM's most important market segment were riddled by mechanical problems. Known inside the company as the X-cars, the code name used by the engineers and designers, the Buick Skylark, Chevrolet Citation, Oldsmobile Omega, and Pontiac Phoenix were the fresh midsize sedans meant to hold the middle segment of the car market, where the big volumes and profits were. As the X-cars reached the dealer showrooms, so did competing offerings from Japan. Automakers there quickly had grasped the same principles used to launch the Datsun 510 to move into the middle of the market with increasingly capable sedans. Though the original 510 was a rear-drive model, the Japanese largely had begun to shed such platforms during this time frame, only to return to rear-drive for their high-end models and true sports cars years later. Front-drive cars, in which the engine is packaged with the transmission in a front transaxle that drives the front wheels, have some handling advantages in poor weather and are cheaper to produce once expensive retooling is completed. Cars from Fiat in Italy and the Mini in England must be credited for developing the front-drive concept. But such cars present serious handling challenges when coupled with more powerful engines in part because of a phenomenon known as torque steer, in which drivers feel like they're wrestling with their steering wheels on hard acceleration. Though GM first experimented with large front-drive cars in the 1960s via the surprising Oldsmobile Toronado, it was significant that the high-end German and Italian manufacturers never abandoned rear drive for their premium cars, which not coincidentally had the highest profit potential per unit. GM ultimately abandoned rear drive in a whole slew of look-alike full-size cars by the late 1980s, too, which in retrospect was a mistake for this end of the market. GM in recent years had been trying to rectify that error with a new generation of well-regarded rear-drive Cadillacs but as with everything else from this company the change was slow-going.

If GM had any hope of completely fending off the imports, the notion was dashed in 1983. The U.S. Justice Department sued General Motors, claiming 1.1 million 1980 X-model autos were delivered with faulty brakes.[36] Even attempts to modernize the top-of-the line Cadillac proved hollow. A new 6.0 liter V-8 that shut down two to four cylinders at highway speed to save gas proved a failure with the unreliable electronics of the time. Oldsmobile gasoline engines converted to high-mileage diesels were out-and-out lemons, leading to massive complaints from unwary buyers, though diesel-powered cars had been a growing trend in Europe. Owners started to trade in their defect-ridden GM models for foreign sedans. Other consumers just didn't like Detroit's new strategy of sharing motors and platforms between different brands — GM specifically stopped touting its Oldsmobile "Rocket V-8" when auto mechanics everywhere pointed out that it was the same engine found in lower-priced Chevrolets (though, it must be said, many companies worldwide now share platforms and engines between different models and brands).

GM now was losing ground in the small, middle, and luxury car classes. By 1990, GM accounted for only about thirty-eight percent of the American vehicle market. Weary of the shoddy workmanship in Detroit, middle-class baby boomers had embraced German and Japanese cars. The demographics of this switch were interesting, and telling. The import buyer overall was much more likely to be younger, better educated, and more affluent than the American car buyer, meaning once they bought an import brand they were likely to buy many more during their lifespan, including the more profitable upscale models that all manufacturers were offering, the Japanese and Koreans included. This in fact was the basis of GM's mildly entertaining ad campaign of several years ago in which the corporation touted certain cars as "Not your father's Oldsmobile." The problem was, many younger consumers believed that this is exactly what GM — and, by extension, Ford and Chrysler — were trying to foist on them. The Oldsmobile nameplate was discontinued altogether in 2004.

Instead of mandating that GM engineers deliver better performing and more reliable piston-engine cars for the models already in its stable of brands, Roger Smith dreamed big in other ways. Ford execs for years had praised electric cars, but put nothing on the road. Determined that electric cars could carry GM into the future, Smith set in motion the $1 billion EV1 project. Certain that technology was the key to competing with the Japanese on quality, which in itself was a promising change from the old GM philosophy that merely being "equal" was good enough, Smith led GM's $2.5 billion acquisition in 1984 of Electronic Data Systems, the Texas computer company founded by Ross Perot. Two years later, GM spent $5.2 billion for Hughes Aircraft, an aerospace giant based in Los Angeles. Smith also launched Saturn, the new small-car division that took more than five years to get off the ground. By the time the first small Saturn sedan rolled out of the new plant near Spring Hill, Tennessee, in 1990, it was deemed capable and reliable by the auto magazines — the best small car ever built by an American car company in America — but still lacking in comparison to Honda's Civic and Toyota's Corolla, which now dominated the small car segment.

Then GM changed horses in midstream. Truck and SUV sales took off in the late 1980s, giving a false sense of security for all of the Detroit Three. By then, Smith was on his way out at GM, ready for retirement. Boardroom coups shook the executive ranks. Realizing that its labor costs barred it from breaking even on the $12,000 price tag on a small car, GM declined to engineer its own Chevette replacement. Instead it acquired stakes in Suzuki and Izusu and brought over models from the second-tier Japanese carmakers rebadged as Chevrolets. Perhaps worse, GM leaders neglected the EV1 and all but forgot Saturn. A Saturn entry into the all-important midsize market also was delayed for years. When that car, the Saturn L, finally was introduced for model year 2000 (a whopping decade after the original small Saturn) it was deemed an also-ran by the auto magazines, merely an okay car based on a European platform with dull styling that excited no one. It did not sell well. Also lost was the notion of Delco Remy as a kind of West Point capable of engineering a new fleet of electric cars. The division, a key to bringing out the EV1, was folded into a larger new business unit called Delphi, which brought control of a welter of parts businesses purchased in the Durant era into the hands of a few executives. Delphi was spun off as a separate company in 1999. In Japan, which has no independent oil supply of its own, Toyota and Honda each had launched hybrid-electric cars for congested Tokyo streets. In America, oil traded for $10 per barrel and a gallon of gasoline still cost much less than a gallon of milk. Instead of pursuing hybrid or electric car technology with great vigor, GM investments now went for new assembly plants in Eastern Europe and China while it shed jobs in the United States. What fed the company were truck and SUV profits, which also was the case for Ford and its best-selling F150 and Ranger pickups and Ford Explorer SUV, and even for Chrysler, which had purchased the iconic Jeep brand and plants from France's Renault and the dying American Motors Corporation partnership. GM actually came to the SUV boom late, bringing out a credible challenger to the Ford Explorer, a benchmark midsize sport-utility, only after a redesign of its Chevy Blazer well into the 1990s. In the economic boom of the decade, GM still made money, even as its share of the market fell to twenty-eight percent by the end of the decade.

GM rolled into the 2000s, shedding jobs, reliant as ever on its trucks. Capable and good-looking new sedans such as the Cadillac CTS, Chevrolet Malibu and Buick Lucerne had been engineered, but most of the affluent baby boomer consumers who had come of age in the 1970s and 1980s, when quality in Detroit was waning, still preferred the cars from Japan and Europe. It was like parents would tell their daughters prior to the sexual revolution of the 1960s — once you've lost your reputation it's hard to get it back. When oil prices spiked in 2006, truck sales eased and GM profits softened. When a recession set in by late 2008 and choked off the market both for gas-guzzling pickups, SUVs, and many family sedans, as well, GM just ran out of time, ran out of ideas, and ran out of cash. Even the collective bargaining agreement of 2007 with the UAW, which had meant to help the company in the long run, was proving calamitous. It was that contract that shifted responsibility for the ruinous retiree health care benefits to the employee-run VEBA, but only after GM (and the other Detroit-based manufacturers) would deposit billions and billions in cash into those health care trusts, forcing them to actually borrow money to fund the VEBAs, money they could not afford to repay once the recession and auto industry crisis set in. By the time of the 2009 bankruptcy, GM held only eighteen percent of the auto and light truck market in the United States and was a ward of the federal government. Toyota, also chagrined by the same recession, quickly offered help for its bankrupt rival — it offered to sell Prius hybrid technology for use in GM vehicles.

It was a staggering turn of events. And it was why Al Koch and his team of financial analysts remained busy on the thirty-eighth floor of the Renaissance Center, busy dismantling General Motors, by then a towering symbol of industrial blight for many in America.

---

1. Michael J. de la Merced, "At G.M., He's in Charge of Selling the Leftovers," *New York Times*, June 5, 2009, B1.
2. Carol Hopkins, "Turnaround Specialist from Bloomfield Hills Will Lead GM Restructuring Effort," *Oakland Press*, June 2, 2009, A1.
3. de la Merced.
4. Dana Milbank, "Obama Taking Taxpayers on the Government Motors Ride," *Washington Post*, June 2, 2009, A02.
5. Ken Bensinger and Martin Zimmerman, "GM in Chapter 11: The Nation's Opinions," *Los Angeles Times*, June 2, 2009, A1.
6. Amy Thomson and Katie Merx, "Whitacre Vows To 'Learn About Cars' as GM Chairman," *Bloomberg News*, June 10, 2009, http://www.buffalonews.com/businesstoday/businessfinance/story/710013.html.
7. Joseph Szczesny, "General Motors Shuffles Executives," *Oakland Press*, April 8, 1997, B8.
8. David Welch, "Henderson's Strategy to Fix GM," *Business Week*, June 19, 2009, http://www.businessweek.com/magazine/content/09_26/b4137002878880.htm?campaign_id=yhoo.
9. Bill Vlasic, "G.M. Insider Wants to Show He's Tough Enough," *New York Times*, June 16, 2009, B1.
10. Paul Ingrassia, "How GM Lost Its Way," *Wall Street Journal*, June 3, 2009, http://online.wsj.com/article/SB124389995447074461.html.
11. Welch.
12. Bensinger and Zimmerman.
13. David E. Sanger, "The 31-Year-Old in Charge of Dismantling G.M.," *New York Times*, June 1, 2009, A1.
14. Jackie Calmes, "President's Economic Circle Keeps Tensions at a Simmer," *New York Times*, June 8, 2009, A1.
15. Bensinger and Zimmerman.
16. John Ketzenberger, "GM's 'Rebirth': May as well Save the Cigars," *Indianapolis Star*, June 28, 2009, 1D.
17. Alan Tonelson, chief economist of the U.S. Business & Industry Council, was interviewed by Ted Evanoff on June 23, 2009.
18. George White, "Investors Want Speedy Payments on GM Swaps," The Deal.com, June 10, 2009, http://www.thedeal.com/dealscape/2009/06/gm_credit_default_swaps_paymen.php.
19. Bruce Schreiner and Dan Strumpf, "RV Sales Shift to Slow Lane," *Columbus Dispatch*, December 6, 2008, http://www.dispatch.com/live/content/business/stories/2008/12/06/rv_blues.ART_ART_12-06-08_C10_2GC57B7.html.
20. Jim Puzzanghera, "GM in Chapter 11/ Government; Obama Vows To Take Passive Role," *Los Angeles Times*, June 2, 2009, B1.
21. Puzzanghera.
22. Milbank.
23. Ken Baker was interviewed by Ted Evanoff on June 14, 2009.
24. Ted Evanoff, "GM Dealer Cuts Under Way," *Indianapolis Star*, May 16, 2009, 10A.
25. James P. Womack, Daniel T. Jones, Daniel Roos, and Donna S. Carpenter, *The Machine That Changed the World* (New York: Rawson Associates, 1990), 128.
26. *The Machine That Changed the World*, 128.
27. Edwin P. Hoyt Jr., *The House of Morgan* (New York: Dodd Mead & Co., 1966), 238.
28. Robert Conot, *American Odyssey* (New York: William Morrow & Co., 1974), 149.

29. Conot, 243.
30. Conot, 243; italics are Conot's.
31. Conot, 243.
32. Retired General Motors engineer Bill Wylam, of Indianapolis, was interviewed by Ted Evanoff on May 4, 2009.
33. Dan Georgakas and Marvin Surkin, *Detroit: I Do Mind Dying* (New York: St Martin's Press Inc., 1975), 7.
34. David Halberstam, *The Reckoning* (New York: William Morrow & Co., 1986), 440.
35. Harry Stoffer, "Lordstown: Man vs. Machine – and GM Was the Big Loser," *Automotive News*, September 15, 2008, Supplement S-206.
36. Leslie Maitland Werner, "G.M. Is Sued by U.S. on X-Car Defects Involving Brakes," *New York Times*, August 4, 1983, A1.

CHAPTER 8

Reuther's Ghost

JUNE 29, 2009, WAS A RED-LETTER DAY for Chrysler employees in Kokomo, Indiana — not less than graduation day for college graduates, or when the doctors let you go home after a long stay in rehab. An eight-week-long, court-ordered shutdown after Chrysler's April 30 bankruptcy petition finally was over. All twenty-nine Chrysler plants in North America had been idle since May 1 and thousands of workers sent home, including 4,500 in Kokomo, where all of Chrysler's automatic transmissions are made. This was a grand reopening of the plants, a grand day under sunny skies and temperatures in the upper eighties in north Central Indiana, and a great day to be going to work again.

Veteran quality control employee Susan Perry was back at work, too. "Today was interesting!" she emailed a friend after her shift was over, exclamation point included. "We had posters and banners up and the plant was extensively cleaned to show a good front for the returning workers. We all hope this works but again, we have seen this show before. . . . Supposedly, if things don't turn around, the plant manager, etc. will be fired. But if the vehicles we make do not sell it is all for naught."

Perry, fifty-one, began at Chrysler in 1978, but was laid off for a ten-year stretch and is far from qualifying for her "thirty-and-out" pension, the holy grail of all autoworkers. She voted for the latest contract modifications in April of 2009, more correctly known as the Addendum to the 2007 Collective Bargaining Agreement, and which included a range of concessions meant to help Chrysler qualify for additional bailout money from both the

American and Canadian governments. GM workers also approved similar concessions to save their company. While there were some minor differences in the modifications with GM and Chrysler, overall they were similar. Besides a two-tier pay scale for some new hires and the establishment of a union-run Voluntary Employees' Beneficiary Association (VEBA) to administer retiree health care benefits already negotiated in 2007, the union now agreed to: accepting company stock to partly fund the VEBA, elimination of dental and vision benefits for retirees, a switchover from a defined benefit pension plan to a 401K savings plan in which both workers and management would make cash contributions, some limitations in the Supplemental Unemployment Benefits plan generally known as "SUB-pay," and changes in work rules that would allow the companies to combine job classifications in the skilled trades, thereby making it easier for management to assign work.

The UAW also agreed to a limited no-strike clause for new contract negotiations set to commence in 2011, meaning the union would not strike over unsettled issues during that time, but would submit them to binding arbitration.

Annual cost of living adjustments were canceled for the time being, and some additional changes in work rules made it easier for the companies to fire bad employees. "They now have a new attendance program," said Perry. "You have six occurrences and on the seventh occurrence you will be fired. It'll be none of this where Joe has been fired seventeen times and the union managed to get him his job back."

Overtime rules were relaxed, too. Hourly rate employees now will be paid overtime only if they work more than forty hours in a week; this allows the employers to keep workers on the line more than eight hours in a single day if needed without immediately worrying about overtime costs.

Other concessions made in 2009 looked minor from the outside, though perhaps only from the outside. "We gave up a break," said Perry. "If you're on the actual assembly line you realize how precious those breaks are."

UAW president Ron Gettelfinger, always succinct, told his membership exactly why the union leadership recommended the concessions in a letter sent to all workers in late April 2009. Gettelfinger rarely speaks directly to media. It was all about making the smaller sacrifices to save the core benefits, about sacrificing the pawn in the name of overall strategy, as one might say in chess. "While we realize the proposed sacrifices for UAW members are painful, we fought to maintain our wages, our health care, and our jobs," he wrote.[1]

Autoworkers agreed, accepting the give backs in overwhelming numbers. At Chrysler, eighty-two percent of production workers, eighty percent in skilled trades, ninety percent of clericals, and ninety-four percent of engineers voted in favor of concessions, the UAW said, while the tally at GM among all classes was seventy-four percent in favor. Other stakeholders in GM and Chrysler also made painful concessions, willingly or not. Nearly 800 Chrysler dealers lost their franchises in early June, and all of GM's Pontiac dealers will lose their franchises either in 2010 or 2011, though many of them also sell other GM products, such as Buick or GMC trucks. Bondholders at Chrysler received less than thirty cents a dollar on money owed them, and GM bondholders were scheduled to receive only a small ownership stake in the new GM for their troubles.

While Gettelfinger spoke of "painful concessions," some autoworkers surmised they had done better than other stakeholders in the auto industry. "I actually thought we came out a little better than I thought we would," said Sylvester Stafford, the veteran GM Marion Stamping Plant die maker who works on body panels for light trucks and the new Camaro. His main gripe? The 2009 contract modification meant he'd have to use thirty-two hours of vacation time to make up for the traditional Fourth of July week the company previously gave to workers gratis as part of the annual summer shutdown; July the Fourth remained a paid holiday, however.

In spite of overwhelming rank-and-file support, some union members and activists were not at all happy with the 2009 modifications, or the 2007 contract for that matter. They understood that jobs had been saved, but at what cost? They harkened back to the philosophical and moral underpinnings of the labor movement itself in the nineteenth and early twentieth centuries. For them, unions existed to protect the entire working class, not just a dwindling membership base for any one union, and certainly not to protect the owners of the means of production.

Walter Reuther, president of the UAW from 1946 until his death in 1970 — a man who had traveled to the Soviet Union in the early 1930s and had worked in an auto factory in Gorky — treated the United Auto Workers as the vanguard of the labor movement in America in pretty much the same way the Soviets viewed the Communist Party as the vanguard of the proletariat. Reuther and his activist brother, Victor, who also had gone to Russia, were early Socialists who wanted to make sure the workingman and workingwoman received the same benefits and had the same decent lives that the professional and business classes in America enjoyed. In particular, early on the Reuthers supported social security for all, national health insurance, and a guaranteed annual wage, whether or not work was available. Walter Reuther, who also led the left-leaning Council of Industrial Organizations for years and was a co-founder of the Americans for Democratic Action, had been a UAW powerhouse long before he was elected president in 1946. His main competition? The Communists, who by one authoritative estimate numbered 500 leadership positions by 1941.[2]

Walter Reuther was both more patriotic and pragmatic than some of his more radical contemporaries. For example, Communists in both the UAW and the CIO preached isolationism prior to the Second World War, wanted to concentrate on working-class issues, and call strikes to bring the capitalists to heel. They knew that a war economy would not tolerate industrial action of this sort. Yet the Communist factions, led in part by Mike Quill of the United Transport Workers, a constituent member of the CIO, abruptly changed his position after the German invasion of the Soviet Union on June 22, 1941; the implication was that the Communists didn't care about protecting England or America, but only the Soviet Union. Walter Reuther made much of Quill's change of heart. "Such complete hypocrisy turns one's stomach," he wrote (to his wife). "What a hell of a spot they will be in if Joe [Stalin] folds up and patches things with Adolph [Hitler]."[3]

The Communist factions either instigated or had supported prominent strikes in the auto industry early in the Second World War, albeit prior to America's formal involvement in the conflict. A major strike at the Ford River Rouge Plant in April 1941 was sparked by the dismissal of several employees who had lobbied fellow workers to join the United Auto Workers; the first Pulitzer Prize for photography was given to Milton "Pete" Brooks of the *Detroit News* for his image of strikers beating a "scab" with clenched fists and sticks just outside the factory walls during the walkout.[4] It was a scene reminiscent of events at the same factory four years earlier, when Walther Reuther and three associates from the UAW were beaten by Ford security men for distributing leaflets, allegedly on company property.

The 1941 Rouge strike was interesting in that most of the strike breakers were African-Americans recently up from the South, while the picketers outside were both black and white.[5] Ford was the last of the Detroit Three to recognize the UAW, but had no choice after the National Labor Relations Board authorized a union certification vote for the workers.

Industrial strikes largely disappeared from the American landscape during the war effort but came back with a vengeance once the war ended. Largely as a result of rationing ending and price caps coming off, consumer prices shot up throughout the nation when the war ended. What $1 could buy in March 1945 cost $1.23 by March 1947, according to the Federal Reserve Bank of St. Louis. The twelve-month period after V-J Day (Japan's surrender in August 1945) saw 4,630 work stoppages involving 5 million workers cumulatively totaling 120 million lost days of work. The biggest was a UAW strike against General Motors in November 1945 that put 320,000 pickets on the streets.[6] The proximate cause of the GM strike was the refusal of management to "open the books" after claiming it couldn't afford the concessions the UAW was demanding. In negotiating an end to the strike, Reuther and Harry Coen, GM assistant director of personnel, engaged in heated conversation.

Coen: Is the UAW fighting the fight of the whole world?

Reuther: We have been fighting to hold prices and increase purchasing power. We are making our little contribution in that respect.

Coen: Why don't you get down to your size and get down to the type of job you are supposed to be doing as a trade-union leader, and talk about money you would like to have for your people, and let the labor statesmanship go to hell for a while.[7]

By the late 1940s Walter Reuther had joined the likes of Samuel Gompers, first president of the American Federation of Labor, and John L. Lewis, the United Mine Workers boss, as one the most recognizable faces in the history of the American labor movement. And as the automobile became more important to the country so did the UAW. It was in 1950, however, that many think Reuther reached a fork in the road. This was the so-called Treaty of Detroit in which industry leader GM made major concessions in terms of health insurance and pension benefits in return for a five-year contract, i.e., labor peace for the corporation. All these benefits mimicked what Reuther had long wanted for all working men and women, but in accepting them for his membership only was he abandoning "labor statesmanship," as Harry Coen had called it, for narrower trade union interests? Put another way, had he abandoned the theory of social democracy and a national welfare state for the corporate welfare state?

"Like almost all other unionists, Reuther had long found company provision of such welfare programs distasteful — their coverage was incomplete, the financing was indeterminate, and they smacked of old-fashioned paternalism," wrote biographer Nelson Lichtenstein. "He favored a public, federal system for financing social provision. During the war both the CIO and the AFL had worked for the passage of the Wagner-Murray-Dingell bill, which would have liberalized and federalized the American social welfare system in a fashion similar to that envisioned by the British government's pathbreaking Beveridge Report of 1942, the blueprint of the Labour government's postwar welfare state."[8]

Ron Lare, a college dropout and former member of Students for a Democrat Society, the radical '60s organization, is a retired autoworker living in the Detroit area and a long-time UAW dissident. He thinks the union leadership sold out the rank and file both in 2007 and 2009. He thinks the turning point, however, was indeed the 1950 Treaty of Detroit.

"I think the UAW made a couple of strategic decisions that are haunting it," said Lare. "One is that they would try to solve the social problems of their members by trying to get things within the contract, like health care. As long as that was all upward a pretty good chunk of the working class was getting help. But they should have been fighting for health care for everyone. Eventually people looked around and said the UAW's got pretty good health care and I don't have any. That leads to resentment, especially as the organized union work force is shrinking."

Though the Treaty of Detroit was to last five years, negotiations were in fact reopened in 1953 in the wake of layoffs attributed to the end of the Korean War. At this time Reuther pushed for an annual wage — not an hourly rate — for his workers. He reached a compromise in 1955, first with Ford, and then with GM and Chrysler, to establish the supplemental unemployment insurance benefits trust fund (SUB-pay), which would be in addition to any state unemployment insurance benefit that laid-off workers might qualify for. Years later the idea of the Job Bank was to grow out of this concept — once unemployment benefits ran out for workers, they might then qualify for make-work paid for by the companies if real work in the factories still was not available. Initially, SUB-pay cost the companies a five-cent contribution for every man-hour worked, covered twenty-six weeks of unemployment, and would make up sixty percent of a worker's regular salary. In time that percentage went up to eighty-five percent of regular pay, with the state unemployment benefit included. "Though a far cry from the guaranteed annual wage, it was the Reuther leadership's greatest bargaining triumph," wrote historian Kevin Boyle.[9]

SUB-pay further set apart the lucky autoworkers from most other industrial workers, who had to make do with whatever the states offered alone. In the state of Indiana as of 2009, for example, laid-off workers receive a sliding scale benefit based on their regular salary, but not to exceed $390 per week. Many autoworkers get about $1,000 per week in unemployment benefits, SUB-pay included. Health insurance benefits remain essentially free for active autoworkers, too, which is much better than what other Americans have to settle for.

Apart from the lack of solidarity with other workers the UAW has allegedly shown in recent decades, Lare says the two-tier pay scale first agreed to in the 2007 contract, along with an opening for a limited number of so-called temporary workers, will backfire. The "temps" don't get to vote on new contracts, but the new full-time hires will "screw" the more veteran workers, to use Lare's word, as much as possible once they begin voting on future contracts. Retirees don't get to vote on UAW contracts, but are always affected by them, meaning current veteran autoworkers who supported the two-tier system will be vulnerable as soon as they retire themselves. He also thinks that accepting company stock to fund the VEBAs, which are supposed to contain more than $25 billion, is sheer folly. He pointed to Caterpillar, the earth-moving equipment company that established a VEBA in 1998 to manage its retirees' health care costs, paying a reported $32.3 million into it. That VEBA ran short in 2004, after just six years, and has spawned a rash of lawsuits, with retirees suing to keep Caterpillar from increasing their share of health care costs and Caterpillar in turn suing the UAW.[10]

"I think [the VEBA] was a bad idea," said Lare. "I distributed leaflets saying it's a bad idea. It's a finite amount of money and it can run out. It did at Caterpillar. I think probably I'll just make it. I'm sixty-two and at sixty-five I'll have Medicare. But if somebody takes a buyout at fifty-two they could be screwed. I don't think it will run out right away. They'll probably take care of it with co-pays and increased premiums for a while."

Chris Ryan, a young labor activist and Chrysler production worker in Kokomo, Indiana, also says the Treaty of Detroit was a sellout. It was a turning point because it marked Walter Reuther's identification with what Ryan calls "business unionism," meaning the UAW became just another business representing the interests of its own narrow base, as opposed to "solidarity unionism," which is for all workingmen and workingwomen equally.

Ryan, thirty-seven, is a third-generation autoworker whose grandparents came up from Appalachia to work in Kokomo. He calls himself a "Wobbly," too, a nickname for the far Left but non-violent International Workers of the World. But he may be the only Wobbly in Kokomo, a town that was noted for Reagan Democrats in the 1980s and hardy resistance to much of the liberal agenda, such as gun control. "In a small town like Kokomo you don't see too much [militancy]," said Ryan. "That's why I like going to Chicago or Detroit. It's like being around people like me."

Ryan attended the National People's Summit in Grand Circus Park, Detroit, in June 2009, a kind of tent city that attracted hundreds of disaffected UAW workers and a homeless coalition in Detroit itself. The immediate aim was to protest a nearby business summit featuring a talk by Dick Dauch, the CEO of American Axle & Manufacturing Holdings, a GM cast off that was struck in February 2007, the only truly devastating strike in the American automobile industry in recent years. The strike, triggered by management's plan to cut wages and lay off workers, lasted eleven weeks and idled thirty GM plants. GM, which was American Axle's largest customer by far, agreed to chip in $200 million to end the strike. The money largely went to cover buyout costs associated with a planned reduction in force of up to sixty percent at American Axle, as well as a "buy-down" that was essentially a series of bonuses for veteran workers who agreed to stay on, but at a lower hourly wage. Buy-outs were worth up to $140,000 and the buy-downs were set at $105,000 over three years. Even with those incentives, wages for veteran workers were set at between $30 and $45 per hour, while new hires would get at least $26.54 per hour.[11]

GM also was shut down for two days in September 2007 when Ron Gettelfinger ordered 73,000 workers off the job before the union and GM settled on a pattern contract that was largely reaffirmed by Ford and Chrysler later, but which also included the major union concessions on the two-tier pay system and establishing the VEBA.

Ryan and other dissidents were furious that the UAW leadership endorsed the 2007 settlement and, further, were dismayed that eligible UAW members voted better than three to one for it. "That's the problem with the business union model," Ryan said. "Basically, we got ours. That's the thinking. That's how unions became exclusive and reclusive. They're set up to take dues."

What most militants and dissidents inside the UAW would like to see is either nationwide strikes, as sometimes still seen in Europe, or perhaps international unions that are truly international, meaning they negotiate wages on a global scale. "The companies globalized. We didn't," a fellow worker once told Ron Lare. He was struck by both the elegance and profundity of the remark.

"It was so succinct," Lare said. "And this guy wasn't left-wing. He was a former marine who once guarded [Panamanian dictator Manuel] Noriega. He was just making a cold calculation."

The history of militancy in the post–Treaty of Detroit era has been spotty. One of the more remarkable series of episodes revolved around the Dodge Revolutionary Urban Movement (DRUM) and other so-called revolutionary union movements. The founding of the movement dates to May 6, 1968, after an African-American Chrysler Corporation employee named General Baker was fired due to his involvement in a wildcat strike at the Dodge Main plant in Hamtramck, a Detroit suburb. The protest was over an alleged speed-up on the assembly line, but that may have just exposed pre-existing raw nerves in the plant. According to one surviving printed document, the movement was filled "with ideals and strategies forged in the crucible of the Civil

Rights movement and the experiences of the Rebellion of '67," also known as the Detroit Race Riots. The group's stated purpose was to fight injustices faced by black autoworkers both inside the factories and in the society at large; its logo was a clenched fist.[12]

Black workers had come to Detroit in significant numbers beginning in the 1920s as part of the Great Migration, that wave of black humanity that moved from the Deep South to the Northeast, Midwest, and Far West in the wake of Jim Crow laws, segregation, and the mechanization of agriculture. First hired by Ford, blacks soon found opportunities all over Michigan, Indiana, and elsewhere, though there was resistance. Many Southern whites also came north, especially as lots of truck farming jobs moved to California in the 1930s. Then there were ethnic Europeans who had long lived in Great Lakes cities such as Detroit and were early workers in the car industry, many of whom may have felt they were being undercut by these new immigrants. The 1941 strike at Ford's River Rouge complex already had exposed racial tensions. But Detroit, and the auto industry and related defense industries, is where progress for blacks was occurring. By one estimate, four percent of auto industry–related jobs were held by blacks at the start of the war, but that number had quadrupled to sixteen percent by the end of the war. This was during a period before the United States military was integrated. The major race riot during the Second World War itself occurred in Detroit in June 1943 and lasted three days. Many of the rioters, or protestors, were recently arrived African-Americans who sought jobs in the newly converted defense industries that occupied former car factories. The federal government already had ruled in 1941 that there could be no racial discrimination in hiring in defense industries that received government contracts for work. Thirty-four people were killed during the riots, twenty-five of them black, before federal troops restored order after three days.

Racial tensions erupted again in Detroit in July 1967 after a police raid on what was believed to be an illegal gambling establishment frequented by blacks. Forty-three people were killed over the next five days before National Guard and federal troops finally squelched the demonstrations.[13]

Yet, overall, the auto industry was good news for black progress in America. "One of the engines of the black middle class has been the auto sector," John Schmitt, an economist who studies the issue at the Center for Economic and Policy Research, a liberal Washington think tank, told *USA Today* in 2009. In the late 1970s, "one of every fifty African-Americans in the U.S. was working in the auto sector. These jobs were the best jobs. Particularly for African-Americans who had migrated from the South, these were the culmination of a long upward trajectory of economic mobility."[14]

Even in the current auto industry crisis of 2008–09 the Detroit Three continued to play a significant role in the black community. Approximately sixty black-owned automotive suppliers employed about 8,000 workers, about seventy percent of them black. An estimated 150 to 200 black-owned new car dealerships also were on the Chrysler and GM hit lists for closure. Additionally, the Detroit Three collectively were widely believed to have been major advertisers in black communities, as well as major contributors to black charities and causes, particularly through richly endowed offshoots such as the Ford Foundation and Mott Foundation, the latter tracing to a former GM axle supplier.

George McGregor told his story to *USA Today* in 2009: he had left his native Memphis in 1968 after a tour of duty in Vietnam and headed for work in Detroit. A fellow black veteran had told him that the pay in the auto industry was two to three times what he could earn at home. "When I got out, I went home and stayed exactly one week," he said. "I got on the Greyhound bus and came straight to Detroit."

McGregor applied at GM on his first Saturday in Detroit and was offered a job the following Monday. He had also applied at Ford and was offered a job there, too, but took the GM job because it was closer to where he was staying. He started at $3.28, more than double what he would have been able to pull down in Memphis. "It felt like fifty times more," he said. "I still have that check. I have it framed."[15]

DRUM employees likely also had it better than their forefathers had it in the Deep South, but they saw the cup more as half empty than half full. Sociologists would call this the phenomenon of rising expectations; others would just say you have full equality or you don't, and if you don't, you must fight for it. Demographics again were an issue — by one estimate, seventy percent of Dodge Main's employees were black, but virtually all of the union Local leadership was white, typically old guard ethnic Polish Americans, as was the local small town municipal leadership.[16]

According to the Detroit Revolutionary Movements Collection at Wayne State University, DRUM was followed by other revolutionary urban movements, such as FRUM at a Ford plant, ELRUM at the Eldon Avenue Chrysler plant, and several others, including a couple of non-auto plants in the area. In the auto plants, the RUMs protested working conditions and the alleged practice of giving the most dangerous jobs to blacks or to Arab-Americans, who represented a substantial population base in the area. They also continued to lobby against the UAW leadership, which they viewed as a kind of oligarchy. The RUMs published occasional newsletters, and during the 1968–69 academic year two of the original Dodge Main founders began the *South End*, technically a student newspaper published at Wayne State University in Detroit. Later in 1969 the League of Revolutionary Black Workers was created as a kind of central organization for the various RUMs, but by 1971 the constituent groups had largely disappeared. General Baker, who continued to work in the auto industry for decades, said most of the RUMs lacked organizational skill.

"We would tell these groups, 'You guys get together and start your own stuff. We've got some typesetting equipment and we can help you with that and we got some [college] kids who can help,' but that's about it," Baker recalled in 2009.

Nevertheless, Baker said the RUMs had a positive impact

overall. For a time black militants within the union — Baker does not flinch from the term, which historically was used in an accusatory manner — would wear necklaces made from 50-millimeter shells expended during the Detroit riots as a sign of their rebelliousness. Yet Baker now supports the same kind of positions as other current social justice movements within the United States, such as national health insurance and international worker solidarity to combat multinational corporations and globalization. In the American auto industry itself, Baker says the '70s saw an increased number of blacks in apprenticeship programs and the skilled trades within the factories, as well as in supervisory roles for the companies and more black union officers.

The next big wave of militancy within the UAW was New Directions, founded in 1986 as a protest to the UAW concessions first made to Chrysler after the 1979–80 crisis and federal and state bailout of the company, but also later concessions to Ford and GM. Congress passed the Chrysler Loan Guarantee Act on December 20, 1979, but also demanded $260 million in union concessions. In time, these amounted to a reduction in the cost of living allowance, fewer holidays, and, most provocatively, a $2-per-hour pay cut for Chrysler workers as compared to Ford and GM hourly rate employees. Doug Fraser, president of the UAW at the time, recalled that he "worked" Democratic senators in Washington to support the bill while Chrysler chairman Lee Iacocca worked the Republican side — that is, labor and management were on the same side of the fence on this issue, a position the dissidents found intolerable.[17] As partial compensation for the union leadership's cooperation, Iacocca offered Fraser a seat on the board of directors in 1979. Chrysler had rejected earlier UAW overtures for a seat on the board.

The acknowledged first leader of New Directions (the name came from a call for a new direction in UAW policy) was Jerry Tucker, then–assistant director of UAW Region 5. UAW Region 5 now covers locals at Detroit Three plants in Missouri and sixteen other western and southwestern states. New Directions was acknowledged when Victor Reuther, by then aged and long retired, made public statements in support of the movement. Its main organ was a publication called the *Voice of New Directions*, which had a mailing list in the thousands. The platform of New Directions was clear: it opposed all wage and benefit concessions; pushed for a union movement committed to labor as a whole, not just members of this or that union (solidarity unionism as opposed to business unionism, as Chris Ryan would say); and an end to "jointness," its derisive term not only for a joint training program funded by autoworkers and the car companies alike, but for the whole concept of a UAW and corporate "partnership" that both sides were touting. The dissidents believed that jointness led union leaders to worry more about the health of the companies than the health of the workers. New Directions was moderately active in the late 1980s and into the 1990s. A goateed Tucker — his dark, swept-back hair thinning on top — spoke about his continuing struggle in a speech at the University of Paris–Sorbonne in 2005. He noted that fewer than one in ten private business sector employees in America were unionized, the lowest figure in decades, and he said jointness wasn't working. "[A]utoworkers have nothing but more economic takeaways and gripping job insecurity to show for it, and the union is now one third the size it was when the jointness strategy began," he said. "American unionism's current dilemma must be discussed in light of a twentieth century history which includes U.S. Labor's longstanding policy of collaborating with corporate capital; the purging of its left ideologies and practitioners; the AFL-CIO's post–WWII 'cold-warrior' status and complicity in America's imperial foreign policy to date; more frequent avoidance than engagement in struggles around race, gender, and sexual orientation; and a conspicuous lack of support for maintaining class-consciousness as well as internal democracy and membership accountability."[18]

Soldiers of Solidarity carries on the New Directions mantle. Largely credited to Michigan autoworker Gregg Shotwell, it, too, is more of a movement than an organization as such. Shotwell is the author of the newsletter "Live Bait & Ammo," which he originally distributed in non-work areas at GM. He says workers in other plants of the country would reproduce it and distribute the newsletter among themselves. He says with a laugh that workers at the Saturn plant in Spring Hill, Tennessee, used company photocopy machines to do it and that managers knew this, but dared not object. "Live Bait & Ammo" now is published occasionally on the Soldiers of Solidarity website. Shotwell, too, believes that jointness was a mistake, including the actual joint training fund, which in time grew to several billion dollars. "Back [in the 1980s] it was called the nickel fund because that's what it was," said Shotwell.

The joint training fund was intended both to help permanently laid-off workers retrain, as well as improve new technology skills for current workers. At first, the contribution to the joint training fund was five cents per hour worked; the contribution eventually grew to nineteen cents per hour for each hour worked, plus a complex schedule for overtime. The companies also paid into the fund. "With jointness the UAW has attempted to negotiate some say in sourcing decisions," said Shotwell. "The UAW has tried to get more input into that. What it amounts to is it allows the union to compete [with non-union producers and suppliers]. The UAW has advocated the competitive model, which is the corporate model. They will try to find a way to cut the costs in order to keep the work. That's not the union model. The union adopted the corporate model where they not only compete with other sources but they compete with other Locals to get the work. That's good for business, but it's not good for the union movement."

Now retired, Shotwell worked for thirty years at both GM, where he was a production worker, and its spin-off, Delphi, where he made fuel injectors at its Coopersville, Michigan, plant. He claims Delphi actually rebadged some of its injectors, which were then sold as Bosch equipment, a more famous name in the field. In spite of his efforts and those of other dissidents within the rank and file of the UAW in recent decades, he says militancy remains quite low. "Reuther made a deal with Detroit in 1950,"

Shotwell said, going back to that famous, or infamous, year. "He wanted to have national health care and pensions and the capitalists were totally against that so he decided, all right, *we'll* have that, and the companies and unions negotiated benefits for themselves. That's where the separation occurred."

Core to the dissidents' thesis is that management primarily was interested in squashing socialism on a national scale and accomplished this by buying off socialism's leading backer in the United States in mid-century, namely one Walter P. Reuther. Put another way, Detroit's behavior over the years is seen as a kind of "divide and conquer" strategy to separate the UAW from the rest of the labor movement. Either way, it's a conspiracy theory. Most industrialists and bankers in America of the era probably were anti-socialist, and there was the Red Scare in the 1950s, a kind of national paranoia that was, however, informed by Communism's massive inroads in the Soviet Union, China, Indochina, much of Europe, and Central and South America. But such a conspiracy theory ignores the power of the pattern contract to bring any one of the traditional Detroit Three automakers to its knees while the other two wait their turn, as well as the fact that the rank and file vote on all contracts anyway in a democratic process. It's a supply side analysis that assumes management supplied the evil collective bargaining agreements, but which ignores the demand side, a rank and file that could be just as greedy, self-centered, and ultimately self-defeating as the other side.

The car companies, along with the UAW, were in a long slow decline as company restructuring, concessions, jointness, and the SUV and minivan craze failed to turn the tide against foreign competition. It was the Delphi bankruptcy in 2005, one of the largest in history at the time, that gave the dissidents a bit of a shot in the arm in the new millennium. Delphi was a new name given to GM's own parts divisions, which were spun off in 1999; shareholders were given twenty percent of their stock in new Delphi shares, while their GM holdings were reduced accordingly. At the time GM was almost the exclusive customer for Delphi products.

By 2005, nearly half of Delphi's sales were from non-GM customers, according to its Chapter 11 bankruptcy filing, yet its share of GM sales had dropped precipitously. Its overall wage and compensation package for hourly workers was said to be $70 per hour compared to an estimated $20 for all its competitors combined.[19]

Most hourly Delphi workers in the United States took buyouts during the bankruptcy. A two-tier pay scale for hourly workers was instituted, ostensibly only for new hires, but most employees in the restructured corporation were, in fact, new hires.[20] Today, many Delphi hourly workers toil at the lower beginning wage, just under $15 per hour.

Danny Hiatt, the former lounge entertainer and shop chairman at UAW Local 292 in Kokomo, which represents Delphi workers, says that many employees there took buyouts, consistent with the national trend at Delphi. The buyouts offered during the bankruptcy amounted to $1,500 for every month of accrued service, up to a $40,000 maximum. "Most of the people have never seen that much money at one time before," he said. "I've seen many people going out and buying big ticket items and they don't have any money."

Chris Ryan says he saw the downsizing and demand for concessions at Delphi coming even before the bankruptcy, and he knew Chrysler would be next in line to face job loss and concessions. "It started at Delphi," said Ryan, who works at Chrysler in Kokomo. "I saw it coming. I told people at Chrysler it's going to happen and they said no, we have all the work we can handle. Well, we see what happened."

Todd M. Jordan helped establish a small chapter of Soldiers of Solidarity in Kokomo after the two-tier system was broached at Delphi and for a time maintained a militant website, Future ofthe union.com, though he has since taken it down. In his early thirties with an angular crew cut, Jordan said in published interviews that he was raised in a single-parent family and was a descendent of a family that had moved north from the coal mining areas of Kentucky — a common scenario in the auto industry. Jordan claimed that at one time "dozens" of Delphi and Chrysler workers came to his Soldiers of Solidarity meetings. A common thread in Jordan's missives and interviews with national media, including *USA Today*, is that he didn't join a union just to see it make concessions to management.

"We talk for three to five hours with other workers at our meetings," Jordan told a socialist magazine in 2006. "We also encourage involvement of people from around the country and world to come spend the day with us. One of the most important things we talk about is how to make this global and the need to form a people's party, a working-class party. Why can't it start in Kokomo?"[21]

One of the goals of Soldiers of Solidarity is direct election of all leadership positions within the UAW, including at the regional and national level. This demand somewhat mirrors the movement led by Senator George McGovern in the early 1970s to move toward an improved primary system for choosing nominees for President of the United States as opposed to party conventions and especially kingmakers making the choice. Right now delegates elect the UAW regional directors and national officers at conventions; the rank and file get to choose the delegates, but the delegates often have a free hand.

In Europe all the big Socialist, Social Democrat, and Labour movements started their own political parties, though none appear to be as militant as they once were. The labor movement in America clearly is associated with the Democrats, however, and in particular the grand coalition that Franklin Delano Roosevelt cobbled together in the 1930s. It is often said in America that the great strength of the Democrats has been to absorb minority movements and dissidents. This may in part be why there is no true workers' party in the United States — the labor movement was absorbed, then somewhat neutered, by FDR. It's instructive that many intellectuals in Europe are overtly behind labor, but that this is actually quite rare in America. Some academic unions exist, but they are more like guilds, protecting their own narrow faculty interests and sometimes promoting a race, gender, and gay rights agenda, but rarely anything that might resemble supporting the working class as such.

Neither Lare, nor Shotwell, nor Ryan say they ever were threatened because of their union militancy, either by the companies involved or the UAW leadership, though rumors persist that Jerry Tucker of New Directions actually won his 1986 election as director of powerful Local 5, which was headquartered in St. Louis. The UAW had declared him and his reform movement the loser by a narrow margin. A United States district court judge ultimately overturned the 1986 result and ordered a special election; Tucker won that in 1988.[22]

Ginny McMillin, president of Local 292 in Kokomo, notes that many current Delphi workers are in the lower wage tier because so many veteran employees took buyouts to sever all ties with the company. Severing ties has a distinct meaning in the auto and auto parts supply world — you give up your right to ever be called back to work, and you give up your retiree health care benefit. "The biggest part of our membership is '06 people so they don't really know any difference," said McMillin, meaning they hired in after the bankruptcy.

In mid-2009, however, the major hope for Delphi was GM's announced plan to take back five of its North American complexes, including one in Kokomo. Whereas at one time GM wanted to sever its ties to the expensive auto parts division, it was now more concerned about continuity in its supply chain, particularly the electronics systems engineered by Delphi Kokomo. GM had poured an astonishing $11.7 billion into the smaller corporation since its bankruptcy in 2005, including accepting responsibility for $3.4 billion in pension benefits, just to keep it afloat. Yet major hurdles remained in order to complete the reacquisition: how much would Delphi's creditors settle for, and would the United States government approve, given that it had the right of approval for all GM expenditures valued at more than $100 million because of the series of bailout loans?[23]

Many in Kokomo remained pessimistic about future events, especially after the Chrysler and GM bankruptcies. Benjamin

Stine's father and stepfather had both retired out of Chrysler after laboring thirty-one and thirty-two years, respectively, for the company. Stine himself had worked on a Chrysler production line until he took the company's $100,000 buyout package in 2007. He is a very disaffected former employee, decrying everything from what he calls the increasing moral decay in his hometown, the decline of Chrysler as a world-class manufacturer, the sloth of company supervisors and autoworkers alike, and the relentless greed of Wall Street.

"I worked at Chrysler for fifteen years and I'd say fifty percent of the people didn't deserve to work there," Stine said one morning while drinking coffee in a Panera restaurant in Kokomo. "If you got mad at a boss — I saw people sabotage machines to slow down the line and get the supervisor in trouble. The bosses were always telling you what to do. They never wanted to listen to you. You might know your machine better than anyone else, but they couldn't understand that. People in the plant got so disenchanted."

Stine, forty, was putting all that behind him, though. A capable six-string guitar player, he said he was going to make a Christian music album and take it to Nashville, Tennessee, in hopes of finding a producer. It was not at all clear that his buyout check would really carry him through to his new, hoped-for stage in life.

Meanwhile, the Canadian Auto Workers, the breakaway union that formed out of a militancy within the United Auto Workers in 1984, hardly was immune to criticism. With 225,000 members (but fewer than one in four is an auto industry or related employee), the CAW made what some saw as unprecedented and humiliating concessions to all of the Detroit Three in 2009. Key among the concessions was a first-time ever mandate that newly hired workers would contribute $1 dollar per hour (Canadian) to their own pensions, up to a $1,700 limit. The workers also would give up a week of annual vacation, agree to a wage freeze until 2012, and accept an increase in the length of time it takes workers to reach top scale, among other concessions.

CAW president Ken Lewenza defended the moves, especially the hot-button pension issue. "It's really how do we send a message to the companies that we recognize the [pension] challenges going forward?" he told the *Globe and Mail*.[24]

Lewenza was being reasonable, not a tag that others would have put on him in the past. He repeatedly said during negotiations with Chrysler and GM that the CAW had done enough and would not make further concessions, that no one would take advantage of the Canadian autoworker. Lewenza, the son of a long-time autoworker and one of eight children, lived for a time in public housing in Windsor, Ontario. The somewhat burly, square-jawed Lewenza — he could be mistaken for a rugby player — began his auto career in the chassis department at Chrysler Canada in 1972 when he was eighteen. A boisterous, long-haired hippie, he collected parts from a warehouse for final assembly. "It was just like you were in a tunnel," he told the *Windsor Star* in 1994. "It was dark, it was dingy, dirty, greasy."[25]

Lewenza was elected head of Local 444 in 1994 (a previous president of the Local had been murdered by a disgruntled employee who later was ruled insane) and was the first Local president to be elected national president of the CAW. He took charge of the union in September 2008, just in time for the worst crisis in North American automobile history. Just like Ron Gettelfinger did in the United States, Lewenza protested against modifications to recently negotiated contracts, but under pressure from the national and Ontario governments, and the prospect of imminent bankruptcy at both GM and Chrysler he agreed to further concessions, which he presented to membership for approval. Particularly galling to him was the acknowledged end of the pattern contract, which the unions justified as guaranteeing the same benefits to all autoworkers (hence the name "pattern"). Lewenza simply acknowledged in April 2009 that greater concessions had to be made to Chrysler than GM: i.e., no more pattern contracts. South of the Canadian-American border, UAW leaders already had signaled their readiness to allow lower wages and different benefits to workers who might make new, energy efficient subcompact cars to keep the selling prices in line with foreign competition from Korea and, down the road, China and India. "There is no pattern anymore," Lewenza told the *Globe and Mail*.[26]

Though approved by large pluralities at all the Canadian Locals, the concessions to Chrysler and GM attracted blistering criticism. A Socialist organization railed against Lewenza's oft-stated purpose that he wanted to maintain a "Canadian advantage" for the Detroit Three operating in his country as compared to their plants in the United States. That is, he was willing to pit worker against worker, one of the most serious violations of worker solidarity imaginable.[27]

By late 2009 every auto industry activist and observer alike knew the UAW was in crisis. In fact, they had known it for years. Membership had fallen from a high of 1.5 million in 1979 to 576,000 in 2007[28] and dropping, especially with the tens of thousands of autoworkers taking the big buyouts of 2008 and 2009. The recent auto industry crisis also hardened hearts against the UAW and CAW among conservative political leaders and the common man alike. Most newspapers have a "comments" section linked to all major stories. While some posters complained about the unfairness of worker concessions at a time when many executives were receiving big bonuses (a truism at bankrupt Delphi) or were cashing in their company stock (as had happened with some GM executives prior to its bankruptcy), just as many condemned the unionized autoworkers, their high pay scales, and the audacity to be asking taxpayers (many of whom were working stiffs far poorer than the autoworkers) for a bailout. Others attacked the allegedly poor quality of vehicles made by the Detroit Three and not a few purportedly former autoworkers themselves told horror stories of lax work habits and even overt sabotage on the assembly line — much like what was reported in the 1970s in Lordstown, Ohio, but on a wider scale, especially in the Detroit area. The common thread among these posters was clear: the chickens have come home to roost, and the autoworkers are getting what they deserve.

Anonymous allegations of misconduct and sabotage are not much better than hearsay, but there is plenty of on-the-record testimony to support the charges, including in the 1992 landmark book *Rivethead: Tales From the Assembly Line*, written by former Flint, Michigan, autoworker Ben Hamper. In it, the self-described GM "shoprat" documents drug and alcohol abuse by workers, but also mind-numbing work and abusive treatment by supervisors.[29]

More recently Marvin Powell, employed at GM's Pontiac, Michigan, assembly plant, which was targeted for closure in GM's bankruptcy, told the *New York Times* what he found inside the massively wide and broad factory when he began there in 1996, as well as in the ensuing years. There were drugs and alcohol for sale, numbers runners, and even "parking-lot girls" who apparently performed oral sex on male workers during lunch breaks, much like at some truck stops. "Anything you can find outside the plant, you can find inside the plant," Powell said, speaking pointedly in the present tense.[30] General Baker, too, says a motel near the old Dodge Main factory openly promoted prostitution, that several professional gamblers ran various kinds of games near the factory, and that as the company began hiring more women sexual contact among employees within the factory itself was not uncommon.

Yet Baker says the work was truly tough at times. He recalled his stint working inside a Ford plant. "Our supervisor used to have a fifth of vodka on his desk and he'd give that to you before you'd climb on top the coke ovens," he recalled, noting that Ford alone among the plants he knew made some of its own iron. "They'd give you wooden slats to put on your shoes because the leather would melt otherwise."

David Green, president of UAW Local 1714, which represents many of the workers at Lordstown today, says conditions and spirits have improved dramatically, but really were terrible in the 1970s when GM produced the ill-fated Chevrolet Vega there. "You were a piece of meat. You were a number. That's how it was," he told *Automotive News* in 2008.[31]

Conditions began improving at Lordstown in the 1990s, and the complex now produces the Chevrolet Cobalt, a competent if uninspired design and GM's only small car made in America. The assembly plant was rated among the top ten most productive auto plants in America by Harbour Consulting, a closely watched industry observer.

Several observers have written about nepotism in auto industry hiring (an issue the transplants such as Honda and Toyota pointedly did not have to contend with). Such practices help explain why so many Detroit Three autoworkers are second- or third-generation employees. When jobs were plentiful and seemingly everyone in the important auto towns had a relative working in the shops, nepotism might not be such an issue, but as the jobs became harder to come by it likely was a sore point. Combine this fact with job transfers protected by UAW contracts, such as Paragraph 96, and it's no wonder there is so much hostility from other working class individuals to the UAW in auto industry–related communities. Marion, Indiana, mayor Wayne Seybold, who cleverly used tax policy to keep a major GM metal stamping facility in his town off the GM closure list in 2009, claimed there hadn't been a local hire "off the street" in years, an assertion that could neither be confirmed nor denied by a union leader inside the plant (i.e., it was probably true). Management does not publicly discuss hiring practices. Seybold wanted the tax base and the economic impact of all those jobs, but few if any of his constituents were likely to get jobs inside the plant themselves, he reckoned. The UAW had become a clique, even another country, when viewed by resentful people from the outside. The plant walls were not altogether unlike a moat surrounding a medieval castle meant to keep the less privileged out.

Another GM plant saved in Indiana is in Bedford. Deep in the relatively lush south central part of the state, it has a population of about 13,000. Aluminum castings for transmission cases as well as pistons are made there. UAW membership at the Bedford plant stood at 322 in 2009, down from 1,200 a few years earlier, plus a handful of electrical workers who have their own union. Scott Moore, a forty-eight-year-old grandfather of two and the epitome of the rural middle class, complete with a swimming pool on his acreage, was elected president of UAW Local 440 in June 2008. The unemployment rate in Bedford and neighboring Lawrence County was 13.3 percent in May 2009, well above the state and national averages. The sleepy little town had seen only a few store closures because of the recent recession, but that was mostly because lots of local businesses had long since closed anyway.

The work continues to be hard inside the aluminum casting plant, though various OSHA mandates, UAW-negotiated safety improvements, and more modern manufacturing processes have improved air quality and safety issues over the years. Still, molten aluminum is poured at 1,200 degrees Fahrenheit and the plant is too large to be air-conditioned, so it's very hot in the summer. The raw aluminum is melted in one area of the plant, then the molten aluminum is transported in a "ladle" via forklift truck and poured into a small holding furnace at each die-cast machine, after which the right amount of aluminum is poured into the sleeve of the die-cast machine. The die-cast machines themselves are huge, as big as Moore's living room at home, he says. That's the process for making transmission cases; the much smaller pistons use a gravity feed into special molds.

Moore said sixty-seven percent of his Local voted to accept contract modifications with GM in 2009, but he remains skeptical about making further concessions on wages. One of his daughters studied computer-assisted design in technical school and had hoped to work for auto parts supplier Dana Holding Corporation in nearby Mitchell, Indiana, the boyhood home of astronaut Gus Grissom, but it closed its doors in 2007 and moved most of the work to Mexico.

"It started in Mexico, moved to Korea, and now they're moving to China," said the mellow-speaking Moore. "Even the Mexicans are getting angry. It doesn't matter what you do. The corporations are going to find somewhere else where the wages are lower. You can never compete with that. I think we as a society have to decide what's important to us. Do we want a higher standard of living for our working class or do we just want the cheapest price for everything?"

Local 440 has a small building on the edge of downtown, clad in small limestone blocks like so many structures in the city, which is famous for its nearby limestone quarries. Moore's small, cramped office features a single window and an old, industrial-looking steel desk and not much else. A marquee sign outside just says "Local 440," sans the usual prideful labor union boasts or announcements about upcoming events. Unlike officers at larger Locals who continue to draw their salaries from the employers, but don't actually do factory work anymore, Moore continues to spend much of his time toiling as a machine repairman, which is a skilled trade inside the plant. The rationale for forcing the companies to pay the salaries of union officers is that they help run the plants and maintain labor harmony, which is true, but union dissidents would see this as a conflict of interest.

The GM plant itself sits on a gently rolling hillside northwest of the city, near the main four-lane that runs by Bedford. It's a huge sheet metal–clad structure, far larger than one would expect to see in an enterprise that has only 322 hourly UAW workers. A smaller, limestone office building houses the salaried and administrative people. A baseball diamond that GM installed years ago recently was paved over; it was available for use by GM employees and their families and anyone else in the community. A PCB-impacted field nearby is covered with huge tarps, part of an expensive, seemingly never ending land reclamation project.

Moore says he's happy working inside a factory. "I went to trade school when I was in high school," he said. "The last half semester of my senior year I went to work in a factory as a machinist. It seems natural to me. But I've had friends who have hired in and they didn't last very long. They just didn't like being confined like that."

Moore was at the "Ren Center," as everyone commonly refers to GM's corporate headquarters, the Renaissance Center in

Detroit, for a series of union meetings on the auto industry crisis and proposed contract modifications in 2008 and 2009. He's part of a sub-council that had to approve the modifications before they were presented to membership for a vote. In late 2008 at one meeting that outlined the difficulties facing the auto companies and how the UAW might help, he says union representatives from GM, Ford, and Chrysler Locals all met together, which was a rare event outside of a national convention.

Like all businesses, nonprofits, and other unions, the UAW deals with cash flow issues — it collects money, then spends it. But how much money, and where does the money go? UAW dues (more correctly known as per capita taxes, or "per caps") are two hours of pay per month, or 1.15 percent of gross wages. This rate has been in force since 1967. The money is divided this way: thirty-eight percent stays with the local union, thirty-two percent goes to the UAW International, and thirty percent goes to the strike fund. Members in good standing draw $200 per week from the International Union Strike Fund if they are on strike and have their health insurance paid from the fund, as well. In recent years the strike fund has stood at a healthy $800 million.[32] The published UAW budget for 2008 listed total receipts of $315,772,004, and had cash disbursements of $310,114,667. About $45 million went into the general strike fund while $32 million went into "union administration."[33]

Salary for UAW staff is hard to discern, though. According to a 2007 report in the *Detroit News*, the UAW actually paid its staff about $90 million in the previous calendar year, including more than $100,000 each to twenty-two regional directors, vice presidents, and some other senior officers. But President Ron Gettelfinger drew a relatively modest salary of about $158,000, including allowances and expenses, surprisingly low for one who heads such a significant union. His salary has been flat during the current auto industry crisis, too.[34]

Federal law prohibits the use of union dues for political action. However, the UAW can and does support candidates via its Political Action Committee, officially named the UAW Voluntary

Community Action Program (VCAP), which is funded by autoworker donations as distinct from dues per se. The union spent about $9.6 million on various lobbying and political activities in 2006, for example, and contributed about $2 million to Senate and House candidates alone in the 2008 election cycle.[35]

Where the union goes from here — its political influence, its commitment to social justice, even its ability to negotiate contracts — is anybody's guess. Mark Crouch is a former steelworker who now teaches in the Labor Studies Department at IPFW, a joint campus of Indiana University and Purdue University in Fort Wayne, Indiana. Crouch earned his bachelor's degree in economics from Emporia State University by studying part-time, and later earned his master's degree in industrial relations at the University of Iowa. He's unabashedly pro-union, but he says the union was misguided in some of its demands over the years. For example, Crouch concedes that the Job Bank was largely an expensive hoax. For a time he taught a class on labor history to autoworkers in nearby Anderson; autoworkers were allowed to register as students, then sign up for forty hours classroom time per week just so they could qualify for their Job Bank pay. "And there were some people who went through that ten times," he said. "There was basically the same curriculum each time. All that was being paid for with GM money."

Crouch also contends that the UAW's administrative structure is badly flawed; he describes it in terms highly reminiscent of Chicago-style machine politics under legendary Mayor Richard J. Daley. "The whole staff is made up of guys who worked in big plants where they could deliver the votes for the Administration Caucus," said Crouch. "Most everybody that's gone on to staff has come out of these big plants, plants with 1,000 to 3,000 people working in them. The elections are held at a national convention and that's where the regional directors are elected as are the national officers. What happens is that the delegates are the ones who get to vote. Within each Local there are elections on who gets to be a delegate. The membership doesn't get to vote [directly]."

Perhaps the most controversial UAW president was Stephen

Yokich, who served in that post from 1995 until retiring in 2002. (He died shortly after, suffering a stroke in August 2002.) It was Yokich who authorized the devastating 1998 strike against GM that lasted fifty-four days and shut down virtually all of the company's factories, though it ostensibly was a strike against only two critical parts plants, forcing GM to lay off virtually all of its other workers, which in turn meant the union did not have to expend all of its strike fund. It was believed to be the costliest strike in the company's modern history, though the UAW's 1970 "thirty-and-out" strike over pension benefits lasted longer.

Yokich won great benefits for autoworkers, especially in the 1999 contracts. Workers won extra pay, received an extra holiday for national elections, and a series of Family Service and Learning Centers, which were like libraries, training facilities, and day cares all wrapped up in one. At the time the Detroit Three also promised not to close any additional factories during the life of the contracts, meaning job security, though the UAW looked the other way when Chrysler sold its machine shop in New Castle, Indiana, to auto-parts supplier Metaldyne, which promptly cut half the 1,600 jobs and reduced wages to $18 per hour. Yokich also oversaw an expansion of the UAW into what were clearly other industries, such as cafeteria workers in Puerto Rico and health care workers in Ohio and Michigan.

But Yokich also spent a lot of union money on such ventures as: the United Broadcasting Network, a radio network that was to combat right-wing talk radio, but failed; a luxury golf course in northern Michigan; a start-up airline Pro Air, which was an investment of $14.7 million; sponsorship of NASCAR racing teams, which cost up to $16 million per year; and more.[36]

Then there was the repeated use of "jointness" funds on junkets, events, and parties accessible only to top leadership, or for investment in new office space when plenty already was available. The joint training fund was begun in 1982. Over the years billions of dollars have gone into jointness funds at all the Detroit Three and much of the money has in fact been used for safety and technology training, craft education, and other personal enrichment programs, as originally intended. Yet a major investigation by the *Detroit Free Press* in 2001 found that accounting for jointness funds often was sloppy at best, including on Internal Revenue Service documents, while workers still didn't have anything approaching joint control over the shop floor, which is what many had hoped for as the program was continued over the years.[37]

The 2009 addendum to the current UAW contract finally changed both funding and expenditures for the fund — the company alone will fund the program going forward based on a formula tied to overtime, and all proceeds will be given directly to the Locals, based on size, for use at their discretion.

Worst of all, according to his critics, Yokich was imperious and inaccessible, and he and union leaders down to the Local level who reported to him allegedly were far too cozy with management. This criticism goes beyond the belief that Yokich simply was following a line of thinking that said companies had to be viable in order to give anything to the workers, a major fault line between socialist and capitalist models. These critics also argued that UAW leaders in the factories repeatedly were paid unworked overtime as a way of buying their cooperation on management decisions and interpretations of contract language, and that Yokich encouraged the practice.

In 2001 Bob Bolton, a member of Local 685 in what was then one of DaimlerChrysler's transmission plants in Kokomo, Indiana, told the *Free Press* that he "wrote to President Stephen Yokich to tell him that our local officials were being bought off by DaimlerChrysler. I called him. I sent him documents and a tape. . . . What happened? An official from the International came down and threatened me in front of 300 people at our union meeting." According to the newspaper, Bolton's confrontation with the International UAW was confirmed by two other UAW members who attended the meeting.[38]

Ruth Needleman is a professor of Labor Studies at Indiana University Northwest, located in Gary. She's studied the steel industry woes in America, auto plants in Brazil, and the UAW.

She's on the side of the dissidents, or to the left of them. Needleman claims that free market economic theories such as those often credited to the late University of Chicago economics professor Milton Friedman — and allegedly supported by the likes of Bill Clinton, George W. Bush, Britain's Tony Blair, and "New Labour" — constitute neo-Liberalism and do not protect the workingmen and workingwomen of the world. She attacks corporations for allegedly only caring about profits and not about the economic impact of their policies on working people, the common good, or the nation as such.

Yet she also blames the UAW and all their demands over the years for the mess it finds itself in today. "It's not that these people were overpaid," she said. "It's that the union was so intent on only taking care of its own in a sense it screwed the rest of the nation."

---

1. Alex P. Kellogg and Kris Maher, "UAW to Get 55 Percent Stake in Chrysler for Concessions," *Wall Street Journal*, April 28, 2009, http://online.wsj.com/article/SB124087751929461535.html.
2. Nelson Lichtenstein, *Walter Reuther: The Most Dangerous Man in Detroit* (Urbana and Chicago, IL, The University of Illinois Press, 1997), 184.
3. "Nazi Jab at Soviet Lands Flush on Plymouth Local," *Detroit News* (undated), cited in Lichtenstein, 184.
4. Walter P. Reuther Library Image Gallery, http://www.reuther.wayne.edu/node/3372.
5. Joseph Cabadas, *River Rouge: Ford's Industrial Colossus* (Osceola, WI: Motorbooks, 2004), 78
6. "GM Rejects Reuther's Call to 'Open the Books': The Post-WW II Strike Wave," History Matters: The U.S. Survey Course on the Web, http://historymatters.gmu.edu/d/5138.
7. UAW minutes, quoted in Irving Howe and B.J. Widick, *The UAW and Walter Reuther* (New York: Random House, 1949), and cited in "GM Rejects Reuther's Call to 'Open the Books': The Post-WWII Strike Wave," History Matters: The U.S. Survey Course on the Web, http://historymatters.gmu.edu/d/5138.
8. Lichtenstein, 282.
9. Kevin Boyle, *The UAW and the Heyday of American Liberalism, 1945–1968* (Ithaca, NY: Cornell University Press, 1998), 95.
10. Susan Kelly, "New GM Slogan: Viva the VEBA," Workforce Management, October 2007, http://www.workforce.com/section/02/feature/25/17/56/251759.html.
11. Nick Bunkley, "Strike Settled, American Axle Details Layoff Plans," *New York Times*, May 29, 2008, Business 2.
12. "Dodge Revolutionary Union Movement," http://sitemaker.umich.edu/motorcityvoices/files/mcv_web_exhibit_panel_3.pdf.
13. "Detroit Riots 1967," http://www.67riots.rutgers.edu/d_index.htm, and elsewhere. Information on both riots is widely available on the Internet and in standard reference works. Most analyses follow a standard sociological model – poverty, racial discrimination, disenfranchisement, and more are seen as the root causes, though a few note the dramatic trends in white flight in Detroit over the years. Politicians typically blamed toughs, hooligans, or militants. A leading black militant of the day, H. Rap Brown, has been widely quoted as saying in 1967 that if "Motown" didn't come around, "We are going to burn you down."

14. Larry Copeland, "African Americans Feel Auto Industry's Pain; Factory Jobs, Dealerships Helped Build Black Middle Class," *USA Today*, January 21, 2009, 9B.

15. Copeland.

16. Martin Glaberman, "The Dodge Revolutionary Urban Movement," *International Socialism*, 1st Series, No. 36, April/May 1969, 8–9, www.marxists.org/archive/glaberman/1969/04/drum.htm.

17. David Sedgwick, "Fraser: Chrysler Was Worse Off Than We Thought," *Automotive News*, April 12, 1999, 44.

18. Jerry Tucker, "U.S. Labor in Crisis: The Current Internal Debate and the Role of Democracy in Its Revitalization," *Monthly Review*, July 21, 2005, http://mrzine.monthlyreview.org/tucker210705.html.

19. For a thorough yet readable summary of events, see David Barkholz, "Delphi Spinoff Was a Spiral of Disaster . . ." *Automotive News*, September 15, 2008, S266.

20. George Will, "The UAW, Marching in Reverse," *Washington Post*, January 11, 2007, A25.

21. Ty Moore, "Inside the UAW Opposition – Justice Speaks with SOS Activist Todd Jordan," *Socialist Alternative*, April 26, 2006, http://www.socialistalternative.org/news/article14.php?id=256.

22. Joseph J. Fucini and Suzy Fucini, *Working for the Japanese* (New York: Free Press, 1992), 201.

23. Jeffrey McCracken and John D. Stoll, "Eyeing Bigger Bailout, GM in Talks with Delphi . . .," *Globe and Mail*, February 9, 2009, B5.

24. Greg Keenan, "Auto Workers Make Historic Concession to Pay Into Their Own Pension," *Globe and Mail*, updated May 16, 2009,
http://www.theglobeandmail.com/news/national/ontario/article1124120.ece#article.

25. Brian Cross, "Lewenza's Rise," *Windsor Star*, December 14, 1994, http://www2.canada
.com/windsorstar/news/story.html?id=44821924-085e-4bdc-b2f8-95cf0fbd775a.

26. Greg Keenan, Karen Howlett, and Shawn McCarthy, "CAW to Chrysler: No More Concessions in Bankruptcy," *Globe and Mail,* April 23, 2009,
http://v1.theglobeandmail.com/servlet/story/RTGAM.20090423.wcaw0423/BNStory/VideoLineup.

27. Keith Jones, "Canadian Auto Workers Union Imposes Concessions on Chrysler Workers," World Socialist, April 27, 2009, http://www.wsws.org/articles/2009/apr2009/cana-a27.shtml.

28. Sharon Terlep and Bill Vlasic, "Sides Hammer Out Two-Tier Wage Deal . . .," *Detroit News*, September 26, 2007, http://detnews.com/article/20070926/AUTO01/709260398/Sides-hammer-out-two-tier-wage-deal.

29. Ben Hamper, *Rivethead: Tales From the Assembly Line* (New York: Warner Books, 1992).

30. Jonathan Mahler, "G.M., Detroit, and the Fall of the Black Middle Class," *New York Times*, June 28, 2009, http://www.nytimes.com/2009/06/28/magazine/28detroit-t.html.

31. Harry Stoffer, "Lordstown – Man vs. Machine, and GM Was the Big Loser," *Automotive News*, September 14, 2008, S206.

32. UAW Local 2195, Athens, AL, updated June 2009,
http://www.uawlocal2195.org/News/Local_News_Page_21.html.

33. U.S. Department of Labor, Office of Labor-Management filing, Statement B – Receipts and Disbursements, File Number: 000-149.

34. David Shepardson, "UAW Officers Get Pay Raise," *Detroit News*, April 13, 2007,
http://www.detnews.com/apps/pbcs.dll/article?AID=/20070413/AUTO01/704130353#.

35. Center for Responsive Politics (opensecrets.org), based on Federal Election Commission data,
http://www.opensecrets.org/pacs/pacgot.php?cmte=C00002840&cycle=2008.

36. Jennifer Dixon and Jeffrey McCracken, "Rich Contracts and Cozy Contacts: UAW's Yokich Has Boosted Perks for Workers but Membership Shrinks as Ties to Execs Grow," *Detroit Free Press*, May 19, 2001, 1A.

37. Jennifer Dixon, "A Shroud of Secrecy Surrounds Joint Funds: Programs Assist Many, But Some Ask if the Millions Are Properly Spent," *Detroit Free Press*, May 18, 2001, 1A.

38. Jeffrey McCracken, "UAW Dissidents Challenge Bosses; A Litany of Wrongdoing Is Alleged at 10 Union Locals; FBI, Labor Department Scrutinize Overtime, Jobs," *Detroit Free Press*, May 17, 2001, 1A.

CHAPTER 9

Saving Our Cities

LOTS OF AMERICANS VISIT ITALY every year: sip the wine in Tuscany, ski the Alps, see the pope in St. Peter's Square. Few go hat in hand, but that's just what Kokomo Mayor Greg Goodnight was reduced to in late July 2009.

Goodnight and a small economic development team that included his sustainability officer, David Galvin, a U.S. Navy veteran who had been stationed in Italy for a few months in the early 1990s, met with several smaller companies and with top executives at Fiat S.p.A. in Turin, though not with the big boss, Sergio Marchionne. Goodnight was looking for investment dollars in his hometown, but diplomatically failed to bring up a more pressing issue — Fiat's leaked position on $5.9 million in property taxes owed by Cerberus-owned Chrysler LLC prior to the bankruptcy. Fiat was refusing to pay them, saying it was the old Chrysler that went bankrupt, not this new Fiat-Chrysler partnership. The reporter from the hometown newspaper had dutifully hounded the mayor on just this issue during a long-distance phone call while he was overseas, but the mayor didn't want to spook anybody. Or provoke anyone. He was dealing from weakness and he knew it. It was something he never liked to do as a former steelworkers' union president and something he detested as a mayor with lots of responsibility but not that much authority. Just smile and talk up his city — that was his game plan. If Fiat could repudiate back taxes what else could it do?

"Old Chrysler did not pay its taxes," Goodnight finally conceded upon his return, speaking from the kitchen of his colonial style home in Kokomo, not far from city hall itself. "If you read the [*Kokomo*] *Tribune* article yesterday it was all, 'What are you going to do? What are you going to do?' Well, unfortunately, like I told my wife today, every time I get this thing figured out somebody changes the rules on me."

The new Chrysler was arguing that it didn't owe the delinquent property taxes to the city because of the 2009 bankruptcy. In Indiana's distinctive tax universe, Chrysler had paid its taxes on the buildings and acreage it owned in Kokomo, but not on the so-called personal property inside the plants themselves (machine tools, presses, even computers and other office equipment) that represented the larger sum. And even though the old, bankrupt Chrysler had sold those good assets to the new Chrysler, somehow the tax liability didn't go with it. Or so Fiat was arguing.

The Chrysler debt represented nearly fifteen percent of Kokomo's total annual revenue projections; other government entities, such as the local school corporations, library board, and sewer district, had additional claims on Chrysler's back taxes that also were at risk, over and above the $5.9 million. And this was on top of a chronic problem facing many communities in Indiana during the great recession of 2009. Property tax collection rates across the board stood at eighty or eighty-five percent in such cities, down from historic averages hovering around ninety-eight percent, said Matt Greller, executive director of the non-partisan Indiana Association of Cities and Towns. "I was in Muncie for a two-hour meeting with city leaders and they're worried about how to pay the electric bill, let alone attract new business," Greller said.

Goodnight said he would appeal to Ed Montgomery, the president's "czar" for hard-hit automotive towns who had visited the city several weeks earlier, but he knew Montgomery had no budget of his own and consequently little real power. Goodnight would consider legal action, too, but that would be costly, time-consuming, and a positive outcome would not be assured. The revenue shortfall could not easily be made up, either, because recent changes in Indiana state law had tied the hands of all local leaders who might want to raise property taxes on others to make up shortfalls. This was the property tax "cap" that had been set at 1.5 percent of assessed value on residential property, 2.5 percent on rental property, and 3.5 percent on business property in 2009, to be reduced by a further half point in each category in 2010. The property tax caps had been pushed through by Republican Governor Mitch Daniels in the wake of sharp property tax increases following the state's phaseout of the business inventory tax earlier in the decade. The property tax increases, often based on antiquated property assessment formulas in use in the state prior to 2007, caused a furor with the electorate statewide, and even cost popular Indianapolis Mayor Bart Peterson, a Democrat, his job in November 2007 when he was soundly beaten by Republican Greg Ballard, an ex–marine officer but a complete political novice. The new tax caps were expected to reduce local property tax revenues by twenty-eight percent statewide by 2010, a challenge for all towns in the state, but more so for hard-hit automotive communities.[1]

In the meantime, all Goodnight could really think to do was turn to the state and borrow enough money to cover about half of the tax shortfall. This is what the city had done after the Delphi bankruptcy in 2005, when that company also skipped out on some of its tax liability. Still, a state loan had not been approved for the Chrysler situation yet, and loans have to be repaid in any case. Consequently, Goodnight could only chip away at costs, as he had been doing for a year and a half. Most recently he had reduced the number of trash pickup routes from twenty-five to nineteen, and he closed an unprofitable city-run day care center. "In Indianapolis I'm known as the face of the battle to save the auto industry in Indiana," Goodnight said. "But in Kokomo I'm known as the guy who made people take their trash out to the other side of the street."

The recession and auto industry crisis was starting to get really annoying. Goodnight took a drink from a bottle of ginger ale he pulled from the refrigerator, then plopped it down on a counter top with an ironic smile on his face.

"They made it clear a lot of their decisions will depend on our national economy, the international economy, and the auto market, especially in the U.S.," Goodnight said, recapping his trip. "I feel very confident they know their product line with Fiat and their product line with Chrysler are different markets, and they made it clear there's not going to be an immediate transition where they'll eliminate Chrysler and emerge afterwards as just the Fiat brand."

The mayor faced other headaches, too, such as the never-ending conflict with the firefighters' union. Via a door-to-door campaign the union had very publicly campaigned against the mayor's call to freeze the payroll. The city and union agreed to enter non-binding arbitration, which the firefighters won, and the city council decided to honor the proposed raises. But the conflict continued when Goodnight made good on his threat to lop off several firefighter positions as a means of paying for raises for the surviving firefighter positions.

"We have more firefighters per resident and per square mile than virtually any other city our size," said a wary Goodnight. "And they're paid very well."

Firefighters had grown accustomed to receiving approximately what UAW workers in Kokomo had been getting in their contracts, including fully paid retiree health benefits. Goodnight wondered just how long this could continue in an era of negative wage growth, however, including the two-tier pay system for automotive workers that brought some starting salaries down to about $15 per hour, well below what firefighters in his city earned.

Specifically, Goodnight canceled the fire department's ambulance service, throwing twelve emergency medical technicians out of work, plus five administrative positions within the department. The EMT duties were all handed over to the two local hospitals in Kokomo; there is no shortage of ambulances in Kokomo. But saying twelve "firefighters" had lost their jobs, thereby endangering public safety, made for good theater, Goodnight complained, which was duly covered in the local press.

These and other layoffs in the city administration were sure to be an issue if and when he were to run for re-election, Goodnight acknowledged. Altogether, in his first eighteen months in office and counting, he had reduced city payroll from 521 to 461 or more than ten percent. None of this made him popular with laid-off workers or their extended families, which could tip the balance in any future mayoral election in a close-knit community like Kokomo.

"I can answer for every decision I've made, what my thinking was and why," he said, sounding more resigned than defiant. "You have to put your faith in the electorate. Good policy should lead to votes."

Goodnight also wrestled with the township trustees over sharing the cost of firefighter services in unincorporated areas served by Kokomo, a pet peeve not just for him but for mayors across the state who had to cope with providing services for unincorporated areas in their region. In Indiana's arcane, nineteenth-century government structure, citizens always lived in a state, county, and township, which were the basic structures, but not necessarily in a city or town. Goodnight wanted $1 million to continue providing fire services to these unincorporated areas near Kokomo (in truth, he just wanted to annex them), but the township trustees turned thumbs down on the demand. One vocal township trustee proposed paying $70,000 per year — less than the salary of one firefighter, benefits included — plus he'd ante up $385,000 for a squad rescue truck for use by the city's fire department, but the township would retain title to the vehicle. Center Township had $6 million in reserves in 2009, Goodnight claimed, and he said the city of Kokomo was staring into a $2.5 million budget shortfall for the next fiscal year. This was separate from the Chrysler back taxes issue, too. Health care benefits for the city's eighty-two retired firefighters as of 2009 alone cost $1.3 million annually.

The tussle over paying for fire protection in unincorporated areas was more good theater dutifully reported by the local press, and reminded many observers of the recent, widely distributed Kernan-Shepard Report in Indiana, which looked critically at townships, but acknowledged the myriad overlapping jurisdictions and government entities in the state such as school corporations, sewer districts, highly gerrymandered House and Senate districts for state government, and more. Citizens not only lived in multiple jurisdictions in Indiana, but they might share a House district with a fairly close neighbor, for example, but not share the same school district (known as corporations in the state), or they might share the same library district but not the same sewer district. It's often been said that the role of a free press is to be a watchdog on government and the administration of justice, but that's impossible when there are just too many government entities to watch. Joe Kernan is a former Indiana governor and Randall Shepard is the reigning chief justice of the Indiana Supreme Court. The report concluded that, at a minimum, township government should be eliminated; townships were just part of an antiquated nineteenth-century reality in Indiana when people had to ride horses to what at the time seemed like distant locales. All township duties could easily be transferred to other, existing jurisdictions, the report concluded, thereby eliminating lots of salaried government positions within the state, as well as the lax oversight for which many townships were known. The Kernan-Shepard Report was considered non-partisan, important in that it was calling for the elimination of lots of elected officials, some of whom were Democrats and some Republicans. It was non-binding, too, and had not been enforced.

Greg Goodnight remains a big fan of Kernan-Shepard, perhaps in part because of his own experiences with his local township over funding the Kokomo fire department. "A lot of people don't even know what township they're in," said Goodnight. "I think it's a question of accountability, but it's also a matter of eliminating a lot of public officials. I always ask people, 'Name me every elected official that represents you — school board, trustee board, trustee, coroner, treasurer, city council.' I think Kernan-Shepard is a good way to start down that path. It's quite reasonable. Look how long it takes us to do an Interstate 69 extension down to Evansville. It takes generations. I think the state needs to take the leadership. They can do what they do in Illinois. If they want to consolidate school districts, the state will pay off the debt of the weaker school district. I talk to school superintendants here and they say they would consolidate, but they don't want to take over the debt of the other school corporation."

In towns and cities across America a host of publicly and privately funded economic development agencies, think tanks, and foundations purport to be working for more jobs, more educational opportunities, and a better quality of life. E. Mitchell Roob Jr. is secretary of commerce for the state of Indiana and chief executive officer of the Indiana Economic Development Corporation. Roob, like many other thinkers, believes that small towns and cities cannot shoulder the burden of attracting and keeping multinational corporations in their midst on their own. In late 2008 the state of Indiana had a key role in bringing a large Honda Civic assembly plant to Greensburg, southeast of Indianapolis. The plant employs about 950, with the hiring of another 1,000 workers for the second shift on hold until the economy recovers. Base wages for production workers start at a new industry standard of $14.84 per hour, also the prevailing industrial wage in an area hit by closings of manufacturing plants. Roob believes that it is state government that can best deal with multinational corporations. Cities or regional economic development agencies can best deal with small and midsize companies, he says, but the plethora of local, regional, and statewide economic development agencies, including chamber of commerce–type groups plus various small business "incubator" programs is no less dizzying to outsiders than is the structure of state and local government itself. It's like the old Abbott and Costello comedy routine, "Who's on first?"

Many observers believe economic development has to be done regionally, whether that means regionally within a state or regionally among several nearby states. Kokomo sustainability director David Galvin has seen the failure to think regionally firsthand. DaimlerChrysler had a deal several years ago with German transmission maker GETRAG for a fuel-efficient dual wet-clutch transmission for a new generation of Chrysler models. The $530 million plant was scaled to supply 700,000 transmissions per year. Kokomo, along with other Indiana communities, vied for the development. The new plant was built, but just over the line in neighboring Tipton County, a bit closer to Indianapolis, and a bit closer to the major interstate highways in the area, always a consideration. At the time Kokomo residents howled that their city and county had "lost" the plant. That was their first mistake, Galvin said. They couldn't think regionally, and they ignored the fact that their friends and neighbors would still have jobs in the new factory.

Then the GETRAG deal went sour altogether. When Cerberus took over Chrysler, auto sales already were weakening. Cerberus and GETRAG began to dicker over the price of each transmission. The relationship soon crashed when Cerberus opposed GETRAG's interest in securing German government financial backing for the project. Cerberus filed a lawsuit, arguing GETRAG misrepresented its ability to finance the plant. Industry analysts opined the underlying reason for the dispute rested with Cerberus. It did not want the German government to hold a lien on the property in the event Cerberus decided to sell off Chrysler.

The factory now sits empty at the intersection of two major state highways between Kokomo and Indianapolis; the only employees are round-the-clock security guards. What was the reaction of some local citizens to the fiasco, according to Galvin? "Maybe we should chalk that up as a victory that we didn't get it," someone told Galvin. He was dismayed. "Well, no, you don't count a failure as a victory."

The UAW and some "buy American" groups have frequently chastised states for giving tax breaks to foreign companies, but no economic development group or local government leader buys that argument. "Is this Civic an American-built car?" Greensburg mayor Gary Herbert asked workers and guests, including

Indiana Governor Mitch Daniels, at the grand opening of the new Honda Civic plant in 2008. "Yes," the crowd boisterously replied in unison.[2]

Subarus and Camrys already were being made in Lafayette, and Toyota Sienna minivans and Sequoia sport-utility vehicles are made in Princeton, which was retooling for Highlander SUV production after the Tundra pickup was moved to San Antonio, Texas. Roob claims that Indiana has the largest concentration of transplants in one state in the country; all the factories were built with various state and local incentives. Roob says incentives and tax abatements should not be confused with bailouts or subsidies. He's all for incentives, which bring jobs, stimulate further growth, and lead to increased tax revenues down the road. But he has no use for propping up inefficient industries, something the Soviet bloc countries tried for many years to ill effect, and which the United Kingdom tried for its ailing domestic auto and motorcycle industries in decades past.[3]

"If Chrysler would have died thirty years ago [in 1979] the people in Kokomo would have reallocated their resources and gone through what they're going to have to go through now eventually," Roob said.

Of course, Chrysler has received tax breaks over the years, including $20 million in state and local incentives for the $1 billion Indiana Transmission Plant No. 1 constructed in the mid-1990s. Nevertheless, incentives for companies in the United States generally pale in comparison to the tax breaks foreign automakers get by inviting bidding wars among the states eager for the jobs that come with a vehicle assembly plant, essentially forcing state leaders to say, "Marry me, marry me," like on some awful reality TV show. Alabama incentives topped $253 million for Mercedes' car plant, $234 million for Hyundai, and $158 million for Honda. Mississippi committed $295 million for Nissan. By that measure, Indiana has been less generous, allocating $26 million in state and local incentives for General Motors to expand truck production in Fort Wayne (GM never tried to wangle more money by pretending it might expand production elsewhere),

$75 million for Toyota in what is now called Princeton West, $86.5 million for Honda production in Greensburg, and $94 million for the original Subaru-Isuzu plant in Lafayette. Toyota asked for no new incentives when it moved some of its Camry production to the Subaru plant in Lafayette in 2007.[4]

Money talks when it comes to attracting business, in other words. But many people also think the quality of local schools is key to bringing in new investment to small and midsize towns. Small business owners and professional people don't want to send their children to weak schools, and larger corporations worry about recruiting managers and technical staff for the same reason. Well-compensated workers would have a choice of private schools in larger markets, but generally not in small communities so the quality of schools actually is more important in smaller towns than in big cities. High school graduation rates have been improving in recent years throughout many small and midsize communities in Indiana, but are not impressive overall. Besides, graduation rates say nothing about the quality of education one is receiving.

Joe Dunbar, a retired social studies teacher and current president of the Kokomo-Center Consolidated School Corporation, concedes that in most schools all you have to do is show up to graduate. To confirm this hypothesis he did his own study of graduation rates for eighth graders who entered Kokomo high schools and how many graduated in four years. "There was a significant number we lost, but the dropout rate numbers were minute," Dunbar said. "They just seemed to disappear."

Graduation rates for Howard County high schools, which include Kokomo, were as low as sixty-nine percent for 2007. The worst rate was for Taylor High School, on the east side of Kokomo. Kokomo High School's rate stood at seventy-seven percent; the state average was seventy-six percent for 2007.[5]

Part of the problem is that Kokomo proper is home to three school corporations, plus another school corporation in Russiaville, an immediate suburb, and a fifth, fully independent school corporation in Greentown, a small community less than ten miles due east. This is yet another violation of principles endorsed by the Kernan-Shepard Report. Too many tax dollars go to support too many administrators and all the duplication of effort. The need to consolidate immediately adjoining school districts is separate from the wave of individual school closings (also known as school consolidation) that swept through rural America beginning in the 1950s. Such consolidation was just one dagger in the heart of community life and identity in very small towns. Small towns benefited from their own schools without the need to bus children miles away from home. But five school corporations in one county of about 85,000 people clearly are too many. In recent years small efforts have been made to voluntarily consolidate some duties of the various Howard County school corporations, such as purchasing and transportation options, as well as a county-wide program for at-risk children but, as with township government, no government employees and bureaucrats seem willing to voluntarily put themselves out to pasture.

Dunbar says local schools have been hurt over the years by various trends. GM, Chrysler, and Delphi executives and engineers often lived outside the county, many in the affluent Indianapolis suburb of Carmel in Hamilton County, because of their belief that local schools were inferior, which became a self-fulfilling prophecy. (This was in addition to GM's policy of relocating managers and engineers from Detroit not to Kokomo, but to Carmel because of the relative real-estate values involved.) Many local children didn't care much about book learning because they were virtually guaranteed good-paying jobs inside the automotive plants, at least as long as they had a parent or close relative already working there. And local school corporations used technical school education and career centers as dumping grounds for discipline problems and other at-risk children rather than actually respecting the value of technical school training and working with one's hands. The latter trend was especially galling to Dunbar, who noted that kids quickly pick up on the fact that they are not respected. Yet Kokomo-Center schools have been unfairly maligned over the years. Its career center has a better-than-average reputation; the school corporation has a strong gifted and talented educational curriculum that begins in kindergarten; and it sponsors full-day kindergarten in most of its schools, something that is not required by state law and is not common in Indiana.

The need for better high schools as a part of community development cannot be overstated, however. While national leaders and pundits alike talk about the value of a college education, citing statistics that purport to show how much more college graduates earn than do workers with a mere high school diploma (comparisons that are not valid because youth who choose to leave after high school are not from the same statistical universe as youth who choose to go on to college, and because degrees from different universities and different majors lead to wildly different income potential), other thinkers note that it is the quality of a high school education itself that is key. "It's not a question of how many graduate. It's a question of what do they know," said Morton Marcus, long-time newspaper columnist and former director of the Indiana Business Research Center who has studied manufacturing communities in the Middle West since the 1970s. "Even more, it's a question of where they go to college after they graduate."

In spite of myriad economic development efforts in the state, it's often individual initiative that makes a difference. Tom Tolen is a native Hoosier and Taylor High School graduate who is an administrator at Howard Haven in Kokomo, one of the last remaining county homes for the poor in Indiana. Howard Haven dates back to the pre–Civil War era in America. "Years ago this home was on the chopping block just like a lot of other homes," said Tolen, forty-one, who has a social work degree from Indiana University–Kokomo. "There was a lot of pressure to close this home. There were very few residents here. There was more staff than residents. It costs a lot of money to operate these homes."

Most county homes in Indiana were in Gothic-looking, brick or wood-frame nineteenth-century structures out in the country;

they were more colloquially known as "poor homes" and residents often had to work in nearby fields for their keep. Howard Haven is in a low-rise, medium-brown brick building just within the Kokomo city limits, across the street from an ordinary looking subdivision. It looks more like a small elementary school than a "poor home." Administrators kept the facility open only through community involvement. During one visit to the home in 2009 a gaggle of teenagers from a local church were doing yard work and tidying up the grounds. Tom Tolen and director Jennifer Vary showed a guest a well-stocked pantry in the basement filled with canned foods, toilet paper, and the like, virtually all of it donated by local businesses or a food bank. Howard Haven, still a government entity, cannot legally receive donations directly from food banks and certain other entities, but Tolen and others incorporated the nonprofit Friends of Howard Haven in order to receive gifts on behalf of the residents. A Designers' Show Home Guild member redecorated all the resident rooms recently — local donors paid $3,000 for new furniture and paint in each of the residents' rooms in return for a simple plaque by each doorway. Almost everything was purchased from local stores, too. An aluminum can recycling container sits at the edge of Howard Haven's parking lot — the first fund-raiser for the home, it proved so successful it's a source of ongoing income. Regular funding comes from the county, state government ($37 a day for each of the home's twenty-seven or twenty-eight residents, depending on occupancy), and the residents' Social Security and disability checks. Eight people work full-time at the facility.

The auto industry itself has had a role in supporting the home, albeit indirectly. Two of the resident rooms are sponsored by UAW Locals 685 and 292, the Chrysler and Delphi unions, respectively. "It was the generosity of the people. But it was also the affluence," noted Tolen. "Where did that money come from? It was the auto industry. We recognize that when people don't have the jobs then there is not the affluence."

In Bedford, deep in southern Indiana closer to Louisville than

Indianapolis, another first-time mayor struggled with an auto industry in retreat and the need to cut expenses in light of dwindling tax revenues. Property tax caps were estimated to cost Bedford $1.3 million in 2009 — a lot for a town of only 13,500 souls. Shawna Girgis was the surprise winner in a three-way race in November 2007 running as an Independent. A former medical social worker, it was her first political campaign. In her thirties with beauty pageant good looks, Girgis is the wife of an Egyptian-American doctor. Girgis has raised utility rates and put the city's various insurance plans up for competitive bidding, thereby saving the city $291,000 per year. (Allegedly there had been sweetheart deals with two local insurance companies prior to her arrival.) She has also restricted the use of "take home" city-owned vehicles by municipal employees.

"When I lay off people these are people I know," Girgis said during an interview in city hall, which is in a historic federal style building painted white near the small downtown and the Bedford Courthouse Square. The tall windows in her first floor office directly face the sidewalk outside.

Bedford, the Lawrence County seat, was founded in 1825, after the state legislature deemed the earlier county seat on the shores of White River unsafe because of a malaria outbreak. The county itself is named for War of 1812 hero James "Don't give up the ship" Lawrence. Bedford is most famous for its nearby limestone quarries and stonecutting mills, but also has a GM aluminum casting plant that employs 322 autoworkers. A Visteon plant — the former parts supply arm of Ford Motor Company that went bankrupt in 2009 — closed the previous year. The downturn in the auto industry was only partly offset by the success of a small company called Stone City Products, which in spite of its name makes metal stampings for most of the major Japanese auto companies doing business in the United States.

Retail in town is distressed. A large grocery store in the local mall closed a couple of years ago and remains vacant, as does a former Goody's Family Clothing store. That national retailer declared bankruptcy in 2008. A Walmart store relocated from busy Sixteenth Street to the edge of town, nearer State Road 37, the major thoroughfare connecting Bedford to the rest of the state. Walmart's old building was only recently occupied by TSC, a farm supply and variety store. Common Sense, a locally owned home décor store, also recently closed under the crush of the recession. Other vacant storefronts dot the city.

Like other small town mayors, Girgis preaches the gospel of diversification. One successful local manufacturer, Bedford Machine and Tool, was founded in the late 1980s by two disgruntled GM managers. The company invested $3 million in wind turbine technology; it machines 37,000-pound castings that house the generator and prop, as well another large part called a hub that bolts onto a shaft in the overall wind turbine design.

In spite of all the talk in Washington about investing in alternative sources of energy and reducing carbon footprints, co-owner Doug Conrad says the wind turbine business was far better before the current recession. "It's just like you read," said Conrad, a former tool engineer at GM who played varsity high school basketball with Boston Celtic great Larry Bird while growing up together in French Lick, Indiana. "The banks aren't loaning money for anything like that. Not even to Boone Pickens."

Conrad continues to sell machined parts for use in GM buses, as well as parts for a new Ford six-speed car transmission. He also runs a separate recycle and reuse company, which is profitable.

In some ways, Bedford Machine and Tool is the future of manufacturing in America — small firms relegated to picking up whatever they can find, in truth no more than second-tier or third-tier suppliers to the multinationals of the world. Conrad describes his firm as a "job shop," meaning it bids on work that larger companies or contractors need done, but doesn't manufacture much on its own. The company pays $19 or $20 per hour for machinists and other skilled laborers, plus benefits. This is far below what the skilled trades in UAW-negotiated contracts continue to get, even after the concessions of 2009. Full-time production workers earn $13 to $14 per hour, plus benefits, half the base wage that veteran UAW production workers are guaranteed, but close to what many new hires in the auto industry will get under the two-tier system approved in 2007. The company normally employs about seventy people in its main plant, but was down to fifty in the great recession of 2009. Bedford Machine and Tool does about $30 million in sales annually and is viable, says Conrad, who fully expects to survive the recession. But it will take thousands of such companies across the country to make up for what's been lost in the automobile industry since the 1970s.

Overall, Bedford and Lawrence County were in an awkward position when it came to the new economy. Three out of four adults age twenty-five or older were high school graduates or better, according to the 2000 census; only one in ten was a college graduate, though. Nearly ten percent of the population was on food stamps in 2008, and about one-third of school children were on free or reduced-fee lunch programs in 2009. The June 2009 unemployment rate stood at thirteen percent, well above the state average.[6]

Over in Connersville, city leaders and former Visteon workers continued their hometown efforts to win a new development from Carbon Motors Corporation, which was set to make a highly specialized police vehicle. At least 1,000 people came out for a so-called American Jobs Rally at the old Visteon plant on Wednesday, July 29, 2009, in what was really a kind of homecoming party just for the start-up company. About a dozen volunteers had spent days cleaning up the old Visteon plant for the occasion. Indiana Governor Mitch Daniels and Carbon Motors executives announced in advance that they would attend the midday festivities, but were mum on just what they might announce. City leaders and residents had previously hosted Carbon Motors executives in May in an effort to win the car building plant — again, it was a "Marry me, marry me" kind of scenario. "We cleaned the showroom, the hallways, the restrooms, the VIP conference room, and out in the big plant," Visteon retiree Ruby Siler told the Richmond, Indiana *Palladium-Item*. "We swept the plant floor to take up the screws that were all over the place."[7]

Carbon executives indeed had something to announce to the citizens of Connersville. "We are creating new American jobs of national importance and it was only appropriate to announce that at a very unique Rally for American Jobs," said Carbon Motors CEO William Santana Li. "It is essential that the local, state, and federal authorities work in concert with the private sector to deliver on our country's moral obligation to provide our 840,000 law enforcement responders the appropriate equipment to secure our homeland against threats, both foreign and domestic. With the unanimous vote of the Board of Directors, we are pleased and honored to announce that the great state of Indiana will become the police car capital of the world."

This was a state-supported economic development effort, and it looked to be a great victory for local residents. With production slated for 2012, Carbon executives estimated that the project would directly and indirectly generate 10,000 jobs, as well as have $3 billion economic impact over the next ten years. Yet cautious reporters noted that Carbon actually had no major source of independent financing yet, and could produce no evidence of signed contracts with police departments to actually buy its vehicles. Playing the economic-incentives game had reached a new high — or low — as pundits speculated that the company wanted a commitment from the state of Indiana first so that it could then approach potential investors and customers.

Up in Marion, Mayor Wayne Seybold appeared to be dealt a slightly better hand than some of his compatriots in other automotive town administrations elsewhere in the state. The city's monster GM metal-stamping plant stayed off the company's closure list after the June 1 bankruptcy, and the corporation announced in early July that it was bringing three presses valued at $247 million to the facility, which would add 100 jobs. The presses were assets being removed from other GM plants that were on its closure list — one city's loss is another's gain, you might say. As a reward for the move, the Marion City Council voted to offer $40 million in economic development bonds for the GM plant, up from a previously announced $25 million.

Of course, some people create their own luck. Seybold had employed an economic development tool known as Tax Increment Financing (TIF) to allow GM to effectively use credits against its property tax bills to pay for improvements to the factory, such as the soon-to-arrive presses. Normally TIF districts are done geographically or for a group of businesses in one area; the city of Marion just made the GM plant into its own TIF district.

The mayor's clever tactics had been noticed. At the behest of government leaders in Columbia, Tennessee, and Maury County, Tennessee, which is home to what was long known as GM's Spring Hill Saturn auto plant, Seybold agreed to participate in a video conference in early June. Spring Hill had made small Saturn cars since 1990, but had recently shifted production to GM crossover vehicles. As 2009 rolled on, the fate of the plant and its 3,000 employees was undecided, even after wealthy Detroit auto dealer Roger Penske agreed to buy the Saturn brand rights from GM, but not the Saturn factory. What to do? The Indiana end of the video conference was held in a highly computerized audio-visual center inside the new Ivy Tech State College Building in Marion.

Only thing was, the Columbia mayor never participated in the video conference; a leading county executive also was missing. An apologetic group of other local Tennessee leaders announced the mayor had decided not to run for re-election. He had simply skipped the meeting he had called. Seybold himself was late for the conference, although he had a better excuse. He was scheduled to appear at the locally syndicated television show *Inside Indiana Business* taping in Indianapolis earlier that morning. He appeared with UAW Region 3 director Mo Davison; the topic was the car industry crisis, of course. Then he drove himself up from the capital city, about seventy miles to the southwest. His aides stood at the large conference room picture windows as they watched the mayor drive his Chevrolet Impala into the campus parking lot "hot," which was mostly empty because of the early summer recess.

The Ivy Tech building, which opened in January 2008, was built with creative financing. Local developers; the independent, nonprofit Ivy Tech Foundation; and the city itself donated land and money to get the $21 million building up and running. (The Ivy Tech Community College system formerly was known as Indiana Vocational Technical College; the word "Ivy" is just a colloquialism for Indiana Vocational.) Seybold had insisted the new campus be built east of the city, just off Interstate 69, which connects Detroit with Indianapolis, because it would serve as a regional campus and an economic stimulus for the area, not just his town.

Mayor Seybold and his key economic development guru, Jay Julian, explained how they had used TIF to cozy up to GM. In fact, earlier in the year they had met several times with GM officials, including representatives from corporate in Detroit, and had convinced them that the city of Marion had a progressive and realistic plan to help the corporation. Clearly, the corporation had wanted to know if local leadership in Marion had the basic competency to work with a major multinational corporation. Not all small and midsize towns do. During the video conference the mayor and his assistants also explained how the city had brought in new retail development with the help of an outside consulting firm, demolished hundreds of vacant buildings, and towed nearly 1,600 abandoned cars in one recent year alone. No new businesses want to come to a town that looks bad, they all agreed.

The issue of tearing down vacant homes is a thorny one for many cities, large and small. One of Seybold's advisers explained a hidden problem — banks often won't bother to foreclose on especially "low-value" homes, leaving them in a kind of legal limbo where no one has the right to touch them. "They would just sit there," he explained. "The property owners would just walk away. The thieves would come in and strip them." But through good cooperation from various local agencies, town leaders in Marion found a legal mechanism ordering the owners of record to fix up the properties, or face demolition.

The Columbia and Maury County leaders marveled at the level of cooperation and even sophistication between various city agencies in Marion. "Everybody's got their finger in it," one unidentified county commissioner down in Tennessee said. "We're very territorial here."

Everyone laughed, but it was a knowing laugh, a cynical, sad laughter in the end. The video conference ended collegially after about an hour; it's not clear what the Tennessee officials learned, however. Mayor Seybold had been working on saving his city since he took office in 2003, yet here were officials from a similarly placed town a little south of Nashville (itself a capital city not much different in size than Indianapolis) who were only now asking what they could do to keep their GM plant open and improve economic development in their area. And this was a week *after* GM had declared bankruptcy.

Seybold had proved time and again that he was pro-active, which sounds a lot like a cliché until you meet someone who actually is. In addition to Seybold's series of tornadic, publicly funded demolitions in the city, he and Grant County officials came up with an even better plan to deal with tax delinquent properties that could not be sold at auction — meaning sold at either a treasurer's office tax sale or a county commissioners' certificate sale. These were properties no one wanted to buy and that government officials didn't really want to pay to demolish, whether or not they could put a lien on the land. The plan, unveiled in July 2009, was for city and county government to simply deed the properties to neighboring property owners for as little as a dollar each; this would allow the neighbors to tear down the existing structures on their own and rebuild, or just have a double lot for their current homes. The city gets rid of problem properties; neighbors add value to their existing properties; and increased future assessments would mean increased revenues.

How did the idea come to the mayor to essentially give tax delinquent or vacant properties to neighbors? The city was mowing hundreds of abandoned properties monthly, then fining owners $150 each time. It would have been a money-making operation for the city, perhaps like writing traffic tickets in a speed trap, except that owners often couldn't be found and the city was in the red on the beautification project. But the mayor and his assistants noticed that some responsible property owners were mowing abandoned properties that adjoined their own anyway, even though they weren't the ones being fined. What Seybold was doing was urban land reform, albeit more for the middle class than the urban poor.

Seybold also went on a buying spree of sorts. While some tax delinquent sites are simply deeded over to the city for free if buyers can't be found, Seybold has ordered his lieutenants to bid on properties at auction if the price was right, thereby speeding up the process of taking control. One case in June 2009 involved a large salvage yard on the historic and wild Mississinewa River, which runs right through Marion. The yard was filled with old tires, loose bricks, and other debris, and the owners had not paid a series of fines related to poor environmental management. Seybold bought the property for $750 at a commissioners' certificate sale; the plan is to clean up the site, then resell it to someone who will develop it for a good purpose. The city also purchased a privately owned parking lot near downtown that will become a city-owned pay lot, as well as a small triangular piece of land in town with no commercial value, but which will serve as a kind of green gateway to nearby businesses.

More significantly, though, Marion turned to what is known as a local option income tax (LOIT), to make up for some budget shortfalls, especially those resulting from the state property tax caps. The local income tax option in Indiana ordinarily provides property tax relief for citizens, that is, money raised through the LOIT can be used as a credit against property taxes owed by citizens. As such, it does nothing for municipalities that already have a shortfall in property tax collections — it's like robbing Peter to pay Paul. However, through a quirk in state law, once that credit is established, a further .25 percent local income tax can be levied, and that money can be used to pay public safety costs such as police salaries. On July 7, 2009, the Marion City

Council endorsed the controversial plan by the narrowest of margins, 5–4. Members of the Grant County Tea Party attended the city council meeting to rudely protest any new tax. Various public safety officials packed the meeting as well, all in support of the new tax. Mayor Seybold, even though a Republican, supported the new tax. "There's no way to cut your way out of this tax," he said after the meeting, referring to various budget cuts and layoffs already in place in Marion.[8]

For all his efforts at containing costs and increasing revenues, Seybold continued to warn that Marion would need between $1.8 million and $2.8 million in further cuts for fiscal year 2010 to balance the budget. "It will not be pretty," he said.

Unemployment in Marion and surrounding Grant County stood at 13.7 percent in June 2009, well above the state average of 10.6 percent at the time, which itself was above the national average. The poverty rate stood at 17.4 percent in 2007, before the current recession, and was 24.8 percent for children eighteen and under. Nearly one in seven residents in the county received food stamps. The poverty figures were worse than those reported for Bedford and Lawrence County, yet educational attainment is better in Marion — nearly eighty percent of adults twenty-five and older have high school diplomas, and 14.1 percent have four-year degrees or better.[9]

One way Marion is trying to turn itself around is via retail development; it turned to Fort Worth–based Buxton Company, which advises cities on such matters, including matching retailers with suitable markets and economic development opportunities. "Retail will bring back industry, because retail brings back people, and people bring industry," said Charles Wetzel, president of the company.

Small towns like Marion that are on the fringe of much larger metro markets (such as Indianapolis and Fort Wayne) suffer "leakage," explained Wetzel, meaning people who live in the smaller communities often take their trade elsewhere when they spend their money. Yet smaller towns represent an opportunity to large retailers and mass merchandisers because there is less competition from other large retailers to worry about. Companies that move in not only can succeed in the market, but dominate it, Wetzel said. It's worth noting that Walmart grew into the world's largest retailer by first setting up shop in smaller towns and on the fringes of major metro markets. But "small town" here means places like Marion, which has a population of about 30,000. As Richard C. Longworth noted in his 2007 book, *Caught in the Middle: America's Heartland in the Age of Globalism*, very small towns, with populations of one or two thousand or less, are losing all their retail establishments, with the partial exception of a single gas station in each that combines a convenience store (or C-store, as they're colloquially known) selling a very few bare essentials like aspirin and toothpaste, maybe fresh milk, and lots of junk food.[10]

Seybold is serious about retail development in Marion, both large and small. He personally attends grand openings of almost any mom-and-pop business in town or local fast-food franchisee. "I love the work, and I just love the process," Seybold said during an interview at an Arby's Restaurant in between meetings at either end of town. "It probably goes back to my training days. I'd be on the ice for seven or eight hours a day, then I'd have to go to work, and you'd do it all over the next day. As a mayor you could put in three or four hours a day, or you could put in twelve."

No city in Indiana was hit harder — or earlier — by sinking fortunes in the American automobile industry than Anderson. Some estimates say there were 24,000 auto industry jobs in Anderson and the immediate environs as recently as a generation ago — virtually all GM employees. Now there are none, though a few hundred may work in new technology start-ups or second-tier automotive suppliers. Up to 10,000 retired GM and Delphi workers are believed to still live in the area, which is a major source of income for the local economy, especially for area hospitals and medical providers — at least until they die off.[11] A new, land-based casino was hailed as a kind of savior for the city when it opened in 2008. The casino employs about 1,000 people and pays $200,000 in taxes per month, yet was threatening bankruptcy by the summer of 2009.

Drew Story, twenty-five, a bartender at Montana Mike's Steakhouse in Anderson, told the *Indianapolis Star* in June 2009 that the casino had helped revitalize the area. "When the factories pulled out of this town, it was almost like pulling the life support out of the community," he said. The casino at Hoosier Park, he said, had "brought the life back."[12]

Hoosier Park, one of two "racinos" in the state, and one of ten casinos overall, paid $250 million in licensing fees to open a casino next to its pre-existing horse racing track in Anderson. With one exception, all other casinos in the state are on boats, either moored in rivers or on Lake Michigan. The logic behind such "riverboat" casinos has always been questionable — some have argued that the gambling is not really in the state if it's on the water, while others have more credibly argued that casino sprawl, crime, and prostitution could better be contained if gambling were restricted to boats, but not allowed on land.

Casinos paid $900 million in taxes to the state of Indiana in 2008, but almost no academics think casinos are the right way to fund state government. Locally, many observers thought the Hoosier Park owners were bluffing when they suggested they'd declare bankruptcy only a year after opening if they didn't get some relief from the admittedly large $250 million licensing fee. What they were doing was akin to sports franchises threatening to leave town if they don't get publicly funded new stadiums to use, a tactic that was allegedly used in recent years by both the Indiana Pacers basketball team and Indianapolis Colts football team, as well as other major sports franchises in the country. Nevertheless, the mere threat to pull the plug and throw another 1,000 people of out work in Anderson had prompted several legislators, but not the governor, to support tax relief for the casino as of the summer of 2009. The game of chicken only intensified in November 2009 when Hoosier Park's parent company, Centaur Gaming, announced it would miss a round of debt payments to its creditors and would close two of its subsidiaries (though not yet Hoosier Park).[13]

Anderson city officials did have some good news in July when $6 million in federal stimulus spending was committed to curb sewer runoff in the White River, which flows through Anderson and several other cities in the state, including Indianapolis. Another $1.5 million was committed to a new water tower near Anderson's Flagship Enterprise Center just off Interstate 69. While much federal stimulus spending clearly was going to dubious road paving projects across America, essentially rewarding highway construction companies (which historically are among the biggest contributors to statewide political campaigns), the Anderson stimulus package had a clear environmental impact and supported what had been an earlier, unfunded state mandate to help clean up the White River.

Anderson city leaders also continued their efforts to bring new business to town. They competed head-on with Kokomo for VGB Starchware, for example, including the offer of paid Ivy Tech State College retraining for new hires, contacts for "creative financing" of any new venture, and especially the offer of a tax-free zone so long as an appropriate portion of production were exported out of the country. Anderson also has control of several former GM plants it could lease at attractive rates, and is closer to a better highway network than is Kokomo, a major advantage. But it's just a scratch-your-way-to-a-living approach for a once proud city with a strong automotive heritage. In October 2009 the city lost out on a bid to lure California-based Fisker Automotive for its new, plug-in automotive plant. The plant would instead be built in Delaware; ironically, Fisker was paying the Motors Liquidation Company (the former General Motors) a paltry $18 million for one of its old plants there. The development is expected to create 2,000 factory jobs and 3,000 vendor and second-tier supplier jobs by 2014.[14]

Taking possession of former factory buildings — a tactic employed in Anderson — has not been done in Kokomo. Mayor Goodnight says he does not want to be in the property management business. In truth, though, he knows that development is going to be an even harder sell in Kokomo than in Anderson, and he doesn't want the city to be stuck with large buildings it can't find businesses to occupy. "You drive that I-69 corridor he's not that far from Fishers," said Goodnight, referring to Anderson mayor Kris Ockomon and to Fishers, Indiana, a prosperous Indianapolis suburb to the immediate northeast of the capital city. "He's a little better positioned than we are."

Then Goodnight added, "I don't really care for competing with other cities, especially that are in close proximity to us. But I didn't make the rules."

Some monies for economic development come via oft-touted job retraining programs in Anderson as well as many other locales in the state and across the country. Many of the laid-off automotive workers in Anderson and elsewhere qualify for job retraining, but there simply aren't any reliable figures on how many actually get new jobs based solely or largely on their new skills. On the contrary, a little-noticed Department of Labor study, first publicized by the *New York Times*, found little or no positive impact of retraining on future job prospects. The 2008 government study compared employment rates and/or current earnings for laid-off workers who received job retraining versus those who did not.[15] The study was labeled by its authors "non-experimental" because it didn't take a cohort of laid-off autoworkers and randomly assign them to "retraining" and "no retraining" groups, then look at outcomes — that would have been a better study, but it would have much more costly and time-consuming, and would have raised sensitive "human subjects" questions.

Michael Luo, the reporter for the *Times*, separately interviewed the authors of the study and other experts as to why something with such a halo effect as "job retraining," including a constant stream of state and federal aid for it over the years, might not be worth much. The reasons he found? "Many workers who have lost their jobs are older and had spent their lives working in one industry," Luo wrote. "In need of a job right away, many pick relatively short training programs, which often have marginal benefits. Job retraining is also ineffective without job creation, a point made by several economists who have long cautioned against placing too much stock in it. Finally, workers trying to pick a new field cannot predict the future of the labor market, especially in a time of economic upheaval."[16]

Unspoken by some observers, perhaps, was the belief that many of the lower skill production workers, people who just do repetitive work all day, had not learned better skills earlier in their lives and probably were never going to, while some workers sign up for retraining just to qualify for extended unemployment benefits in some areas.

Nevertheless, some retraining does work, just like some smoking cessation programs succeed and so do some diets, even if the failure rates are high. One certain growth area for jobs in this country is in the medical arts. Indiana, one of the fattest states in the union, cannot be an exception. That's what Lance Schattner is counting on; he was one of the last Guide employees laid off in Anderson before the automotive lighting manufacturer moved to Mexico. Schattner was scheduled to complete a two-year medical assistant program at Ivy Tech Community College in late 2009. "It's been a really big switch for me," Schattner told the *Indianapolis Star*. "I was never a poor student to begin with [in high school] . . . but for the first time, I know the reason I'm sitting in a class. Knowing why I'm there is important to me. It's easier to know that after going roughly two years in school, I'm going to hopefully get a new career."[17]

Another Anderson resident grabbing the bull by the horns is Randy Good, owner of Good's Candy Store. The business dates to 1981, when Randy's mom and dad, a former GM Delco Remy employee, opened a part-time donut shop. Randy bought the business from his parents and expanded it into a home-made candy store and ice cream parlor with comfortable seating inside a country style, gambrel-roofed building on the edge of Anderson.

What's remarkable about Randy Good's success — his store looks clean, homey, successful, and has a large parking lot — is that he built his business right in the face of Anderson's historic decline. He even put up a new building just five years ago as the last of the "GM orphans," which the spin-offs sometimes were called, were in their final tailspin. Local retail was hurting, but he noticed that Walmart, Lowes, Meijer, and other big box stores still were opening in or near Anderson. "I knew there is money being passed around," said Good, fifty, who is a striking look-alike for actor Michael York. "I wanted to carve out my niche and get my share."

Good says his idea was always to make his shop into a regional destination, not just a neighborhood store, and he even has a full-time traveling salesman who sells his fresh candies across the state. That's part of his key to his success — Good actually has a business plan. Even more remarkable is the fact that Randy Good runs any business at all. While politicians tout the value of small business in job creation, the fact is that so much very small or mom-and-pop business creation in America is done by immigrants, but not people from earlier generations of Americans, namely whites or blacks. From Hispanic-owned grocery stores to Pakistani and Indian restaurants to Arab American–owned residential rental properties, such small businesses by and large are owned by recent immigrants. The immigration debate's focus on illegal immigrants doing low-wage labor in jobs "Americans don't want to do" completely misses this part of the picture. It's as if only immigrants understand the American dream, or believe in it. Or, more alarmingly, retain the requisite drive and skills to actually start and run their own businesses, not merely train for a job or a career where someone else takes the risks, gives the orders, and cuts the checks.

Perhaps money has just come too easily for lots of Americans, especially in the triumphant, post–Second World War years, or maybe lots of Americans just don't want to work seventy or eighty hours per week, as Good often does. Some middle-class Americans will open artsy businesses or new technology ventures, of course, while turnkey franchise operations, such as McDonald's restaurants or Subway Sandwich Shops, abound. Yet the former are really few and far between, while the latter are all capital-intensive businesses where ownership more often than not is absentee anyway. People who own such businesses may be investors, but most are not true businessmen or businesswomen. The evidence is overwhelming, if anecdotal, that most Americans no longer start and run their own businesses, or even are willing to take over their parents' small businesses — the kind that really made up Main Street in small towns and neighborhood shopping districts in big cities across America for generations.

Like Randy Good, Jerry Alexander is an exception to the above rule. His family goes back generations in Indiana; most of his relatives in recent decades worked in the auto industry. "My uncles and aunts all worked for General Motors," said Alexander, a tall, middle-aged businessman with a ruddy complexion. "My friends all worked for General Motors. Guys I went to school with. I was encouraged by my dad to work for GM and I did apply. The only thing is, I applied for a sales job and I didn't get it."

Alexander is a true entrepreneur with his finger in several pies, but he's been struggling under the weight of Anderson's failing economy, as well as the ever present and oppressive armada of local, state, and federal regulations. He owns seventy residential rental units sprinkled through a handful of apartment buildings and homes in Anderson, plus a medium-size commercial building in downtown Anderson that once housed a locksmith and a local bike shop. Residential tenants rarely completed their leases anymore, he lamented. The turnover rate in some of his properties can be several hundred percent per year, suggesting not only big losses for him but huge turmoil in the lives of those tenants. Alexander said he had at least $200,000 in judgments against former tenants, but doesn't expect to collect on any of them.

Alexander is co-owner of a commercial property downtown. When he bought into it a few years ago he found nearly 200 abandoned bicycles that customers had brought in for repair, but never bothered to claim. They could buy a new, made-in-Taiwan or Chinese bicycle at Walmart for little more than the price of repairing that old made-in-America Schwinn or Huffy, so they stuck the bike shop owner with the repair bill. The locksmith moved to a small shop across the street and is open part-time only; he subsists on his Social Security check and runs the business mostly as a hobby now. Alexander's main use for the downtown property was a banquet facility and rental hall that he operated for three years, but it lost money every month. Early in 2009 he remodeled the first floor and opened a restaurant that is upscale by Anderson's standards; it's kind of grand tea room in the old style. It, too, is struggling. He wanted to put in an elevator to the second story of his building and open it up for rental space for professionals and artisans alike, but building codes mandated that he would then have to put in a modern sprinkler system, which was prohibitively expensive. There was just no chance for a return on investment at that point. He could have legally opened the second floor to business without either improvement — the "as is" quality of the building would have been grandfathered in — but he knew almost no customers or clients in America are willing to walk up one flight of stairs under their own power anymore to do business. Altogether Alexander has more than $440,000 of his own money and secured loans tied up in the new restaurant venture. "It's all on the line," he said.

Besides regulations there are the payments he has to collect and/or make, including sales tax, Social Security contributions, unemployment insurance dues, and more. He has a business student from a regional campus of Indiana University who helps him with the books in exchange for a small salary and college credit. "There are so many things that hamstring an independent business," said Alexander. He was speaking during peak lunch hour on a weekday in his restaurant, but only about half the tables were filled, and every diner was old. "Then, once you open up, you realize there are so many things you hadn't thought of."

Like many old-timers, Alexander recalls the days when Anderson streets and sidewalks were jammed not only on Saturdays, but on weekday lunchtime, too. "Downtown businesses were thriving," he said. "There was a lot of foot traffic walking from store to store. It was not uncommon to have several thousand people downtown at one time. A lot of the intersections, they had police directing traffic. Looking back, the nostalgia of it, that was an impressive time."

Now, he feels he's staring into the abyss. Charles Dickens could not have had a darker vision of the future. "I saw something the last couple of weeks I never thought I'd see here in Anderson, street people with grocery carts," Alexander said. "I had never seen people in Anderson do that before, but in the last six months they're going through the dumpsters. I see it here at the restaurant. They're going through it for the metal and the cans. I'm at a point [with rental properties] where multiple families are moving in together. That used to be just Hispanic families. But now it's white families and black families. It's brothers and sisters moving in together with their families. You think you're renting to two, three people, but you're really renting to eight or nine. I'm in court every week evicting people."

Indeed, the city of Anderson faces monumental problems. There are all those retired automotive workers still receiving GM pensions, but that won't last forever. And the city has lost an astounding twenty-five percent in assessed valuation in recent years, even before the property tax caps are factored in.[18] No amount of gambling is going to reverse that process in and of itself.

Anderson is the seat of Madison County. The county has a population of about 130,000, while 56,000 are age forty-five or older. More than 20,000 are age sixty-five or older. About eighty percent of residents age twenty-five or older have a high school diploma or better, while slightly fewer than one in seven have a college degree or better. The state average for college-educated adults is one in five. The poverty rate is high — nearly fourteen percent overall and more than twenty-two percent for children under age eighteen as of 2007, the last year for which complete data are available. Nearly one in nine residents in the county is on food stamps, and the June 2009 unemployment rate was 11.4 percent. The latter figure is higher than the state average, but better than other automotive cities in the state. Many residents simply commute to jobs in the Indianapolis metro market, of course, or to prosperous northern and northeastern suburbs of Indianapolis.[19]

If truth be told, there will be winners and losers in Indiana's automotive towns, as will be the case in former manufacturing towns across the United States and Canada. This is not quite the same thesis as Richard Florida's prediction that only cities attractive to the "creative class" will survive. The creative class consists of highly educated, technologically savvy, artsy, and racially and sexually diverse individuals who, according to Florida, will save some of North America's best cities by making them more attractive to other creative people and therefore more conducive to business and entrepreneurial development. This is not Kokomo or Anderson. In places like these, it will be the quality of public schools, the local crime rate, cost of living, tax policy, quality of the labor market, highways and rail lines, energy costs — all the classic ingredients of growth.

Back in Kokomo, newspaper publisher Wayne Janner worried, too. Well into his sixties, Janner is a lifelong Kokomo resident and former GM Delco Electronics worker. His weekly newspaper, the *Kokomo Herald*, is the smallest of three papers regularly published in the city. Most stories are the kind of notices and announcements you'd find in any weekly "shopper," but he'll cover the schools, local tax controversies, and the jobs market, as well, which is what local newspapers have always done well. He's socially and politically conservative and, like Anderson's Jerry Alexander, likes the old days better than what he sees around him today.

"I began to look for a job in 1961," after graduating high school, Janner recalled. "There were many factories in Kokomo at the time, a goodly number of small factories. I made the rounds looking for a job. Things were very unproductive in that regard and I contemplated going into the military. Something finally popped and came through in the fall. At the time it was known as Delco Radio. Later on they upgraded it to Delco Electronics. So I had a career there in the factory. I went into skilled trades for most of my time there. I was in skilled trades twenty-three years out of my thirty-one years at GM. . . .

"I don't think there's any doubt back in those days when I hired in at General Motors I felt fortunate to get a job that paid fairly well. The smaller factories in town paid considerably less. But there was Chrysler, there was Delco and the steel companies. The smaller companies were suppliers, like a feeder system, both for companies and for workers. It seemed like there was a lot of mobility in those days, especially in the smaller factories where it wasn't quite so critical. If you weren't happy where you working, you could quit your job and go across town to where you might be more happy. They seemed to always be expanding. Compare that to today, where there are very few or almost no jobs."

Janner retired from Delco on a Friday in 1993; the next Monday he took over his mother's newspaper business and has been running it since. It makes very little money; he's mostly survived on his GM pension, Social Security and, now, Medicare insurance, he says.

Janner says that growing up in Kokomo was "calm and relaxed" with very little crime. This is how many Americans remember the early post–Second World War years and well into the 1950s. The working classes didn't yet have much, but they never felt poor, and the quality of life and sense of community was better, at least for most. He even likes Indiana's continuing "blue laws," which ban most alcohol sales on Sundays, but were much tougher in the old days. "Nothing was open on Sundays, except maybe a couple of restaurants and some things you needed for emergencies," he said. "You'd go to church, then you'd go for a ride in the country."

If Janner can wax nostalgic for the old days, a kind of *Leave It to Beaver* and *Father Knows Best* world that actually did exist for many, if not all Americans, he is not indifferent to the future. "How bad can things get? Oh, it can get much worse in Kokomo and in the country. The track that we're on in this country and the lack of political statesmanship we have in this country, in some cases the lack of integrity, does not give me any hope. . . . Thirty years ago it never would have occurred to me that we would be having this conversation."

And that's where Goodnight and other local leaders come in. Much closer to the people than millionaire senators who all send their children to private schools in Washington, D.C., or even congressmen and congresswomen whose districts cover large, meandering swaths within a state and who represent many hundreds of thousands of voters each, and who are always running for reelection anyway, it's the mayors who always know what is happening first. That's why Greg Goodnight went to Italy — he knew the cavalry might not be coming, so he had to fend for himself.

"Personally, I loved Italy," said Goodnight. "It was different. I had never been to Europe. They're not as excessive as we are. Not as much air conditioning as we have here. I had a lot of business meetings and they used natural lighting. We walked between floors to go to different rooms. I never saw an escalator, though my wife said she saw one at a train station."

The mayor came back with no firm commitment to keep any jobs in Kokomo, but nevertheless believed the trip was a success. "It wasn't just a quick handshake, photo op, and out the door," Goodnight said. "They were very clear that some of the products they offer won't be sold here because the American consumer is just not ready to change their ways. They're not going to try to dump a bunch of products on us and hope they will succeed. They do have one or two products they will sell here."

Overall, this was good news because it suggested that Fiat knew it would have to make some products for the North American market in North America.

Goodnight and his team also met with about ten other Italian companies in their week-long visit, including alternative energy and green companies. Brian A. Howey, editor of the highly regarded *Howey Politics Indiana*, likes Kokomo's stated focus on a green future and especially its investment in K-Fuel as one way of moving the city ahead, and says he's surprised the concept has not taken off elsewhere in the state. "They're using K-Fuel to steer away from what I call the long-term Indiana love affair with the internal combustion engine," Howey said. "I did a column on [K-Fuel] that runs in twenty-five newspapers across the state. I would have thought [city leaders] would be beating a path to Kokomo."

The challenges confronting Kokomo are immense. In June 2009 unemployment rose to 19.7 percent, the highest in the state and close to Great Depression levels, when one in four Americans was out of a job. And while Chrysler jobs were safe for now, many Chrysler models remain the least competitive of the traditional Detroit Three manufacturers in a highly competitive market with continued overcapacity worldwide. Goodnight wasn't throwing in the towel quite yet, though. He keeps a heavily marked-up copy of Longworth's *Caught in the Middle* in his house like some people keep the Bible, and he recommends it and its gospel of regional economic development to anyone who will listen. Goodnight also believes that some cities will be winners in the days and years ahead, and some will be losers. He wants to be one of the winners. As we talked, Goodnight could only take another swig from a bottle of ginger ale, sigh, and wax philosophical. "I feel like things happen for a reason," he said. "I was union president at my former employer when we went through a bankruptcy. I feel this is probably what I should be doing now."

1. Mike Smith, "Legislature Approves Property Tax Caps," *Chesterton (Ind.) Tribune*, March 14, 2008, http://chestertontribune.com/Indiana%20News/3153%20Legislature_approves_property_t.htm and "The Facts on Property Tax Caps in Indiana," http://www.elwoodindiana.org/content/facts-property-tax-caps-indiana.

2. Andrea Hopkins, "Honda Opens New US Plant as Detroit Seeks Bailout," Reuters UK, November 17, 2008, http://uk.reuters.com/article/idUKN1751884720081117.

3. For a good summary and analysis of British government efforts to save its once dominant motorcycle industry in the 1970s, see Abe Aamidor, *Shooting Star: The Rise and Fall of the British Motorcycle Industry* (Toronto: ECW Press, 2009), Chapter 6.

4. Ted Evanoff and Michele McNeil Solida, "No End in Sight for Incentives," *Indianapolis Star*, December 29, 2002, A1, and additional research from *Indianapolis Star* library.

5. Indiana Department of Education, "Indiana High School Graduation Rates Released," January 22,

2008, http://www.iyi.org/resources/pdf/databook-education.pdf.

6. STATS Indiana, "Lawrence County IN Depth Profile," http://www.stats.indiana.edu/profiles/pr18093.html.

7. "Connersville Preps for Police- Car Plant Rally," *Palladium-Item*, July 27, 2009, http://www.indystar.com/article/20090727/BusINESS/90727003/Connersville+preps+for+police-car+plant+rally.

8. Maribeth Holtz, "LOIT OK'd at 1 Percent: City Council Says Statewide Property Tax Reforms Reason," *(Marion) Chronicle-Tribune*, July 8, 2009, http://www.chronicle-tribune.com/articles/2009/07/08/news/doc4a542b3446a8f904320792.txt.

9. STATS Indiana, "Grant County IN Depth Profile," http://www.stats.indiana.edu/profiles/pr18053.html.

10. Richard C. Longworth, *Caught in the Middle: America's Heartland in the Age of Globalism* (New York: Bloomsbury, 2008), 93–94.

11. Longworth, 48.

12. Bill Ruthart and Amanda Hamon, "Facing Long Odds: Cities Have Much To Lose if Casinos' Struggles Continue," *Indianapolis Star*, June 22, 2009, A-01.

13. Bill Ruthart, "Anderson and Track Face a Tough Future," *Indianapolis Star*, November 2, 2009, http://www.indystar.com/apps/pbcs.dll/article?AID=2009911020352.

14. Randall Chase,"Fisker to Build Hybrid Cars at Idled Del. GM Plant," Associated Press, October 27, 2009, http://abcnews.go.com/Business/wireStory?id=8925649.

15. Jacob M. Benus, et al., "Workforce Investment Act Non-Experimental Net Impact Evaluation: Final Report," prepared by Impaq International, http://wdr.doleta.gov/research/FullText_Documents/Workforce%20Investment%20Act%20Non-Experimental%20Net%20Impact%20Evaluation%20-%20Final%20Report.pdf.

16. Michael Luo, "Job Retraining May Fall Short of High Hopes," *New York Times*, July 6, 2009, http://www.nytimes.com/2009/07/06/us/06retrain.html?_r=2&hp.

17. Ted Evanoff, "Too Little Stimulus Cash for Indiana?" *Indianapolis Star*, March 8, 2009, A1.

18. Editorial, "Shared Sacrifice Will Help City," *Anderson Herald-Bulletin*, June 14, 2009.

19. STATS Indiana, "Madison County IN Depth Profile," http://www.stats.indiana.edu/profiles/pr18095.html.

CHAPTER 10

Electric Shock

WHILE KOKOMO MAYOR GREG GOODNIGHT flew off to Italy, hoping to secure a guarantee from Fiat that it would keep jobs in his Indiana city, Japanese automaker Nissan was hoping to secure a commitment of a different sort — a $1.6 billion loan from the United States government. What happened next revealed the unusual forces starting to weigh on Middle America's factory towns. Goodnight returned home empty-handed. Nissan closed the deal.

One struck out, one scored — a sign the automotive world created in Detroit a century earlier was splintering. Nissan would spend the federal loan preparing its complex at Smyrna, Tennessee, to produce electric cars by 2010. Handing an advantage like a federal loan to a foreign company in direct competition with the automakers in Detroit surviving on an infusion of taxpayer dollars caused hardly a stir in Washington. The future might be green from the vantage point of President Barack Obama, but salvaging Detroit and ushering new, environmentally friendly cars onto American roads were not considered one and the same.

The White House had committed $77 billion in taxpayer money to rescue General Motors and Chrysler from the recession, and take them in and out of quick bankruptcies. At the same time, $25 billion was available from Congress for retooling plants to assemble new, ultra fuel-efficient autos. Chrysler and GM, however, were for the time being barred from this green-car loan fund, the Advanced Technology Vehicles Manufacturing

(ATVM) program, until they could show financial stability.[1] Obama had campaigned in favor of putting more hybrid cars on American roads. No one seriously thought GM would be shut out from green-car loans, but playing second fiddle to Nissan, which intended to debut the Leaf electric car on American roads by 2012, was clearly a departure from the old ways. Obama did not stand in the way of Nissan's loan, even though the Japanese automaker could gain a competitive advantage over the Detroit companies just emerging from bankruptcy. "It's important to remember that the Obama Administration has its own agenda and it doesn't always jibe with business imperatives," reasoned *Business Week* magazine auto writers David Welch and David Kiley.[2]

Left unsaid was that America was seriously behind in automotive research. For the last year, GM executives had touted the proposed Chevrolet Volt, a $40,000 plug-in hybrid car scheduled to reach dealers in late 2010. But the car was widely considered too costly to be GM's main offering in the coming market for green cars. GM needed a car nearer half that price, something a middle-class commuter could afford. What insiders understood, however, was that green-car leadership necessary to devise such a vehicle had been draining out of Detroit and the United States. While GM and Chrysler struggled during the summer of 2009, rival automaker Hyundai wrapped up a four-year, $200 million research program aimed at delivering a subcompact hybrid expressly designed to take on the popular Honda Civic hybrid on Hyundai's home turf of South Korea. Powered by high-tech batteries and propane, a common fuel in South Korea, the $15,800 Avante LPi debuted in the summer of 2009 and was priced less than the Civic model.[3] It paved the way for a number of gasoline-electric hybrids expected to reach the United States in 2010, including a hybrid version of the Sonata sedan.[4] The Avante's innovative distinction was located beneath the floor — the nest for lithium polymer batteries, which Hyundai engineers decided were cheaper to make and smaller in size than the lithium-ion technology others in the auto industry were trying to perfect.

While Hyundai was coming late to the hybrid party — the Toyota Prius had been around since 1998 — it was at least coming in with a car whose appeal was both a low asking price and fuel economy. "A race is heating up for green cars," Hyundai spokesman Noh Jin-seok announced at the Avante's unveiling in Seoul. "Hybrid cars in the green-car race will be vital for Hyundai."⁵

But if the Koreans took the race seriously, General Motors was still trying to find the track. Only weeks before the Avante was unveiled in Seoul, GM canceled the Chevrolet Malibu Hybrid, selling fewer than 1,000 of the gas-electric sedans in May in the United States. The gasoline-only Malibu long had impressed critics as a plush and sporty ride rivaling the midsize Honda Accord. Some called the Chevy an equal to upscale European road cars. But the hybrid version disappointed. Held back by a very small electric motor, the hybrid offered little thrust and didn't mesh well with the transmission. "The result is a queasy sensation of surging and relaxing, especially in heavy traffic and hilly terrain," *New York Times* auto reviewer Lawrence Ulrich reported. "Drop off the gas to coast, even at freeway speeds, and the clumsy power-regenerating mode makes the car feel as if it is dragging an anchor."⁶

Mediocre performance might have been overlooked, except Americans quickly figured out the $26,275 list price dimmed the hybrid Malibu's appeal. The fuel economy was sound at 26 miles per gallon in the city and 34 mpg on the open road, yet a four-cylinder gasoline Malibu with a six-speed transmission zipped along at 22 mpg in the city, 33 mpg highway, and was priced $2,325 below the hybrid model. "The feds estimate that the hybrid will save you — wait for it — just $146 a year in fuel compared with that four-cylinder sibling," Ulrich said. "Even accounting for a one-time $1,550 tax credit, this hybrid won't put you in the black through fuel savings. . . . It's time to add the Malibu Hybrid to the growing pile of hybrid failures from General Motors."

Canceling the hybrid Malibu was a sobering counterpoint to an Obama administration advocating hybrids and electric vehicles as the keys to easing America's half-century-long reliance on imported oil. Detroit auto executives, particularly at General Motors, never had been enamored of hybrids in the first place. Hybrids were viewed as a Tokyo solution to brief commutes on congested urban streets. GM engineers had believed an exotic form of electric car known as the fuel cell could satisfy America's penchant for long drives. Since the 1990s, GM had spent more than $1 billion on the fuel cell, but shelved the half-completed program in the mid-2000s largely for want of cash, but also the lack of a suitable battery after years of research by a government-industry consortium. Now, Japan and South Korea were the acknowledged intellectual homes, not only for hybrids, but also for what was considered absolutely essential in next-generation cars, whether fuel cells or hybrid electrics — powerful, massive batteries derived from lithium technology. China claimed its strides in electric vehicles soon would make it the center for EV technology. German carmaker Daimler, girded with a $2.7 billion infusion for green technology research from the sovereign wealth fund of Abu Dhabi, was staking its lead in Europe, where GM was thinking of selling off its own massive Adam Opel AG operation, once a center for green-car research.

It was not as if Detroit was starting from nothing. But it was not clear which form of green technology would become the leader, or whether green was even a sound investment for an automaker's resources. Obviously, energy prices were a decisive factor. When oil prices surged, reaching $145 per barrel in July 2008, eager Americans bought all of Toyota's imported Prius hybrids. As oil prices fell by half over the next year, sales weakened, and Toyota shelved plans to build a Prius assembly plant at Tupelo, Mississippi. The price of oil — fluctuating in part because of America's weak dollar and massive appetite for imports — was whipsawing the auto industry's strategic planners. Even though it was outselling GM, Toyota nevertheless lost about $7.7 billion in its 2009 financial year. Almost all the loss originated in the United States. No automaker could afford to bet its future entirely on green cars, yet a major decision faced auto executives. They had to decide which form of technology was the best bet.

Electric cars, hybrids, plug-in hybrids, clean diesels, natural gas, and biofuels were at the leading edge of technology available to achieve the government's new edict for sharply higher fuel economy in 2015. Electric cars, hybrids, and/or plug-in hybrids seemed to be the front runners in 2009, at least in the North American market, yet no one was quite sure if electric vehicles or plug-ins could be made affordable enough to be truly best sellers for ordinary commuting and driving chores. In the auto world, an electric car like GM's old EV1 had no engine and moved entirely on power furnished to an electric motor from batteries recharged from wall outlets. A plug-in like the Chevrolet Volt was powered by an electric motor running on batteries and recharged by a small gas engine under the hood or plugged into an electric power outlet. A conventional hybrid like the Prius mated a conventional gasoline engine to an electric motor that assisted during acceleration and was recharged by the engine. Either an electric or plug-in freed the driver from the fuel pump for a round trip of less than fifty or seventy miles. Both types ran on electric power drawn from sophisticated lithium-ion batteries. No battery of this type and size ever had been mass-produced. Prototypes weighed as much as 600 pounds and cost $14,000 apiece in 2009 — as much as a small gasoline-powered car. But lithium-ion batteries promised to ease the world's dependence on expensive oil. This was the holy grail.

What battery engineers had to do was scrape out the weight and cost. The only way to do that was to lavish money on research, make generations of the big batteries, and produce them in sufficient quantities so the research costs could be spread over long production runs. And the cost of manufacturing the rest of the car also had to come down, to make the whole package affordable. Because unless it was a pure electric vehicle, the car still came with an engine, and the cost of the electric motor, batteries, and electronic controls (meshing the motor, batteries and engine) had to be added on. This took considerable research and development talent. The problem in Detroit was that while Ford had some research money on hand in 2009, GM and Chrysler were all but broke.

With 250 million cars and trucks in use in America, and nearly twice that number around the world, the very idea of plug-in hybrids and electric cars seemed like clean and modern solutions to real problems. After all, exhaust emissions fouled urban air with brown skies of smog. In 1997, smog was responsible for six million asthma attacks in the United States each year plus 159,000 emergency room visits and 53,000 hospitalizations, according to reports cited in California environmental regulator Terry Tamminen's book, *Lives per Gallon*.[7] America long had been trying to clean the air, but with half-hearted measures like the 1975 Corporate Average Fuel Economy law, which played out unevenly over the years. CAFE led to the ubiquitous window stickers on new autos, showing the average miles per gallon in city and highway tests, and did force automakers to improve fuel economy, but the results were a compromise.

When buyers resisted little cars capable of 35 mpg, engineers tuned and tweaked bigger engines and transmissions into modern power trains. These improved mileage but sacrificed greater fuel economy for higher horsepower, a compromise meant to satisfy both CAFE and the customers who shunned the small cars' size and arthritic acceleration. By the late 1990s, a roomy family sedan like the Buick LeSabre ran twenty-eight miles on the open road on a single gallon of gasoline, about double the fuel economy of full-size Buicks from the 1970s. While the gain was impressive, urban skies did not suddenly clear. The number of vehicles in use had doubled in a generation as the baby boomers and their offspring started driving, and as more women went into the labor force and needed cars to get to work, one result of American wages stagnating in the 1970s while the consumer appetite didn't. People drove farther, too. Beginning in the 1950s, the nation's new interstate highway system spawned distant residential suburbs for middle-class families who worked in the city and commuted home by car. In time, big Buicks weren't the preferred ride for suburbia. The top choices were midsize Japanese and Korean cars, as well as Detroit's commodious minivans and high-riding pickup trucks and sport-utility vehicles, 12- and 15-mpg luxury models with air conditioners, four-wheel drive systems, and sturdy tow packages — all of which cut fuel economy though, to be sure, a conventional two-wheel-drive minivan like the Ford Windstar managed 24 mpg on the freeway. Minivans were built of lighter car parts while SUVs evolved from pickups built on sturdy steel frames for heavy-work chores.

With oil trading for as little as $10 per barrel after the East Asian economy crashed in the speculative lending bubble of 1997, gasoline prices hardly concerned Americans. Most buyers of new autos, after all, were in the upper third of the income bracket and readily accepted the $28,000 average transaction price on a new SUV reported by GM in the late 1990s. And interest rates were so low that leasing a big SUV truck for $200 per month was cheaper than buying a four-cylinder sedan for $300 per month. By 1999, pickups and SUVs outsold coupes and sedans in nearly every state. America was in the midst of the truck craze. Toyota had put up three truck plants in Indiana and Texas to capitalize on the insatiable demand for trucks. GM brought out the Hummer, a slab-sided army truck that looked like an SUV on steroids but conveyed the public mood during a roaring economy fueled by cheap oil and a tech-stock euphoria. When GM market researchers surveyed American teens after the quick 1991 Gulf War, the boys talked of two images. There was the supremacy of American technology (television news had shown armed American cruise missiles miraculously navigating Iraqi streets to fly precisely into the window of the target building). And there was the modern jeep in the form of the rugged Humvee. Essentially a jumbo SUV, the army truck was assembled by AM General Corp. of South Bend, Indiana, and equipped with a superior four-wheel-drive system. The Humvee was also called the Hummer, both names being soldier shorthand for the Pentagon's unlikely

277

designation for the truck, High-Mobility Multipurpose Wheeled Vehicle. Sensing that American society was shedding the anti-military bent common among many baby boomers since the Vietnam era, GM execs figured the Humvee could be an aspirational vehicle for the next generation of drivers longing for a vehicle that suggested the individuality of the owner. GM bought the Hummer brand name from AM General (then owned by Long Island billionaire Ira Rennert, and now owned by corporate raider and lipstick magnate Ronald Perelman of Revlon fame). General Motors ginned up luxury SUVs in the Humvee's image — the Hummer H1, H2, and H3 — and revived its fading Cadillac brand around a design theme of art and science said to reflect American prowess in technology. One of the first top sellers was the Cadillac Escalade SUV. As the truck boom in America crowded the roads with pickups and SUVs, various nations had tried to make efforts to scale back pollution with flimsy accords like the Kyoto Treaty of 1998. But better fuel economy was less a concern for United States government policy makers than oil exploration. In 2000, Washington provided annual tax breaks and subsidies for oil companies exceeding $10 billion, and spent another $55 billion guarding the pipelines and sea lanes plied by tankers carrying oil to American ports, *Lives per Gallon* says.[8]

By the time Barack Obama was elected president, America used 21 million barrels of oil each day, burning about half of it, 440 million gallons, chiefly in automobiles and big freight trucks, but also trains, planes, buses, lawn mowers, tractors, combines, harvesters, road graders, boats, and ships. In 1950, the United States produced half the oil used in the world, but fifty years later the nation wasn't supplying even half of its own oil. By 2009, Americans were paying foreign oil producers more than $800 million each day — or more than $290 billion per year, a massive outflow of money, part of it borrowed from China on credit through the sale of United States Treasury bills. About 60 percent of the oil used in the United States was imported, chiefly from Canada and Mexico, but also the Persian Gulf, Europe, and South America. So much cash flowed out of the country for oil and other imports, the dollar's value fell overseas. Faced with an ebbing dollar, oil producers counteracted the eroded buying power with higher prices, which in turn raised gasoline prices for American consumers. So did China's quick economic rise — which depleted oil surpluses — and speculators betting on oil's price gyrations in the global markets.

Slapping a $2 per gallon federal tax on gasoline would have encouraged Americans to park the SUVs and buy small cars. It also would have set off a heated political debate among a citizenry in no mood to pay more taxes. The one, quick policy response Washington could wield against the rising oil bill was CAFE. For decades auto executives in Detroit and a multitude of lawmakers in Congress had fended off stricter fuel economy measures. There was an economic logic to this in Detroit that also made political sense in Washington. Trucks accounted for seventy percent of Chrysler's sales volume, sixty percent of Ford's, and just over half of GM's. Seriously tweaking CAFE could benefit the foreign automakers' sales of small cars, and batter the golden goose for the half a million autoworkers and literally thousands of managers and owners of auto-parts manufacturing companies tied to the Detroit Three.

Once the global economy collapsed in the rubble of Wall Street, though, Obama was elected along with a tide of fellow Democrats. Little complaint was heard when Obama, in one of his first moves in office, let the CAFE administrator impose sharply higher mileage standards, beginning in 2015. In fact, most Americans favored the move. The standards were far beyond anything the auto execs had imagined could come out of the docile precincts of Capitol Hill, but Detroit's clout had vanished. In a new sign of the times, GM negotiated the sale of the Hummer brand rights to an obscure Chinese manufacturer of construction equipment (although AM General continued manufacturing the H2 model in Indiana). Not only were Chrysler and General Motors surviving on lifelines tended by the White House, but the United States government owned a controlling sixty percent stake in GM. Obama insisted GM going forward would produce a larger volume of fuel-efficient cars, an echo of his campaign theme of putting 1 million plug-in hybrids capable of 150 mpg on American roads by 2015. The United States government also allocated another $2 billion for green-car technology on top of the $25 billion appropriated earlier by Congress.

Washington's largesse had opened a new era for hybrids, plug-in hybrids, and pure electric cars. While the technology sounded ultra sophisticated, Obama actually was circling the country back to its automotive roots. Not only had the electric car been on hand for the dawn of the automobile age, it was France's electric tricycle of 1881 that actually ushered in the auto era. Electricity and steam power, not gasoline engines, were the familiar technologies for many of the leading nineteenth century entrepreneurs bringing out automobiles. Americans were weary of travel by horse and buggy on the often muddy and usually rutted roads found in every county and most cities. Demand for the original battery-powered electric cars soon surpassed steam-driven models, but electric cars fell by the wayside to that interloper, the gasoline internal combustion engine. Gas cars quickly caught on and were preferred for the freedom of the long drive. No battery stored enough energy for hours of driving. That was true then. And it is true today.

Always avid travelers, Americans had welcomed the rapid construction of the Clipper ships and steamboats, canals and locks, interurbans and railroads. But it was getting to the stations and docks, indeed just getting around, that always proved trying. By 1891, Connecticut bicycle manufacturing tycoon Albert Augustus Pope had created the nation's first road lobby, the League of American Wheelmen, by writing in his pamphlet, "Highway Improvement," that "American roads are among the worst in the civilized world and always have been."9 Seen largely as a toy of the affluent, the early car was written off as a costly novelty by a chronicler of tony American society in the magazine *Country Life in America.* But after Pope had recast his bicycle plants to make electric cars, a dozen other entrepreneurs soon matched his example. Improvements like enclosed cabins rapidly made the cars desirable to drayman, physicians, and others who traveled constantly. In 1899, manufacturers sold 1,575 electric cars, a volume that outpaced steam cars and certainly gasoline cars, but was hardly a harbinger of what was to come.[10]

The gasoline internal combustion engine was still the loud, cantankerous, and difficult-to-master newcomer on the scene, while electric cars were regarded as quiet, reliable and easy to operate. Indiana Bicycle Company had made its first electric vehicle in 1898, the Waverly, and by 1903 was selling 2,000 per year. Merging with Pope, it advertised six Pope Waverly Electrics in 1905 — the $850 Road Wagon, the $1,400 Stanhope, the $1,450 Coupe Top Chelsea, the $1,500 Surrey, and the $2,250 Station Wagon. The fastest model was the $950 Speed Road Wagon. Boasted one ad: "We have succeeded in producing a carriage that will do 18 miles per hour."[11]

What finally did in the electric car was what limits it today — the range of the batteries. Range became a serious liability among Americans a century ago after the astonishing developments at Spindletop, Texas, and Highland Park, Michigan. Spindletop meant oil, a gusher, more than anyone ever had believed could be underground. And when drills going more than 1,000 feet below the surface of Texas finally reached it in 1901, the sea of oil not only ensured easy access to petroleum for generations of Americans, it spawned Gulf Oil, American Oil (later, Amoco), Humble Oil (now part of ExxonMobil), and a host of other oil companies, all of whom competed, and in that rivalry held the price of gasoline to around ten cents per gallon, or about two dollars in today's money. Gasoline was suddenly plentiful, relatively cheap, and, up on the outskirts of Detroit, Henry Ford was about to do what never had been done — not even by the innovative industrial engineers of England, France, and Germany. He was going to mass-produce the car, turn it from the object of affection for the wealthy to an everyday conveyance affordable even for ordinary Americans.

Ford took the car out of the hands of his craftsmen and put it on the assembly line he had created — first in Highland Park though he soon expanded nearby in colossal proportions at the Rouge. The latter was the 100,000-employee complex built on the edge of Detroit at River Rouge, the name of a creek dredged to open turning basins for the 500-foot-long steamships coming off Lake Huron laden with iron ore for the new Ford steel mills. In 1910, the price of a basic Ford Model T was comparable to Pope Waverly Electrics' $950 Speed Road Wagon. By 1915, the price of the Model T had plunged almost in half to $490, or about $10,000 in today's money. By 1920, a new Model T went for $290, notes Lindsay Brooke's authoritative history, *Ford Model T: The Car That Put the World on Wheels.*[12]

Ford purposely designed the car to ride high over muddy roads and gave it 3.5-inch wide tires to handle the ruts. The rugged, reliable, inexpensive gasoline Model T not only did more than any other vehicle to put America on wheels, it also dispatched the electric car, with the aid of legions of mechanics who improved the design of the gas engine, and now largely forgotten innovators like Charles Kettering. His Dayton Engineering Laboratories Company brought out the electric self-starter in 1912, a device that finally made the gasoline car start easily with the turn of a switch, just like an electric. In 1913, the electric car business peaked. A decade later, it had all but vanished.

Ford himself was entirely familiar with steam and electric power, having worked his early years laboring in a Detroit River shipyard and then the nearby shop of Thomas Edison, the genius whose inventive mind brought forth the lightbulb, the phonograph, and batteries for the early electric cars. Edison had worked on durable storage batteries and finally perfected his iron-nickel version, but by then most motorists favored his old understudy's Model Ts for the absolute freedom gasoline cars provided on open roads. In the *History of the Electric Automobile*, Ernest H. Wakefield writes of Pope manufacturing boss Hiram Maxim waxing eloquently in print in 1897 about something then entirely foreign to most Americans, country jaunts to one town after another in an electric automobile going 12 miles per hour. "Maxim . . . probably earliest caught the sense of what would become 'touring,' a phenomenon that would transform America. It would cause a transcontinental network of roads to be established, transform the petroleum companies, and cause the West to drill for oil in the Middle East," Wakefield wrote. "Tourism would prove a poison for electric vehicles, and a tonic for gasoline-powered automobiles. For the first time, the range of a vehicle became significant. A fully charged battery would propel Hiram Maxim's electric 25 miles; a full tank of gasoline would move . . . [a] Gasoline motorcar 200 miles! The tank could be refilled in five minutes; a battery recharge required five hours. What was true in 1900 is, unfortunately, valid at the close of the twentieth century." [13]

When Wakefield, an electrical engineer who had worked on the Manhattan Project atom bomb program during the Second World War, published his book in 1994, what he didn't know — what hardly anyone in the world knew — was that Toyota was going to put a car on the road in a few years that was part electric, part gasoline, and this hybrid would compel people to think of the electric car as something entirely capable of dethroning the gas automobile from its preeminence on the highway. That car was the Prius, the very vehicle that would inspire Washington in 2009 to start spending money on electric vehicles. While even engineers in Detroit admitted the Prius design and the packaging of the internal systems was almost flawless, Detroit insisted the Prius was not really about fuel economy on American highways. From the very start, Toyota engineers agreed.

Prius had been designed in the mid-1990s for Tokyo's congested streets. It was engineered to solve a specific problem, curbing fuel use on short city treks. Introduced to America in 1998, the hybrid sedan caught on in the middle-class suburbs, but caught on slowly as a fad. Oil prices then were low, making the Prius an expensive showpiece for consumers who wanted to tout their green acumen. Toyota priced the auto at about $20,000 but subsidized the cost for years in the American market. There was some resistance to the first generation Prius in part because of its styling. The original was very small and unattractive, calling attention to itself more like a bumper car let loose from a carnival rather than a serious mode of transport. The similarly styled Honda Insight looked just as hokey (one auto writer compared it to a tadpole in appearance), was produced from 2000, and also did not sell well, though the ordinary-looking Civic Hybrid sold better. It was the second generation Prius that really lit a fire under hybrid sales — it looked chic, not gimmicky, while still proclaiming its new technology. The third-generation Prius, introduced in 2009 with a kind of "flower power" advertising theme, largely kept the styling cues from the second generation Prius. Honda's new Insight, also introduced in 2009, is an extremely close stylistic copy of the Prius.

Two power plants — gasoline engine and electric motor that charged a battery — pushed up the subcompact car's costs along with the computers and electronic controls that meshed everything together. A conventional gasoline engine propelled the Prius on the highway. The electric motor took over for stop-and-go urban traffic, or assisting the engine in accelerating the car, or running the heating and cooling systems when the car was idling. Friction from braking was channeled to the battery as electric power, allowing the battery to power the car in stop-and-go traffic while the gasoline engine stayed off unless a burst was needed for acceleration. This is why hybrids show better mileage on city streets than on open roads. The 2009 Toyota Prius averaged 48 miles per gallon in the city and 45 miles per gallon on the highway, reported the U.S. government website Fueleconomy.gov. Prius mated a 1.5-litre engine to a small motor supplied from 1.6 killowat-hour nickel metal hydride batteries. The virtue of these batteries was lower cost than the lithium-ion version. Nickel metal types, however, had one serious drawback. They stored much less energy than the lithium-ion model, which limited the Prius' all-electric highway range to only a few miles. Lithium-ion promised a breakthrough. A 20 kilowatt-hour capacity battery pack serving a big electric motor could run the car forty to sixty miles in the city, or an hour on the open road.

Prius, of course, was a gas-electric hybrid. On the horizon were plug-in gas electric hybrids such as the planned 2012 Chevrolet Volt. Making use of its small gas engine let plug-in hybrid advocates boast of potential mileage on city streets of 100 mpg. This was tantalizing fuel economy. And it was largely the reason a race was on to scale up the lithium-ion battery, long used in tiny forms for powering cell phones and small computers, for use in automobiles. The first automaker with an affordable electric or plug-in family car in the showroom would most likely take a big sales lead over rivals. The leader might even scoop up enough business to collapse weaker carmakers, just as Ford's prowess generations earlier had dispatched once common nameplates like the Pope Waverly Electric Speed Road Wagon. The leader could become the world's resident expert in electric propulsion, bring enormous wealth, and employ thousands of engineers, scientists, researchers, and technicians.

There was just one problem from the standpoint of Detroit and the industrial Midwest. While America was not without green-car knowledge, it was no longer concentrated in Detroit, or any other one location. Craig Irwin studied the prospects of the green-car business as a financial analyst for San Francisco investment advisor Merriman Curhan Ford. What he found were technology pockets in San Francisco and Denver, Austin and Indianapolis, Toronto and Boston. But the research in the various places — at least by the time the $1.6 billion in federal loans had gone out to Nissan — had not coalesced into an industry on a common course and sure of its goals, particularly on lithium-ion research. "The lack of a large entity [like GM] caused the shrinkage of the intellectual economy in North America around battery technology," Irwin said. "There's actually been a scarcity of talent" in Detroit.[14]

Serious engineers with years of Detroit experience concurred with Irwin. Kenneth Baker had been GM's vice president for global research and development. His hallmark was the innovative

EVI. After he retired in 1999, Baker remained acutely interested in electric cars, and was named to the board of directors of Ener1, the New York–based owner of EnerDel, a lithium-ion battery researcher in Indianapolis whose family tree extended to GM Delco and Charles Kettering's Dayton Engineering Labs. Despite all the current talk of electric cars powered by lithium-ion batteries, Baker was cautious. "The reality is there is not a lot of field experience" in lithium-ion batteries scaled up for cars, he said, "and not a lot of manufacturing experience in high-volume production."

Baker took umbrage with Obama assailing Detroit for failing to anticipate a rapid run-up in fuel prices, as if any industry could have anticipated $145-per-barrel oil, and failing to have a hybrid like the Prius on hand when it did happen. Rather than a $23,000 Prius, a consumer might have been better off with a $14,000 Chevrolet Aveo capable of 36 miles per gallon on its gasoline engine — even when oil prices spiked in 2008. But now the government controlled GM. The auto company's future was being staked in large part on bringing out greener cars.

"The administration may chastise GM for not having the right product but people need to want to buy those vehicles," Baker said. "I find it hard to believe that consumers are ready for just little cars and electrics."

Detroit was worried too. Pickup trucks like General Motors' full-size GMC Sierra were the crucial profit makers. Now, Washington was steering the auto industry in the direction of vehicles like the Ford Fusion. Consumers and critics favored the car for its quality and mileage — 41 mpg city, 36 mpg highway, or 39 mpg combined. But the truth was, the $28,000 Fusion sold in the tens of thousands, while the big pickups sold in the hundreds of thousands. Even so, Detroit had to find a way to stay in business with new mileage standards coming in the future.

In May 2009, Obama had outlined new CAFE rules that would require an automaker's fleet of new vehicles in 2015 achieve fuel economy of 35.5 mpg when every car and truck model offered by a particular automaker was averaged together. This thirty percent improvement over existing rules would help clear smoggy skies and reduce oil imports, but the challenge for Detroit was daunting. The GMC Sierra showed the problem. The $29,000 four-wheel-drive GMC Sierra 1500 averaged 15 mpg in combined city and highway driving with its 5.3-liter V-8. Adding a hybrid system, a $9,000 option, pushed the average to 20 mpg. Replacing the gasoline V-8 with a diesel engine, a $6,000 option if one were made available, would stretch fuel economy to about 25 mpg — saving about 400 gallons of fuel per year for the driver going 15,000 miles annually. This in turn cut the yearly fuel bill $1,000 with fuel prices at $2.50 per gallon on average. But the downside was clear. Saving $1,000 per year at the fuel pump meant the truck would have to be used for years to pay off either the diesel or hybrid options. Although each option would pay for itself in the long run — six years and nine years, respectively — it's not clear that most new vehicle buyers thought this way. As every auto and light truck salesperson knows, it's the monthly payments on the vehicle most customers worry about first, and that's directly related to purchase price. What was worse, from Detroit's standpoint, was the CAFE rule itself. Even if GM had nothing on dealer lots but the 36-mpg Aveo subcompact and a 25-mpg Sierra diesel hybrid pickup truck, the resulting corporate average of 30.5 mpg would miss the new fleet standard of 35.5 mpg. GM would have to find some kind of technology like the lithium-ion battery to put cars capable of substantially higher fuel economy on the road.

A generation earlier, GM most likely could have marshaled its engineers and scientists to find a solution. In the 1970s, GM had invented the catalytic converter. In the 1980s, it had put up and staffed its own semiconductor chip fabrication plant in Kokomo. In the 1990s, the EV1 program had cost $1 billion. By the end of the 2000s though, projects of that scale were a thing of the past. With the pressures on the Detroit Three, the companies were laying off thousands of workers permanently. "We're seeing 1,000 applications for one engineering ad — people we couldn't have touched a year ago," Scott Harrison, chief executive officer of Azure Dynamics, said in 2009. Much of the heavy research and product development activity already had been shifting to suppliers such as Azure, an Oak Park, Michigan, developer of hybrid systems for work trucks. Pinched by tight profit margins, the automakers had turned to suppliers for forty percent of the industry's $16 billion in R&D work by 2003.[15] Historically, the Detroit Three had done most of their own work on the engine and transmission — that is, the power train, what the engineers thought of as the heart and soul of the car. Suppliers usually handled peripheral products such as traction systems and entertainment devices like DVD players.

But in a new era of tighter fuel economy rules, Detroit was in danger of losing its complete grip on the power train. Trying to quickly gain insight into lithium-ion technology, the automakers turned to outside producers. Batteries for the Chevrolet Volt plug-in hybrid and other General Motors models would come not from GM supply lines, but LG Chemical. The South Korean company was putting up a $200 million Michigan plant with $122.5 million in state tax incentives.

Ford turned to Johnson Controls Inc. for lithium-ion batteries. JCI, a Milwaukee auto-parts maker, had teamed on the technology with French battery maker Saft. The $220 million JCI-Saft plant was destined for Michigan, which again offered $122.5 million in state tax breaks.

Chrysler, controlled by the UAW, made a deal with A123 Systems, a battery researcher in Cambridge, Massachusetts, founded by Indian billionaire Gururaj Deshpande. A123 was planning a $600 million Michigan battery plant and had applied for a $1.8 billion loan from the green-car fund administered by the United States Department of Energy.

By late summer, Obama's administration ponied up $2.4 billion in grants to get the battery technology rolling in the United States. LG Chemical indirectly pulled in $154 million for its GM venture, while JCI landed $299.2 million and A123 got $249 million. In turn, GM obtained a $105 million grant for green car technology, and rivals Ford and Chrysler received $62.7 million and $70 million, respectively. [16]

Detroit was playing catch-up on battery technology, but catch up was widely regarded as the proper course for Detroit. The domestic automakers had to learn from someone how to make the batteries. A123, LG, and Saft were considered three of the best. Turning to outside producers for crucial components, however, underscored another significant change in Detroit. General Motors for decades had made most of what it needed. So had Ford and, to a lesser extent, Chrysler. Now this process of vertical integration was on the way out. The automakers had to deal with a whole raft of tech companies like A123 outside the realm of Detroit. "Here's a company that has worked vertically for many years and the world has shifted to a horizontal model," Baker, GM's former R&D head, said of General Motors. "GM has to learn how to make that shift."

Going horizontal in Detroit was not necessarily painless for old industrial cities like Kokomo. Not only would the Detroit Three outsource critical components, but the components did not have to be manufactured near the vehicle plants. Kokomo had prospered for years precisely because its central location reduced shipping costs on the heavy metal pieces produced by Chrysler and GM in the local factories. The Kokomo transmission works was on a network of roads that put truckers within a few hours drive of Chrysler assembly lines at Detroit and Windsor, Ontario; St. Louis; Belvidere, Illinois; and Toledo, Ohio.

Being located in central Indiana, though, was not necessarily an advantage in an electric-car industry. Lithium-ion batteries, and the battery packs they rested in, were so heavy that they would be made closer to the final assembly plants. Meanwhile, the systems that channeled the power to the wheels — electric motors, electronic controls, wiring harnesses, circuit boards, and other necessary electrical paraphernalia — were light enough to be shipped from as far away as Asia. Chrysler or GM might import electrical parts and assemble them into, say, power controls in Kokomo, but the design, engineering, and manufacturing of the pieces could be outsourced. Even the finished product, the power controls or the tiny engine in the plug-in hybrid, could be outsourced. Deep into 2009, no domestic content rules required anything in the electric car be engineered or made in North America, noted economist Alan Tonelson.[17] Nor had the United States government been adept at marshaling American technology into an industrial base able to support Detroit. When the White House Office of Science and Technology Policy put on a tech fair in 2008 at Oak Ridge, Tennessee, only two of the 250 people in attendance represented American industrial companies; China had more people in attendance.[18] Now, foreign manufacturers stood to reap profits in an electric-car era. Shaving $200 off the cost of a vehicle by using electrical parts made in, say, China might not lower the asking price on a new $28,000 plug-in hybrid. But that $200 could be a good piece of the automaker's profit margin when multiplied by hundreds of thousands of units sold.

As 2009 came to a close, just how the switch to hybrid and electric technology would all play out, of course, was not clear. But the very fact that the American government was proferring billions of dollars for a new fleet of high-mileage cars was promising to splinter the car industry. "Obama's stimulus," Baker said, "has gotten a lot of manufacturers interested in moving into the market, names we've never heard of before."

GM's collapse was clearly shaking up the industry, opening business and technology plays where none had existed when the carmaker dominated the market. Bright, Coda, Electric Motors, Fisker, Miles, Tesla, Think, and a host of other new and obscure companies were angling for federal loans. Bright was near Indianapolis, but the others were scattered throughout the nation. That meant auto-parts suppliers in the industrial Midwest might have to relocate plants to be closer to the Thinks and Teslas of the world, or might not even get any business.

California-based Tesla, producer of a $107,000 electric sports sedan, had secured a $465 million federal loan from the same fund as Nissan. Powered by tiny lithium-ion batteries, the elegant-looking Tesla Roadster was a pure electric car capable of sports-car acceleration rates of zero to 60 miles per hour in four seconds. Tesla executives wanted the loans to make electric cars and components on the West Coast. Not only was Tesla a newcomer to the auto world, but in a further sign of the splintering of Detroit, analysts suggested Germany's Daimler, maker of the Mercedes brand, might furnish the batteries.[19] Buoyed by a $2.7 billion green-car investment from Abu Dhabi, Daimler had formed a joint venture with German battery maker Evonik and bought ten percent of Tesla.

Middle Eastern money flowing into Daimler was nothing new for the owner of the Mercedes luxury brand. One major shareholder, Deutsche Bank, long had had the government of Kuwait as a shareholder. Some analysts had suggested that the decision to sell off Chrysler had been shaped partly by those investors' impatience with Chrysler's profit-draining problems. But the flow of Middle Eastern and, for that matter, overseas entrepreneurial wealth into the suddenly alluring field of American vehicle propulsion *was* new. For example, Altair Nanotechnologies, a battery researcher based in Las Vegas, Nevada, had opened a plant in Anderson, Indiana, to make use of the old GM Delco Remy staff that had helped develop GM's EV1. Dubai investor Al Yousuf LLC had made two large capital infusions to prop up the Nevada company's research. EnerDel, the Indianapolis battery researcher, traced to the wealth of Russian pulp and paper billionaire Boris Zingarevich, though EnerDel also had impeccable American lineage. The "Del" was an echo off GM's old Delco Remy division and its modern Delphi name.

Delphi and Zingarevich's Florida technology company, Ener1, formed the EnerDel battery joint venture with Japanese electronic supplier Itochu. Ener1 moved its office from Florida to New York, sold shares of stock in a public offering, and acquired by-then bankrupt Delphi's stake in EnerDel. Ener1 also fed $30 million in loans into the battery venture in 2008 to keep it going.

By the summer of 2009, despite its Delco Remy credentials, EnerDel was on the outside looking in as Saft, LG, and start-up A123 landed big contracts. Nissan had not immediately identified the battery supplier for its electric fleet, although EnerDel was angling for the business. EnerDel also was supplying Volvo with test batteries in Europe and talking to Magna International, the Canadian auto-parts supplier. Magna was getting ready to supply Ford with electrical systems and, in a separate venture, had partnered with Russia's Sberbank on a possible deal to buy Opel and Vauxhall, the heart of GM's massive European operations, though that deal was eventually called off by GM executives. If the deal worked out, EnerDel lithium-ion batteries might have powered Opel models in Europe and possibly even Saturns in North America. Opel had designed some cars for Saturn, and there was the possibility that Opel might continue the Saturn design work. EnerDel had hoped the Russian bank could steer deals to the Russian compatriot, Zingarevich, and perhaps line up battery business with the GAZ car company, the number two Russian automaker. Controlled by tycoon Oleg Deripaska, GAZ had recently hired away a senior GM executive in Detroit, Bo Andersson, a European who had been in charge of global procurement for General Motors.

In any event, by late summer, EnerDel had landed a $118 million matching grant from the U.S. Department of Energy, money it could use to tool for production as part of a supply contract with Norwegian electric car maker Think. EnerDel's grant was part of $400 million in battery-technology grants flowing to Indiana companies including the Delphi operation in Kokomo. Just what would happen to Delphi and EnerDel, though, was hard to say. China was full of enterprises large and small boasting of advances in high-tech batteries for Chinese carmakers. Reported a London newspaper, *Sunday Times*, shortly after GM filed for bankruptcy: "The centre of gravity of the world's car industry shifted perceptibly towards China. Here, some of the biggest strides in motor engineering are being made."[20] China's electric-car success in some measure was the doing of Americans, such as entrepreneur Miles Rubin. His start-up firm, Coda Automotive of Santa Monica, California, planned to sell a $45,000 midsize sedan with a ninety-mile range that would be eligible for a $7,500 United States green-car tax credit taking the price down to $37,500 for the buyer. The electric car's body would be made by Hafei Automobile in China and it would use lithium phosphate iron batteries produced abroad by a Hafei venture with Tianjin Lishen, a Chinese battery supplier.[21] The idea of foreign automakers like Hafei benefiting, even indirectly, from a United States government program had started some grumbling in Washington among conservative lawmakers. But with cars like the Coda using BorgWarner transaxles, Delphi steering systems, and Lear power converters — the trio were based in suburban Detroit — defenders of the loan program said it was difficult to define just what was an American car anymore.

That was true. It was hard to say what was American. And it was ironic, incredibly so, because not that long ago the electric car was the province of one company, General Motors. GM's EV1 was regarded as the modern icon of electric cars. It was the car that, had GM persevered, could have launched the electric revolution. Instead, GM backed off. Richard Wagoner, the chairman of the company, later acknowledged this was a big mistake, but by then it was too late. The demise of GM's EV1 was regarded by electric-car enthusiasts as a baffling indictment of a company and an American system in which government officials, lobbyists, and oil companies had weighed in to sideline the car. Despite its short life, the car was a product of the Midwest, an example of automotive ingenuity, an aerodynamic vehicle with a seventy-mile range powered entirely by batteries recharged from the wall outlet.

The EV1 came about after GM chairman Roger Smith, the Roger reviled in the Michael Moore film *Roger & Me*, realized electric cars offered GM a competitive edge heading into the 1990s. Aero Environment, a California company backed by GM, had created the experimental Sunraycer, an electric car that had bested a fleet of other experimental electric cars racing in Australia. In an era marked by high oil prices and smoggy cities, Smith took the limelight at the 1990 auto show in Los Angeles. He showed off an electric concept car based on the Sunraycer, and crowed GM would have an electric car on the road in North America within the decade. GM engineers were pleased, perturbed, and staggered. This was like the company mounting a mission to the moon. "Roger Smith kind of loses his mind and says we're going to mass-produce that car," former GM Delco Remy engineer Bill Wylam remembered.

In California, government air quality officials heard Smith. They soon did something that rattled auto executives in Detroit even more. California decreed that two percent of the new autos sold in the state in 1998 had to be ZEVs — zero emission vehicles — and ten percent of the new autos sold in 2003 had to be ZEVs. Zero emission meant the tailpipe could leave no sulfur, nitrogen, or other pollution in its wake. The idea of clearer skies traced to the 1970 Clean Air Act of the Nixon era. California's new mandate was clearly intended to usher in the electric car using modern technology such as durable solid state electronics refined in part by the space program. Massachusetts, New York, and Vermont usually copied California's air quality laws, so there would be a built-in market in the four states for annual sales of at least 250,000 to 500,000 electric vehicles. As high as this number was, it was low for automobile execs accustomed to thinking in millions. Sales of new autos usually numbered about 15 million vehicles per year in the United States. Each company feared the expense of staffing and tooling one little plant merely to satisfy regulators. Five or six automakers each producing 50,000 to 75,000 electric cars per year would not even make a profit on so slim a sales volume. Less than a decade earlier, a senior Ford exec had spouted off publicly about the coming future of electric cars. Chrysler had talked for years of turbines. No one had held Detroit's feet to the fire. Now, here was Roger Smith chortling about a vehicle not even on the drawing boards, heady with the recent acquisitions of Hughes Aerospace and Electronic Data Systems. He was eager to have Hughes' and EDS's engineers migrate their technology into GM and its cars, and just as eager to fend off contentions he had squandered cash by buying two companies outside the auto business. When he boasted of an electric car, even an electric car no one ever had seen, California air regulators took him at his word and set the ZEV mandate. In Washington, auto lobbyists and their oil industry colleagues quickly geared up to get lawmakers to head off California. But that was behind the scenes. On the surface, the race was on. Chrysler's approach was halfhearted, while Honda, Toyota, Ford, and General Motors quickly put some of their best engineers on ZEVs. As always in electric cars, the battery would prove to be the problem.

General Motors R&D chief Ken Baker, relying on a $1 billion budget and more than 1,000 engineers, scientists, researchers, and technicians, beat all rivals to market. Baker's crew crafted the stylish and aerodynamic EV1. Powered by a big electric motor and old-fashioned lead acid batteries — there was no engine — the first EV1 zipped along California streets before Toyota had its electric car on the road. "The EV1 was the most energy-efficient vehicle ever invented, even today," Baker said.

Bill Wylam was in the middle of it for GM. He had always believed in electricity as a positive feature in cars. "Electricity is what makes the car worth having," the retired engineer said one day during an interview in his home in a comfortable Indianapolis lakeside community. He was right. He also could have said it made a car fun and safe, even smart. Air conditioners, antilock brakes, traction control, CD changers, stereo speakers, key fobs, six-way seats, even the superior fuel economy of the modern automobile, and conveniences large and small relied on sensors and microprocessors pulsing electricity through wires and circuit boards. The automobile had become like an electric power plant on wheels furnishing energy to a wide array of computers and devices. GM's Delco Remy division and its old cousin, Delco, had been the place for electrical engineers devising those systems. Graduating from Purdue University in 1955, Wylam had gone to the heart of Delco Remy, a complex of shops and offices in Anderson, Indiana, that would employ 19,000 workers in time. Delco Remy turned out all manner of generators, alternators, and electrical systems in the millions of units every year, but it was also keen on developing quality standards used in industries all over America when Wylam arrived there. He had always regarded Delco Remy as GM's special grooming ground for execs bound for upper-echelon engineering and administrative duties.

Delco Remy had had a can-do spirit, although as Wylam found, that spirit was ebbing. In the 1980s, he was director of international business for Delco Remy, living in Asia to open parts-making ventures in South Korea and China. Delco Remy's clout in GM meant he also opened ventures for other GM parts operations such as AC Sparkplugs, Harrison Radiator, Inland Fisher Body, Guide Lamp, Packard Electric, and Rochester Carburetor. After Delco Remy reorganized into five business units, part of GM's reshuffling in response to the flood of imported cars from Japan, Wylam was brought back to Anderson to run an engineering operation separate from the five business units. It was 1989. Wylam quickly learned his unit had just engineered a big and quiet electric motor for a new United States Navy torpedo. "Forget where it goes [in torpedoes]," Wylam remembered an engineer told him. "These motors are going into cars." The engineer was right. Roger Smith was about drop his bombshell at the Los Angeles auto show.

When Smith gave the final go-ahead to design the EV1, Wylam quietly brought together a handful of the engineers in his office and relocated them to an obscure industrial park on the edge of Indianapolis where they could work in secret. No one in GM wanted Ford or Chrysler to know what they really were doing. Although Wylam had a budget of $40 million per year, GM's legendary conservative culture soon confronted him. The other five Delco Remy managers, set on their own production goals, were loathe to hand off many of their engineers to Wylam. "It took years to get the resources we really needed," Wylam said. "It took time for them to realize the top people in GM were saying do what it takes. None of the division managers wanted to take it on. They'd say, 'Hell, I'm not going to do that. Electric cars are something for the chairman to play with.'"

Eventually half the engineers in Wylam's "skunk works," as

it was known, came from outside Delco Remy, with the bulk streaming in from Continental Engineering in Anderson as well as Hughes Aerospace and Electronic Data Systems. They invented very little from scratch. What they were doing was putting a long row of lead-acid batteries in a big package, connecting the package to the electronic controls and cooling mechanisms, and then continually trying to engineer weight, bulk, and cost out of this battery pack. They succeeded. Wylam, who came to be known as Battery Bill in Delco Remy, rolled the battery packs for the EV1 out of his skunk works on deadline.

But the enthusiasm for an electric car was leaking out of GM. A boardroom coup put Jack Smith atop the company and ushered in years of strikes, attrition, and belt tightening. Delco Remy and the array of businesses acquired during Durant's empire building era were rolled into Delphi, a massive business employing 203,000 people worldwide. Donald Runkle, who had made his mark as Chevrolet's chief engineer, took charge of what became a business within Delphi, the Engine and Management unit in Flint, Michigan, which inherited Delco Remy. Don Runkle and Jack Smith didn't kill the electric car program, but with oil dropping to $10 per barrel, they had little interest in subsidizing its development.

In all, 1,117 electric cars were built at a shop GM tooled specially for EV1 production in Lansing, Michigan. The graceful car contained a number of advanced features such as anti-lock brakes, traction control, keyless entry, and thermal glass for heat rejection, along with seats made on light magnesium frames, dent resistant side panels on an aluminum frame, and extremely light magnesium alloy wheels. Saturn dealers in Los Angeles, Phoenix, San Diego, and Tucson distributed the cars. They were made in two generations, notes automotive tech writer Bill Siuru of *Green Car Journal*. The first 660 were labeled model year 1997 and were sustained by twenty-six Delco 12-volt lead acid batteries capable of driving the vehicle fifty-five to seventy-five miles between charges. Model year 1999 cars contained twenty-six GM Ovonic 13.2-volt batteries that extended the range to as much as 150 miles. Some first generation models were later refitted with 100-mile-range Panasonic batteries from Japan. An innovative recharging unit that resembled a wooden paddle was developed by GM to make it easy for drivers to recharge the vehicle. The recharging took about eight hours.[22]

It soon was clear the EV1 would never make a profit for GM. Had there been a realistic price on the car, it would have topped $80,000, including $30,000 for the batteries alone. Instead, GM subsidized the model to attract drivers, offering it only on lease to make payments affordable. By the time a few hundred samples were produced, prospective customers, including some Hollywood celebrities, were carefully screened to make sure they at least understood the mileage limitations. The EV1 was priced at about $34,000 to $40,000, keeping the lease payments at about $400 per month. The low sales volumes and price would not cover the cost of tooling and staffing a plant. And that was a problem for the executives. Roger Smith, had he stayed on longer, might have inculcated an appreciation in the GM boardroom for the EV1's potential. But Don Runkle, Jack Smith, and the board now had little appetite for electric cars. Runkle himself had been groomed in the high-horsepower era. GM captured fifty percent of the American market only after it rolled out fast cars like the 1964 Pontiac GTO. Designed expressly to appeal to young drivers — in the same demographic vein occupied today by male fans of NASCAR — the inexpensive GTO was the average man's race car. A 1964 Pontiac brochure shows a photograph of a rakish GTO roaring along a dirt road over the words: "There are few great moments in life. This is one of them." The idea was solid gold. The car became iconic. "Win a guest role on the *Monkees* TV show and this customized Pontiac GTO," crowed a 1968 Kellogg's magazine advertisement for Rice Krispies cereal.[23]

Later, that very appreciation of the big gasoline engine would blind GM's culture to the potential of electric vehicles just as it had dulled the response when small Japanese sedans began to take away its car business. "The desire to win has not been sufficiently instilled into the engineers of beleaguered Detroit — a city which is still not aware of the gravity of its problem," journalist Brock Yates perceptively warned in his 1983 book, *The Decline and Fall of the American Automobile Industry*. [24]

Distracted by the Delphi reorganization, still enamored of gasoline engines, Runkle scheduled a meeting with Wylam in Flint in the late 1990s. Wylam drove in from Anderson, fearing GM was about to commit one of its bigger bonehead moves. Runkle "was a piston guy," Wylam said, surrounded by piston guys. Wylam feared they would disband the electric car program.

He was right. "They didn't want to work on the electric vehicle," Wylam remembered. "They told me to shut down my shop." Wylam immediately resigned. The engineers he'd hired scattered. Many wound up later at start-up battery researcher EnerDel, which occupies the same building that had housed Wylam's skunk works.

Could the EV1 have been saved? Powerful new batteries might extend its range, but the United States Advanced Battery Consortium, a research arm created by the Detroit Three and the American government, had discovered no suitable breakthroughs in the 1990s. Nor were the GM execs willing to spend corporate money on lithium-ion research when oil was so cheap that pickups were becoming the new station wagon of the American suburbs. And in the middle of America's truck craze, few states were talking about adopting California's ZEV mandate. Even California was preparing to relax the edict. If there was no legal requirement to market the EV1, GM execs reasoned, why do it? As leases expired, GM took back and scrapped the cars.

Taking the EV1 off the road triggered a wave of conspiracy theories. Most pointed at auto and oil execs, while some blamed Washington, others California regulators, and castigating them all was the 2006 documentary *Who Killed the Electric Car?* The decidedly pro-EV1 cult film — narrated by actor Martin Sheen and drawing on the commentary of consumer advocate Ralph Nader and actor Ed Begley Jr., also an electric car enthusiast — contended that that the EV1s "were so efficient, they were on the brink of altering the future of driving in America — perhaps the world," but that GM had wantonly canceled the program. It was telling, years later, that GM had no superior technology it could pull off a hidden shelf and use as a silver bullet against the fuel crisis of 2008, when crude reached $145 per barrel. It was hard to believe that GM execs had been part of a wider conspiracy when the company, battered by falling sales of its trucks, tumbled into the hands of the United States government largely because it did not have a solution to the fuel crisis in the dealer showrooms.

Yet, in the late 1990s and early 2000s, environmentalists sensed the oddity of a company backing off so completely from what was at least a promising engineering development. Terry Tamminen, who became secretary of the California state Environmental Protection Agency in 2003, placed the blame on Detroit and oil execs in his book *Lives per Gallon*. Fearing electric cars could ruin the prosperous truck business, Tamminen asserts, the Detroit executives played along with California regulators only until they could dilute the 1998 deadline for zero emission cars. He claimed their choice of action was to create the United States Advanced Battery Consortium, a Detroit Three research arm funded largely by the United States Department of Energy. Rather than let USABC hit on something profound, Tamminen contends, the auto execs made sure the group was unable to find a suitable replacement for the short-range lead-acid batteries. That, of course, was the conspiracy theory.

If there was a conspiracy in the making, however, Baker and Wylam say they didn't see it. And it was never mentioned in the most thorough accounting by a journalist of the EV1's actual development. For several years the company gave Michael Shnayerson regular access to GM executives working on the electric car business. His 1996 book, *The Car That Could*, says that late into 1994 Baker and the other GM execs were rushing to create a hand-built fleet of fifty Impacts, as the electric car was known then. What Shnayerson discovered was an intense dissatisfaction at Ford and Chrysler over GM's decision to create a battery-making business called GM Ovonics and let it commercialize USABC technology, a move that looked as if GM was trying to corner this high-tech battery for itself. GM Ovonics was a joint venture of General Motors and the Ovonics arm of Energy Conversion Devices, the battery firm that had hired Robert Stempel, the GM chairman fired in the 1992 boardroom coup. Baker and other execs favored the brilliant owner of the battery company, Stanford Ovshinsky, because he had a slew of solid patents on nickel metal hydride technology, a type of battery considered in the 1990s one of the best replacements for lead-acid models. Ford was then pursuing sodium-sulfur batteries while Chrysler waited to see what came out of USABC.

Alarmed as Ford and Chrysler execs were over the formation of GM Ovonics, Shnayerson pointed out GM was not trying to keep the Ovshinsky technology to itself. GM soon agreed to sell the GM Ovonics batteries at cost to Ford and Chrysler. As it turned out, GM Ovonics was formed as a defensive measure by the automaker to ensure the battery supply was ample, Shnayerson's scenario suggests. GM execs took control of battery manufacturing to lift the burden off Ovshinksy. Running short on cash, Energy Conversion Devices was too weak to make batteries, and was fighting patent disputes with a United States–based arm of Saft, the French battery company.

The controversy swirling then around GM Ovonics later would help fuel the conspiracy theories. Tamminen contends Ovonics was "close to perfecting the very batteries the automakers wanted to claim could not be made."[25] In any event, in 1995 California regulators decided to push back the 1998 deadline for zero emission cars. Tamminen recounts heavy political pressure on California officials from oil lobbyists. Mobil Oil ads hammered on the notion the batteries were not feasible, and the electric car amounted to a government subsidy for Mobil's competition.[26] At the same time, Ovshinsky himself was loudly proclaiming his batteries were ready for production. However, GM execs were constantly correcting him, *The Car That Could* points out, and explaining it was one thing to make a few dozen batteries, and it was quite another to make them by the tens of thousands. Nor did the batteries have the 100-plus mile range the inventor insisted they would have. Hearing the GM Ovonics batteries were not ready for mass production, California regulators moved the original ZEV deadline to 2003. Later, the officials would altogether scrap the deadline and turn to other ways to clear smog. When they did, GM formally canceled the EV1.

Even so, GM didn't entirely pull out of high-tech propulsion. True, the execs took a dim view of hybrids, the technology that a decade later would enthrall Obama. But even after Toyota brought the Prius to the United States in 1998, GM executives went off on a different tack, taking hybrids to commercial fleets. GM officials scoffed at hybrids used in small cars, calling them overly expensive vehicles that would never repay drivers in fuel savings. Larry Burns, Baker's successor in GM R&D, contended hybrids made more sense in stop-and-go city buses, garbage trucks, delivery vans, and similar work trucks. There, the fleet owners could recoup the hybrid's hefty price because the system would save thousands of gallons of fuel every year. GM's Allison Transmission in Indianapolis became the company's hybrid research center and combined with the old GM remnants, Delphi Delco in Kokomo and Remy International in Anderson, to produce hybrids for commercial vehicles. But it was never a huge market. Although a hybrid bus got 5 miles per gallon, double the mileage of regular buses, GM Allison's technology failed to catch on widely with bus fleets. That was because Allison made only automatic transmissions, and these cost more than the manual kind. Adding this to the cost of hybrid technology stretched the asking price beyond the budget of many bus fleets.

Even as regulators in California scrapped the ZEV deadlines, GM kept a portion of its R&D staff focused on high-tech propulsion. Wagoner was the new president of General Motors. He decided to leapfrog the hybrid and explore something different. It was an EV1 drive train mated to a remarkable chemical battery called the fuel cell, a device regarded as more advanced than the lithium-ion type. Fuel cell research had been quietly carried out for years under a talented European engineer, Peter Hanenberger, head of the GM Opel engineering complex in Rüsselsheim, Germany. When the engineer was reassigned to Australia as part of the shake-up induced by Jack Smith, he was replaced by an American troubleshooter named Frank Colvin. Colvin soon was spending almost two days a week on the fuel cell research.

Never used in cars before, the technology was well known among GM Hughes Aerospace engineers. Since the 1960s, fuel cells in spacecraft had produced astronauts' drinking water, heat, and electricity. The device never ran down like a battery as long as it was furnished oxygen and a fuel like hydrogen. This set off a chemical reaction that created electricity and streamed pure water as its only exhaust. GM execs figured the fuel cell could well extend the EV1's range — if the battery could be made on an assembly line and the price brought down.

Looking for insight into the manufacturability of fuel cells in 1999, Wagoner invited Colvin to fly to Europe with him on a GM jet. Having banked more than $20 billion in cash amid the truck boom, Wagoner knew he had the resources for more fuel cell research, but he wanted to ask one of the company's problem solvers if the things could actually be mass-produced for automobiles. Wagoner and the Stanford MBA talked for an hour. "I told him everyone thought this was something we could do and should do," Colvin recalled later in an interview with the *Indianapolis Star*. Colvin said Wagoner concurred and replied: "You don't have to talk to me a lot about this. I don't have to understand exactly what you're trying to apply. But you have to bring the business plan together, bring the commercialization of this to me, if I'm going to bet my company on this."[27]

Returning to the United States, near the Lake Ontario shoreline at Honeoye Falls, New York, Colvin oversaw the renovation of a GM engineering lab into a test facility for manufacturing fuel cells. GM soon began running an experimental $100,000-plus Chevrolet S10 pickup powered by a fuel cell. Burns and other execs gave talks suggesting that by 2010 GM would manufacture high volumes of suitcase-sized fuel cells as backup power for skyscrapers, shopping malls, and hospitals. By spreading development costs over these stationary fuel cells, the price for the automobile fuel cell would reach an affordable level. At least that was the idea.

Just how far Wagoner or America would have gone with the fuel cell isn't clear. Certainly there was no infrastructure. The oil companies never rushed to equip service stations with hydrogen pumps for refueling fuel cell cars. And it wasn't at all clear that the auto industry had settled on a way to safely store the volatile hydrogen aboard the car. In any case, the manufacturing costs remained sky-high. Analysts expected that an affordable fuel cell car would not be available before 2020. Joseph Romm, a hydrogen official at the United States Department of Energy in the 1990s, concluded in his 2004 book, *The Hype About Hydrogen*, that Detroit and the country had gotten caught up in the tech euphoria of the late 1990s. He called experiments such as the California Fuel Cell Partnership worthwhile for automakers, giving engineers valuable experience in running fuel cell cars and buses on regular urban routes, but stopped short of a full endorsement, noting that while fuel cells could power cars, the costs would be very high.[28]

Indeed, fuel cells can power cars even today. In 2009, for example, sponsored by the California Fuel Cell Partnership, Daimler, GM, Hyundai, Nissan, Toyota, and Volkswagen ran fuel cell vehicles in a 1,700-mile trek from Mexico to British Columbia. No failures were reported in the press and the range for each vehicle was about 400 miles between refills. But, just as Romm contended, many more years of development would be necessary to bring down the technology's cost. Exotic as the fuel cell might be, Daimler and Toyota never wavered in their commitment to research fuel cells. Despite the Obama administration's penchant for hybrid cars, a Toyota executive said in 2009: "It is relevant to point out that over the last five years fuel cell technology has probably progressed at a faster rate than has advanced battery technology."[29]

Of course, all of this had become a side issue for GM earlier in the decade as its $20 billion bankroll disappeared. Once the 2001 terrorist attacks on New York and Washington scared Americans from shopping or traveling, GM cut its already discounted prices on vehicles to get consumers buying and keep the plants running. The price cuts, taking the form of consumer incentives, came shortly after officials in the Bush administration staged a televised visit to the Cadillac assembly plant in Detroit and urged GM to do what it could for the economy. From that point, GM launched the heavy incentives. A price war broke out with Chrysler and Ford, and quickly began to shrink GM's cash hoard. Colvin soon retired and the fuel cell program was rarely mentioned in public.

For all of "the General's" failures, President Obama and the public at large have been too hard on GM, says Ken Baker, the former R&D chief. "What GM was highly criticized by the government for was not being strategic in investing properly, in not having an energy efficient vehicle in anticipation of a fuel crisis," Baker said. Yet GM, despite its cultural limitations, had tried. Now it would be up to the United States government to usher into place what the country's largest industrial company and the $1 trillion auto industry had so far failed to do.

What few people understood in 2009 was the vast cost of continuing on with the process of developing hybrid and plug-in hybrid cars, said Michael Lew, a technology analyst studying the potential green-car business for San Francisco investment advisor Think Equity. Although deep into 2009 the government had committed $27 billion on the endeavor, Lew said the final price tag easily could double that amount, particularly to get the battery technology commercially viable. "Everyone looks at the Asian battery companies as the goliaths — they know how to build batteries," Lew said. "But the format for the car battery is a lot larger than the button-sized batteries they're building [now for consumer electronics]. This is going to come down to who can build the battery the fastest."

The first company with an affordable, dependable battery could corner the car market, especially if technical or manufacturing hitches held back its rivals. Developing batteries may have been expensive, but in the end, the Obama administration decided to proceed. Making yet another appearance in hard-hit Elkhart County in northern Indiana on August 5, 2009, the president unveiled technology grants totaling $2.4 billion for forty-eight companies to create batteries and supporting systems for hybrids, plug-ins, and electric cars. Seven of the grants went to Indiana companies, second in number only to Michigan, but the recipients were actually spread throughout twenty-five states, a signal that auto technology was being dispersed throughout the nation rather than centered in Detroit and the Midwest. Much of the money was committed to the partners in the lithium-ion battery joint ventures going into Michigan: Johnson Controls and France's Saft, and General Motors' partner, South Korea–based LG Chemical. Also significant was the award to the arm of Arizona-based Ecotality to support a Japanese automaker. The Arizona firm would install a network of recharging systems in western states specifically for the Nissan Leaf electric car that the Japanese automaker planned to make in Tennessee in a plant retooled with the earlier $1.6 billion federal loan.

"For too long, we failed to invest in this kind of innovative work, even as countries like China and Japan were racing ahead," Obama said in a speech at a recreational vehicle plant that truck-maker Navistar International had purchased in the spring from bankrupt Monaco Coach. Navistar now planned to make several hundred electric delivery trucks and rehire more of the 1,400 idled Monaco workers, using a $39.2 million grant handed out by Obama through the 2009 American Recovery and Reinvestment Act.

The president spoke about both designing and manufacturing high-tech batteries and alternative energy systems in America. But it was clear the White House's green-car initiatives would benefit many foreign companies like LG. And despite the money being lavished on lithium-ion batteries, no one was certain the technology was even affordable. Indianapolis battery maker EnerDel had received a $118.5 million grant from Obama and would use the cash to double the size of its plant. But clearly, it was not enough just to make batteries, said Charles Gassenheimer, chairman of EnerDel owner Ener1. Electric utilities would have to step up and make the batteries affordable for consumers through a complicated arrangement, still being worked out, of buying power from motorists' electric cars, Gassenheimer said. Without that kind of buyback system, lithium-ion batteries' price might not come down enough to make electric cars price competitive with gasoline models.

As it was, battery power looked quite uncompetitive to some observers. Silicon Valley venture capitalist Vinod Khosla, a cofounder of Sun Microsystems, figured the most economical and least polluting model might not be a high-tech lithium-ion electric car, but a conventional gasoline sedan equipped with what was already available, an everyday flex-fuel engine burning gasoline mixed with fifteen percent ethanol. Khosla, a major investor in ethanol fuel producer Coskata, a partner of GM, quite obviously stood to make money on ethanol, but he was also doing something that was missing on the surface of America in 2009. He was trying to decide if it made sense for government policy to favor hybrids or plug-ins over any other form of technology. He concluded that from the standpoint of costs to the owner as well as tailpipe emissions, including the exhaust from the smokestacks producing electricity that would feed into the nation's grid to replenish car batteries, the best bet for America was not the hybrid or the plug-in. By his measure, a plug-in Chevrolet Volt, even if it was priced at $30,000, would cost a driver $623 per month for the car loan, fuel, and conventional electricity replenishing the battery from a wall outlet. A $21,000 Prius hybrid would cost $490 per month for the car note and fuel, compared to a conventional flex-fuel Toyota Corolla's $355 per month. The Corolla also would emit the least greenhouse gases — 88 grams of carbon dioxide per mile, compared to the Volt's 144 grams and the Prius' 238 grams, a measure which included the emissions from the power plants producing electricity for the cars, Khosla said. He put his thoughts into a research paper. In it, he said ethanol that was derived from wood waste, weeds, and other cellulosic material would be superior to corn ethanol. He wrote that little analysis of all these competing technologies has been conducted in large part because corn ethanol has been negatively cast in the public mind "by the oil companies' marketing machine and farm policy critics, and impractical environmentalists. . . . [Meanwhile] the Prius and hybrids have been positioned by Toyota's marketing machine."[30]

Whether Khosla was a disgruntled investor or astute observer, hybrids like the Prius had caught on in the American imagination as the right vehicle for the times. There had been rapid advances in diesel technology and, as Khosla pointed out, biofuels like ethanol, but auto analysts concurred that the immediate deadline posed by the United States government was going to force the industry to scramble to get fuel economy on the road by 2015. Auto designers would turn to smaller vehicles and reach for the already obtainable hybrids and plug-in technology capable of achieving that new standard of 35.5 miles per gallon. Electrics, hybrids, plug-in hybrids, clean diesels, natural gas, biofuel — they might all find a place in time. But that left the industrial Midwest in a curious state of mind.

While places like Kokomo were trying to figure what part of the car they would continue to manufacture in their local plants, the automakers were trying to figure out what power plant they might produce. For instance, diesels ran cleaner than they ever had, and even California had relaxed its prohibition on diesel cars, making the diesel a logical power plant for suvs and pickups. But with a $5,000 premium on the diesel engine, would an automaker try to build a business around a diesel, which was still foreign to most U.S. consumers, or go with the gasoline hybrid, which cost as much as a diesel, but at least was now familiar to Americans? Moreover, diesel fuel had been priced higher than gasoline in the United States prior to the recession in part because oil companies had done little to expand refining capacity. Diesel pricing is odd in America — when gasoline prices are low, diesel always costs more. But gasoline prices rise much more rapidly than diesel fuel; the break-even point in recent years was about $2.69 per gallon, meaning that's the price point when the two fuels cost the same. Of course, Americans were different in their attitude toward diesels compared to the Europeans, where diesel cars were favored for fuel economy twenty-five percent to thirty-five percent greater than that of gasoline cars. Most European nations had long accepted diesels' dirtier tailpipe emissions, dirtier at least than what California air quality regulators would tolerate. Consequently, Europeans were now familiar with the cars and wholly embracing the cleaner diesels coming from automakers. Diesels had become nearly half the market in Europe, where there is much less fuss about hybrids and plug-ins. But in Indianapolis in 2009, Navistar permanently closed the plant that had been supplying Ford with diesels for its pickup trucks since the early 1980s.

In the United States, trying to figure out future strategy was splintering the culture of Detroit, shifting it off old moorings. If the heart and soul of the vehicle was the power train, what would Detroit market in the age of electric cars, when stepping on the acceleration pedal brought not the throaty rumble of a V-8 but the almost noiseless sound of a high-tech electric motor spooling up? *Washington Post* writer Michael Leahy discovered this curious ambiguity when he arrived to meet the dean of the Detroit auto industry, Robert Lutz, the vice chairman of General Motors, in the summer of 2009. Lutz, the guru behind GM's styling and engineering renaissance in the 2000s, was lavishing praise on the 400-horsepower Chevrolet Camaro set to make its debut in a few weeks. But out at the airport, GM had put on prominent display its Volt plug-in hybrid.

Which would be GM's halo vehicle — Camaro or Volt? Lutz's heart clearly was with the muscle car, but his head nodded to the plug-in. "Obama has said that he wants a million plug-in vehicles on the market by 2015," Lutz told Leahy. "Think where GM would be now if we had not made the decision to productionize the Volt a year and a half ago. That is the real question. You could argue that we were late but that the Volt has now become the focal point, the rallying point for the pro-GM forces. We can say, 'See, we can transform the automobile; we can be the company that electrifies the automobile.' We can say, 'Yes, we can.'" [31]

1. "Automakers Get $8b Jolt," *Grand Rapids Press*, June 24, 2009, A11.
2. David Welch, David Kiley, "The New Detroit," *Business Week*, June 8, 2009, 28.
3. Kim Deok-hyun, "Hyundai's First Hybrid Car Gets Over 1,000 Orders," *Yonhap News Agency*, July 2, 2009, english.yonhapnews.co.kr/business/2009/07/02/3/0502000000AEN20090702003100320F.html.
4. "Hyundai Blue Drive Hybrids," *Green Car Journal*, Winter 2008/2009, 34.
5. Deok-hyun.
6. Lawrence Ulrich, ". . . And One That's Off Key," *New York Times*, June 21, 2009, AU1.
7. Terry Tamminen, *Lives per Gallon: The True Cost of Our Oil Addiction* (Washington, D.C.: Island Press, 2006), 20.
8. Tamminen, 60; Table 3.1 cites oil industry subsidies reported by Evan Harrje, *The Real Price of Gasoline* (Washington, D.C.: International Center for Technology Assessment, 2000).
9. Tom Lewis, *Divided Highways: Building the Interstate Highways, Transforming American Life* (New York: Viking Penguin Books, 1997), 7.
10. Ernest H. Wakefield, *History of the Electric Automobile* (Warrendale, PA: Society of Automotive Engineers Inc., 1994), 124.
11. Dennis E. Horvath and Terri Horvath, *Indiana Cars: A History of the Automobile in Indiana* (Indianapolis, IN: Hoosier Auto Show and Swap Meet Inc., 2002), 107.
12. Lindsay Brooke, *Ford Model T: The Car That Put the World on Wheels* (Minneapolis, MN: MBI Publishing Co., 2008), 13.
13. Wakefield, 128.
14. Craig Irwin, a vice president for research at San Francisco investment advisor Merriman Curhan Ford, was interviewed by Ted Evanoff in July 2009.
15. Thomas Klier and James Rubenstein, *Who Really Made Your Car?* (Kalamazoo, MI: Upjohn Institute For Employment Research, 2008), 20.
16. David Shepardson, Alisa Priddle, "Big 3, Michigan Win Big in Battery Grants," *Detroit News*, August 6, 2009, 1.
17. Alan Tonelson, senior economist the U.S. Business & Industry Council, a trade group in Washington, D.C., was interviewed by Ted Evanoff on this subject at various times in 2008 and 2009.
18. Richard McCormack, *Manufacturing a Better Future for America* (Washington, D.C.: Alliance For American Manufacturing, 2009), 48.
19. Ted Evanoff, "The Big Potential of Little EnerDel," *Indianapolis Star*, July 26, 2009, D3.
20. Ben Younkman, "Shanghai Surprise: China Cracks the Electric Car," *Sunday Times*, June 7, 2009, 4.
21. Bill Siuru, "Miles Coda Battery Electric Car is Coming in 2010," *Green Car Journal*, June 5, 2009, http://www.greencar.com/articles/miles-coda-battery-electric-car-coming-2010.php.
22. Bill Siuru, "5 Things You Need to Know About the GM EV1," *Green Car Journal*, July 3, 2008, http://www.greencar.com/articles/5-things-need-gm-ev1.php.
23. Jim Wangers, *Glory Days: When Horsepower and Passion Ruled Detroit* (Cambridge, MA: Robert Bentley Publishers, 1998), 171, 219.
24. Brock Yates, *The Decline and Fall of the American Automobile Industry* (New York: Random House Inc., 1983), 213.
25. Tamminen, 147.
26. Tamminen, 149.
27. Ted Evanoff, "GM Cranks Up Its Fuel-Cell Technology," *Indianapolis Star*, June 2, 2002, E7.
28. Joseph J. Romm, *The Hype about Hydrogen* (Washington, D.C.: Island Press, 2004), 112.
29. "Hydrogen Hits a Speed Bump," *Green Car Journal*, Summer 2009, 7.

30. Vinod Khosla, "Pragmentalists vs. Environmentalists (Part I): Prius: Green or Greenwash?" http://www.khoslaventures.com/presentations/Hybrids.pdf.

31. Michael Leahy, "Behind GM's Attempt to Change Its Image Is Ambivalence About Its Car of the Future," *Washington Post*, June 7, 2009, A1.

CHAPTER 11

What's Good
for Wall Street . . .

As 2009 DRAGGED ON, it was clear something huge — and in its own way malevolent — was loose in Middle America. Across the industrial states and into Canada, mayors and union leaders inched forward with their recovery plans, but forces greater than they could control were at work. The recession had not quite hit bottom yet. Globalization was in full swing. Few analysts believed all the idled North American industrial workers ever would be recalled to their shops and factories. Yet the political Left and Right were gripped by an internecine cultural war, arguing about what was effectively European-style Social Democracy on one side and a radical laissez-faire economics on the other. Each tore the other down for allegedly being anti-American on one side, or racist and fascist on the other, but hardly noticing the disintegration of the American tax base and American communities. A battle of elites, in other words.

In the Midwest, communities were isolated like islands in an economic storm, their local leaders largely cast adrift. They were like soldiers in the Old West being told, "Hold the fort, reinforcements are on the way." In spite of cash infusions as part of Obama's $787 billion stimulus package, the truth was becoming more apparent every day — there were no reinforcements, or at least not many. Local leaders might be part of the battle to save Middle America, but they could hardly lead or direct the fight. Towns and cities might compete for factories, jobs, and investment — as they do for pro sports franchises — but it was like gladiators competing in the Roman Coliseum. Sure, one would win, another lose, but it was a zero sum game for America. And the town that managed to land that warehouse from Dollar General or even some green technology start-up more than likely already had lost a pair of huge factories. The mayors were fighting just to tread water. Through it all, the middle of the country was aching.

Americans once lived on farms, grew fruits and vegetables in their gardens. Women knew how to sew dresses. Men knew how to chop wood and children invented their own games. It had been a time of self reliance. People could weather storms. Now, everyone had been reduced to *homo economicus* — economic man. All most people knew was how to make money, and when the money dried up, they didn't know what to do. Many hardly knew how to cook meals for themselves, and suddenly they could no longer afford to eat out. "People don't know how to live poor anymore," observed Kokomo community activist Tom Tolen.

Cities struggled to "live poor," too. Kokomo mayor Greg Goodnight was ecstatic that a local shopping mall operator had recently announced it would pay its real-estate taxes on time; this had been in doubt for months. Anderson mayor Kris Ockomon was reduced to putting a brave face on his disappointment that President Obama had not included Anderson firms in a round of financing for hybrid and electric-car development. Obama had just flown to Elkhart County to announce the names of companies that would get $2.4 billion worth of grants. "We were invited to the factory where the president was going to speak," Ockomon told his hometown newspaper. "We weren't really sure why in particular we were invited. We thought there might be an announcement for [us]."[1]

As the recession dragged into its twenty-second month late in the summer of 2009, it was a time of trying to hang on by kindling hopes, wishes, and dreams. Yet it also seemed as if Middle America was at a pivotal time in its history. Factory layoffs were part of the boom and bust manufacturing cycle going back to England's Industrial Revolution. But now, it looked like fewer than half of the 200,000 industrial jobs lost in Indiana since 2000 would ever come back. Dozens of factories had closed, the work automated or offshored. Technology was the buzzword, but it left a gaping question. Could a place like Anderson succeed? "At one point, most Americans who made a living did it by making items," said Hindy Schachter, a management professor at the New Jersey Institute of Technology. "Today most American workers are employed in providing services. High-end service jobs such as financial or media positions congregate in 'high end' locations with good education and entertainment systems. The 'solution' for your mayors is to rework their cities into becoming likely destination spots for Google/Intel/Hedge Fund companies. Can most cities do this? Probably not. The new system will have winners and losers."

What was happening was the decline of the Midwest. And it portended something that was in many ways something worse. It was the decline of an empire — America — into a country of haves and have-nots.

Not all that long ago, many Americans believed that Japan would own the twenty-first century. Late in 2009, this certainly looked to have come true from the standpoint of Middle America's worn factory towns. General Motors and Chrysler had just emerged from bankruptcy reorganizations, bankruptcies inflicted in large measure by the unsurpassed quality and value of Japanese automobiles. Yet the collapse of the real-estate bubble in Tokyo had backfired on Japan, miring the nation in an economic slump stretching back to the 1990s. Now, opinion leaders of every political stripe and in every part of the United States accepted the idea that the new century would belong not to Japan, but to China. And the acceptance of this idea, that China would be the global manufacturing center, would put the industrial Midwest on a crash course with the rest of the United States. The "smart people," so to speak, had no faith the United States could do what Japan had done earlier and what China was now trying to do — manufacture its way to prosperity. If they were right — meaning if the American worker, foreman, engineer, and plant manager really were incapable of withstanding international competition — then investors were right to put their money elsewhere than in Middle America. After all, why throw good money after bad, you could argue. But what was "right" for the investors might not be right for Middle America, in itself proof of a huge rift in the nation. Wall Street was all about finance, and California was technology, but the specialty in great swaths of the interior was the design, engineering, and production of manufactured goods. Yet, when it came to manufacturing, it was as if the people on the coasts had no attention span. America was at the crossroads.

Yes, the government had bailed out Chrysler and General Motors. Many autoworkers had returned to factories that had been closed for much of the spring and summer in 2009. But it was clear that the reorganization of the companies was not the only ingredient necessary for a successful turnaround. Beyond the bailout were public policy moves that, if put in place, could not only sustain the domestic auto industry, but assure a fresh burst of new industrial work in Middle America, and even refloat an American economy foundering on deficits. Debts had mounted as the United States borrowed money to bring in goods from abroad in massive quantities. Even amidst the recession, in the month of June 2009, American imports of $152.8 billion surpassed the volume of exports by $27 billion.[2] This trade deficit endured month after month, year after year. Many economists understood this was unsustainable. The country either had to import less, which would lower the standard of living, or it had to produce more. It had to become a manufacturing nation again, whatever the naysayers on the East and West Coasts might think. In the industrial Midwest, a region rich with engineering colleges and the production capacity of the downsized Detroit car companies, like a voice in the wilderness, there remained an abiding belief that this could be done.

What the region needed to go forward was two-fold — a cease-fire agreement with Wall Street and a coherent industrial road map emanating from Washington. The Midwest had had neither of those in place since the start of the pivotal 1980s.

While the decline of Detroit would flow largely from the bad decisions of the auto executives, including unsustainable labor agreements made in concert with the UAW, it was also true the decisions in New York and Washington in the 1980s, decisions that enriched the men and women on Wall Street, markedly intensified the pressure on manufacturing executives, and took away jobs from the men and women in Middle America's factories. Boarded plants in Kokomo, shabby bungalows in Anderson, and cold foundries in Indianapolis resulted from decisions made, and decisions avoided, during the last decades of the Cold War. It perhaps would be going too far to say the United States sacrificed its rich industrial base for the principle of containing communism. But there had been a plan: We would buy stuff made abroad, which would build prosperity as a hedge against the spread of communism, and we'd get cheap goods here and get rid of the kinds of jobs all the smart people didn't think were important anyway. "What's said [in Washington] is we want to engage China," said Indiana Congressman Joe Donnelly, whose district represents part of Kokomo. "If we took more action they would get extraordinarily angry. Instead of dealing with it what Washington did year after year was to accommodate China so they wouldn't get angry."

The pawns in all this, the grunts who would end up like body counts in war? It was the workers themselves.

"Kokomo is Delphi and Chrysler," said Ruth Needleman, a labor studies professor at Indiana University Northwest. "People who lived there were the mythical middle class. I say mythical because the term was invented. . . . It was a term that eliminated the need to talk about the working class even though they were the essential working class. The country moved away from a definition of the working class that was rooted in what you did and how much autonomy you had, and moved it into how much you could buy."

Today, of course, no one can go back and reclaim what was once here. There is, however, an opportunity for a fresh start that can reinvigorate Middle America. And in this, the White House has been lacking. In the summer of 2009, President Barack Obama and his automotive task force were lauded in many quarters for Detroit's rescue. Even so, a sense of disquiet grew in America. Yes, the auto companies were alive, recast by the White House to survive the full-blown depression scouring the entire automotive industry as sales of new vehicles fell forty percent off the pace of 2007. But the White House had squandered an opportunity. Stripped of its resources and scale, no longer could GM in particular drive the industrial economy forward. Obama's auto task force treated the GM rescue as if it were a merger or acquisition of just another manufacturer. When it came to reviving the industrial Midwest, the government had no real strategic plan; there was nothing like the Manhattan Project in Franklin Roosevelt's administration during the Second World War, or even the kind of space shot to the moon John F. Kennedy had supported a generation later. It was as if the White House had built an island called GM and forgotten to install the bridge to the rest of America and its foundering economy.

Hiring by manufacturers had helped end previous economic downturns. Roger Smith's GM tech spending binge had done just that on the heels of the 1981–82 recession. From December 2007 through June 2009 more than 1.9 million manufacturing jobs were lost in the United States.[3] Bad enough, but industrial jobs had also vanished in the United States throughout the first decade of the new millennium. Each year in the decade left less of a manufacturing base to rekindle the economy. Obama had inherited the economic turmoil left by the Bush administration and Wall Street, and he was trying to restore order. His fight had no cohesive strategy, though, drawing criticism that the country was drifting off course.

"My overarching fear is the Obama economic strategy pays a lot of attention to restarting the financial markets and lending, and restarting spending, but it is not paying a lot of attention to restarting production. That's dangerous," said conservative economist Alan Tonelson.[4] Only twice in the last seven decades had the American unemployment rate reached double digits, and now it was creeping past nine percent.

As the layoffs mounted, *New York Times* columnist Bob Herbert urged a massive program on the order of the Great Depression initiatives to restore jobs. "The joblessness the nation is experiencing is crushing any hope of a real economic recovery . . ." Herbert wrote. "The best and the brightest in Washington may have a theory about how to get the economy booming without dealing with the employment crisis, but I'd like to see that theory work in the real world."[5]

An executive from Silicon Valley, epicenter of high-tech America, chimed in with criticism, too. Andrew Grove, former chief executive officer of Intel Corporation, pointed out the government was not actually positioning Detroit for the future. "The U.S. government is investing in the automobile industry with the intention of preventing jobs from being lost," Grove said. "But there is no comparably large investment being made to develop the capabilities that could serve the companies in a new era of electric cars."[6]

With the administration moving ahead on the tangled issue of health care reform, and the president himself traveling abroad on occasion, Obama sought to head off critics, defending the $787 billion stimulus bill that had come out of Washington in March. The measure had been derided for spreading the money over thousands of projects, many of them set for construction in 2010, and many of them relatively minor in economic impact, such as repaving rural airport runways, a necessary task, but one which would create only a few temporary jobs. Meanwhile, in the summer of 2009, Los Angeles City Hall was curbing civic projects, causing layoffs of 2,300 construction workers.[7] Critics estimated that two to three million jobs would be lost in 2009, while Obama administration supporters countered that those lost jobs were being replaced by four million jobs. So many numbers were being bandied about that Americans were confused. Lost — or suppressed — in the discussion were the millions of jobs held by illegal aliens, and the fact that programs targeting chronically unemployed young black males were almost non-existent. Recessions were always messy and uneven, but the urban black underclass rarely had *not* been in a recession. Nevertheless, the president preached patience. "We must let it work the way it's supposed to, with the understanding that in any recession, employment tends to recover more slowly than other measures of economic activity," the president told the nation.[8]

Only days after GM emerged from its remarkably short bankruptcy, the economy *was* showing signs of improvement. The jobless rate remained at a recession level, 9.4 percent in late summer, but stock prices were firming up. Quarterly profits had risen twelve percent for French luxury handbag maker Hermes International. Jaguar, the marque Ford sold to India's Tata, was readying the $72,500 aluminum-bodied XJ sedan for the luxury market. American sales of new autos, while not getting better, were month by month a little less worse than in the preceding month. And then there was the short-lived but successful "Cash for Clunkers" program in August 2009 which did spur auto sales, albeit more for Japanese nameplates than the traditional Detroit Three, with the exception of Ford. "I'm so low on car [inventory] right now it's laughable," Indianapolis dealer Jerry Harvey said. "Dealers are screaming at Ford for more production."[9] Intending to scrap some of the aged and polluting vehicles in the fleet of 300 million cars and trucks on American roads, the administration offered consumer incentives to trade in old autos. Drivers quickly responded, another sign the economy was coming out of the doldrums. Dealers sold nearly 650,000 new autos in July and August under the Cash for Clunkers program, which cost the United States government about $2.8 billion in incentives.

With GM and Chrysler out of bankruptcy, Obama's auto task force had accomplished the difficult chore of stabilizing the two automakers. Steven Rattner, the Wall Streeter chosen by Obama to head the task force, stepped down as the unit's chief. Although he gave no speech or hints of what he would do next, his quiet departure struck a curious note. Wall Street and Detroit had been intertwined for decades. The bankers allocated cash and the auto execs invested it in new plants and equipment. During this time, auto execs had largely called their own shots, right up until Obama had sent in a task force of investment bankers led by Rattner with orders to right GM and Chrysler. The bright young banker seemed just like the head of a cavalry troop riding in to protect the settlers from raiders — the cavalry was coming for Detroit executives and auto industry workers, if not for manufacturing towns themselves. Or was it?

By the beginning of the twenty-first century, Wall Street's interests and Detroit's were out of alignment. Indeed, Wall Street's interests were no longer the interests of Middle America. The old days of staid and traditional investment banking were tottering as the East Coast lost interest in the slow process of financing and building an American manufacturing base. The investment bankers did not set in motion the forces that created the Rust Belt, although they benefited from the changes wracking the region. From the 1980s' spree of leveraged buyouts to the 1990s' offshoring trend, the investment banks in New York prospered, and put Wall Street increasingly at odds with Middle America's stagnating incomes. In his 2008 book, *Bad Money*, former Nixon speech writer Kevin Phillips points out, "The economic uncertainty and disillusionment of Middle America has become a commonplace. . . . [T]he chance that a household would at some point experience a fifty percent drop in income rose from minimal in 1970 to almost one in five in 2002."[10]

While the industrial Midwest fretted in the 2000s about preserving its blue-collar middle class, Wall Street was immersed in its own warfare that made debate about the Midwest irrelevant in New York. As Columbia University faculty member Richard Goldberg noted in his 2009 book, *The Battle for Wall Street*, the staid mainline firms that had reigned on Manhattan for a century had been trying since the end of the 1990s to stare down robust competition from upstart hedge funds and private equity firms, as well as huge pension funds and university endowment funds, all wielding huge pools of investment dollars.[11] Looking for fast growth and easy money, the aggressive funds were changing the climate of New York in favor in megaprofits on obscure instruments such as collateralized debt obligations. The upstarts were clearly pushing Wall Street into ever more exotic financial instruments in search of double-digit profits. Phillips, in *Bad Money*, quotes Wall Street economist David Hall to underscore the culpability of the investment bankers in the meltdown of the American economy. In November 2007, as the financial crash began, Hall pointed out, "Wall Street has produced a credit crisis for banks by securitizing more than $900 billion worth of subprime loans. The ultimate default rate on these loans could rise as high as twenty to twenty-five percent, so there is $200 to $250 billion of bad paper now circulating in the financial system."[12]

Of course, Rattner himself did not preside over the collapse of Wall Street. But the polished young banker was a product of a heady era that produced extraordinary wealth in Manhattan, and set it apart from the rest of America as a hugely influential and almost invincible caste. British journalist Gillian Tett noted 1,852 American bankers were prosecuted during the 1980s' savings and loan scandals, and another 2,558 were jailed, but two years into the meltdown of Wall Street "and the level of retribution so far seems almost nonexistent," Tett wrote, pointing out that "the sheer number of powerful parties that typically participated in complex financial deals" made rounding up the transgressors difficult. "Not many law firms want to fight numerous Wall Street banks, particularly since the Supreme Court has made it difficult to win securities cases in the last couple of years by raising the bar for evidence."[13]

If Manhattan was about financial engineering of ever more exotic securities, Detroit was about actual engineering. And yet as Rattner stepped down from Obama's auto task force, neither the young investment banker nor Obama had anything to say about bringing the engineers of the Midwest to the task of reenergizing the economy. It was as if Rattner had looked at Detroit as a banker looks at a potential client. He demands it pare back union wages, cut out production capacity, reduce the labor force. Little was said about reconstituting GM and Chrysler as real engines of manufacturing wealth and job security. "Historically, the success of the U.S. economy was high productivity, which in turn fueled economic growth," said labor analyst Harley Shaiken, a professor at the University of California at Berkeley. "What we have forgotten in the rush to demonize the unions is that the flip side of high wages is high purchasing power." Not only were UAW wages on the down slide in Detroit Three plants — many new hires (skilled trades excepted) would start at less than $15 per hour — but Toyota had announced that going forward its wages in new plants would be linked to the prevailing industrial wage in the region it was entering rather than the UAW scale set in Detroit. Midwestern pay scales were coming down.

At the same time, there was no certainty the engineering corps in Detroit would get a significant piece of the electric car research money necessary to invigorate R&D in the region. Shaiken, noting Ford's source for lithium-ion batteries was France's Saft, said he feared "the R&D brains go to France. That affects the future of our economy. If you manufacture batteries in China, you will do R&D in China. That's why China wants to manufacture batteries. China understands what we've forgotten, I think. We have a tendency to think manufacturing is twentieth century if not nineteenth century. But manufacturing is at the heart of any largely advanced economy in the world. China, Germany, and Japan understand that. We, I think, have ignored it."

In the lore of Detroit, Henry Ford, Billy Durant, Walter Chrysler, Lee Iacocca — these were manufacturers, car guys, businessmen at home in the clanking, noisy, dangerous setting of an automobile factory. Though their world was distant from Wall Street, they moved in the same orbit. J. Pierpont Morgan had bankrolled autos, steel, tractors, and electrical gadgets in hopes of concocting lucrative manufacturing monopolies. Over the years, though, the financial world gradually had separated itself from the manufacturing side of America. Washington claimed that Detroit — and, by extension, all of Middle America with its manufacturing towns — was ignorant of the buying realities of consumers in 2009. Yet Wall Street was itself unhinged from the real needs of Middle America, beginning at least a quarter of a century earlier. By 1983, the unbridled merger and acquisition era had taken hold. Buyouts and mergers would begin to denude the Midwest of its factories, and shape and influence Washington and many of the deal makers later selected for Obama's auto team. When the era first came on, Detroit already was wallowing in poorly made cars; the UAW was mugging the Detroit Three for ever more money and benefits; and Washington was impervious to the ills of America's single largest industry. Focused on eroding incomes or, in many cases, personal indulgences, the society itself was out of synch. Public high schools were graduating failing students wholly unversed in either the Bill of Rights or rudimentary mathematics — meaning neither side in the growing culture wars in America, neither the Left nor the Right, could be happy. Meanwhile Indian, Japanese, Korean, Pakistani, and Taiwanese immigrants filled seats in American engineering classes. The United States was educating the next generation of gifted foreign engineers, the very people who would grasp the computer, electronics, and battery technology designed in America, take it to Asia, and sell it back to Americans under brand names like Sony and Samsung. American educators were mostly interested in promoting the liberal arts, humanities, finance, and sociology to our citizens, however, as if all the talk about a post-industrial society really were valid, which it wasn't.

Through it all, Manhattan was exuberant, engorged on the sudden new wealth. Marketers even coined a phrase in the early 1980s: yuppies, short for young urban professionals, newly minted lawyers and MBAs hired by Wall Street firms suddenly in need of thousands of hardworking troops in offices handling M&A — mergers and acquisitions. The M&A department suddenly became *the* place to work in the 1980s; the writer David Halberstam described Wall Street as having turned wonderfully golden (complete with high fees and fancy hourly billing rates) for the yuppies whose duty was to concoct and script the buyout or breakup of companies that businessmen in another era had created. "All the best young people wanted to be in M/A . . ." Halberstam pointed out in his 1986 book, *The Reckoning*. "Some of them liked to speak about their days as anti-war activists or Nader's Raiders [consumer activists], though roles of social conscience seemed well behind them. Almost no one, as far as they were concerned, was as smart as they were. The only people they seemed to respect were their opponents, people exactly like them in rival houses. . . . They spoke a brittle shorthand with each other, a language that seemed to reek of contempt for the world of business. Everyone, in their argot, was trying to 'screw' everyone else. . . ."[14]

Out of that milieu came distinct trends that would harm middle-class factory workers across the industrial Midwest. One was the rapid inflation of stock market prices, which put an unwavering focus on quarterly profits. Suddenly, businessmen "were under pressure not to run their companies well, or to produce a better product, but to maximize their stock and make the books look better," Halberstam explained.[15] This pressed executives to back off on upgrading plants and eventually offshore some production and spin off divisions.

Another trend was the grooming of the self-absorbed yuppies into hardcore deal makers. From the M&A era emerged extravagantly rich financiers such as Ivan Boesky, Carl Icahn, and Michael Milken. Household names by virtue of their new wealth in the 1980s, they were the swashbuckling mentors for the next generation of nouveau riche Streeters like Steven Rattner and Stephen Feinberg, the latter a Milken protégé who went on to form Cerberus and buy and sell Chrysler as if it were a piece of used furniture.

It is not well remembered in America why the wheeling and dealing M&A era originated, but it did not come out of thin air. A sudden tide of money flowed to Wall Street, a tide set loose by an unusual confluence of decisions and events that shook the country in the 1970s. For many economic historians, the tragedy of Detroit and the stagnant wages of ordinary factory workers trace to a key point: the beginning of the 1970s. When the decade opened, the United States was unarguably the richest country in world history. Millions of veterans educated on the Second World War GI Bill had reached their prime earning years, and their well-tended offspring were comfortably ensconced in some of the best colleges on earth. Having spent lavishly on the Apollo moon shots, the construction of the interstate highway system, more than 300,000 troops in Europe and Japan, and a major war in Vietnam, America was booming, its economy stimulated by federal outlays of cash. Overseas, companies were gorged on dollars for chemicals, metals, and materials shipped to the United States — especially to sustain the force of 500,000 troops in Vietnam in the late 1960s and early 1970s. Richard Duncan notes in *The Dollar Crisis* that exporters abroad, unwilling to hold so many greenbacks, began exchanging the paper bills for American gold, sending a veritable river of the ore flowing out of the U.S. stronghold at Fort Knox, Kentucky.[16]

President Richard Nixon suspended the exchange of dollars for gold. He declared the dollar's value would be set in the currency exchange markets. This meant the perceived strength of the American economy would determine the dollar's value in Tokyo or Riyadh or anyplace else that took greenbacks. In a roaring American economy, a currency trader might accept, say, 200 Japanese yen for a single dollar. If the U.S. was slumping, the weak dollar might be worth 100 yen. Leaving the gold standard would have deep repercussions on America's old-line manufacturers. For one thing, strategic planning would become difficult against rivals in Japan and China, where strong government backing would enable export-minded enterprises to take the long view and absorb years of losses. For another, it exposed consumers and the Detroit automakers to wild fluctuations in commodity prices, such as the escalation of oil from $10 per barrel in 1998 to $145 by 2008. In Europe and Asia, the White House decision left governments with little choice but to let their own currencies rise and fall in relation to the U.S. dollar. Since the American economy was preeminent around the world following the collapse of Asia and Europe in the Second World War, the American dollar became *the* accepted currency. This would create turmoil around the world. When the dollar was weak, United States manufacturers could export their own products at discount prices and elbow aside foreign competitors unable to match the low prices. European and Asian nations, including Japan and eventually China, set in place sophisticated barriers to protect homegrown industries, much to the chagrin of fair traders who argued the United States was not doing enough to maintain level trade. They were heard particularly when the dollar was strong. Then, low-price imports could flow into the United States, eviscerating American manufacturers.

But in 1973, when the United States formally went off the gold standard, the turmoil to come was only hinted at. Overshadowing the exchange rate issue was political upheaval. There was the U.S. withdrawal from the Vietnam War and, in 1975, the eventual loss of South Vietnam to the Communist North, as well as Nixon's 1974 resignation in the Watergate domestic spying and break-in scandal. Then the rapid erosion in buying power undermined working Americans as gasoline prices doubled and a recession set in with the oil embargo triggered by the 1973 Arab-Israeli war and Saudi-dominated Organization of Petroleum Exporting Countries, or OPEC. The decade ended in military humiliation when America was unable to free several dozen U.S. hostages held in Tehran after Iran's 1979 Islamic revolution.

In 1980 a surly public elected Ronald Reagan president of the United States. He was a handsome former movie actor whose sunny confidence and staunch conservatism had already won him two terms as governor in California. Campaigning against him for a spell in 1980, former CIA director George H. W. Bush, scion of an old oil and railroad family, complained of Reagan's "voodoo economics" strategy. Promising to restore America's status in the world as the "shining city on the hill," Reagan was swept into office. He presided over crucial changes: deregulation of the old savings and loan industry, deep tax cuts, a massive military build-up, and a promise to restore prosperity to the country by attracting cash into the United States from around the world. On Wall Street, investors were delighted. Despite the 1960s' boom, in 1980 the stock market had been slack for fourteen years, and bonds had been in a bear market since 1945, notes financial writer Bill Bonner in *Empire of Debt*.[17]

New Yorkers were not necessarily in favor of war, but the net effect of higher defense spending and lower taxes — the locus of Bush's "voodoo" analysis — was tonic for a parched Street. Not only would aerospace and defense electronics companies borrow money to finance the build-up, but Americans could invest the income freed up by tax cuts with Wall Street firms. Moreover, Wall Street would get lucrative new work from another quarter. Without the tax revenue coming in, the American government would have to borrow money from investors, offering them United States Treasury bills that promised repayment later. Massive government borrowing tended to push up interest rates harmfully for Detroit's automakers, but federal debt was money in the bank for Wall Street. It got to peddle U.S. Treasury bills. As United States Treasury notes were hawked around the world, old-line economists warned the rising federal strategy "facilitated the extraordinary misallocation of corporate capital," in the words of Richard Duncan, a World Bank Asian markets advisor.[18] But there was no stopping the binge. Between 1980 and 1993, federal debt soared from twenty-two percent of gross domestic product (GDP) to fifty percent.

Working also in Wall Street's favor was the Federal Reserve Board. The Fed had been begrudgingly created in response to the 1880s' populist cry by legions of American farmers starved for currency prior to the Alaska gold rush. One century later, the modern Fed, the manager of the money supply, was in tune with Wall Street. Weary of the inflation eating at corporate profits, Wall Street demanded from the White House and got an inflation fighter in Paul Volcker, who had been head of the Federal Reserve Bank of New York. Appointed chairman of the entire Federal Reserve system in 1980, Volcker promptly cranked short-term interest rates to more than twenty percent. Bludgeoned by the unaffordable rates, consumers stopped buying and stores cut prices. Inflation was tamed, but the fall in spending set off a recession that devastated the industrial Midwest, just as the automakers were trying to come to grips with the car imports from Japan. The Detroit Three alone idled more than 250,000 autoworkers in the 1981 and 1982 recession. In the auto plants, Ginny McMillin found herself laid off for four years in her home-town, Kokomo, when GM Delco cut back in 1981. "I didn't have a year in so I couldn't transfer to [GM's] Marion [plant]," she recalled. "I was shit out of luck at home with three kids. I was on food stamps. I remember going to Marsh [Supermarket] at midnight so my friends wouldn't see me."

Startled by the downturn, the worst since the Great Depres-sion, the UAW soon began to cooperate with auto executives on plant productivity improvements, but also pressed for guaran-tees of job security. Hard as the recession was on Detroit, Wall Street blossomed. Investors around the world began moving their money to America to take advantage of the high interest rates. Cranked up by Volcker to fend off inflation, American rates were higher than Europe's or Asia's. Investors abroad saw a good deal. Foreign cash flowed into Treasury bills, bank certificates of deposit, real estate, and stocks.

Wall Street was becoming flush with cash, but what put it over the top, at least on the M&A side, and set in motion a spate of factory closings, was the deregulation of the savings and loan banks. Very few of these exist today, although for a century they were a fixture in literally thousands of neighborhoods. Blue-collar families especially relied on them for low-rate home loans. Known as thrifts, or S and Ls, they long had been protected by a web of rules disbanded in the deregulation climate swept in by Reagan. When Volcker surged interest rates, however, thrifts were hammered worse than Detroit. Having booked thirty-year mortgage loans at interest rates of six or seven percent, S and Ls were failing by the dozens as the cost of money soared beyond fif-teen percent. They were paying more for money than they were getting in repayment on loans. Congress swiftly guaranteed deposits up to $100,000, so even if the S and L went under, the American taxpayer would protect the customer.

This prevented runs on the thrifts, although what made S and Ls the lucrative honeypot for Wall Street was one final piece of deregulation. In an effort to shore up profits, thrifts were allowed to invest the money deposited by customers — the deposits guaranteed by the American government — in endeavors promising high income. Dreamers, scam artists, hustlers, and the plain incompetent began lining up for loans from thrifts, by then operating under loose federal supervision following the downsizing of bank regulatory agencies. By 1990, the S and L industry would implode under the greed of the speculators and trigger a $250 billion federal bailout to repay depositors in failed thrifts. Out of the carnage emerged a new breed of lender, mortgage giants such as Countrywide. These unregulated mortgage firms in tandem with unrestrained Wall Street derivatives traders would create the next financial debacle, the global credit crisis of 2008, which in turn helped bankrupt GM and Chrysler. But back in the 1980s, when the thrifts still were standing, their easy-to-get loans financed a staggering array of speculative skyscrapers, golf courses, shopping malls, residential developments, and corporate takeovers. One of the biggest users of the easy money was Michael Milken, the junk-bond king.

Milken, a graduate of the Ivy League business school at the University of Pennsylvania, was hired on at Drexel Harriman Ripley in 1970, pursuing an idea to market the risky bonds of struggling companies with low credit ratings. Traditionally, companies considered risky bets for bankers were assigned low credit ratings because they had problems that made them less likely than top-notch corporations to repay loans. The lower the score, the higher the interest rate charged by the bank to make up for the risk. Drexel, a very distant offshoot of the old J. Pierpont Morgan banking dynasty, was a second-tier firm in New York, where Milken himself was regarded as an outsider among the old patriarchs on Wall Street.[19] Seeing a redeemable quality in struggling companies, he called them "fallen angels." Milken insisted their debt was risky but worthy because of the sky-high interest paid on the bonds. Milken's idea gleamed when Reagan tax policies unleashed a torrent of demand for loans. Corporate borrowers could deduct the interest on the debt from their income taxes. Milken made junk bonds part of the everyday language of finance. U.S. corporations accumulated debt like never before, issuing not just junk bonds, but taking on all kinds of loans, knowing they could cut their income taxes. Between 1980 and 1990, the volume of credit debt rose from 180 percent of GDP to nearly 250 percent.[20]

Among his peers, many thought Milken's genius lay not in simply hawking junk bonds with a preacher's zeal, but in proffering the bonds as essential tools for hostile corporate takeovers, first for small-time wheelers and dealers ignored by the patriarchs of Manhattan, then by the buyout titans of Wall Street whose business was buying and selling other businesses. "There was a crude, bullying quality to the Drexel organization, which gave the firm the air of a Mafia family," Edward Chancellor reported in his book, *Devil Take the Hindmost*.[21] In 1984, Thomas Boone Pickens, an Oklahoma oil tycoon trying to take over Gulf Oil, came to Drexel for junk-bond financing, the first corporate raider to knock on the door of what by then was named Drexel Burnham Lambert. "Without actually having the funds necessary for the takeover," Chancellor writes, "Drexel produced a letter stating it was 'highly confident' of raising the capital through the sale of junk bonds. Although this bid failed, the 'highly confident' letter symbolized Drexel's ability to finance deals of limitless size." Pickens may have been first, but he certainly was not the last. Hundreds of deals followed including what then was the titanic $6 billion in Drexel junk bonds in 1986 for the buyout firm Kohlberg Kravis Roberts' takeover of mighty Beatrice, the conglomerate whose holdings ranged from Avis car rentals to Samsonite luggage. Weary of the staid traditions of Manhattan, Milken moved his Drexel staff to Los Angeles, where he arranged more than $200 billion worth of junk-bond deals during the 1980s, financing an array of mergers and acquisitions that gave Drexel a piece of 150 companies. S and Ls bought a huge volume of the bonds as investments. By 1990, just as the thrifts imploded, Drexel collapsed in bankruptcy. Milken paid a $600 million fine and was briefly imprisoned for securities fraud. Although he was widely berated for spreading so much risky debt, he pointed out the bonds had aided many cash-starved companies. And if they were junk bonds rather than the AAA-rated bonds, well, that was the new way of America. "Everything we like is junk, junk food, junk clothes, junk records," Milken said. "Everything that stands the test of time is junk."[22]

While Milken peddled junk bonds, and American businesses larded up on debt, and Reagan White House policy encouraged a borrow-your-way-to-prosperity ethic among the citizenry and corporations, the industrial base of America was slowly dissolving. Auto executives in Detroit would be assailed for failing to head off the imports flowing into the United States in the 1980s. Detroit's failure in those years, however, was in many ways emblematic of the boardrooms of manufacturing companies throughout the country. In a nation whose high standard of living for a century had been tied to its manufacturing prowess, the business leaders in America were standing down rather than trying to compete head on with imports. This was happening in boardrooms in every city. And it was happening in large measure because of Volcker's inflation fight. Sky-high interest rates had sent the dollar's value soaring. Imports flooded into the United States, hammering essential industries. CEOs, pressed by Wall Street to come up with regular quarterly gains in profits, turned to junk bonds and mergers and acquisitions, rather than try to compete all-out with the surging tide of products from overseas that could be priced less than the American version. A strong dollar favored producers abroad. By the mid-1980s, "a Toyota, once delivered in San Francisco for $10,000, could now be marketed in America at a real cost to the Japanese of only $7,500," pointed out journalist William Greider in his book, *Secrets of the Temple*.[23] Whether in grain, steel, computer chips, machine tools, or cars, foreign producers "grabbed a larger and larger share of the domestic market," Greider wrote.

Milken and Wall Street were not the architects of industrial decline. They were simply its bankers. Using junk debt meant an obscure businessman without the assets to borrow heavily from a bank could go to a junk-bond dealer like Drexel, arrange the financing, buy the company, and make the newly acquired business pay off the junk-bond debt — a transaction known as a leveraged buyout. Even rich corporate raiders could avoid traditional lenders. Instead, money was raised by selling junk bonds to an S and L. And the subsequent debt was piled on the books of the acquired company, which in turn wrote off the debt on its income taxes. By 1987, the annual value of merger activity in the United States neared $300 billion, with top-tier Wall Street firms leading the way, each averaging 110 to 200 deals per year, and each collecting as much as $100 million in takeover fees every year, noted economic historian Charles Geist in his book, *Wall Street*.[24] While the era was making the men and women of Manhattan rich, workers in Middle America were seeing wages stagnate and jobs vanish. Between 1980 and 1990, American companies opened 1,000 plants in Mexico. Between 1990 and 1995, another 1,000 plants opened there. While not all of these south-of-the-border plants emanated from corporate takeovers, many did. For example, Drexel junk bonds enabled wealthy Los Angeles investor Andrew Galef's Spectrum Group to take over New Jersey lightbulb maker Universal, which was moved to Matamoros, Mexico, where wages were $1.91 per hour, compared to $7.91 in New Jersey.[25]

As a driver of the economy, the industrial base was losing power, though much of America was unaware or simply did not care, figuring it was coming into the post-industrial, information-based society talked about in the colleges since the 1960s. Or, perhaps, they really thought a service economy could provide good jobs for all, not understanding that "service" and "servant" have the same root word. Only one union, the United Steelworkers, staunchly fought the North American Free Trade

Agreement, and the USW lost. The pact cut taxes on shipments between Canada, the United States, and Mexico, although by the time it was enacted in 1993 many executives of big businesses that wanted plants in Mexico already had them. Free trade agreements are supposed to be win-win arrangements, in which each country does what it does best, and everyone benefits from higher productivity, better quality, and lower prices. But if some countries cheat and other countries really can't do much about it, then it looks like predatory trade. As industrial jobs went abroad, manufacturing dropped off the radar scope of concerns for most Americans. By 2009, hardly anyone on the East Coast or the West Coast came to the defense of Chrysler when the Obama administration steered it into the arms of Italy's Fiat.

For many people in the great cities on the American coasts, Chrysler and General Motors were the insular denizens of a déclassé region, a place you were from. Once educated in the professions, its own people often moved away. And when they remembered the Midwest in their writings, they were fashionably derisive. "Every house had a station wagon in the driveway and a skinny tree from the nursery ailing in the front yard," the writer Susan Choi reminisced from New York about her childhood home near South Bend, Indiana. When the novelist William Gass, who lived for fifteen years in Indiana while teaching at Purdue University, wrote fiction about life in a small Midwestern town, even the climate was grimly remembered. "[I]t is snow without any laughter in it. . . . [O]f course soot covers everything." And the natives? Boorish. "Sports, politics, and religion are the three passions of the badly educated," Gass wrote. "They are the Midwest's open sores."[26]

Midwesterners might shrug off the musings of Gass and Choi as old-fashioned ribbing. But these gifted writers pointed to something larger. Once, the great interior of the country had been a thought leader at the forefront of a whole host of civic reform movements. Peaking as a cultural force in the 1920s, the region had devolved slowly into the New Appalachia of the new century. Even the urban landscape — restaurants and theaters, breweries and newspapers, factories and hardwares, coffee shops and department stores — no longer was in the hands of local families known to everyone in town. The region had become little more than a commercial colony, a province of vast national chain stores and franchise operations tended from distant cities. When urban scholar John Austin of the Brookings Institution examined the region in 2006, he concluded it has a "workforce ill-prepared to obtain or create jobs in the new economy. Its landscape is dotted with hollowing city centers, emptying manufacturing towns, and isolated farm, mining, and timber communities, which continue to bleed mobile, educated workers. And, perhaps most importantly, within much of the region the culture of innovation that helped make it a leader has been lost."[27]

Just why the entrepreneurial resolve vanished is open to debate. But obviously there was nobody anyone could point to at the top of a major company who was an outright manufacturing man like Chrysler, Ford, or Durant. Certainly, when the currency exchange rates began working *against* Japan later in the 1980s, following a spike in oil prices, the Japanese automakers didn't give up. Showing the same élan as entrepreneurs, Japanese companies moved assembly lines to America and redoubled the efforts of their engineers, taking costs out of their designs. By 2009, there was little evidence of this kind of élan in Detroit.

On the day in April 2009 when Chrysler manufacturing star Tom LaSorda announced he would step down as vice chairman, the news caused no ripples outside Detroit. LaSorda had been the latest in the long line of talented engineers over the decades who had kept the wheezing and fitful machine that was Chrysler alive. Outside Detroit, the Canadian-born LaSorda was hardly a household name. And the fact that he would leave, or Chrysler would fade into Fiat, was hardly a concern. Hardcore factory men were few and far between. This was not accidental. America's business leaders had been getting out of manufacturing for years. In the mid-1980s, the writer David Halberstam had suggested that perhaps it wasn't so much that Detroit couldn't compete with Japan, but that it didn't want to compete.[28]

In an era when the tectonic plates were being shifted by M&A yuppies, soaring federal deficits, massive corporate debts, uncomfortable swings in currency exchange rates, the 1980s flood of imports from Japan gave the financiers at the top of the car companies in America an excuse to throw in the towel. They could do what they had long wanted to do — break up the auto parts divisions, move the factories abroad. When Halberstam brought this up two decades ago with Harley Shaiken, a labor analyst at the University of California, Shaiken said he worried that America's leaders had given up on manufacturing because they were not manufacturing men. In 1986, Halberstam wrote that Shaiken believed "that the men who headed these large American industrial corporations would not stand and fight against the Japanese, or at least would not fight very hard. . . . It was significant, Shaiken thought, that they were not men of the plants, not manufacturing men who, finding they had lost the lead, would push hard and fight to regain it. Rather, they were men of finance, and they were trained to think not in terms of loyalties to products and to factories and locales and men who worked for them but of profit and profit alone."[29]

A quarter of a century after those words saw print, it would be hard to say that much had changed in the boardrooms of America. Corporate executives were still castigated for having little loyalty to their customers, employees, communities, or flag. What had changed, Shaiken noted in 2009, was that finance clearly had trumped manufacturing in its perceived importance. "In the twentieth century," he said, "America was thought of as the center for knowing how to make things. In the twenty-first century, we've become known as the center of financial instruments." In 2009, ten months after United States Treasury officials had panicked Congress into the $700 billion bailout for Wall Street, Goldman Sachs declared its best quarterly profit in 140 years, and reserved $11 *billion* for future payment of employee bonuses. The joy at Goldman Sachs, a Manhattan goliath whose alumni included Henry Paulson, the United States

Treasury secretary presiding over the bailout in the Bush White House, was bitter news for millions of Americans whose jobs had vanished in a recession fueled by Wall Street excess. Jon Stewart told viewers of his national comedy show: "Goldman Sachs makes $3.4 billion profit from April to June. I guess the bailouts are working. For Goldman Sachs."

Taking note of Stewart's deadpan humor, *New York Times* writer David Segal focused on the public cynicism. "It's the widespread sense that winners in this economy are produced by a game that's rigged. . . . If these companies can return to the festivities so quickly, were they really having the near-death experience they and the government claimed? And if taxpayers risked their money when they backstopped Wall Street's misadventures, why aren't they sharing in the upside now that the party has started again?"[30]

Of course, Goldman Sachs' good fortune traced to the sudden collapse of most other Wall Street titans. It was easy to make money when there was so little competition. But the gross disparity in Goldman Sachs even having $11 billion for bonuses, while the rest of the country suffered a staggering unemployment rate, was nothing new. Wall Street long had been on a course outward bound from Middle America. Paulson himself, along with Thomas McLarty, who had been chief of staff for President Bill Clinton, were new investors in Coda Automotive, a California upstart that in 2009 decided to produce $45,000 electric cars equipped with batteries purchased from China's Tianjin Lishen, and car bodies made by China's Hafei Automobile Industry Group.[31] Paulson, a former Wall Street investment banker at Goldman Sachs, had led the U.S.-China Strategic and Economic Dialog as United States Treasury secretary.

By the summer of 2009, the trans-Pacific dialog was long forgotten. Washington lawmakers were grilling the former Cabinet official for his efforts the prior autumn while in the White House to prop up Wall Street and Goldman Sachs. "Is it possible that there's so much conflict of interest here that all you folks don't even realize that you're helping people that you're associated with?" Cliff Stearns, a Republican from Florida in the U.S. House of Representatives, asked Paulson at a congressional hearing.

"I operated very consistently within the ethic guidelines I had as secretary of the Treasury," Paulson replied.[32]

While Paulson fended off the inquisition in Congress, his investment in Coda Automotive, which was raising $24 million in total from investors, pointed to a key irony. Wall Street was investing in an assembly plant in America — the $24 million. But it was investing in a luxury car whose electric vitals originated in China and would enhance Chinese R&D, all the while presenting a rival in the car market for luxury models manufactured by Detroit. In one respect, this was nothing new. The borrowing binge of the 1980s actually starved the American industrial base. Kevin Phillips, a former Nixon White House official, writing in *Bad Money*, quoted Harvard economist Benjamin Friedman: "'The 1980s,' Friedman said, 'has been by far the worst period for business investment in physical assets like plant and equipment since World War II. Instead of borrowing to build new facilities or even to build liquidity, the corporate business sector as a whole has mostly used the proceeds of its extraordinary volume of borrowing . . . [for] mergers and acquisitions, leveraged buyouts and stock repurchases.'"[33]

Rather than spend that money on machine tools, engineering design computers, research labs, or other goods that could fight off imports and create income and jobs for years, the CEOs had been like lottery winners blowing windfalls in Las Vegas. Progressive and New Left theorists were incensed, suddenly sounding more nationalistic than the many flag-wavers on Wall Street. "There's more to decision-making than how much profit I can make," fumed Indiana University Northwest's Ruth Needleman. "They may talk like that in the board rooms but they don't care about the tax base, about the standard of living. They are making decisions without any commitment to the nation."

Yet business leaders were not mavericks. They were logical. Building a business from scratch, or trying to grow profits in a mature business, was risky and time consuming, especially in the face of low-wage foreign competition reaching America. Profits could be more quickly shown by buying a plant in the next state. Just adding the income of the acquired business to the balance sheet had a way of making the acquirer's stock price climb. Because executive pay was tied in part to the stock price, the deals produced hefty bonus checks. At the root of the buyout mania, fueling the process, was United States tax policy. Interest payments on corporate debt were deductible. The policies were meant to stimulate investment. Instead, they eviscerated the industrial core. Taxpayers helped foot the bill. In the 1980s, "the interest deduction became an instrument to dismantle America — not to build it," journalists Donald L. Bartlett and James B. Steele wrote. "Businesses borrowed money to raid other businesses and sell off their assets. That led to the closing of factories, the elimination of middle-income jobs, and the paying of astronomical sums to owners, investors, and corporate executives who brought it all about. All this was subsidized by taxpayers — through the deduction for interest payments."[34]

Not only did Wall Street finance the merger mania of the 1980s, it relentlessly drummed into CEOs the absolute need of turning in higher profits quarter after quarter after quarter. This had always been the case, but it became more so in the 1980s as the mergers swelled corporate profits. And it would figure in the decision of business leaders to cave in rather than fight imports, not just in Detroit, but across the country — just think of all the domestic TV tube and power tool and other appliance manufacturers that didn't even last as long as the car companies. By the winter of 2009, Obama and Rattner would rebuke and fire Richard Wagoner, General Motors' chairman, for the company's disastrous financial situation. Ironically, GM's ills were rooted in the decisions of the 1980s, when it *had* tried to fight imports, however ineptly, building a series of high-tech plants expressly to fend off Honda, Nissan, and Toyota. Too big to quickly turn around, an immense enterprise sized in the monopoly era of J. Pierpont Morgan to dominate the market, General Motors was one of the few American manufacturers that didn't turn tail and run for the easy profits dangled by Wall Street in the merger mania of the Reagan era. Two decades later, Wagoner would be chastised, and GM scaled back radically by Obama and Rattner, who held the view that now, as a smaller company, GM could be made profitable. But those were the blandishments of lawyers and financiers, not manufacturers.

Halberstam sensed all this in 1986, writing back then that "there was a growing split, indeed chasm, between what was good for Wall Street and what was good, in the long run, for productivity for America."[35] It was not only Detroit's automakers confronting the chasm then, but CEOs in an array of industries, including the Silicon Valley, alarmed by the vicissitudes of American capitalism. In another era, the government had helped the old patrician, J. Pierpont Morgan, or at least looked the other way while he bundled rivals into huge concerns such as General Electric, all to avoid competition that ruined profits. By the M&A era, however, Wall Street and Washington were gripped by the notion of laissez-faire. Hoping to slow the tide of imports in the early 1980s, a host of major companies called on Washington to protest these winds of change. Earlier, Reagan had helped Detroit weather the recession by temporarily restricting car imports to a certain volume. When the corporations asked specifically for a thirty-five-percent surcharge on a wide array of Japanese imports to offset the price advantage bestowed by the strong dollar, the Reagan White House refused. In doing so, the administration defined the issue not in terms of the chasm Halberstam described — Wall Street versus American productivity — but free trade or protectionism. Although it was well understood the free-trade stance would erode jobs, Harvard economist Martin Feldstein, then a top Reagan economics advisor, called the trade-off necessary. "A weaker dollar and smaller trade deficit would also mean less capital inflow from the rest of the world and therefore a lower level of domestic investment in plant and equipment and in housing," Feldstein said.[36] Of course, as Benjamin Friedman, his Harvard colleague, would later point out, much of that capital inflow was squandered on mergers and acquisitions rather than plant and equipment. But at the time, many leading Americans agreed with Feldstein. Free trade was the mantra.

Although the big corporations had gotten nowhere with Reagan, the idea of stemming the imports didn't quite die. Former Nixon White House advisor Clyde Prestowitz also set out to do something about imports, supported not only by the Detroit automakers, but executives at a long line of top-drawer electronics companies. Earlier, in the Nixon years, Prestowitz had negotiated trade deals with countries including Japan. He had been struck by how the rich Americans viewed free trade as an abstract principle, while the guiding focus of the Japanese government had nothing to do with free trade. It was purely trade: build a standard of living for the Japanese people around manufactured goods made specifically for export to the world, particularly the richest market in the world, the United States. Having scant resources in the ground like coal, oil, or ore, the Japanese ruthlessly protected their home industries, putting up barriers to a wide variety of imports. American cigarettes were almost impossible to find in Japanese stores, just as one example.[37]

Prestowitz pressed for trade restraints. But with the Cold War still under way, Washington was reluctant to offend an ally by putting up full blown trade barriers that could be seen as the opening salvo of a trade war. Prestowitz, interviewed years later, said the stance then was ruinous for the economy of Middle America and is still in place today in the Obama White House and remains wrong.

"We think we're playing a free-market, free-trade game," Prestowitz said. "When I was in the government, we assumed Japan was playing the same game. They weren't. Japan was playing a game called catch-up — or export-led growth. We were constantly in conflict with them. Memory chips, automotive, grapes, and walnuts. Each time there was a conflict the pattern was the same. Japan would enter the U.S. with imports, but the U.S. couldn't get its exports into Japan. We'd see our factories close and accuse Japan of dumping goods here and not letting us into their markets. They'd say wait a minute, your quality is low, or the steering wheel is on the wrong side, or your delivery is late.

"A series of American industries were impacted," Prestowitz continued. "Machine tools. Memory chips. I finally said [to colleagues in Washington] I realized that we and Japan were playing two different games. Their idea of an open market is a tool and not an end in itself. Japan's objective is to have strong industry. If the [open] market doesn't help them, they'll find a way to get there. What they did is what we did until 1945."[38]

A young economist in Prestowitz's office, Alan Tonelson, remembered the government stance back then. Washington refused stern action on the imports, so American corporations no longer pushed for import restraints. Instead, they began to move pieces of their own businesses to low-wage nations. For Tonelson, it was less the principles of free trade that shaped the White House decision than it was the politics of the Cold War, the containment of the Iron Curtain, a strategy faithfully adhered to by every American administration since 1945. The United States had put troops ashore in Korea and Vietnam to fight communism, and one tangible benefit for Japan had been the shipping routes in the Western Pacific near China, kept open and protected by American military power. Yet, there was a sense in Washington that a trade war might somehow move Japan out of the American camp just when the United States desperately needed Japan's bankers. Grown wealthy on exports, Japan was at its economic peak late in the 1980s. So rich were its holdings of U.S. dollars and Treasury bills, Japan had succeeded Saudi Arabia as America's biggest creditor. Much as they worry about China today, Americans back then worried Japan was not to be ruffled or disturbed in any way, for fear it might unload assets or stop financing the American debt explosion.

Once the big corporations put their seal of approval on off-shoring, the trend became a stampede. General Motors began to uproot auto parts product lines in Anderson, Flint, Kokomo, and other cities and move the work abroad. By 1998, GM was the largest private employer in Mexico, employing 78,000 auto-workers there.[39] The 1998 wage difference: $2 per hour in Mexico; $22 per hour in the United States. By the 2000s, GM had cut its labor force in Indiana, where it had been the state's largest employer, from 40,000 workers in the 1980s to fewer than 6,000. Americans were largely silent. Many perceived the lesser quality of Detroit automobiles to be the responsibility of coddled UAW members. But by the time the quality gap between Japanese and American automobiles narrowed in the late 1990s, a result of better engineering in Detroit, few baby boomers cared. They had turned their backs on Detroit.

Across the nation, NAFTA encouraged the move of factories to Mexico, and in turn gave way to the movement of plants to Taiwan, South Korea, and the Philippines, and finally Vietnam, China, and India. And the move did not stop simply with facto-ries and assembly line jobs. In 2004, the *Times of India* bannered the headline "Silicon Valley Falls to Bangalore." The report claimed 150,000 information technology engineers were employed in Bangalore, 20,000 more than in the California tech center.[40] For executives in U.S. companies, the reliance on low-wage labor overseas helped the profit margins requisite for good earnings demanded by Wall Street. But the practice was haunting Middle America and other sections of the country. "Our finan-cial mess is a result of a mindset focused on shareholder return. But this mindset failed us," Prestowitz said. "It's brought us a catastrophe."[41]

Just as offshoring cost manufacturing jobs, some economists suggested the rise of educated classes in India and China in par-ticular, along with the ready access to information technology, might soon eviscerate millions of American *office* jobs, even for highly paid lawyers and tax accountants and the like. Princeton University economist Alan Blinder, vice chairman of Promontory Interfinancial Network, studied the offshoring trend and "esti-mated that 30 million to 40 million U.S. jobs are potentially offshorable" in the coming years, he wrote in a 2007 opinion piece for the *Washington Post*. "These include scientists, mathematicians, and editors on the high end and telephone operators, clerks, and typists on the low end," Blinder wrote. "Obviously, not all of these jobs are going to India, China, or elsewhere. But many will."[42]

Once research and scientific work shifts overseas from America in large volume, the level of productivity could tend to diminish in the United States. Starving the United States in this way could be a dangerous path because it is productivity — the ability to do more and more with fewer inputs — that helps sustain the nation's high incomes. Ron Hira, a Rochester Institute of Technology public policy professor, notes former IBM research chief Ralph Gomory saw nothing necessarily beneficial for American society in the shift of white-collar and high-tech work abroad. "When U.S. companies build semiconductor plants and R&D facilities in Asia rather than in the U.S.," Gomory told a congressional panel, "then that is a shift in productive capability, and neither economic theory nor common sense asserts that shift is good for the U.S. even in the long run."[43]

If there was a danger, it was clear the White House was not addressing it. By the late winter of 2009, Obama's decision to fire the head of General Motors, scale back GM, and prop it up with taxpayer cash was right out of the old Wall Street playbook of the 1980s. Downsizing a manufacturing corporation was standard procedure in the M&A departments that groomed Steven Rattner and Ronald Bloom — the former Lazard banker who succeeded Rattner as leader of the auto task force. Of course, fat corporations *had* to be trimmed. And the net effect of the GM bankruptcy orchestrated by Obama was to cut away the high debts dragging on the company. Yet, there was no sense of robust confidence that GM might avoid a second bankruptcy in a few years.

For one thing, Obama's plan hitched GM's fortune largely to small cars. "No high income country on earth has made small cars profitably while keeping import markets open to them," said Tonelson, the economist at the United States Business and Industry Council in Washington. Doubts also centered on battery technology. "The battery challenge has yet to be overcome even as the government is pushing plug-in vehicles in a big way," *Green Car Journal* pointed out.[44] On top of the technical and small-car hurdles, there were all the other distractions. When GM executives let out that plants in China might supply little high-mileage autos, the UAW, which now controlled 17.5 percent of the company, quickly blocked the idea. Then, when GM put its Orion Township plant (a suburban Detroit assembly line constructed during the 1980s' high-tech plant spree) on the will-be-closed list, the government suddenly intervened. GM quickly announced Orion would make a future small car. And when GM tried to pare the number of car dealers, Congress intervened, forcing the auto executives to argue the closings were necessary. Then a new GM board of directors, installed by the Obama administration, reversed the decision to sell off Opel, GM's German automaker. And the deal for Saab, GM's Swedish automaker, soon unraveled.

It was a conundrum for GM. Sure the old company was out of bankruptcy, but it was having a hard time gaining traction. And to Tonelson, the economist in Washington, it pointed to a larger issue. The government was not serious about reinvigorating the industrial base of Middle America. "The end goal of the administration was to achieve the orderly contraction of the U.S. auto industry," Tonelson said. "The goal should have been to promote the expansion of the industry, but their bottom line seems to be the same unfettered free trade and import of automotive products we've seen for two decades."

While electric-car startups such as Coda, Fisker, and Tesla promised a wave of innovation in automobiles, nothing compelled the companies to use parts produced in the United States. Americans might drive a high-mileage sedan, but all the components could be imported. Consequently, much of the engineering brainpower that went into the design of high-tech automobile components might wind up resident not in the United States, but Beijing, Stuttgart, Seoul, or Tokyo. While it was good to have 2,000 jobs on a car assembly line for workers earning $25,000 per year, it was even better to have a job for a $100,000-per-year engineer to go along with those 2,000 jobs. It was better because the engineer, having designed one component, could use the knowledge to innovate the next component and the next, and in that way secure the jobs for those 2,000 autoworkers into the future. This had been one secret of Japan's success. Having taken hold of the electronics business, Japanese engineers devised generations of newfangled products, from cassette recorders to DVDs, all creating wealth for Japan. The restructuring of Detroit, however, was rapidly hollowing out the engineering corps, making it likely that much of what went into a "Detroit" car would have been acquired from a supplier. "They just don't have the ability to do R&D anymore [in Detroit]," said Kenneth Baker, former vice president of research and development for General Motors.[45]

The diminished R&D capability was a key issue for the success, even the survival, of the domestic auto industry. Without a creative technology base in place, the billions put in GM by taxpayers would be squandered. Long a critic of Detroit executives, stock analyst Maryann Keller bristled when Washington lawmakers cast the bailout of Detroit as unnecessary when the foreign-owned automotive plants, including suppliers from abroad, employed more than 100,000 Americans. "No wealthy industrialized nation can exist without a healthy automobile manufacturing industry," Keller said. "I'm really just appalled by the uninformed comments from a lot of our legislators when they equate Japanese assembly plants with automobile manufacturing. Automobile manufacturing is not putting pieces of a car together. Putting cars together does not add to the technical base of a country. Just because Toyota is going to put a plant in Kentucky does not enrich the United States in the technology necessary to know *how* to build a hybrid car. The technology, the knowhow, is staying in Japan. There's a big difference between design technology and engineering and assembly. It's the design technology you want as a country. We're getting the assembly and some of the engineering" from abroad.[46]

For Tonelson, and others who had examined the decline of

the industrial Midwest, the solutions were obvious and plentiful. It boiled down to an array of ideas, large and small. What was clear was the automakers had to be harnessed to a larger plan to salvage the industrial base and create industrial jobs across the region. As part of this, Detroit needed to refocus on American battery technology at companies such as EnerDel in Indianapolis, or A123 in Cambridge, Massachusetts, rather than rely on France's Saft or South Korea's LG Chemical. This point was clearly asserted in *Fortune* magazine by business writer Paul Keegan. "Industrialists the world over understand what is only now dawning on Detroit: the handful of companies that end up controlling the battery industry will also control the car industry," Keegan wrote. "Because battery technology will become the core competency that defines the modern car company, it will hardly be the kind of intellectual property you'd want to outsource to a foreign auto-supply company. Sure, GM can assemble those T-shaped battery packs for the Volt domestically. But the most crucial aspect is developing a safe, reliable chemistry and using that proprietary technology to mass-produce the hundreds of cells required for a single battery pack. Too bad for GM that the cells for the Volt actually will come from a Korean company, LG Chemical."[47]

Another obvious place to start was bigger tax credits. Much of Wall Street had been blown away in 2008, but the bias against manufacturing still existed among many investors. Tax initiatives could steer money to the sector and help entrepreneurs in manufacturing attract financing. Idle automotive and recreation vehicle plants were available for transformation and reinvention throughout the region. "In World War II it took no time to retool the plants for war," said Indiana University Northwest's Ruth Needleman. "Why aren't we using all these [auto] plants for public transportation and energy efficient vehicles, or machinery that would let us go green?"

Also helpful would be an end to the use of quarterly earnings reports. Trying to satisfy Wall Street's appetite for growing profits every three months tends to focus executive attention on the short term, rather than investing in long horizons. Even some military planners have urged an end to Wall Street's focus on quarterly profits, contending it was one in a bevy of reasons for the gradual gutting of the U.S. manufacturing base. Throughout the industrial Midwest, 1,991 metal works plants had closed between 1998 and 2004 and dismissed 80,000 workers, raising concerns in the Pentagon that American manufacturers might not be able to sustain the armed forces in a major war. "One area of utmost concern for the Defense Department and defense industry is manufacturing machine tools," wrote Lawrence Farrell Jr., a retired United States Air Force lieutenant general, in the February 2005 issue of *National Defense* magazine. "There is a compelling case to be made that both the federal government and the private sector need to step up their investments in manufacturing technology, so we can remain competitive with economic powerhouses such as Japan, Germany, and China."[48]

What also could quickly help preserve jobs, at least in the auto sector, are tougher domestic content rules that insisted vehicle components must be engineered or at least made in the United States. When the Europeans dropped their barriers to Japanese auto plants, they also demanded and got strong domestic content laws. Tonelson said this saved thousands of jobs in plants that make smaller pieces used in larger components. In the United States, many of those small pieces are still imported across a range of industries, especially in autos. Tonelson, who studies import and export trends, said that "since the start of 2005, imports of tires, electrical equipment, seating and trim, and vehicles from Japan have risen. Imports of tires, lighting systems, stampings, and miscellaneous parts from Germany have grown. And imports of every parts category from Korea are up except for electrical systems and vehicles themselves. Just as surprising, many categories of parts imports from Germany and Korea have risen significantly since 2005, notably lighting, stampings, and air conditioning systems from the former, and brakes, transmission and power train–related items, and seating and trim products from the latter."[49]

And there was the big issue, the thorny one that took on international implications. This was trade reform. Peter Morici, who had been the chief economist for the United States International Trade Commission under the Democratic administration of President Bill Clinton in the 1990s, believed whether it was on the agenda now or not, Americans would have to confront foreign trade issues eventually in a way they had not confronted them for three decades. That was the key to the economy. Just as in the 1980s and 1990s the United States had run up huge deficits with Japan, it was now splurging on goods from China. With China paving the way by loaning the United States money for the imports, China's holdings of U.S. Treasury bills had exceeded $750 billion, the United States Department of Commerce reported. But for economists fixated on trade reform, the trade deficit and heavy borrowing were not only unsustainable — the U.S. could not run up endless debts — it was holding back the American economic recovery. The United States, Morici argued, could not recover until people had jobs and they could not have enough jobs until China stopped fiddling with its currency to maintain a low price on goods shipped to the United States. Said Morici: "The U.S. economy cannot again achieve robust and sustainable growth, unless *either* consumers spend more than they earn and Americans finance it all by borrowing from abroad *or* the trade deficit is significantly reduced to redirect more U.S. spending to domestic suppliers of goods and services."[50]

Legendary investor Warren Buffett, chairman of the Berkshire Hathaway conglomerate, weighed in on the same point, but made it earlier — in 2003. Noting the sagging value of the dollar abroad, he contended investors overseas were losing patience in holding onto so many dollars flooding out from the United States to buy oil and other goods. Their reluctance to keep dollars was pushing the value of the American currency down, and as it slumped, foreign investors could cheaply buy American real estate. Worse, the weak dollar did nothing to improve the balance of trade with China, as China had linked its currency to the dollar in any case. Buffett proposed bucking up the dollar through a mechanism that essentially sought to restrict the flood of imports flowing into the United States. "Our trade deficit has greatly worsened, to the point that our country's 'net worth,' so to speak, is now being transferred abroad at an alarming rate," Buffett wrote in *Fortune* magazine. "In the late 1970s the trade situation [produced] . . . deficits that initially ran about one percent of GDP. That was hardly serious. . . . Since then, however, it's been all downhill, with the pace of decline rapidly accelerating in the past five years. Our annual trade deficit now exceeds four percent of GDP. Equally ominous, the rest of the world owns a staggering $2.5 trillion more of the U.S. than we own of other countries. . . . In effect, our country has been behaving like an extraordinarily rich family that possesses an immense farm. In order to consume four percent more than we produce — that's the trade deficit — we have, day by day, been both selling pieces of the farm and increasing the mortgage on what we still own."[51]

Since Buffett wrote those words in 2003, the trade deficit has only grown. Policy makers in Washington and investment bankers on Wall Street have paid only token attention to solutions. Across the industrial Midwest, the pain was felt in job losses accelerated by the recession that came on at the end of 2007. Ed Montgomery, the Harvard-trained economist whom President Obama had named director of recovery for auto communities, slogged across the countryside in 2009, visiting a town here, pledging some dollars there, but actually managing to effect little change. Local newspapers that had splashed his picture across their pages in the spring learned to ignore him, in part because he rarely granted meaningful interviews, but only offered sound bites. The appointment of the pleasant academic by Obama came to resemble other White House initiatives — long on good intentions, short on attention to detail, and ultimately diluted in their ability to help the region.

Meanwhile, social critics, urban planners, and futurists tried to come up with their own prescription for Middle America. Former *Chicago Tribune* reporter Richard C. Longworth's reissued book, *Caught in the Middle: America's Heartland in the Age of Globalization*, focused on a region where the bulk of the cityscapes were dominated by chain stores. One of the book's great insights was the loyalty of family businesses to a community, a loyalty far in excess of what multinational corporations demonstrated. Longworth's larger point was that Midwesterners were unaware that globalization had devastated the entire region or were only slowly rising to the challenge. And yet what the talented writer seemed to have overlooked was that cities and towns, more than ever, *are* aware of what has happened. But they are largely on their own in dealing with the impersonal forces of globalization and in many cases are overwhelmed. Longworth urges a regional strategy to help Middle America, not merely state or local incentives, but in truth a national economic development policy is in order, perhaps like Japan and Germany had after their devastating defeats in the Second World War. Short of national endeavors, local leaders adjusted as best they could.

"I'm a firm believer that the world is a global market and you have to play in the global market," said Wayne Seybold, the Republican mayor of Marion, shortly before setting off on a trip to Shanghai in September 2009 with the governor of Indiana, Mitch Daniels. The goal of the trip was to lure Chinese entrepreneurs to set up plants in his city. Making his third industry recruiting visit to China in eight months, Seybold had only to look around Indiana to see the fruits of previous efforts to attract investment, not from China, but from Japan, when its own economy was booming in the 1980s. Throughout Indiana, more than 200 Japanese factories opened between 1988 and 2008, employing more than 40,000 workers in 2009, including almost 8,000 workers on Honda, Subaru, and Toyota vehicle assembly lines. "I'm all for global business," Seybold said. "I think that's how we're going to grow in the future."

Yet, for every Seybold trying to attract a Chinese entrepreneur, there are scores of small cities sinking in decline. Part of the reason is that towns in rural areas have lost their primary appeal as low-wage places for manufacturers. Mexico and Asia are the low-price havens. Purdue University economist Patrick McNamara notes midsize and larger cities have retained more of their industrial bases in the 2000s in part because the plants are highly automated, and managers of the high-tech plants want to be close to the engineering, accounting, and logistics services that bigger cities offer. The days of 3,000 people laboring in one rural plant are gone. In American manufacturing, at least what is left of it, technology is king. According to the United Steelworkers union even in northern Indiana's shabby looking steel country just southeast of Chicago, 10,000 steelworkers are still employed, producing as much in a year in the recently modernized mills as the 90,000 steelworkers who toiled there in the 1970s. Still, Seybold sees the cup as half full, not half empty. He believes that modern technology mixed with foreign capital and foreign entrepreneurs can produce jobs in America, even in hard-pressed cities like Marion, because of an ingredient especially appealing to Chinese families. Shut out from China's prestigious universities, or in need of finance and marketing MBAS, Chinese entrepreneurs are interested in the state's universities, Seybold says, and want their own children to immigrate here for the schooling. "They love our education system," Seybold said. "They're really wanting to make a lifestyle investment so their kids can go to our universities."[52]

If even a handful of Chinese firms set up manufacturing shops in Marion, the 500 to 1,000 new jobs would boost the city — though not enough to replace the nearly $1 million in taxes lost after the Thomson TV tube plant vanished. Looking at the disparity in jobs attracted and jobs lost, it is clear that investment from abroad could not really undergird the region, but only begin to replace what has been there. By late 2008, Marion contained only half of the 10,500 industrial jobs that had sustained the city a decade earlier with high-wage factory work. The same pattern was evident regionwide. Deindustrialization haunted the Midwest. Futurists such as Richard Florida coined the idea of a creative class of smart, progressive, hip, and sexually aware young people as the force that will save some cities in the future. Like cities around the Midwest, Marion is aware of the notion of a creative class, and has converted an abandoned railroad bed into a parkway bicycle path, razed dozens of abandoned homes, and repaired sidewalks in neighborhood after neighborhood. Yet, Marion can never be a New York or San Francisco, or London or Frankfurt, or Toronto or Vancouver. Few cities can. Nor should they want to. The creative class doesn't create manufacturing, doesn't create agriculture, doesn't create community beyond its own community, and doesn't even create much culture — the creative class consumes culture. In truth, Florida's bottom-line thesis is just as pessimistic as that of New Jersey Institute of Technology scholar Hindy Schachter's — there will be winners and losers. Very few industrial towns will be successful going forward.

Richard C. Longworth's solution for Middle America looks somewhat attractive on the surface. He supports regional planning that effectively does away with state borders. High on the list of regional planning would be regional high-speed rail transportation, for example. But is it plausible? Indiana can't even get rid of arcane township government, and statewide officials will always protect their turf because people vote by state, not by region. There are multiple layers of overlapping jurisdictions all across America, in fact. State government itself will have to be eliminated before people will stop thinking in terms of their states in competition with other states, and it will take a constitutional convention to get rid of the states. That will never happen.

And even if regional development could be done without giving any state a de facto veto power, not everyone agrees it would be a panacea. "Development doesn't happen in *Indiana*. It happens in 'some place' Indiana," said Mitchell Roob, head of the state's main economic development agency. "It happens in South Bend, Indiana, or it happens in Bedford, Indiana. So the community where development happens is important." Yes, that's true, if all we care about are cottage industries. But this is no way to save a great country.

And yet the allure of regional development across state borders continues to entice planners. A study by John Austin of the Brookings Institution specifically turned on the theme. His recommendations, laid out in *The Vital Center*, a 2006 research report written with Britany Affolter-Caine of the University of Michigan, centered on organizing the region — Ontario and the states of Indiana, Illinois, Michigan, Ohio, and Wisconsin, along with parts of western New York and Pennsylvania, and eastern Iowa and Missouri — into a bloc that looked out for its own self interest. One idea: use federal money to pay most tuition for college students in the region. Another: harness the universities to work in concert on projects.[53]

Those last points, the universities, are not to be overlooked. The region may be in decline, but the universities refute the notion of the Midwest as a lost cause. The states in the region came into the union following the Northwest Ordinance of 1787, a piece of legislation rooted firmly in New Englanders' belief of compulsory public education for all. This was what brought about America's original land grant universities. Midwesterners took this to heart. Today, nineteen of the 100 leading universities in the *world* are in the Great Lakes region as defined by Austin. Yet the universities also are the frontline in the current culture wars where one side demands virtually open enrollment and emphasis on the liberal arts and humanities and perhaps some soft sciences, but not the hard sciences. That the purpose of higher education is to train citizens for democracy, not to compete in the global economy, is a mantra heard everywhere on campus today in one form or another. It suggests a false dichotomy — why can't citizens be trained both for democracy and to compete in the global economy?

At the same time, thousands of engineers and scientists are already in place residing in the Midwest. The region's problem is the long and now accelerating decline in manufacturing. What can turn around the situation and keep this knowledge base from scattering is a concerted national effort, not to simply retrain laid-off industrial workers and put them on the bullet train to Chicago to work in a bank, but more broadly, to revive manufacturing and make use of their skills. "That whole notion that we can move to higher ground and do sophisticated stuff and [in other nations] they're going to just do low-tech stuff, it was stupid, it was condescending," Prestowitz said. "Implicit in that kind of thinking is a huge assumption that there's no cost of adjustment. You can't move seamlessly from steel and machine tools to software and biotechnology. This is where our economic analysis has really been foolish. In actuality, a U.S. steel worker doesn't quickly become a knowledge worker in software."

Prestowitz, in an interview in 2009, recommended the United States employ a broad arsenal of tools to help the entire country rebound and in the process reenergize the Midwest industrial base. "The French are very good at attracting foreign investment to their country," Prestowitz said. "Many nations entice manufacturers to move abroad with tax abatement, tax holidays, capital grants, free infrastructure, or paying for half the investment.

"In the United States," he continued, "each state has an economic development policy, but the states individually don't have the resources a country has. So typically, the U.S. does not have a way to counter these financial investment incentives from abroad. Nationally, we ought to have the Department of Commerce form a war chest the government can use. If Israel or China or another country makes an overture to a U.S. company, then we can match it.

"We can also pursue industries," Prestowitz said. "A quick analysis shows a lot of environmental equipment, parts of solar panels, wind mills, this equipment is not made in the United States. If we're going to make a big push on creating a greener energy policy, part of that ought to be how do we arrange for this company making windmills to move from Denmark to the United States."[54]

If local leadership can't really save Middle America, and if a national industrial policy does not really exist, but only a national fiscal policy, and if regional development across state borders is ultimately a pipe dream, and Washington is inured to the dissolution of the American industrial base and reluctant to deal with the trade deficit, then what is to be done? Central to the question is another question. What is the true middle in America?

The fight between the Left and the Right sometimes looks like a fight between supporters of radical laissez-faire economics on the Right, and a renewed demand for what is essentially socialism on the Left. But the fight is really about the heart and soul of American civilization. Both sides speak of personal liberties in strikingly similar ways. Yet on the right, personal liberty means the right to keep one's accumulated wealth, the right to bear arms, and the right to keep government away. And the other side speaks of the right to privacy and the right to an abortion. Both sides are telling the government, and anyone else for that matter, to stay out of its business. Both sides are arguing for liberties that protect their own narrow interests, in other words. No one speaks for Middle America, however, where the economy has disintegrated while the intellectual leaders debate personal rights. Who speaks for the entire country? No one.

---

1. Aleasha Sandley, "Bright Automotive Not Among Grant Recipients," (Anderson, IN) *Herald Bulletin*, August 5, 2009, http://www.theheraldbulletin.com/breakingnews/local_story_217234603.html.

2. U.S. Bureau of Economic Analysis report, August 12, 2009, http://www.bea.gov/newsreleases/international/trade/tradnewsrelease.htm.

3. Nayla Kazzi and Heather Boushy, "Uneven Job Losses . . .," Center for American Progress, July 17, 2009, http://www.americanprogress.org.

4. Alan Tonelson, chief economist of the U.S. Business and Industry Council, a trade group in Washington, D.C., was interviewed at various times by Ted Evanoff.

5. Bob Herbert, "The Human Equation," *New York Times*, July 11, 2009, A17.

6. Andrew S. Grove, "What Detroit Can Learn From Silicon Valley," *Wall Street Journal*, July 13, 2009, A13.

7. Jim Carlton, Bobby White, "State's Cities Brace for More Sacrifice," *Wall Street Journal*, July 22, 2009, A3.

8. Mark Apuzzo, "Give Stimulus Time, Obama Tells Nation," Associated Press, *Indianapolis Star*, July 12, 2009, A6.

9. Ted Evanoff, Tom Spalding, "'Cash for Clunkers' Riddled with Question Marks," *Indianapolis Star*, July 13, 2009, A1.

10. Kevin Phillips, *Bad Money: Reckless Finance, Failed Politics and the Global Crisis of American Capitalism* (New York: Viking Penguin, 2008), 97.

11. Richard Goldberg, *The Battle for Wall Street: Behind the Lines in the Struggle That Pushed an Industry into Turmoil* (Hoboken, NJ: John Wiley, 2009), 7.

12. Phillips, 96.

13. Gillian Tett, "More Prison Sentences May Renew Financial Credibility," *Financial Times*, September 4, 2009, 18.

14. David Halberstam, *The Reckoning* (New York: William Morrow & Co., 1986), 677.

15. Halberstam, 678.

16. Richard Duncan, *The Dollar Crisis* (Singapore: John C. Wiley, 2003), 10.

17. Bill Bonner and Addison Wiggin, *Empire of Debt* (Hoboken, NJ: John C. Wiley, 2006), 213.

18. Duncan, 4.

19. Charles R. Geist, *Wall Street: A History* (New York: Oxford University Press, 1997), 317.

20. Duncan, 101.

21. Edward Chancellor, *Devil Take the Hindmost: A History of Financial Speculation* (New York: Farrar, Straus and Giroux, 1999), 259.

22. Chancellor, 257.

23. William Greider, *Secrets of the Temple: How the Federal Reserve Runs the Country* (New York: Simon & Schuster Inc., 1987), 592.

24. Geist, 339.

25. Donald L. Bartlett, James B. Steele, *America: What Went Wrong?* (Kansas City, Mo.: Universal Press Syndicate Co., 1992), 55.

26. William Gass, *In the Heart of the Heart of the Country and Other Stories* (New York: Harper and Row, 1968).

27. John Austin and Britany Affolter-Caine, "The Vital Center," Brookings Institution Metropolitan Policy Program, 2006.

28. Halberstam, 678.

29. Halberstam, 693.

30. David Segal, "Windfall for Bankers, Resentment for the Rest," *New York Times*, July 19, 2009, W4.

31. Coda Automotive, "Driven to Lead" special advertising section, *Green Car Journal*, summer 2009, 19.

32. Gretchen Morgenson and Don Van Natta Jr., "Paulson's Calls to Goldman Tested Ethics," *New York Times*, August 8, 2009, http://www.nytimes.com/2009/08/09/business/09paulson.html.

33. Phillips, 40.

34. Bartlett and Steele, 55.

35. Halberstam, 678.

36. Greider, 599.

37. The once-prominent British motorcycle industry made the same arguments in the early 1960s against free trade agreements between the UK and Japan that ultimately favored Japanese motorcycle manufacturers, but not British concerns BSA and Triumph. See Abe Aamidor, *Shooting Star: The Rise and Fall of the British Motorcycle Industry*, (Toronto: ECW Press, 2009), 90.

38. Ted Evanoff, "Q&A: Trade," *Indianapolis Star*, May 21, 2009, http://blogs.indystar.com/commonsense/2009/05/qa_clyde_presto.html.

39. Sam Dillon, "International Business; A 20-Year G.M. Parts Migration to Mexico," *New York Times*, June 24, 1998, D1.

40. Lou Dobbs, *Exporting America: Why Corporate Greed Is Shipping American Jobs Overseas* (New York: Time Warner Book Group, 2004), 83.

41. Evanoff, "Q&A: Trade."

42. Edmund Conway, "The future's bright . . . But Not for Lawyers and Accountants," (London) *Daily Telegraph*, May 8, 2007, 12.

43. Ron Hira, "Globalization of R&D," *Manufacturing A Better Future For America* (Washington, D.C.: Alliance For American Manufacturing, 2009), 153.

44. "Hydrogen Hits a Speed Bump," *Green Car Journal*, summer 2009, 7.

45. Kenneth Baker, who headed General Motors EV1 electric car program in the 1990s, was interviewed by Ted Evanoff on June 25, 2009.

46. Financial analyst Mary Ann Keller, author of *Collision: G.M., Toyota, Volkswagen and the Race to Own the 21st Century*, was interviewed by Ted Evanoff at various times in 2008 and 2009.

47. Paul Keegan, "The Great Electric Car Race," *Fortune*, April 27, 2009, 59.

48. Ted Evanoff, "A Losing Battle: Our Industrial Base," *Indianapolis Star*, October 10, 2006, D1.

49. Alan Tonelson, "Congress Must Ensure That the Big Three Bailout Is Made-in-America," American Economic Alert newsletter, December 10, 2008, http://www.americaneconomicalert.org/view_art.asp?Prod_ID=3091.

50. "Recalibrating U.S.-China," New America Foundation, June 11, 2009, http://www.newamerica.net/publications/policy/recalibrating_u_s_china.

51. Warren Buffett, "America's Growing Trade Deficit Is Selling the Nation Out from Under Us," *Fortune*, November 10, 2003.

52. Ted Evanoff, "In Search for Jobs, Indiana Turns to China," *Indianapolis Star*, September 6, 2009, D1.
53. John Austin and Britany Affolter-Caine, "The Vital Center," Brookings Institution Metropolitan Policy Program, 2006, 19.
54. Evanoff, "Q&A: Trade."

CHAPTER 12

Into the Brink

INDIANA HAD BEEN THE HOME of Eugene Debs, the early twentieth-century union firebrand and presidential aspirant, and it was still the state with the largest number of industrial workers as a share of the workforce. But you would never have known it from the tenor in worn manufacturing cities around the state as Labor Day 2009 rolled around. The continuing recession, the worst economic downturn in America since the Great Depression, and one that was much more sudden, may have been partly behind the somber mood.

In Indianapolis, only a few hundred spectators stood on the sides of downtown streets or in University Park, a narrow stretch of urban greenspace known for a war memorial, flags of the fifty states, and patriotic statuary ranging from Abraham Lincoln to Benjamin Harrison. They watched a motley crew of labor union representatives, both public employee and industrial, walk or glide down the center of the streets in open top cars and floats. Only about twelve percent of American workers belong to unions, and fewer than eight percent of workers in the private sector do so.[1] But even in manufacturing oriented Indiana, there was no demonstration of brash unionism. Entertainment was provided by a handful of high school marching bands, none too lavishly dressed or rigorously trained. Things looked sparse, uninspired. There was no energy in the air at all.

Local economies were looking up a bit, but not much. "Turned the corner" and "bottomed out" were the buzzwords both ordinary folk and political pundits alike now used. The recession had officially ended in France and Germany, albeit only marginally. Housing sales were up two months in a row in the United States. The word "recession" was a mathematical construct anyway — if the economy shrinks two quarters in a row, then you're in recession. When it stops shrinking, you're out of recession. The more popular definition of recession always made more sense — when you're out of work yourself, it's a recession. When you get a job yourself, the recession is over. Unemployment remained in the low- to mid-double digits in many counties in Indiana, so it was still a recession for many people there.

In Kokomo Labor Day 2009 had special significance. Mayor Greg Goodnight and Democratic Congressman Joe Donnelly met with dozens of autoworkers at the UAW Local 685 union hall. Local 685 represents the Chrysler transmission workers in town, but many Delphi workers from Local 292 also mingled, a solidarity spurred not by ideology, but by adversity. "A year ago, we didn't know if we'd be successful getting Chrysler to the other side," Donnelly, who represents part of Kokomo and Howard County, told the crowd. "But we knew if we got to the other side, what an enormous victory it would be, and what a bright future we'd have. Together, we're going to have as strong an auto sector as we've had in decades and decades."[2]

People applauded and some even cheered, but it was hyperbole. It was a campaign speech, in fact, as congressmen in America are always running for re-election every two years.

Ginny McMillin, the Local 292 officer, threw cold water on Donnelly's upbeat message, anyway, as she revealed that $89 million in federal stimulus spending to help build green-energy vehicles may not come to Delphi in Kokomo as earlier projected. A wrinkle had emerged in the plan, but maybe "fissure" was the more apt term. GM had taken back control of the local Delphi complex, which was good news on one level. GM was looking more secure than Delphi, which had gone into bankruptcy four years earlier than its prodigal parent and in 2009 was trying to slash the pensions of 15,000 salaried retirees. Now rumors swirled that GM would elect to use the $89 million at another plant. Local union workers snarled and hissed when they heard this. It seemed not to matter that these were fellow Americans, not to mention fellow union workers. Rank territorialism continued to bleed America.

Two weeks later, tempers also flared inside the union hall when more disturbing news was revealed. Several dozen retired Chrysler workers from Kokomo had made a six-hour bus ride in July to help protest the announced closing of a Dodge truck and minivan plant in Fenton, Missouri, which once had employed 6,000. The effort was not entirely selfless — the UAW veterans knew that seniority rules would allow displaced workers in Fenton to move elsewhere in the company and take away jobs from local citizens with less seniority, perhaps even in Kokomo. In September 2009 that's just what happened. The new Chrysler Corporation announced that 178 veteran workers had claimed slots in Kokomo, where the transmission plants and a casting plant had been kept open. But no one was adding jobs — 178 locals would just be pushed down the seniority ladder, maybe risk being put on the street. They'd collect unemployment and their SUB-pay for a while, but then that would be it.

"It's not fair to them or to us," said Holly Brenton. Her husband has worked at Kokomo Transmission Plant for twelve years, and she was speaking after a tumultuous, four-hour, standing-room-only meeting at Local 685 on September 19 as workers clamored to know if they or a loved one were on the local hit list, yet to be announced. "They closed their plant, but now they can come here and take our jobs. That's not fair, but that's how the contract was written. I don't agree with the rules. I don't know anyone who does, but they are the rules we have to follow."[3]

It was worker against worker, in other words, hardly reflective of either good industrial or labor policy.

Several days after the Labor Day gathering Mayor Goodnight admitted that the road ahead would not be less fraught than in the recent past. Kokomo and Howard County's unemployment rate topped nineteen percent in June, then recovered to the middle fourteen percent range in July and August. The worst was over, but had a new baseline been established? Taking a break from his busy schedule, Goodnight strolled with a visitor through a decorated and paved, European-style alley in the heart of Kokomo's downtown on his way to Jamie's, a corner coffee shop popular with retirees, delivery truck drivers, and office workers on their lunch breaks. Jamie's is the kind of place with ceiling-high picture windows fronting the sidewalk and chrome rings around all the stools at the front counter. Its small, billboard-style menu is posted high on the wall behind the lunch counter with items spelled out in movable black plastic letters; prices are in red letters. It looks just like 1955 inside Jamie's, but without trying to be retro or trendy. It *is* the 1950s inside Jamie's.

The mayor was still reeling from the news that Fiat was serious about not paying $5.9 million in 2008 property taxes that were due in June 2009, citing the Chrysler bankruptcy as an excuse. It was a very different, very private position from what he had expressed in the local press when he told reporters that he was "very comfortable" with Fiat's ability and willingness to meet its tax obligation. The money had already been budgeted. But Fiat's heart was as hard as the Biblical Pharaoh's. There was a short-term solution in the works as the state might step in and offer Kokomo a ten-year, low interest loan to make up the short-fall. It's what the state had done on a smaller scale with the Delphi bankruptcy several years earlier. But when cities can't repay their debts they go bankrupt, just like businesses do. Goodnight had heard that President Obama's auto town adviser Ed Montgomery and Congressman Donnelly were currently lobbying Fiat to at least pay some of the bill, in a kind of "pretty please" scenario, but it was so pathetic and Goodnight himself had been left out of the negotiations. And the mayor was worried that Fiat wouldn't pay its 2009 debt due in 2010, either, citing the same bankruptcy. Fiat was virtually given Chrysler, but what was given to Kokomo?

In fact, this is what came to pass by late fall in Kokomo. Fiat would not pay the back taxes technically owed by Old Carco LLC, the legal fiction created by the scripted Chrysler bankruptcy, an entity that owned all assets belonging to Chrysler that Fiat didn't want. The name itself was like a bad joke. Montgomery, as usual, achieved nothing, and the mayor was reduced to dickering with the state of Indiana on just how much interest he'd have to pay on a loan to cover Fiat's — make that Old Carco LLC's — tax default. He wanted a one percent maximum interest rate; the state was offering a three percent minimum, and the issue remained unresolved.

"The president, I support him on a whole host of things," Goodnight said inside one of the coffee shop's many vinyl-lined booths. "I think he's doing a good job considering the hand he's been dealt. I'm probably greedy, but I do wish he would come to Kokomo. He's been to Elkhart County three times."

Elkhart County in northern Indiana had become a kind of national poster child for the hurting economies of Middle America, but for a time Kokomo and Howard County had a higher unemployment rate than its northern neighbor. Recreational vehicles are made in Elkhart, but automobile transmissions and auto parts are made in Kokomo, and until America has a national mass transportation policy the country needs cars a lot more than RVs, Goodnight argues.

There *was* some good news in recent weeks for the city, however. Local firefighters agreed to rescind their two percent pay raise in light of a pay freeze Goodnight had negotiated with the American Federation of State, County and Municipal Employees (AFSCME) and local government workers. Maybe it was belated civic-mindedness on the part of the first responders; maybe they were just shamed into making the gesture. If not a united front in the face of recession between city and citizen, then at least a truce had to be called in the usually adversarial relationship between employer and employee. The city had earlier announced that about one-third of its employees would lose their "paid lunch" hour. About 140 employees worked 8 a.m. to 4 p.m. weekday schedules and were paid for forty hours work, even though they had an hour for lunch. Those workers would now go on a forty-five-hour week for their forty hours of pay.

And Goodnight had won over both civic and business leaders in his bid to create a special "river district" along Wildcat Creek and elsewhere in the central city; this would be a tax district permitting new bars and restaurants to obtain "three way" liquor licenses for the knockdown price of only $1,000. Such licenses, which allow establishments to serve the full gamut of beer, wine, and hard liquor, normally sell for $70,000 to $100,000 in Howard County. Some residents had opposed any expansion of drinking in town, while some current bar owners didn't want the competition, but the mayor insisted it was good for economic development.

There's a saying in business that you can't cut your way to profitability, but that's what Goodnight was trying to do in Kokomo. He also was putting the finishing touches on a plan to remove a dozen traffic signals from the city and convert the intersections to four-way stops where appropriate. Removing the signals would save at least $1,000 at each intersection every year in the cost of electricity alone, and each signal required a full inspection and bulb replacement annually, also expensive. But the main goal was to increase traffic and business downtown. None of this was the stuff of multi-billion dollar bailouts, but it was what you do if you're in the trenches like Goodnight was. He was going to yank dozens of parking meters from downtown streets, too. The parking meters only generated ten cents per hour, hardly worth the cost of collection. Goodnight had to count every penny and husband all his resources in a time of severe economic downturn he could.

The real power in Kokomo speaks Italian, of course. Chrysler Group CEO Sergio Marchionne had essentially stood up Greg Goodnight when the latter visited Turin over the summer, inflicting a hurt the mayor had to keep inside for appearance's sake, if nothing else. The Canadian-Italian businessman also had been mum on just what his plans for the American market might be, leading to high anxiety and pointless speculation by all strata in Kokomo. Finally, though, in early November 2009 Marchionne came to Auburn Hills, Michigan, for a press conference to announce strategy for both the Fiat and Chrysler brands in

America. Much to his relief, Mayor Goodnight received a personally signed invitation from Marchionne to attend a reception with Fiat executives after the press conference. Goodnight and a city attorney made the long drive from Kokomo to Detroit in a city-owned Dodge the night before the press conference, then drove back the next day.

"Here's how I met [Marchionne]," Goodnight said later. "When I got there before the program started they came to me and asked me to sit at his table during the luncheon. I was one of eight people seated with him. I got a couple of minutes face time with him. I told him who I was and he was familiar with the city. He knew about my visit to Italy. He asked me if I enjoyed Italy. It was mostly small talk."

Goodnight said he avoided any mention of the tax problem Fiat had stuck the city with, however.

Brian A. Howey, the independent Indiana journalist and publisher of *Howey Politics Indiana*, rated Goodnight's first two years in office favorably. "He's been a pretty good mayor given the scope of the challenges his city faces," said Howey, offering the mayor the same kind of qualified support the mayor had given Obama. "Part of being a mayor is keeping a lid on things. If a city administration is seen as being rudderless that can affect business development."

Nevertheless, Howey is very cautious in rating the chances for a full recovery of any Indiana city. "When Jill Long Thompson ran for Governor in 2008 [as a Democrat] she said she's going to save every Indiana city," Howey recalled. "I had to tell her that Indiana is littered with cities that were built along the rivers, then went by the wayside with the building of the canals. Then with the coming of the railroad those earlier cities withered and now cities are going in along the interstates."

It's a thesis not much different than that of Richard Florida, or Richard C. Longworth, or a host of other pundits in America. There would be winners and losers. Kokomo had good power and water supplies, important for future manufacturing, but was thirty miles from the nearest interstate.

Going green remained a theme of the mayor, and his city. The atrium lobby in Kokomo City Hall had a new installation late in the summer of 2009 — a Skystream 3.7 wind turbine, made by a company called Southwest Windpower, based in Flagstaff, Arizona. Goodnight had encouraged a local franchise dealer to place the device in the lobby, along with his business cards, as a way of showing visitors the city's commitment to green energy. This was on top of the growing use of K-Fuel biodiesel in city vehicles, which was brewed at Kokomo's sewage treatment facility. The Skystream 3.7 is an interesting innovation that allows home-owners and small business to generate their own electricity via a smaller-than-average wind turbine, then sell back excess capacity to their local utility company as long as they remain connected to the grid. But the local utility company for Kokomo does not allow customers to sell back electricity, itself a reflection of the lack of a true national energy policy in this country. And though the Skystream 3.7 is said to made in the United States of America, it is not made anywhere near Kokomo. Additionally, the city had just lost its bid for a new EnerDel facility. The automotive lithium-ion battery manufacturer already had two plants in the Indianapolis area; Kokomo had hoped to be a third site. Local reports speculated that Central Indiana would indeed get EnerDel's proposed new plant, but it would be closer to a main interstate highway, as well as closer to Indianapolis itself. The region would be helped, but Kokomo not so much. Cities were still pitted against cities.

Late in 2009 all Americans had to wonder if a new baseline for employment, wealth, and prosperity had been established. Economists openly spoke of a "jobless recovery." Yet the return of big bonuses to Wall Street firms led to a revival of the acrimonious discourse that had accompanied the fall 2008 financial market bailout. There was a renewed feeling that Wall Street and Big Business had gotten away with something. Indeed, corporations had become a new kind of entity on the world stage, neither animal, nor vegetable, nor mineral, and not part of any industry or human basic endeavor, actually. While the Left's objection to globalization and multinational corporations was really an objection to capitalism per se, corporations were proving about as loyal to American cities as NFL teams that sneak out of town at midnight because they could get a better deal elsewhere. Corporations just existed to feed themselves; there was no loyalty even to the nation. But many Americans also distrusted Big Labor.

The United Auto Workers, though not necessarily other members of the working class, had gotten away with something, too. For all its talk of concessions, the UAW easily paid the least cost for the automotive bailout of 2009 of any stakeholders. The historic decline in private sector union membership may trace to union misdeeds as much as corporate pressure, and the profound distrust of government heard on right-wing talk radio in America may trace to contempt for public employee unions, too. Like the battle between the Left and the Right in the culture wars, Middle America was the odd man out in a war between Big Capital and Big Labor.

Still, investment always starts with capital and that means Wall Street. But what if Wall Street were right, meaning investment in manufacturing in America was pointless, a money pit that could never give positive returns on investment? The truth is that wristwatches and phonographic equipment and small power tools and even pots and pans that used to be made in America are no longer made here. Jobs in those industries largely dried up decades ago. Capital seeks the best return on investment and lowest-cost labor like water seeking its own level — it's a law of nature, not a character flaw. The reality is that Americans will have to work for lower wages in order to be competitive, and that's not necessarily bad. Politicians used to talk about lowering the cost of living, not merely raising the standard of living — and that can still be done through a combination of better health insurance programs, improvements to mass transit, higher standards in good public education, and more. *Homo economicus* isn't going to cut it anymore — we can't just assume we'll put more money in people's pockets. We might also require an overhaul in the common attitude to work summed up in the old Johnny Paycheck song, "Take This Job and Shove It."

Susan Perry, the veteran Chrysler worker in Kokomo, saw all the cracks in union solidarity even as production ramped up under the new Fiat leadership in the fall of 2009. "This week the plant manager held town hall meetings with all employees. He showed a fifty-five-minute video of clips from the big November 4 meeting," she said in late November 2009. That was the meeting Goodnight attended in Auburn Hills. "The message was upbeat and promising, but the workers are in a wait-and-see mode. The St. Louis people were scared — they said the only time they had town halls was when they got bad news."

The 177 "St. Louis workers" — as they were called, even though they were from a shuttered Chrysler plant in Fenton, Missouri, a St. Louis suburb — had arrived in Kokomo earlier in the fall. "That always makes for an interesting time, the integration of workers," Perry said. "The ones that came so far have more seniority than our people, so we moved down the seniority list. That causes some anger and resentment, plus they laid off our people to make slots for them. . . . It's interesting to study the dynamics of the integration of higher seniority workers and the effects on the current workers. We have a set of workers with twelve to twenty years that have never experienced an influx of higher seniority workers and don't understand that they, too, would like to have the right to go to another plant to finish out their time to retirement. I spend a lot of time explaining this to younger workers as they are angry they can't buy a job because a higher seniority worker from St. Louis is getting it first."

Maybe new job creation will come from immigrants, not from what traditionally has been a corporate welfare state, including the Detroit Three auto manufacturers. When people speak of the Manhattan Project and suggest we need one for new energy sources in America — a good idea, actually — they forget that Enrico Fermi was an Italian immigrant, and that many other top scientists and engineers either were British subjects seconded here to work on the project, or were Jewish refugees from Nazi-occupied Europe. Ditto for the craftsmen who did much of the brick-laying and bridge building in the muscle years of America — immigrants. Even small business creation today is heavily dependent on immigrants. Maybe more of those foreign students studying in our graduate schools will settle in America. If America is — or was — a success story, it may have nothing to do with American character, American ingenuity, or anything of the kind. It might be the American ideals of opportunity and freedom; let's open the doors to people who are willing to move here and make America greater.

Many policy makers have embraced the notion of education as America's salvation. President Obama has spoken of sending 100 percent of our high school graduates to college. But it's a fantasy, a cruel hoax. For one thing, who might employ all those grads? EDS, the giant Texas computer data company, employed forty-three percent of its workforce in low-wage nations by 2008, up from nearly zero six years earlier.[4] EDS was not alone in its international quest. "Intel can succeed without ever hiring another American," said Craig Barrett, chief executive of the California electronics giant.[5]

And even if the jobs were there for grads, America's high schools are notably subpar. As Indiana University economist Morton Marcus has argued, what good is it to talk about college if so many high schools are no good? It's long been known that the first two years of college are to make up for a shoddy high-school education anyway. Tragically, the whole debate over the quality of American schools and the demand for universal college attendance has been caught up in the culture wars, with the Left in denial about the need for Americans to compete globally, especially in manufacturing and engineering, and the Right being accused of elitism and wanting to keep power for itself by efforts to raise standards and restrict enrollment. Yet students who come out of a dismal high school do need something of consequence to make a living at. Are such people to survive on welfare, live as itinerant deer hunters, raise families on the $12-per-hour paid by the Dollar General warehouse in Marion? That is why states like

Indiana are promoting modern job skills through their community college systems. That will help some people who don't want to go to a liberal arts college. But we still need more jobs for people who will never work at a skilled trade, and that will be production jobs in a factory. It does no good to pretend we are going to have a nation exclusively of scientists, information technology experts, entrepreneurs, artists, and so on. Only a minority of people in any advanced society have such jobs, and both the Left and the Right do a good job of making sure it is their children who have first claim on them.

Those policy makers who talk about educational reform and universal college matriculation are tricksters — they send their children to private high schools or to good high schools in safe university towns, and then they send their children to elite colleges where it's expected they'll step into the best jobs. They're not sending their own children to Indiana University–Kokomo. Witness the experience of every president with school-age children in Washington, D.C., and virtually all senators who live there year-round. They send their children to private schools, then usually to top colleges, reinforcing the notion that America has become a plutocracy, not a democracy. Yet privilege is as dear to the Modern Language Association and the American Association of University Women as it is to United States senators and Fortune 500 presidents. To have good jobs for all, the country needs a strong industrial base. A return of the family farm and the small farmer wouldn't hurt, either.

Years ago a top executive at IBM was asked if he was troubled by all the people getting MBAs at a plethora of graduate business programs opening across the United States and applying to work at his company, which then was still one of the most powerful in the country. Not so, the executive answered, because IBM only hired the top ten percent of graduates from the top tier graduate schools anyway. Talk of universal college is just a sop — the elites, whether on the Right or the Left, both of which are privileged classes, would always take care of themselves and their children first.

The truth is that the divide between rich and poor, the haves and have-nots, a bifurcation in American society not unlike what's been going on in Central and South America for generations, is growing in the United States. It's been documented.[6] Thinkers and political pundits, whether on the Left or the Right, and policy makers, whether Democrats or Republicans, represent their own interests first. The true intentions of such elites in this country were made strikingly clear beginning with school desegregation in the 1960s — leaders on both sides of the debate almost completely exempted themselves and their children from this great experiment. Something similar happened in the anti–Vietnam War movement of the 1960s, as well, which largely subsided in all elite colleges as soon as the best and brightest, whether Republican or Democrat, Right or Left, figured out how to beat the draft. That's why, for example, serious anti-war protests moved from Columbia University in New York City in 1968 to places like Kent State University in Ohio by 1970. The exact same phenomenon was repeated in Congress's vote to support George Bush's war in Iraq — almost nobody in Washington saw any of their children in harm's way. Even the Left's opposition to the Iraq War was largely framed in anti-corporate and anti-Israel rhetoric; the Left had very little itself at stake in the war. NBC broadcaster and author Tom Brokaw's "greatest generation" is not quite dead yet, but their children and grandchildren were nothing of the kind.

Liberal social critic Lewis Lapham, former editor of *Harper's* magazine, has condemned the entire political structure of Washington. He described Republicans and Democrats alike as a single political class, abetting "the transformation of democracy into something more closely resembling a plutocracy. . . . It seems like politics has just been reduced to trivial entertainment. So long as we could buy an SUV or a condo in Florida, what the hell difference did it make who was running the country?"[7]

Conservative social scientist Samuel P. Huntington makes a complementary observation on the elites who clearly run America — whether Left or Right. They care more about internationalism and globalization, not American jobs or American identity or

Middle America at all. "[T]he extensive international involvements of American business, academic, professional, media, nonprofit, and political elites lowered the salience of national identity for those elites, who now increasingly identified themselves, their interests, and their identities in terms of international and global institutions, networks, and causes."[8]

Ideology always serves the interests of those who advance it, no matter what the ideology. Middle America, sadly, does not have its own ideology, though plenty of people claim to be looking out for it. Who really is looking out for Middle America, though? Not right-wing Republicans like Dick Cheney, the patron saint of Halliburton, nor Democrat Nancy Pelosi, nominally a former housewife, but really the darling of the San Francisco Bay area, one of Richard Florida's favorite "creative class" cities. Perhaps it is the vice grip of pluralism — there are only constituencies and special interest groups competing for power and privilege in a country like America, but no common good at all. That great American success story known as Barack Obama — and it is a great success story, for him and for America, a nation founded in large part on immigration and opportunity, not merely on exploitation and "manifest destiny" — so far is an enigma. He is somewhat hawkish on the war in Afghanistan in spite of his earlier opposition to the Iraq misadventure; he is fully committed to health care reform although stumbling badly in his efforts; and he is amazingly silent on the issue of race, which is always the elephant in the room in America. For all of President Obama's talk about protecting the middle class and Middle America, however, which does suggest he at least understands the catastrophe that will befall us all if we become like Central or South America, there continues to be that growing divide between people with good professions and good-paying jobs, with real autonomy and wide horizons in their lives, and an underclass filled with people who don't own anything, have no vision for their own or their children's futures, who have had poor public school educations, and who drift from one part-time or dead-end job to another.

The catastrophe is even worse in the African-American community as corporations and universities alike compete for that talented tenth that W. E. B. DuBois always talked about, either because they really believe in diversity, or just want to inoculate themselves from the charge of racism. Either way, we are heading toward Richard Florida's vision of a future America — a few winners, and lots of losers. It is a fatal vision.

Sarah Palin, former Republican vice-presidential candidate, was mocked for many things in 2008, including saying she was so happy to be back in "the real America" during one campaign stop in a small, mostly white town late in the campaign. "We believe that the best of America is not all in Washington, D.C.," she said. "We believe that the best of America is in these small towns that we get to visit, and in these wonderful little pockets of what I call the real America, being here with all of you hard-working very patriotic, um, very, um, pro-America areas of this great nation."9

Whatever one thinks of Palin's abysmal performance during the campaign and after, she was not wrong about small-town America, or at least the ideal of small-town America. Yet all the pro-diversity pundits and urban sophisticates took target practice at Palin like shooting ducks in a pond. The Washington, New York, and San Francisco elites apparently think all small towns in the Midwest are all white, and not worth saving. But if those critics had visited Kokomo, Anderson, or Bedford they'd know something has been lost in America. (They'd also see that small towns in America are not all white, and that small-town virtues have no color boundaries.) In spite of the good efforts of hardworking, forward-thinking leaders like that of Greg Goodnight, Kris Ockomon, Wayne Seybold, and Shawna Girgis — none of whom went to Harvard, none of whom is a lawyer, none of whom loves Europe more than America — and in spite of the hard fight in the trenches led by blue-collar, in-your-face union men like Danny Hiatt, Mo Davison, and Richie Boruff, cities and towns really are sliding into the abyss. These are the real faces of Middle America. Who is looking out for them? As Indiana editor Brian

A. Howey has said, "You can't foreclose on Middle America."

It is time for "the middle," not the Left and not the Right, to take back America. Neither Wall Street nor Berkeley should rule in Washington. People inside the beltway can teach us nothing about American culture and community. When both the Right and the Left appear mostly interested in attacking each other, then returning to their Scotch whiskey and lattes, then everyone must know that Middle America is going to have to save itself.

Greg Goodnight sat in his booth inside Jamie's finishing his Coca-Cola and he got to thinking about the election campaign in 2011. Yeah, he'll probably stand for re-election, but maybe not after that, he said, assuming he is re-elected. "Teddy Roosevelt said this after he won that first election, 'I can promise you that I'll just stay in office for four years,'" Goodnight recalled. "He really regretted that later. That really handcuffed him. People treated him like a lame duck. So I'm not going to say that. People will think they can run right over me."

There was some good news for the mayor to chew on — sort of. Zuna Infotech, an "onshoring" company, announced in a well-attended press conference that it planned to bring up to 400 high-tech and IT consulting jobs to a new headquarters in Kokomo. Such jobs normally go "offshore" because most of the work can be done online anyway. Mayor Goodnight, appropriately dressed for the occasion in a steel gray business suit and tie, along with a beatific-looking Governor Mitch Daniels and others sat on the rostrum inside the city's Inventrek Technology Park with Zuna CEO Jim Harter, a former Kokomo resident, to announce the deal. Incentives valued at $1.8 million from various public agencies clearly brought Zuna to the party, but Goodnight in particular hailed the business for bringing diversification to the local economy. Yet only fifty of those 400 jobs were expected in calendar year 2010, and Harter was vague on whether the company's high-tech and IT employees would really be full-time equivalents, or merely subcontractors who were on call, sort of like working at the car wash. Zuna would base its local operations in Inventrek at heavily discounted rent; as a publicly owned facility Inventrek pays almost no property taxes and can easily undercut private sector rental office space.

The new General Motors also completed its reaquisition of the local Delphi operation, using some of its bailout money to close the deal. The move immediately saved 827 hourly rate UAW jobs and 336 salaried positions from extinction. A Delphi "world headquarters" sign on US 31 was not immediately replaced, however. "We will look into correct signage in the next few months but it's not money we are ready to spend now," said GM general manager Bill Shaw, speaking during a conference call with local media.[10]

Additionally, during that November 4 press conference in Auburn Hills, Fiat chairman Sergio Marchionne had announced a five-year plan that called for a complete makeover for the car line by 2014, including four all-new Dodge models. If it was true — if — the transmissions likely would be built in Kokomo. However, Chrysler would back off earlier plans to develop hybrid electrics models using millions of federal dollars; instead, Fiat would contribute the fuel-efficient cars. No one knew what this would mean for the Chrysler Kokomo works.

At the same time, investment banker Steven Rattner, a key architect of the Detroit bailout, finally chimed in about his stint as the White House's auto czar. Late in October 2009, after he had resigned from the task force, Rattner's piece in *Fortune* magazine described his surprise at the unsophisticated finance department of GM and the riveting attention shown the task force on its initial visit to Detroit. "What we didn't prepare for," Rattner wrote, "was the intense public interest in our visit to these hard-hit communities. Throngs of reporters awaited us at every stop while a news helicopter buzzed overhead. More peculiarly, the ensuing press coverage seemed wildly over-focused on our test drive of the Chevy Volt, as if the company's salvation rested on this one vehicle. We applauded GM's increased emphasis on new technologies, which seemed to be driven by both commercial considerations and public relations, but we recognized that they couldn't possibly have any meaningful impact on GM's finances for at least five years. Everyone knew Detroit's reputation for insular, slow-moving cultures. Even by that low standard, I was shocked by the stunningly poor management that we found, particularly at GM, where we encountered, among other things, perhaps the weakest finance operation any of us had ever seen in a major company."[11]

Rattner never said what line of work he would pursue next. In any event, things had bottomed out in Kokomo, and perhaps were improving. Goodnight had steered a steady course through the shoals and debris of the great auto industry crisis of 2009 and he and his city had survived, albeit worse for the wear, yet Goodnight clearly was thinking about a future out of office, in spite of his Teddy Roosevelt disclaimer. By penny-pinching worthy of *Hints from Heloise,* Goodnight had managed to keep his city from bankruptcy itself, if not quite make it prosperous once again. He had a lot to be proud of, though he was not narcissistic at all, unlike so many other American politicians who think looking the part is being the thing itself. His attitude was more like a soldier who had survived a great battle, but who knew there would be many more in a long war. He was thankful and relieved, but that's all. The future was not assured, but neither he nor his city had been defeated. Not yet. Not this time. Goodnight paused inside the coffee shop to take a call from his wife. She was at the doctor's office. He told her he would stop home soon. The mayor had a private life, a fact easy to forget when talking to any public figure. And people came and went inside the shop — Goodnight had to acknowledge all of them, of course, sometimes getting out of his seat to greet them, sometimes just having to look up and smile as they approached him.

Then Greg Goodnight announced a surprising thing in his life. He was going back to college. He had registered for a geology class at Indiana University–Kokomo for the fall '09 term and would work toward a bachelor's degree. This would not be something symbolic, either, like multi-millionaire basketball player Shaquille O'Neal completing his degree while playing in the NBA. The former steelworker and union president cum small-town mayor wants to be a high school civics teacher one day, he said. He knows plenty of school superintendants and principals who can help him get a job, he noted. This ambition looked so modest compared to generations of, say, Defense Department officials who so often get high-paying jobs with defense contractors after their service careers are over.

"My father, my late father, in my last year of high school, I teased my father and asked him, 'How am I going to pay for college?'" Goodnight recalled. "We agreed the only choices I had were either to find a job or join the service. I really wish there was more force, that he had taken an active role, and made me go to college."

1. "A Hopeful Year for Unions," *New York Times*, February 7, 2008, citing Bureau of Labor Statistics, http://www.nytimes.com/2008/02/07/opinion/07thu3.html.
2. Scott Smith, "Organized Labor Celebrates at UAW Local 685," *Kokomo Tribune*, September 7, 2009, http://www.kokomotribune.com/archivesearch/local_story_250232035.html.
3. K.O. Jackson, "St. Louis Workers Headed to Kokomo," *Kokomo Tribune*, September 19, 2009, http://www.kokomotribune.com/local/local_story_262223641.html.
4. Ron Hira, *Manufacturing a Better Future for America* (Washington, D.C.: Alliance for American Manufacturing, 2009), 154.
5. Hira, 154.
6. Elizabeth Gudrais, "Unequal America: Causes and Consequences of the Wide – And Growing – Gap Between Rich and Poor," *Harvard Magazine*, July-August 2008, http://harvardmagazine.com/2008/07/unequal-america.html.
7. Gary Younge, "Lion of the US Left," *The Guardian* (London), March 5, 2003, 4.
8. Samuel P. Huntington, *Who Are We? The Challenges to America's National Identity* (New York: Simon & Schuster, 2004), 257–58
9. Quoted in Sam Stein, "Palin Explains What Parts of America Not 'Pro-America,'" *Huffington Post*, October 17, 2008, http://www.huffingtonpost.com/2008/10/17/palin-clarifies-what-part_n_135641.html.
10. K.O. Jackson, "GM introduces itself to Kokomo," *Kokomo Tribune*, November 5, 2009, www.kokomotribune.com/local/local_story_308231144.html.
11. Steven Rattner, "The Auto Bailout: How We Did It," *Fortune*, October 21, 2009, http://money.cnn.com/2009/10/21/autos/auto_bailout_rattner.fortune/index.htm?postversion=2009102109.

Bibliography

Donald L. Bartlett, James B. Steele, *America: What Went Wrong?* (Kansas City, MO: Universal Press Syndicate Co., 1992).

Bill Bonner, Addison Wiggin, *Empire of Debt : The Rise of an Epic Financial Crisis* (Hoboken, NJ: John C. Wiley, 2006).

Lindsay Brooke, *Ford Model T: The Car That Put the World on Wheels* (Minneapolis, MN: MBI Publishing Co., 2008).

Edward Chancellor, *Devil Take the Hindmost: A History of Financial Speculation* (New York: Farrar, Straus and Giroux, 1999).

Robert Conot, *American Odyssey: A Unique History of America Told Through the Life of a Great City* (New York: William Morrow & Co., 1974).

Lou Dobbs, *Exporting America: Why Corporate Greed Is Shipping American Jobs Overseas* (New York: Time Warner Book Group, 2004).

Richard Duncan, *The Dollar Crisis: Causes Consequences Cures* (Singapore: John Wiley & Sons, 2003).

Richard Florida, *The Rise of the Creative Class: And How It's Transforming Work, Leisure, Community and Everyday Life* (New York: Basic Books, 2002).

William Gass, *In the Heart of the Heart of the Country and Other Stories* (New York: Harper and Row, 1968).

Charles R. Geist, *Wall Street: A History* (New York: Oxford University Press, 1997).

Dan Georgakas, Marvin Surkin, *Detroit: I Do Mind Dying*, (New York: St Martin's Press Inc., 1975).

Richard Goldberg, *The Battle for Wall Street: Behind the Lines in the Struggle That Pushed an Industry into Turmoil* (Hoboken, NJ: John Wiley, 2009).

William Greider, *Secrets of the Temple: How the Federal Reserve Runs the Country* (New York: Simon & Schuster Inc., 1987).

David Halberstam, *The Reckoning* (New York: William Morrow & Co., 1986).

Ben Hamper, *Rivethead: Tales From the Assembly Line* (New York: Warner Books, 1992).

Dennis E. Horvath, Terri Horvath, *Indiana Cars: A History of the Automobile in*

Indiana (Indianapolis, IN: Hoosier Auto Show and Swap Meet Inc., 2002).

Edwin P. Hoyt Jr., *The House of Morgan* (New York: Dodd Mead & Co., 1966).

Samuel P. Huntington, *Who Are We? The Challenges to American National Identity* (New York: Simon & Schuster, 2004).

Charles Hyde, *Riding the Roller Coaster: A History of the Chrysler Corporation* (Detroit, MI: Wayne State University Press, 2003).

Thomas Klier, James Rubenstein, *Who Really Made Your Car?* (Kalamazoo, MI: W.E. Upjohn Institute for Employment Research, 2008).

Tom Lewis, *Divided Highways: Building the Interstate Highways, Transforming American Life* (New York: Viking Penguin Books, 1997).

Nelson Lichtenstein, *Walter Reuther: The Most Dangerous Man in Detroit* (Champaign, IL: University of Illinois Press, 1997).

Richard C. Longworth, *Caught in the Middle: America's Heartland in the Age of Globalism* (New York: Bloomsbury USA, 2007).

Richard McCormack, *Manufacturing a Better Future for America* (Washington, D.C.: Alliance For American Manufacturing, 2009).

Kevin Phillips, *Bad Money: Reckless Finance, Failed Politics and the Global Crisis of American Capitalism* (New York: Viking Penguin, 2008).

Joseph J. Romm, *The Hype about Hydrogen* (Washington, D.C.: Island Press, 2004).

Terry Tamminen, *Lives per Gallon: The True Cost of Our Oil Addiction* (Washington, D.C.: Island Press, 2006).

Ernest H. Wakefield, *History of the Electric Automobile* (Warrendale, PA: Society of Automotive Engineers Inc., 1994).

Jim Wangers, *Glory Days: When Horsepower and Passion Ruled Detroit* (Cambridge, MA: Robert Bentley Publishers, 1998).

James P. Womack, Daniel T. Jones, Daniel Roos, and Donna S. Carpenter, *The Machine That Changed the World* (New York: Rawson Associates), 1990.

Brock Yates, *The Decline and Fall of the American Automobile Industry* (New York: Random House Inc., 1983).